Indigenous Elites and Creole Identity in Colonial Mexico, 1500–1800

Modern Mexico derives many of its richest symbols of national heritage and identity from the Aztec legacy, even as it remains a predominantly Spanish-speaking, Christian society. This volume argues that the composite, neo-Aztec flavor of Mexican identity was, in part, a consequence of active efforts by indigenous elites after the Spanish conquest to grandfather ancestral rights into the colonial era. By emphasizing the antiquity of their claims before Spanish officials, native leaders extended the historical awareness of the colonial regime into the pre-Hispanic past, and therefore also the themes, emotional contours, and beginning points of what we today understand as "Mexican history." This emphasis on ancient roots, moreover, resonated with the patriotic longings of many creoles, descendants of Spaniards born in Mexico. Alienated by Spanish scorn, creoles associated with indigenous elites and studied their histories, thereby reinventing themselves as Mexico's new "native" leadership, and the heirs to its prestigious antiquity.

Peter B. Villella is Assistant Professor of History at the University of North Carolina at Greensboro.

Cambridge Latin American Studies

General editor

Herbert S. Klein

Gouverneur Morris Emeritus Professor of History, Columbia University and Hoover Research Fellow, Stanford University

101

Indigenous Elites and Creole Identity in Colonial Mexico, 1500–1800

(continued after the index)

Indigenous Elites and Creole Identity in Colonial Mexico, 1500–1800

PETER B. VILLELLA
University of North Carolina, Greensboro

CAMBRIDGE
UNIVERSITY PRESS

CAMBRIDGE
UNIVERSITY PRESS

32 Avenue of the Americas, New York, NY 10013-2473, USA

Cambridge University Press is part of the University of Cambridge.

It furthers the University's mission by disseminating knowledge in the pursuit of education, learning, and research at the highest international levels of excellence.

www.cambridge.org
Information on this title: www.cambridge.org/9781107129030

First published 2016

Printed in the United States of America

A catalog record for this publication is available from the British Library.

ISBN 978-1-107-12903-0 Hardback

For Judy

Contents

Figures

Abbreviations

AGN: Archivo General de la Nación, Mexico City, Mexico
BN: Bienes Nacionales
I: Indios
RC: Reales Cédulas
RCO: Reales Cédulas Originales
TR: Tributos
U: Universidad
VM: Vínculos y Mayorazgos
AGI: Archivo General de Indias, Seville, Spain
ECJ: Escribanía de Cámara de Justicia
I: Indiferente
J: Justicia
MX: Audiencia de México
PR: Patronato Real
UCB: Bancroft Library, University of California, Berkeley
HL: Huntington Library, San Marino, CA
LC: Miscellaneous Manuscript Collection, Library of Congress, Washington, DC
LL: Lilly Library, Indiana University, Bloomington, IN
PRT: *La nobleza indígena del centro de México después de la conquista*
Emma Pérez-Rocha and Rafael Tena, eds. (México: Universidad Nacional Autónoma de México, 2000).

RLI: *Recopilación de las leyes de los reynos de las indias*
Archivo Digital de la Legislación en el Perú, Congreso de la
República del Perú. www.leyes.congreso.gob.pe/leyes_indias
.htm

Acknowledgments

Beyond the pioneering work of many who have gone before, this book reflects the expertise, patience, and generosity of numerous mentors, colleagues, peers, and sponsors, both at home and abroad.

The idea for this research derived from my doctoral studies under Kevin Terraciano at UCLA. It was Kevin who first directed me toward the study of indigenous nobles in Mexico, whose thoughtful and steady guidance transformed my sophomoric enthusiasm into a productive historical inquiry, and whose effective pedagogical style has been the model for my own. I was also privileged to work with the master Hispanists Teofilo Ruiz and Anthony Pagden, both of whom encouraged me to broaden my contemplation of colonial Mexico and include a trans-Atlantic context. Anna More's knowledge of the arcane baroque intellectual world of New Spain helped shape and focus my own investigations, while José Moya's insights on method and approach were invaluable during the early stages of my work.

As a graduate student, I also benefitted in countless ways from many peers and friends, all of whom model and contribute to UCLA's grand tradition of ethnohistory. The tireless Dana Velasco Murillo offered good cheer and friendship as well as indispensable scholarly criticism, and her suggestions greatly improved earlier drafts of this book. Whether in Los Angeles, Mexico City, or Seville, I learned consistently from a most inquisitive and insightful cohort, including Xochitl Flores, Zeb Tortorici, Benjamin Cowan, Brad Benton, Pablo Sierra, León García, Verónica Gutiérrez, Owen Jones, and Miriam Melton-Villanueva. As a scholar, I am ultimately a product of UCLA's unique and wonderful intellectual ferment, exemplified by long afternoons in Kevin's office, poring over

Nahuatl documents while sharing research, ideas, food, laughter, and perhaps a *mezcalito*.

It is difficult to overestimate the importance of informal guidance and correspondence on the early development of junior scholars. Susan Schroeder's reputation for generosity in this regard is only exceeded by her universal esteem as an historian, and I am deeply grateful for her criticisms of an early draft. Rebecca Earle kindly assisted with some early research, while John Chuchiak, Camilla Townsend, David Tavárez, Stafford Poole, Matthew Restall, Greg O'Brien, and Kris Lane have freely offered scholarly expertise and advice over the years. I am grateful to the late Peer Schmidt, who introduced me to an entire corpus of non-Anglophone scholarship, as well as Jim Muldoon, who convinced me that everything modern has a medieval antecedent. Last but not least, in its final form this book reflects the careful and thoughtful input of Herb Klein, Deborah Gershenowitz, and the anonymous readers at Cambridge University Press, all of whom spent considerable energy helping me to refine a rough idea into a coherent history.

My work has also relied heavily on generous institutional support. I am indebted to the experts at numerous libraries and archives, in particular the Archivo General de la Nación and the Biblioteca Nacional in Mexico City, as well as the Archivo General de Indias in Seville, Spain. My foreign research over the years was enabled by the UCLA Graduate Division, the UCLA Latin American Institute, and the UNCG Office of Research and Economic Development. I was also priviliged and honored to reside as a research fellow at the John Carter Brown Library at Brown University, the Young Research Library Special Collections at UCLA, the Lilly Library at Indiana University, and the Huntington Library in San Marino, CA. Most importantly, a generous fellowship from the American Council for Learned Societies in 2012–13 afforded me the time and freedom necessary to compile my data, refine my ideas, and craft them into the present form.

There is a psychological challenge to writing, which can be an isolating endeavor. I could not have completed this project without consistent emotional support and encouragement from those whom I love the most. I thank my father and stepmother, my brothers, and my late mother, all of whom kept me afloat in ways never fully articulated or even understood. Finally, I extend eternal gratitude to my beloved wife Judy, whose wisdom, strength, and good humor I rely on every day.

Note on language

The texts examined and often excerpted in this volume are highly eclectic, and present problems of spelling and translation. This is magnified in the case of proper names, which vary considerably between authors, and even within the same texts, in both early modern Nahuatl as well as Castilian-Spanish.

When quoted directly, names and words in both Castilian and Nahuatl have been left as they are found in the primary sources. Where necessary, I clarify the most ambiguous or confusing cases in parentheses.

Outside of direct quotations and paraphrases, all Castilian-derived names and places are modernized to match standard contemporary spellings; the same is true for Mexican place names. The spelling of Nahuatl-derived place names that do not match contemporary Mexican usage, meanwhile, has been regularized according to the orthographical system adopted by James Lockhart in *Nahuatl as Written: Lessons in Older Written Nahuatl* (Stanford: Stanford University Press, 2002). All other Nahuatl words also follow Lockhart's spelling conventions.

The name of the ninth ruler of Tenochtitlan varies as much today as it did in the sixteenth century. I have chosen "Moctezuma" because it is the most familiar variation in modern usage. The same goes for other well-known Nahua leaders. As regards Nahuatl reverential formulations – the suffix – *tzin* indicating honor or importance – I follow the authors of the texts being analyzed.

As for the colonial-era natural lords, in all cases I address them with *don* or *doña* and a Christian name. This is how they would have expected to be addressed, and how their own compatriots would have done so.

All translations from any language, unless otherwise indicated, are my own.

I

Introduction

We wish now to relate some information, so that Your Majesty may understand our ancient state, and thus be persuaded to more easily concede that which we ask.

Don Antonio Cortés Totoquihuaztli, tlatoani of Tlacopan, 1552[1]

King Nezahualcoyotl demonstrated [greatness through] vast personal wealth as well as an estimable spirit . . . His household expenditures [were so vast that I would not have believed it] if . . . I had not had in my possession the true and correct amount as recorded in the accounts written by his grandson, who after becoming Christian was named don Antonio Pimentel. . . . And while some people lie, I esteem myself in writing the truth, [as] this is not some romance novel . . . but a history in which everything I say is true and fully credible.

Fray Juan de Torquemada, 1615[2]

In 1740, a young theology student from Mexico experienced a divine marvel, although he was unaware of it at the time. José Mariano Díaz de la Vega was the sacristan for the Franciscan priory in Tlaxcala, east of Mexico City, during a terrible drought. As they had before in such times of need, the indigenous leaders of the Nahua community in Tlaxcala turned to heaven for succor – more specifically, the Virgin Mary, whose painted wooden image, titled the Virgin of Ocotlan, they honored in a

---

[1] Don Antonio Cortés to Emperor Carlos V, Tlacopan, Dec 1, 1552, in PRT, 174–75.
[2] Juan de Torquemada, *Los veinte y un libros rituales y monarquía indiana . . .* 3rd edn., 7 vols. (México: Universidad Nacional Autónoma de México, Instituto de Investigaciones Históricas, 1975–83), v. 1, 231–32.

I

local sanctuary.[3] Díaz was impressed by the Tlaxcaltecas' deep reverence for the statue, which they brought out for the traditional nine-day cycle of prayers and processions.

Afterward, the Franciscans decided to honor their own church by temporarily relocating the Virgin of Ocotlan there for another round of devotional acts. It fell to Díaz to prepare the sanctuary to receive the image, which was placed on the lower portion of the altar. Yet he was dissatisfied with the results; such a holy image, he thought, demanded a more exalted throne, and although it was already late in the day and the others had left he resolved to raise the Virgin to a more prominent spot himself. She was heavy – heavier than anything he had ever lifted before – but he succeeded in lifting her to the altar's upper level. It was not until later that he discovered what the people of Tlaxcala already knew: The Virgin of Ocotlan could alter the weight of her image. Carved of strong and dense wood, the statue normally required four men to lift, yet at other times a single person might be sufficient, and even find it as light as a feather.

Recalling the episode forty-two years later, Díaz noted that this marvel was merely one of countless many by which heaven had favored Mexico, and especially its native inhabitants. In Díaz's vision, signs of divine immanence were everywhere across and within the Mexican landscape for those who had the eyes and faith to see them, tucked beneath its hills and hidden within its forests. However, he lamented, these wonders had gone unheralded among Mexico's educated, Spanish-speaking elites, and had been exiled by silence and time to an undeserved obscurity and forgetfulness. Fortunately, the humble Indians – and especially their leaders, pious Christians descended from the ancient noble houses of pre-Hispanic Mexico – had shepherded this "ancient and glorious" knowledge into the modern era, despite lacking the pens and ink with which to record it. Suffering widespread scorn and mistreatment, for centuries they quietly tended the shrines and preserved the secrets of Mexico's proud heritage. To uncover the Indians' esoteric wisdom, therefore, was to understand the triumphant truth: That although they were "unhappy, abject, and disdained among men," they were "beloved, favored, and exalted" in heaven. Díaz exhorted his skeptics to see for themselves; "come to Mexico," he exclaimed, and speak with the blessed native folk

---

[3] The Nahuas are the Nahuatl-speaking peoples of central Mexico whose ancestors are sometimes remembered as the "Aztecs."

"to whom the Sacred and Holy Empress Mary has appeared on repeated occasions."[4]

Díaz de la Vega described the cult of Ocotlan as an ancient indigenous tradition, but its historical origins exemplify the intricately blended and syncretic culture for which Mexico – and Latin America more generally – is justly famous. During the eighteenth century, the devotion flourished as a rich and elaborate example of baroque religiosity, complete with chapels, paintings, and devotional acts, and in 1755 the city of Tlaxcala proclaimed the Virgin of Ocotlan as its official patroness.[5] Yet the earliest news of the cult dates to the late-seventeenth century, and its spread can be attributed to Tlaxcala's leading families seeking to promote civic pride and boost their town's reputation within the composite monarchy of Spain.[6] Thus, while Díaz was not wrong to describe devotion to the Virgin of Ocotlan as a venerable "Indian" tradition, her advocates were products of and participants in a dynamic colonial social and political arena.

Díaz's vision was not typical, but neither was it unique. Many of his fellow educated *creoles* (American-born Spaniards) were likewise inclined to locate patriotic symbols and legends among what they portrayed as the primordial traditions of Mexico's diverse native population. To them, Mexico's Indians – and especially its leaders – were the guardians of a secret ancestral wisdom. They were the unchanging human expressions of the Mexican landscape, and therefore symbols or proxies of an eternal Mexican spirit. By adopting native symbols as their own, creoles who identified as American rather than European distinguished themselves from their Spanish grandparents and retrofitted their young, colonial society with an ancient, prestigious, and distinctly American heritage. Yet like the cult of Ocotlan, many of the "Indian antiquities" and memories the creoles cited were in reality artifacts of a more recent colonial experience, developed within colonial legal and religious parameters, for specific immediate purposes, and with the participation of numerous non-native authorities, observers, and sympathizers. By representing native memories as inherently timeless and ancient, the creoles ignored an entire history

---

[4] José Mariano Díaz de la Vega, "Memorias piadosas de la nación mexicana," UCB M-M 240, ff. 49–52.

[5] Jaime Cuadriello, *The Glories of the Republic of Tlaxcala: Art and Life in Viceregal Mexico*, trans. Christopher J. Follet (Austin: University of Texas Press, 2004), 151–61.

[6] Rodrigo Martínez Baracs, *La secuencia tlaxcalteca: orígenes del culto a Nuestra Señora de Ocotlán* (Mexico: Instituto Nacional de Antropología e Historia, 2000), 13–63.

of colonial interaction and change, domination and violence, negotiation and adaptation.

We sometimes reproduce this fallacy in our own era. By investigating creole identity without also critically examining the indigenous symbols upon which they were built – or by researching those symbols without acknowledging the colonial legal regime within which they were produced – we have implicitly accepted Díaz's erroneous premise: That the "Indian memories" he explored were ancient (because they were Indian), and therefore unreflective of any historical process. By historicizing elite native self-representation and its relationship to creole historiography, the present study targets this imbalance. To be specific: How did the historical reconstructions of native leaders reflect their unique and precarious status within the colonial world, and how did these practical concerns inform and facilitate the broader creole appropriation of native memories, symbols, and texts? This book explores the political and legal activities of the hereditary indigenous nobility of central Mexico under Spanish rule (1521–1821), and traces their personal, thematic, and textual intersections with the contemporaneous development of Mexican creolism. It argues that, for different reasons, many native leaders and some erudite creoles preferred similar interpretations of the Mexican past, leading the latter to sympathize with and emphasize the authority of the former. As a result, there was a distinct indigenous role in the creole project to imagine a Mexican nationhood emphasizing native roots.

Known generically as *caciques*, for three centuries indigenous nobles and their descendants engaged colonial authorities and institutions hoping to secure, preserve, and expand their relative status in the colonial order. Citing Spanish laws acknowledging the inherited rights of native leaders who aligned with the Spanish crown and the Catholic Church, in their negotiations with the colonial regime many caciques strategically portrayed themselves as lords of ancient pedigree as well as loyal vassals and pious Christians. Such visions of alliance and cooperation between native dynasties and the Spanish crown were sometimes explicit, and sometimes sublimated into accounts, both historical and semimythic, of indigenous champions of Hispanism and Christianity. Their purpose was to reduce the perceived cultural and political distance between local noble lineages and the colonial regime, thereby rendering pre-Hispanic history and its attendant indigenous identities marginally less controversial to Spanish authorities. Thus did they represent themselves, not as the defeated remnants of a vanquished order, nor merely as provincial bosses with inherited rights, but as co-architects of the Hispano-Catholic colonial entity known as "New Spain," and therefore deserving of special prerogatives and protections by its own standards.

Going further, the caciques' accounts often invoked precolonial precedents to validate colonial pursuits of social prestige and local authority – or, conversely, retrofitted local, ancestral memories with colonial values and concerns. In doing so they implicitly asserted continuity between pre-Hispanic and colonial Mexico, thereby reinterpreting New Spain as the cultural and political "heir" to the native civilizations that preceded it. This historical vision, in which the roots of colonial society lay not with the Spanish conquest of 1521 but rather Mexico's ancient indigenous legacy, resonated strongly with the patriotic longings of Mexican-born Spaniards, many of whom were eager to adopt a distinctly American identity while remaining loyal to the colonial, Hispano-Catholic principles underlying their own elite status. Both directly, through personal interactions and shared genealogy, and indirectly, through texts and artifacts, certain influential creoles incorporated the caciques' icons and memories into their own. By the eighteenth century, a number of patriotic legends circulated through the erudite creole world, many derived explicitly from elite indigenous accounts. Thus did the caciques' legal, political, and intellectual efforts to secure their place in the colonial order help infuse neo-Aztec sentiments into the patriotic historiography of New Spain – and therefore modern Mexican nationalism, which embraces an indigenous historical identity within and alongside Hispano-Catholic institutions, laws, and beliefs.[7]

This is not a story of one-way memory transmission, but rather of resonances, dialogues, intersections, and parallels. The cacique agenda of self-fashioning developed in tandem with creole historiography, with both informing one another over generations as caciques navigated colonial laws and prejudices via references to ancestral history, and as creoles

---

[7] As an ethnonym or demonym, "Aztecs" is only properly applied to the twelfth- and thirteenth-century ancestors of the Mexica of Tenochtitlan and Tlatelolco before they joined the sedentary civilization of central Mexico; that is how the seventeenth-century Nahua chronicler Chimalpahin employed it. In this book, "Aztec" refers less to an historic culture than to an object of recall – that is, how pre-Hispanic central Mexico has been represented and invoked since 1521 in Mexican testimonies and historiography. "Neo-Aztec," then, refers to post-1521 people, practices, and ideas that explicitly invoke or represent themselves as direct derivations of the pre-Hispanic culture of central Mexico. Domingo Francisco de San Antón Muñon Chimalpahin Cuauhtlehuanitzin, *Codex Chimalpahin: Society and Politics in Mexico Tenochtitlán, Tlatelolco, Texcoco, Culhuacán, and Other Nahua altepetl in Central Mexico.*, trans. Arthur J.O. Anderson and Susan Schroeder, 2 vols. (Norman: University of Oklahoma Press, 1997), v. 1, 29.

mined cacique accounts for patriotic symbols to call their own. Their immediate goals differed, but as both were served by similar visions of Mexican history they became historiographical allies, citing and collaborating with one another across time.

By revealing an indigenous role in the emergence of Mexican creolism and, by extension, the long-term construction of Mexican nationhood, this volume seeks to bridge the perceived gulf between Latin American nationalisms and local expressions of American indigeneity. Recent scholarship has explored how, over the long colonial era, local native identities gradually gave way to broader categories of class, race, and nation – for example, how "Indians" became "Mexicans."[8] The present study, in contrast, asks how native memories informed and shaped those broader categories – how the national category of "Mexican" came to connote a certain brand of indigenous heritage – as well as how that heritage was itself derived from a colonial history of negotiation and adaptation. Mexico's richly intricate synthesis of Hispano-Catholic and neo-Aztec sympathies was not merely the passive result of ethnic and racial mixture, I argue, but also an indirect legacy of calculated campaigns by indigenous leaders to preserve their inherited authority by reconciling it to the colonial order. In their own and the creoles' imagination, they were the heirs and guardians of Mexican antiquity in the modern era, but it was an antiquity reinterpreted according to the needs and longings of the guardians themselves.

Attributing ancient roots to a colonial society

Modern Mexico is a land where Hispanic political and legal structures overlay indigenous cultures and histories. "Any contact with the Mexican people, however brief," Octavio Paz famously observed, "reveals that the ancient beliefs and customs are still in existence beneath Western forms."[9] This mixed heritage – often referred to as a *mestizo* (mixed) culture due to its association with widespread racial and ethnic blending between Native Americans and Europeans – derives from the three long centuries

---

[8] See R. Douglas Cope, *The Limits of Racial Domination: Plebeian Society in Colonial Mexico city, 1660–1720* (Madison, WI: University of Wisconsin Press, 1994); David Frye, *Indians Into Mexicans: History and Identity in a Mexican Town* (Austin: University of Texas Press, 1996); and Colin M. MacLachlan, *Imperialism and the Origins of Mexican Culture* (Cambridge, MA: Harvard University Press, 2015).

[9] Octavio Paz, *The Labryinth of Solitude and Other Writings*, trans. Lysander Kemp, Yara Milos, and Rachel Phillips Belash (New York: Grove Press, 1985), 89.

of the colonial era, in which the Spanish regime in Mexico imposed itself upon preexisting indigenous structures without entirely erasing them.[10] As historians have demonstrated, one of the deepest and most characteristic features of Spanish America was the tendency for indigenous identities and cultural practices to survive, adapt, and resurface in often surprising ways, despite pervasive and hegemonic processes of race-mixing and cultural Hispanization.[11] Spanish imperialist efforts to restrict and smother indigenous ways of thinking and behaving often failed. In many cases native practices survived in occult, underground forms; yet just as often, they adopted new, superficially amenable guises, paying overt obedience to colonial authority while simultaneously subverting and mocking it. Mexican traditions of art and literature have drawn freely from a deep well of eclectic traditions ever since. Like the "Indian symphony" of Carlos Chávez, which inserts Mesoamerican instruments and themes into the formal structures of European orchestral music, they deliberately confuse where the indigenous ends and the Hispanic begins: A world of seamless contrasts that explicitly proclaims unity even as it revels in dissonance and tension.[12] In today's Mexico the Virgin Mary is often identified as a Mesoamerican deity, while neo-Aztec dancers regularly offer veneration to the Virgin Mary. The ruined temple of Tenochtitlan occupies the same physical space as the Metropolitan Cathedral of Mexico City, and both are essential symbols of national patrimony and heritage.

Mexico's layered identity also informs its conventional narrative of national history as presented in schools, museums, and other public spaces. Mexican historiography traces the nation's origins not to independence from Spain in 1821, nor to the Spanish conquest of 1521, but

---

[10] See Colin M. MacLachlan and Jaime E. Rodríguez O., *The Forging of the Cosmic Race: A Reinterpretation of Colonial Mexico* (Berkeley: University of California Press, 1980).

[11] See, for example, the latest research into "urban Indians," which demonstrates that native peoples who lived in Spanish cities nonetheless maintained distinct cultural practices derived from indigenous precedents, and even developed new ones. Dana Velasco Murillo, Mark Lentz, and Margarita R. Ochoa, eds., *City Indians in Spain's American Empire: Urban Indigenous Society in Colonial Mesoamerica and Andean South America, 1530–1810* (Portland, OR: Sussex Academic Press, 2012).

[12] "Mesoamerica" refers to the densely populated pre-Columbian culture area stretching from roughly Nicaragua in the southeast to the modern Mexican states of Jalisco, Nayarit, Zacatecas, and Colima in the northwest. On the eve of contact with Europeans, the area in and around Mexico City and the states of Mexico, Tlaxcala, Puebla, Hidalgo, Morelos, and Veracruz were the most prosperous, with an estimated population of about twenty-five million.

to the Mesoamerican past.[13] This tendency, present in the nineteenth century even under Hispanophilic, conservative governments, became even more explicit and visible following the Revolution of 1910. Yet while the emphasis on native roots – what Rebecca Earle has called "Indianesque" nationalism – is rather obvious and banal to many Mexicans today, it was not an inevitable result of the colonial experience.[14] Mainstream national history in the United States, for example, only rarely admits Native American themes and memories – and even then typically represents them as parallel, rather than foundational to, the national character; dubbing it "the great nation of futurity," the heralds of Anglo-Saxon expansionism did not envision the US as the heir to any indigenous tradition, but rather a purely new entity that had emerged, like Athena, entirely from the minds of its Founding Fathers.[15] The opposite is true in much of Latin America, and especially Mexico, where neo-Aztec sentiment is prominent and the "imagined community" of the nation-state does not pretend to be unmoored from history.[16] In showcasing the great artifacts of pre-Hispanic Mesoamerica, the National Museum of Anthropology in Mexico City explicitly represents itself as a treasury of national patrimony. In Washington, DC, meanwhile, the Smithsonian's Museum of the American Indian and Museum of American History lie in two separate buildings.[17]

Yet if the composite, neo-Aztec nature of Mexican identity was not inevitable, neither was it coincidental. To a large degree it is the legacy of the distinct Spanish approach to colonization in America: Rather than treating native societies as sovereign nations to be subdued, removed, or segregated, the colonizers forcibly integrated them as corporate vassals of the crown.[18] Yet this volume argues that it was also a consequence of active efforts by indigenous elites, especially in the Nahua-dominated

---

[13] Michael J. Gonzales, "Imagining Mexico in 1910: Visions of the *Patria* in the Centennial Celebration in Mexico City," *Journal of Latin American Studies* 39, no. 3 (2007).

[14] Rebecca Earle, *The Return of the Native: Indians and Myth-making in Spanish America, 1810–1930* (Durham: Duke University Press, 2008).

[15] John L. O'Sullivan "The Great Nation of Futurity," *The United States Magazine and Democratic Review* 6, no. 23 (1839).

[16] Benedict Anderson, *Imagined Communities: Reflections on the Origin and Spread of Nationalism* (New York: Verso, 1991).

[17] Paz himself placed this distinction at the root of his assessment of the essential differences between Mexico and the United States. Paz, "Mexico and the United States," in Paz, *The Labryinth of Solitude and Other Writings*: 359–63.

[18] Charles Gibson, "Conquest, Capitulation, and Indian Treaties," *American Historical Review* 83, no. 1 (1978).

central areas around Mexico City, to grandfather patrimonial rights into the postconquest world. As Frederick Cooper argues, "colonial regimes and the oppositions to them reshaped the conceptual frameworks in which both operated"; by demanding inclusion in the colonial hierarchy via the telling and re-telling of their own histories, native leaders extended the historical awareness of New Spain into the pre-Hispanic past, and therefore also the themes, emotional contours, and beginning points of what we today call "Mexican history."[19]

In the decades following the 1521 Spanish defeat of Tenochtitlan, the most powerful entity in pre-Hispanic Mesoamerica, central Mexican indigenous leaders saw their populations collapse and alien institutions co-opt their customary social, religious, and political modes of authority. While many resisted violently, others pragmatically engaged the colonial regime itself, negotiating for a measure of autonomy. By conceding allegiance to the Spanish monarch, they sought to avoid the harshest terms of colonialism and preserve the integrity of local political structures – and with it, their traditional rights to govern and extract tributes from their communities. Yet such arrangements were never secure. Almost immediately, frustrated native leaders – especially Nahuas from in and around the emerging Spanish nucleus of Mexico City – were appearing regularly before imperial officials complaining of plundered patrimonies and trampled rights. Dispossessed and increasingly incapable of projecting direct power over native commoners, they turned instead to the realm of words and rhetoric, demanding justice, protection, and even restoration from their conquerors. Yet to be effective the caciques had to craft their pleas carefully, and attune their self-advocacy to the myriad prejudices and ideologies of the colonial authorities who determined their fates. At stake was their survival as a discrete provincial elite.

Seeking a persuasive moral and political case for recognition, the caciques relied on history, the location of their greatest glory. Invariably, whenever and wherever they engaged the colonial regime – in petitions, disputes, and legal testimony – native elites implied that preconquest modes of local authority retained their legitimacy despite (or even because of) the imposition of Spanish rule, Christian evangelization, and the relentless flood of European fortune-seekers into America. They were, they argued, the heirs to a grand and ancient legacy who had willingly embraced the Spanish monarch and the Catholic Church at the

---

[19] Frederick Cooper, *Colonialism in Question: Theory, Knowledge, History* (Berkeley: University of California Press, 2005), 25.

first opportunity. They typically ignored or de-emphasized any sense of tension in this version of history; in fact, they insisted, their eagerness for baptism and Spanish vassalage not only secured their position in the colonial order, but was also evidence of their own meritorious virtue, nobility, and wisdom as inherited from antiquity.

The recurring themes of primordial greatness, fealty to the king, and religious orthodoxy were not coincidental, as they spoke directly to Spanish laws and conceits, valorizing native lineages according to Hispano-Catholic criteria while nullifying the neo-Crusader justification for conquest and domination. If most Spaniards thought nothing of depriving naked savages of their freedom and wealth, it was difficult, even for the most strident of imperialists, to disregard the claims of sophisticated and pedigreed aristocrats who had converted to Christianity and committed themselves to the Spanish monarch at the first opportunity. Not only did such stories invoke Spanish laws promising autonomy to those who submitted voluntarily to the crown, it resonated emotionally and theologically with the archetypal conversion story of St. Paul on the road to Damascus. Thus, although the caciques' strategies reflected the imperatives of Spanish colonial justice, they also contained a substantial political substance: They were implicit arguments for autonomy and noble privilege, within Spanish imperialism yet derived from pre-Hispanic antiquity. They reimagined themselves as Mexican vassals of the Spanish suzerain, reconciling their inherited legacies to the colonial regime so as to promote their status within it. They were also highly critical of colonial misrule, if not colonial rule as such, as they called upon the king to make amends for the abuses of Spanish settlers and provincial officials.

Going further, stories of ancient splendor, services to Spain, and Christian piety implied harmony and alliance between Mexico's ancient native lineages and the new colonial regime – a vision that necessarily de-emphasized the role of conquest and rupture in the creation of New Spain. In the Mesoamerican context, conquest could unmake political sovereignty, but if the ruling lineage persisted, so did the ethnic polity they represented.[20] It is appropriate, then, that the caciques did not announce or concede the displacement of their own noble traditions as they integrated into the colonial order, but rather insisted on their survival and continued relevance within that order. But in doing so, they retrofitted it

---

[20] Susan Schroeder, "Introduction: The Genre of Conquest Studies," in *Indian Conquistadors: Indigenous Allies in the Conquest of Mesoamerica*, eds. Laura E. and Michel R. Oudijk Matthew (Norman, OK: University of Oklahoma Press, 2007), 12.

with their own memories and legacies. In their accounts, it would seem, the Spanish-speaking, Catholic society of "New Spain," forged in conquest, had a long and distinguished history before the first Spaniards had even appeared.

Cacique history and the creole *patria*

The cacique vision of continuity between ancient Mesoamerica and colonial New Spain resonated with the patriotic longings of another group in the colonial world, one that likewise considered itself "native" to Mexico: the creoles, children and descendants of Spaniards born in America. By the seventeenth century, many educated urban creoles had come to identify patriotically with Mexican antiquity as their own heritage. According to Anna More, the creoles' imagined *patria*, or homeland, was not only the geographical entity known today as "Mexico," but also an ethnic and genealogical community of Spanish-descended compatriots with "an emotive connection" to the American landscape and its native heritage.[21] One foundation of Novohispanic creolism, then, was a sense of proprietary rootedness in the indigenous Mexican past, especially the high urban civilization of fifteenth-century central Mexico: the densely populated volcanic lake basin the Nahuas called *Anahuac* ("Near the Water"), with the imperial capital of Tenochtitlan at its core.[22]

A simmering rivalry with "peninsular" Spaniards fueled expressions of creole distinction. Tensions between creoles and peninsulars arose almost immediately in the wake of the conquest, as those who had fought to subdue the New World perceived that undeserving latecomers were usurping their hard-won spoils. The conquistadors desired to become grandees of their own American kingdom, with perpetual rights to collect rents and command personal services from local laborers. The crown, however, preferred to view them as mere frontier captains, and erected a series of legal and procedural barriers to the perpetual inheritance of conquest-derived fortunes. Exacerbating and confirming their ire was the disdain

---

[21] Anna More, *Baroque Sovereignty: Carlos de Sigüenza y Góngora and the Creole Archive of Colonial Mexico* (Philadelphia: University of Pennsylvania Press, 2012), 41–42.

[22] "Novohispanic" refers to the colonial administrative entity of New Spain. As New Spain acquired a discrete and proprietary array of political and social networks – and because "Mexico" in the colonial era referred only to Mexico City or to the native people who inhabited it before 1521 – I use "Novohispanic" as an imperfect, but useful label to refer to that which arose within and pertained to the colonial entity, but not the indigenous "Mexico" that existed before nor the national "Mexico" that came after.

they perceived from peninsulars, who frequently scorned creoles as a degenerate and perhaps impure breed of Spaniards tainted by their proximity to Indians, Africans, and the exotic American environment itself.[23] The creole identity, then, was based not on ethnicity or culture – which they shared with peninsular Spaniards – but rather a sense of grievance: They suffered a painful disjuncture between their second-tier status and their lofty self-understanding as the descendants of conquerors.[24] They responded by rejecting notions of American inferiority in a variety of ways, one of the most spectacular of which was an extended apologia for native peoples and their histories.

The creole identification with native history is well known to modern scholars.[25] In New Spain, this tendency revolved largely around the grand antiquity of central Mexico, and in some cases extended to the Indo-Christian cultures that followed the conquest. However, the creoles did not wish to reject their Hispanic heritage and become "Indians." They had no desire to associate or equate themselves with the living, breathing culture of their indigenous contemporaries, whom they (along with their peninsular cousins) scorned as superstitious and perhaps idolatrous. Creoles identified not with native history as such, but a hermetic and abstract version of it – the soaring pyramids and floating gardens of Anahuac. This was one of the most enigmatic, yet characteristic features

---

[23] See Bernard Lavallé, "Del indio al criollo: evolución y tranformación de una imagen colonial," in *La imagen del indio en la Europa moderna* (Seville: Escuela de Estudios Hispano-Americanos, 1990); Rebecca Earle, *The Body of the Conquistador: Food, Race, and the Colonial Experience in Spanish America, 1492–1700* (New York: Cambridge University Press, 2012).

[24] See, for example, the angry protests of the conquistadors' children in Cabildo of Mexico City to the Viceroy, Feb 10, 1567, in Manuel Orozco y Berra, ed. *Noticia histórica de la conjuración del Marqués del Valle* (Mexico: R. Rafael, 1852), 481–83.

[25] This issue is discussed in Jorge Cañizares-Esguerra, *How to Write the History of the New World: Histories, Epistemologies, and Identities in the Eighteenth-Century Atlantic World* (Stanford: Stanford University Press, 2001). 204–345; David A. Brading, *Prophecy and Myth in Mexican History* (Cambridge: Cambridge University Press, 1984); David A. Brading, *The First America: The Spanish Monarchy, Creole Patriots, and the Liberal State 1492-1867* (Cambridge: Cambridge University Press, 1991). 293–313; Enrique Florescano, *Memory, Myth, and Time in Mexico: From the Aztecs to Independence*, trans. Albert G. Bork and Kathryn R. Bork (Austin: University of Texas Press, 1994); Enrique Florescano, *Historia de las historias de la nación mexicana* (México, D.F.: Taurus, 2002); Anthony Pagden, "Identity Formation in Spanish America," in *Colonial Identity in the Atlantic World, 1500–1800*, eds. Nicholas Canny and Anthony Pagden (Princeton, NJ: Princeton University Press, 1989); Anthony Pagden, *Spanish Imperialism and the Political Imagination: Studies in European and Spanish–American Social and Political Theory, 1513–1830* (New Haven: Yale University Press, 1990), 93–97.

of New Spain's creoles: The tendency to imagine a complete division between their colonial culture and the grand native past they attributed to it.[26] "Creole patriotism," according to David Brading, was the "perennially ambiguous" perspective of a people who embraced the civilization their own ancestors had annihilated.[27] The result was what Anthony Pagden has called an "inchoate" and "bizarre mixture [of] diverse, culturally incompatible elements."[28] Yet for all these incongruencies, the indigenous heritage provided the symbols and legends by which New Spain's creoles sublimated their grievances and attributed a prestigious antiquity to their patria.[29]

An indispensable key to this delicate and selective appropriation of the Mexican legacy was the native elite, whom the creoles understood as the embodiment of that legacy. In the creole imaginary, noble Indians, unlike native commoners, innately understood Mesoamerican history and were the most authoritative guardians of its secrets. Once baptized and remade into good Christians, caciques became, to the creoles, acceptable bearers of historical wisdom, thus serving as the critical links between the creoles' colonial culture and the native history they claimed as their own. Much of this process occurred via texts; according to More, the creoles located the Mexican legacy in an "archive" of physical documents – the most valuable of which were pictorial and alphabetic texts produced by caciques, the older, the better.[30] By stressing their mastery of an archive rather than any participation in an ongoing native culture, they posited and described a hermetic, romantic, and forever static Anahuac – and then claimed it as the roots of their own American patria. In this way – by associating and collaborating with caciques, by compiling and investigating their records, and by reproducing their histories – the American Spaniards cast themselves as the "new" caciques: A "native" ruling class unjustly denied its proper birthright by the haughty and imperious "foreigners" who arrived on every ship from Spain.

[26] Jorge Cañizares-Esguerra, "Creole Colonial Spanish America," in *Creolization: History, Ethnography, Theory*, ed. Charles Stewart (Walnut Creek, CA: Left Coast Press, 2007), 32–36.

[27] Brading, *The First America*: 459.

[28] Pagden, *Spanish Imperialism and the Political Imagination*: 131.

[29] This parallels the process, recently chronicled by Danna Levin Rojo, by which indigenous geographical and historical knowledge determined early Spanish understandings of and approaches to Nuevo México (New Mexico), See Levin Rojo, *Return to Aztlan: Indians, Spaniards, and the Invention of Nuevo México* (Norman, OK: University of Oklahoma Press, 2014).

[30] More, *Baroque Sovereignty*: 15–16.

However, while the creoles portrayed the caciques as the bearers of an ancient American wisdom, the majority of their texts were postconquest artifacts derived directly or indirectly from a colonial agenda of noble recognition and autonomy, in which they sought to reconcile preconquest patrimonies to New Spain by aligning them with Hispano-Catholic laws and values. Indeed, this aspect of the caciques' accounts helps explain their profound appeal to patriotic creoles who longed, paradoxically, for a heritage rooted in ancient America, yet that remained nonetheless thoroughly Hispanic and Christian. In this sense, the Mesoamerica depicted in creole writings was a second-order reinterpretation, one that reflected not only pre-Hispanic memories but also the efforts of postconquest lords wielding words to protect lands and legacies they could no longer defend with weapons.

Native perspectives and the politics of history

This study is heavily informed by recent scholarship concerned with the reinterpretation of colonial texts and testimonies, particularly those by indigenous authors. In doing so, it draws upon several now-familiar and interrelated post-Enlightenment conceptions of history-keeping and its purposes. Specifically, it presumes that the past and history are different things,[31] and it accepts that just as the powerful wield history to justify their power, so can the less powerful to protest their marginalization.[32] History-telling (as opposed to the past), therefore, is potentially a political act, a means by which different factions may challenge one another and promote their interests.[33] As Kevin Terraciano argues, "history is not a fixed narrative of events dictated by the victors but a contested field of claims and counterclaims that we continue to revisit and revise from new and different perspectives."[34] This is especially true in colonial

---

[31] Hayden White, *The Content of the Form: Narrative Discourse and Historical Representation* (Baltimore: Johns Hopkins Press, 1987).

[32] Margaret Macmillan, *Dangerous Games: The Uses and Abuses of History* (New York: Modern Library, 2009), 53–78.

[33] Keith Jenkins defines history as "a shifting, problematic discourse, ostensibly about an aspect of the world, the past," that is circumscribed in its possibilities not only by the factual record, but also by "the range of power bases that exist in any given moment and which structure and distribute the meanings of history along a dominant–marginal spectrum." Keith Jenkins, *Re-Thinking History* (New York: Routledge, 1991), 26.

[34] Kevin Terraciano, "Competing Memories of the Conquest of Mexico," in *Contested Visions in the Spanish Colonial World*, ed. Ilona Katzew (Los Angeles: Los Angeles County Museum of Art, 2011), 77.

situations, where competing visions of history coexist almost by definition.[35] According to Ethelia Ruiz-Medrano, the advocacy of alternative versions of history has been and remains especially critical to the native peoples of the Western Hemisphere "as a resource for undertaking social action in the present."[36]

Native leaders who reconciled their ancestral heritages to the administrative and religious structures of Spanish colonialism exemplify the political potential of history-telling, as they did so while demanding the support of colonial authorities. Frances Kartunnen distinguishes between indigenous texts intended for outsiders and those that were not; stories of noble native champions of Hispanism were everywhere and always a "public" mode of indigenous expression, one intended to favorably influence colonial officials and institutions.[37] Such stories were carefully crafted accounts of past events intended to persuade. In this sense, I address the caciques' testimonies not only as historical texts, but also as self-conscious rhetoric attuned to contemporary laws, conflicts, and possibilities.

In this endeavor I benefit from scholarly trends that reassess colonial-era phenomena according to local and non-European perspectives. In recent decades historians have greatly expanded our awareness of the diverse array of human societies and cultures in America before and after the Columbian encounter of 1492. Due to the comparative availability of ethnohistorical sources, the urbanized, sedentary culture groups of Mesoamerica – and in particular the Nahuas who dominated central Mexico – have been among the most extensively researched. This scholarship, exemplified by the philological analysis of native-language records pioneered by James Lockhart and his students, demonstrates that, in contrast to widespread perceptions of cultural stasis and stagnation, indigenous ways of living and interacting under Spanish rule were remarkably resilient, despite colonial mechanisms explicitly

35 Stephanie Wood, "Collective Memory and Mesoamerican Systems of Remembrance," in *Mesoamerican Memory: Enduring Systems of Remembrance*, eds. Amos Megged and Stephanie Wood (Norman, OK: University of Oklahoma Press, 2012).

36 Ethelia Ruiz-Medrano, *Mexico's Indigenous Communities: Their Lands and Histories, 1500–2010*, trans. Russ Davidson (Boulder, CO: University Press of Colorado, 2010), 110.

37 Frances Kartunnen, "Indigenous Writing as a Vehicle for Postconquest Continuity and Change in Mesoamerica," in *Native Traditions in the Postconquest World*, eds. Tom Cummins and Elizabeth Hill Boone (Washington, DC: Dumbarton Oaks, 1998), 428–35.

committed to their eradication.[38] As Lockhart argued, by the late-colonial era "almost nothing in the entire [Nahua] cultural ensemble was left untouched, yet at the same time almost everything went back...to a preconquest antecedent."[39]

The revelations of the "New Philology" suggested the inadequacy of earlier models of colonial change presuming an inexorable and unidirectional "acculturation" to European modes of thinking and behaving, especially in areas of relatively dense indigenous population. Earlier historians revealed much about the eclectic political makeup of Spanish America, but over-reliance on Spanish-language sources also tended to echo the Spaniards' misrepresentations of native societies as essentially static, socially undifferentiated, and politically passive.[40] The newer scholarship, by contrast, suggests a more dynamic reality, one in which native peoples frequently pursued locally determined political and ethnic agendas both in reaction against and orthogonal to the facts of European colonization.[41] Accordingly, modern research accounting for non-Spanish perspectives – what has been called the "new conquest history" – is neither a heroic nor a tragic epic with a clear beginning and a conclusive end, but rather a synthetic mosaic of local experiences that do not immediately lend themselves to a concise overall narrative.[42] The legacy of this process is visible in today's Latin America, the supposed Ibero-Catholic uniformity

---

[38] This scholarship is exemplified by, among others, Sarah L. Cline, *Colonial Culhuacán, 1580–1600* (Albuquerque: University of New Mexico Press, 1986); Robert Haskett, *Indigenous Rulers: An Ethnohistory of Town Government in Colonial Cuernavaca* (Albuquerque: University of New Mexico Press, 1991); Rebecca Horn, *Postconquest Coyoacan: Nahua–Spanish Relations in Central Mexico, 1519–1650* (Stanford, CA: Stanford University Press, 1997); Kevin Terraciano, *The Mixtecs of Colonial Oaxaca: Ñudzahui History, Sixteenth Through Eighteenth Centuries* (Stanford: Stanford University Press, 2001); Matthew Restall, *The Maya World: Yucatec Culture and Society 1550–1850* (Stanford: Stanford University Press, 1997).

[39] James Lockhart, *The Nahuas After the Conquest: A Social and Cultural History of the Indians of Central Mexico, Sixteenth Through Eighteenth Centuries* (Stanford, CA: Stanford University Press, 1992), 5.

[40] Eric R. Wolf, "The Vissicitudes of the Closed Corporate Peasant Community," *American Ethnologist* 13, no. 2 (1986).

[41] See James Lockhart, "Double Mistaken Identity: Some Nahua Concepts in Postconquest Guise," in *Of Things of the Indies: Essays Old and New in Early Latin American History*, ed. James Lockhart (Stanford, CA: Stanford University Press, 1999).

[42] For an overview of this scholarship, see Matthew Restall, "The New Conquest History," *History Compass* 10, no. 2 (2012); see also Ilona Katzew, ed. *Contested Visions in the Spanish Colonial World* (Los Angeles: Los Angeles County Museum of Art, 2011).

of which belies the true diversity of its many cultural, ethnic, linguistic, and religious traditions.[43]

The present study extends the ethnohistorians' findings to the art of history-keeping. As elsewhere in the Americas, indigenous communities in New Spain produced and preserved many "systems of remembrance" – textual, graphic, oral, and performative – that differed substantially from European and Spanish histories.[44] Eurocentric narratives, whether heroic or tragic, portray the Spanish conquest as the unambiguous end to an earlier era and the obvious beginning of a new one – a "limit event" splitting history in two.[45] Yet native memories were typically both narrower and deeper, emphasizing the historical experience of a single community or ancestry within a much longer time horizon.[46] In their telling, the arrival of Europeans was neither an end nor a beginning, but rather a middle chapter within a much longer ethnic history with remote, semilegendary origins.[47] Modern Mexican identity, which locates the nation's origins in the distant Mesoamerican past, reflects this "indigenous" historical vision rather more than the Eurocentric insistence on new beginnings.

This is not to say, however, that there was a coherent indigenous (or elite indigenous) understanding of Mexican history; as Terraciano notes, there simply was no "single 'Indian' view."[48] Some lamented or harshly criticized the atrocities of Spanish imperialism, some were coldly indifferent, and still others were zealously triumphalistic. Many blended all three sentiments into an ambivalent and fragmented totality that is difficult to

---

43 Andrew B. Fisher and Matthew D. O'Hara, eds. *Imperial Subjects: Race and Identity in Colonial Latin America* (Durham: Duke University Press, 2009).

44 Amos Megged and Stephanie Wood, eds. *Mesoamerican Memory: Enduring Systems of Remembrance* (Norman, OK: University of Oklahoma Press, 2012); see also Susan Schroeder, ed. *The Conquest All Over Again: Nahuas and Zapotecs Thinking, Writing, and Painting Spanish Colonialism* (Portland, OR: Sussex Academic Press, 2011); Martin Lienhard, *La voz y su huella* (México: Ediciones Casa Juan Pablos, 2003).

45 I borrow the term from Kerwin Lee Klein, who deploys it in reference to the Holocaust in the collective memory of the postwar Jewish community. Kerwin Lee Klein, "On the Emergence of Memory in Historical Discourse," *Representations* 69, Winter (2000).

46 See Amos Megged, *Social Memory in Ancient and Colonial Mesoamerica* (New York: Cambridge University Press, 2010).

47 Olivia Harris, "The Coming of the White People: Reflections on the Mythologization of History in Latin America," *Bulletin of Latin American Research* 14, no. 1 (1995): 9–24.

48 Terraciano, "Competing Memories," 64.

characterize.[49] One commonality that did exist, however, derived from the conditions in which such texts were produced. A primary site of negotiation and interaction between native leaders and Spanish officials – the forum in which they most consistently recounted their histories – was the colonial justice system, an inconsistent network of overlapping legal jurisdictions with the viceroy (ultimately) at its helm. This does not change the political essence of their stories, as litigation *was* politics, one of the few means by which individuals and corporations could actively defend their vital interests. Susan Kellogg notes that the Novohispanic legal system functioned both as a site of colonial acculturation and hegemony as well as "an instrument of cultural resistance" against that hegemony.[50] Far from static and rigid, the early modern "Law of the Indies" was a contested arena in which colonial subjects of all castes – including native peoples and their hereditary elites – pursued what Brian Owensby calls a "politics of engagement" with imperial authorities: Recurring litigation in pursuit of goals shaped and reshaped by an ever-shifting sea of social conflicts and alignments.[51] One result was a tradition of sustained strategic negotiation via colonial law that Yanna Yannakakis calls "indigenous juris-practice," in which "native legal cultures were not only an artifact of colonialism but also integral to its making."[52]

Some indigenous leaders were quite receptive to Spanish ways of legal justice, which derived from the composite model of monarchy of Hapsburg Spain (1516–1700).[53] Under the Hapsburgs – and to a lesser but

---

[49]   Robert Haskett, *Visions of Paradise: Primordial Titles and Mesoamerican History in Cuernavaca* (Norman, OK: University of Oklahoma Press, 2005); Stephanie Wood, *Transcending Conquest: Nahua Views of Spanish Colonial Mexico* (Norman, OK: University of Oklahoma Press, 2003); Lisa Sousa and Kevin Terraciano, "The 'Original Conquest' of Oaxaca: Nahua and Mixtec Accounts of the Spanish Conquest," *Ethnohistory* 50, no. 2 (2003).

[50]   Susan Kellogg, *Law and the Transformation of Aztec Culture, 1500–1700* (Norman, OK: University of Oklahoma Press, 1995), 214.

[51]   Brian Owensby, *Empire of Law and Indian Justice in Colonial Mexico* (Stanford: Stanford University Press, 2008). 302. See also Nancy van Deusen, *Global Indios: The Indigenous Struggle for Justice in Sixteenth-Century Castile* (Durham: Duke University Press, 2015); and José-Juan López-Portillo García-López, "Another Jerusalem: Political Legitimacy and Courtly Government in the Kingdom of New Spain (1535–1568)" (Ph.D. diss., Queen Mary, University of London, 2011), 176–83.

[52]   Yanna Yannakakis, "Indigenous People and Legal Culture in Spanish America," *History Compass* 11, no. 11 (2013): 932.

[53]   James Lockhart has suggested "receptivity" as a useful way of understanding certain forms of non-coercive cultural change: A people were receptive to foreign practices if they found them self-evidently useful within their own contexts. James Lockhart, "Receptivity and Resistance," in *Of Things of the Indies: Essays Old and New in Early*

still significant degree the Bourbons of the eighteenth century – there was no cohesive empire, but rather "a confederation of principalities held together in the person of a single king."[54] While this discouraged solidarity among the many discrete peoples subjected to Spanish rule, it envisioned native lords as direct vassals of the king (via his American proxy, the viceroy). Caciques responded accordingly, emphasizing an ideal of intimacy and reciprocity between themselves and the crown. This contrasts somewhat with the juris-practice of native commoners – the vast bulk of the native population – who had fewer incentives to highlight histories of cooperation and alliance, and instead tended to stress mistreatment by Spaniards, outsiders, and even their own caciques.[55]

We should recognize the collaborationist flavor of much cacique rhetoric as a pragmatic response to dispossession and disempowerment, a means of coping with and mediating the meaning of foreign rule. As Homi Bhabha teaches, the "mimicry" of the colonizers by the colonized – many caciques, for example, adopted the dress and iconography of the Spanish nobility – can be "potentially and strategically an insurgent counter-appeal" by visibly challenging presumptions of racial and cultural inferiority.[56] Thus, cacique testimonies stressing their own alignment with Spain and the Church were not always (or simply) abject expressions of sympathy for the colonizer. They were what Susan Schroeder has termed "loser histories": The perspectives of those who sought, through the retelling of history, to correct or soften the consequences of perceived historical wrongs and injustice.[57] In New Spain, loser histories by native subjects often downplayed the relevance of violent conquest by glossing over or ignoring it altogether. This phenomenon, according to Stephanie Wood, was a means by which indigenous subjects could "transcend" their ancestors' trauma and thereby "ameliorate or at least negotiate" their own subjugation.[58] Their stories were both symptoms of and protests against decline, fragmentation, and dispossession.

In short, those who reconciled their Mesoamerican legacies to the ideologies and institutions of Spanish colonialism were the displaced

---

Latin American History, ed. James Lockhart (Stanford: Stanford University Press, 1999), 331.

[54] Pagden, *Spanish Imperialism and the Political Imagination*: 3.
[55] Brian Owensby has developed a broadly useful typology regarding the kinds of cases that native litigants brought before Spanish justice. See Owensby, *Empire of Law*.
[56] Homi Bhabha, *The Location of Culture* (New York: Routledge, 1994), 91.
[57] Schroeder, "Introduction: The Genre of Conquest Studies," 9–13.
[58] Wood, *Transcending Conquest*: 147–48.

icons of a vanquished order seeking to retroactively salvage what they could of their ancestors' preeminence. Paradoxically, like a plea bargain, by preemptively (if largely implicitly) accepting a foreign sovereign, savvy caciques opened a small space from which to assert another kind of relevance more germane to the colonial order. It was not "resistance" per se, but rather "negotiation within domination" which, according to Owensby, demonstrates that "social relations cannot be reduced to the mastery of overlords and the subjugation and victimization of subalterns."[59] More specifically, caciques pursued a pragmatic path reflecting their interests as a "liminal" group in colonial society: Local hereditary elites who were dependent on the colonial regime, yet who also lamented the loss of ancestral grandeur.[60] In this way they avoided the despair of King Lear (and other kings bereft of kingdoms) by recasting themselves as something new, complete with their own explanatory historical narrative. They were the "caciques" and "natural lords" of New Spain: Aristocrats by birth, Spanish vassals by choice, and Christians by grace, they merited recognition according to law, custom, and decency.

The historical accounts of caciques exist within a broad variety of colonial records. While a select group of narrative histories are invaluable, there are precious few. Legal testimonials, produced both with and without the assistance of Spanish intermediaries, are far more copious, and with careful interpretation reveal much regarding how elite Indians chose to represent themselves to colonial authorities. Kellogg argues that colonial legal texts have "plots," and that despite their mediation through layers of colonial hegemony, bureaucracy, and ritual, we can nonetheless consider indigenous litigants to be their "authors."[61] Indeed, historical reconstructions are embedded within many legal records, as generations of indigenous leaders seeking colonial favors told of noble ancestors who converted to Christianity, allied with the Spaniards, and helped win Mexico for the king of Spain. Caciques demanded legal privileges by linking themselves to preconquest noble lineages, and they claimed land

---

[59] Brian Owensby, Foreword to Ethelia Ruiz-Medrano and Susan Kellogg, eds. *Negotiation Within Domination: New Spain's Indian Pueblos Confront the Spanish State* (Boulder, CO: University Press of Colorado, 2010), xii.

[60] David Cahill, "A Liminal Nobility: The Incas in the Middle Ground of Late Colonial Peru," in *New Worlds, First Nations*, eds. David Patrick Cahill and Blanca Tovías (Portland, OR: Sussex Academic Press, 2006).

[61] Kellogg, *Law and the Transformation of Aztec Culture*: 43, n. 6.

rights by reference to the historic domains of their ancestors. The voluminous records resulting from such legal and ritual encounters attest to the tenacity with which native leaders fought to secure the rights promised them under the Spanish crown, as well as the routine relevance of pre-Hispanic memories to postconquest legal and political negotiations.[62]

Organization

This book proceeds both thematically and chronologically, corresponding roughly to identifiable patterns in the content and shape of cacique legal and political engagement as well as its links to major figures in the creole intellectual tradition. Following the sources, there will be a special, but not exclusive emphasis on the Nahuas of Anahuac – especially Tenochtitlan, Tlatelolco, Tetzcoco, and Tlacopan – as well as Tlaxcala and the Otomí lords of Querétaro and the Bajío region, as these areas gave rise to some of the most frequently recurring Indianesque motifs within patriotic creole literature. In hailing what they portrayed as their American origins, late-colonial creoles typically highlighted Anahuac as the epicenter of high culture and civilization in pre-Hispanic Mexico; Tlaxcala as Spain's most important native ally and a model of Christian piety; and Querétaro, which boasted of divinely inspired indigenous origins. The spread of legends from these areas reflects the efforts of both patriotic creoles as well as local caciques.

Each chapter identifies and historicizes one major mode of cacique legal action and historical testimony, and explores its personal, thematic, and textual intersections with contemporaneous Hispanic representations of Mesoamerican and early colonial history, adhering to three general organizing premises. First, cacique strategies of self-fashioning at each stage were attuned to both contemporary social and political challenges as well as the inconsistent and shifting application of imperial laws. Second, there were Spanish and creole observers in every era who, for patriotic,

---

[62] See, for example, Rolena Adorno, "Court and Chronicle: A Native Andean's Engagement with Spanish Colonial Law," in *Native Claims: Indigenous Law Against Empire, 1500–1920*, ed. Saliha Belmessous (New York: Oxford University Press, 2012); R. Jovita Baber, "Law, Land, and Legal Rhetoric in Colonial New Spain: A Look at the Changing Rhetoric of Indigenous Americans in the Sixteenth Century," in *Native Claims: Indigenous Law Against Empire, 1500–1920*, ed. Saliha Belmessous (New York: Oxford University Press, 2012).

religious, or self-interested reasons, sympathized with and drew information from the native lords, thereby adapting and transmitting their visions to a broader Hispanic audience. Finally, the creoles' information reflected not only pre-Hispanic historical knowledge and memory, but also the concerns of the colonial native lords who were their informants and sources.

All together, the book traces cacique contributions to the tenor and scope of Novohispanic creolism – the emotive identification with Mexico's indigenous past – through three major epochs. The first was the formative era of the sixteenth century, when Spanish and creole authors worked with the heirs to native dynasties to uncover and record Mesoamerican history in both alphabetic and pictorial texts. Next was the long baroque era of patriotic myth-making, roughly 1640–1740, when indigenous nobles and erudite creoles alike hailed legendary preconquest and conquest-era heroes, the former to establish their own merit, and the latter to ennoble their own partially imagined patria. Last was the rational–empirical late-colonial stage, approximately 1740–1810, marked by the triumphant "rediscovery" of indigenous "antiquities" – in reality artifacts of the sixteenth and seventeenth centuries – and its effects on late-colonial controversies over the nature and legal status of Indians. At every stage, highly consequential collaborations between native lords and creole antiquarians, united by a shared identification with Mexican history, anchored the development of the cacique–creole vision (Figure 1).

Chapters 2 and 3 address the incorporation of the caciques into colonial governance during the sixteenth century, and its effects on postconquest remembrances of preconquest history. The primary protagonists are the bilingual sons and grandsons of preconquest rulers and their (often likewise Nahuatl-speaking) Spanish teachers, acquaintances, and sympathizers. During the 1530s and 1540s, surviving native leaders – along with several Spaniards who had married their daughters and nieces – articulated the premises behind the argument for cacique autonomy under Spanish rule: An emphasis on ancestral greatness combined with assertions of loyalty to the crown and religious orthodoxy. It was a synthesis that was to become the most iconic mode of self-representation among Mexico's indigenous elites for centuries; it also ushered preconquest political relationships into the postconquest era, effectively casting New Spain as the "heir" to Anahuac. By the 1550s, caciques throughout central Mexico were waging sophisticated legal and epistolary campaigns, demanding crown support for their inherited rights.

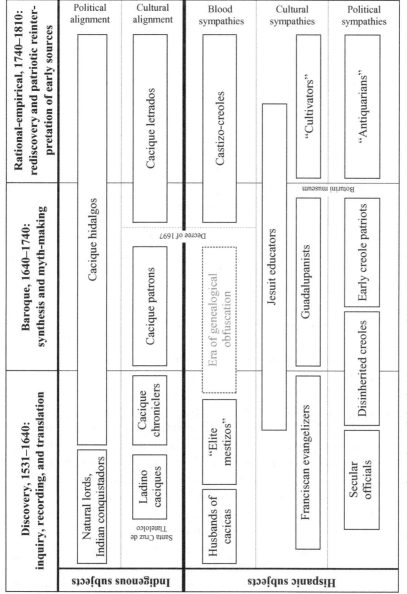

FIGURE 1 Conceptual timeline of the development of Mexican creolism

23

Yet for all their assertions of loyalty, the cumulative result was an ambivalent, if not resentful awareness of their own diminishment, an effect of the
contrast between their memories of historic grandeur and their own relative penury and powerlessness. Meanwhile, these same caciques, simultaneously Indian lords and vassals of Spain, collaborated actively with
those Spaniards – primarily Franciscan friars but also some influential
secular allies – who, for religious, moral, or even selfish reasons, invested
in uncovering and recording the events of Mesoamerican history. One
result was an eclectic series of pictorial and alphabetic histories, genealogies, and legends that not only formed the core of the incipient cacique–
creole archive, but also defined the major themes and motifs that later
generations would identify as "Mexican history." Such texts, whether
primarily authored by Spaniards or caciques, often evince the caciques'
iconic declinism – the sense, even by the 1530s, that a certain historic
luster had been lost, or at least diminished.

Chapter 4 explores the monumental works of the indigenous and mestizo chroniclers active at the turn of the seventeenth century: The grandchildren and great-grandchildren of the lords who had first received favors
from the Spanish regime. Bilingual and educated in Spanish letters, the
cacique-chroniclers echoed stories they inherited from previous generations, and like the testimonies of their predecessors, the rhetorical power
of their chronicles was rooted in tales of pre-Hispanic greatness combined with expressions of loyalty to Spain. The Franciscan influence was
prevalent, inasmuch as the chronicles echo their tendency to interpret
pre-Hispanic history as America's Old Testament, rich with providential
overtones foreshadowing the inevitable triumph of Hispanic Christianity. By synthesizing such ideas with native oral and pictorial traditions
and "translating" them into patriotic narrative accounts, they imbued
cacique memories with the epistemological imprimatur of history. As
accessible exemplars of "Indian history" recorded by Christian caciques,
the chroniclers had an enormous influence on the subsequent development of creolism, especially by way of Juan de Torquemada, a contemporary Franciscan, whose vast and erudite account of Anahuac was the
foundational creole text for over a century and a half.

Chapters 5 and 6 center on the baroque period, a time of patriotic
myth-making in New Spain, as caciques and creoles alike reinterpreted
and reoriented the fragments of Mesoamerican history they inherited for
new purposes. During this period, the development of Mexican creolism
acquired a distinctly Jesuit flavor, inasmuch as it increasingly emphasized
the Indians' capacity for reason. Soon after their arrival in 1572, the

Jesuits organized a network of schools for cacique children; such institutions produced a small but steady stream of two colonial types likely to adopt the historical visions underlying the ideal of continuity between Anahuac and New Spain: educated bilingual caciques, and their creole teachers and collaborators.

By 1600, New Spain had acquired a class of people who were culturally and linguistically Hispanic and who did not boast of ancestral estates, yet who nonetheless continued to proclaim the traditional identity of caciques. Unlanded, mestizo caciques with only the remotest of ties to preconquest patrimonies continued to demand and defend noble privileges such as tax exemptions by citing both ancestral heroes and a tradition of unyielding loyalty and church patronage. Whereas previous generations had merely declared their peaceful submission to Church and crown, seventeenth-century caciques were likely to go even further, portraying their ancestors not only as willing Christians, but also as crusaders who had fearlessly tamed and evangelized the savage lands of America. By turns both direct and indirect, such cacique myth-making intersected frequently with a small but influential network of creole elites who considered themselves linked – primarily by land but also, in some cases, by blood – to the Mesoamerican heritage. Substantiating their patriotic longings were the cacique histories of previous generations, which the creoles held forth as patrimonial treasures. Importantly, the most influential creole texts – in which accounts of miracles and arcane baroque exegesis coexisted seamlessly with an overt emphasis on empiricism – derived from several highly consequential collaborations with cacique lineages.

Chapters 7 and 8 focus on the late-colonial era, a time of patriotic rediscovery, when certain caciques and sympathetic Hispanic leaders alike appealed to the cacique–creole archive within disputes over the proper place of Indians within a Spanish monarchy increasingly devoted to centralization and cultural homogenization. The 1690s marked an important transition, detailed in Chapter 7. Like other provincial elites in the early modern Hispanic world, many native lords saw the potential for social mobility in the bureaucratic structures of the Church and the viceregal apparatus. Encouraged by imperial reforms, numerous cacique families began placing their children within New Spain's network of colleges and seminaries toward 1700 and after, most of them run by Jesuits. This resulted in the emergence of a small, but important vanguard of educated caciques that represented themselves as Indian lords as well as clergy and viceregal functionaries, enforcing colonial hierarchies even as their very existence subverted them. Some creoles, meanwhile – particularly their

Jesuit acquaintances – held such men to be authoritative representatives of the native legacy, and even went so far as to retroactively Indianize the reputations of deceased ecclesiastical luminaries so as to promote them as symbols of Novohispanic erudition.

The eighth and final chapter examines a select cohort of native writers and intellectuals in the eighteenth century. An analysis reveals that they remained dispositionally committed to their indigenous heritage even as they moved within an overwhelmingly Hispanic arena, operating as "Indian ambassadors" and defending native history in colonial debates. Leveraging their ability to speak as priests and royal functionaries, they participated in some of the major disputes of the Enlightenment-era Atlantic world, such as the perennial controversy over the "nature" and capacities of America's native peoples. Many sided with the Jesuits and the Franciscans, their traditional collaborators and teachers, who had long validated native peoples by way of apologetic histories. By engaging Spanish conceits on their own discursive and formal grounds, the cacique-intellectuals challenged those who justified and enforced the social and legal subordination of non-Spaniards. Others, meanwhile, lent their presumed expertise to the Bourbon agenda of imperial consolidation.

Conclusion

In Mexico City in early 1600, the Spanish-speaking Juan Cano de Moctezuma painted a commemorative portrait of his great-grandfather, the famous ruler of Tenochtitlan.[63] To mark the occasion, native and Spanish leaders organized festivities that included a theatrical appearance by the late emperor himself, impersonated by his Nahuatl-speaking grandson don Hernando Alvarado Tezozomoc, a well-recognized nobleman of San Juan Tenochtitlan, Mexico City's indigenous sector. Adorned with ceremonial robes and precious feathers, the crowd bore don Hernando on a litter in the pre-Hispanic style to the Spanish administrative center of Mexico City, where he paid respects at the Metropolitan Cathedral and the viceregal palace.[64] Thus did both Moctezuma's "Spanish" and

---

[63] Juan Cano de Moctezuma was a grandson of doña Isabel Tecuichpochtzin, a highborn daughter of Moctezuma, and Juan Cano de Saavedra, an early Spanish conquistador. Chimalpahin Cuauhtlehuanitzin, *Codex Chimalpahin*: v. 2, 86–88.

[64] Domingo Francisco de San Antón Muñon Chimalpahin Cuauhtlehuanitzin, *Annals of His Time: Don Domingo de San Antón Muñón Chimalpahin Quauhtlehuanitzin*, trans. James Lockhart, Susan Schroeder, and Doris Namala (Stanford: Stanford University Press, 2006), 66–67.

"Indian" heirs, via a highly idealized interpretation of historical events, jointly proclaim the integration of native Mexico into the Spanish crown.

Writing almost two centuries later, José Mariano Díaz de la Vega – whose account of Tlaxcala's Virgin of Ocotlan opened this chapter – would likewise invoke the authority of native leaders and the authenticity of their memories in his defense of Indian Christianity. Importantly, neither the pageantry of 1600 nor Díaz's account of 1782 acknowledged any rupture or conquest in Mexican indigenous history; both imagined perfect alignment and comity between the native heritage and the Hispano-Catholic structures of their own time, and both enlisted cacique memories to substantiate such notions. Yet these were not "ancient" memories; both Tezozomoc and the Tlaxcalteca caciques were participating in a colonial culture that accepted indigenous nobility only once it had been sufficiently Christianized and reconciled to Spanish rule. Indeed, creoles privileged them as "Indian authorities" precisely to the extent that they enabled the fiction of Indo-Hispanic harmony.

Calling for further research, Lockhart once noted the existence of educated native elites who straddled the colonial divide, thereby introducing aspects of indigenous identity to their Hispanic contemporaries.[65] Similarly, in demonstrating the degree to which Spaniards relied upon and absorbed Nahua geographical and historical understandings of the far north, Danna Levin Rojo has called upon scholars to be more attentive to the ways that colonizers can be impacted by the cultures of the colonized.[66] Such concerns animate the research behind the present volume. For different reasons, both native lords and erudite creoles advocated broadly parallel and complementary visions of history in colonial Mexico. This nexus was both inspired and reinforced by their shared emotive attachment to the Mexican landscape and its human legacy, especially *vis-à-vis* outsiders such as Spaniards and *castas* (people of mixed background). This sentimental alignment, however, never coalesced into a coherent or self-conscious program of mythic nationalism or a unified political identity. In tracing cacique political strategies and their role in the emergence of Mexican creolism, then, I refer not to a shared immediate political agenda, but to deeper rhetorical and thematic patterns that become apparent only when we assess the broad arc of cacique self-representation and creole historiography over many generations – a

---

[65] Lockhart, *The Nahuas* 592–93, n. 59. Lockhart was writing of don Manuel de los Santos, a Tlaxcalteca nobleman (d. 1715) addressed in this volume.

[66] Levin Rojo, *Return to Aztlan*, 10–12.

persistent undercurrent rather than an explicit or self-conscious argument. Yet in the long run, by invoking memories of Anahuac within colonial-era negotiations and controversies, native elites and their creole contemporaries appended a proud indigenous past to the mixed colonial society of New Spain – and therefore to Mexico, the modern nation it spawned.

2

The natural lords

Asserting continuity, 1531–66

[Is the witness aware] that for one, ten, twenty, thirty, forty, and fifty and sixty years, and for so much time that the memory of men cannot contradict it, the aforementioned lords of Tatelolco (sic) . . . have held and possessed these lands, availing themselves of their macehuales . . . and reaping their fruits tranquilly and peacefully?

Inquest on behalf of the caciques of Tlatelolco, 1536[1]

All together, people have lived . . . in this land for a total of 765 years, and according to the [Indian histories] perhaps eight or nine years more (unless I have not counted correctly). . . . I have wanted to inform Your Majesty of this so that you will know of those who inhabit this your land of New Spain . . . and to warn Your Majesty that there are people of lineage here . . . [who] are currently disfavored, [but] it was not [they] who caused the war and uprising against the Spaniards, but the other Mexicans . . . because once defeated and subjugated . . . they did not regret it, and they have been profitable [allies] ever since. We believe it . . . unjust that they should pay the debts of the sinners, nor is it right that those who were vassals should trample their superiors, nor is God served when there is hatred among those who are already Christians, or when others reap benefits while those to whom the land originally belonged go about poor and lost.

Franciscan friar on behalf of Juan Cano and doña Isabel Moctezuma, 1532[2]

[1] Probanza of the Lords of Tlatelolco, July–Oct 1536, AGI-J 159, N.5, f. 1331v.
[2] "Origen de los mexicanos," in Joaquín García Icazbalceta, ed. *Nueva colección de documentos para la historia de México: Pomar-Zurita, relaciones antiguas (Siglo XVI)* (Mexico: Editorial Salvador Chávez Hayhoe, 1941), 278–79.

In 1566, a group of Nahua nobles in Mexico City commissioned an illustrated genealogy of Tezacatl and Acazitli, two of the original founders of Tenochtitlan. It was an expression of both civic heritage and aristocratic identity. Four *tlacuiloque* (painters) produced the image on a large *tilma*, or woven fabric, and artistically represented the ancestral tree as a great nopal cactus with multiple branches. On Easter, they paraded the tilma through the streets of the colonial capital to the Indians' church of San José de los Naturales, where they hung it outside for all to see.[3]

European cartographers may have labeled it a *mundus novus*, but no one in sixteenth-century Mexico could have been unaware of its true antiquity. From well-used bridges and roads to irrigated fields and dams, and from elaborate historical manuscripts to songs and oral traditions, reminders of Anahuac were everywhere. While posterity would often perceive the conquest as a transformational cataclysm decisively severing Aztec Mexico from the Hispano-Christian society that replaced it, in reality colonial institutions initially presumed to commandeer and administer an already ancient civilization. Accordingly, contemporaneous records plainly demonstrate that native political identities and agendas not only survived, but remained consequential well into the sixteenth century and beyond, inflecting postconquest interactions between indigenous groups, and between natives and Spaniards.

This chapter illustrates the prevalence and significance of legal and moral appeals to Mexican antiquity during the first postconquest decades – a time not only of upheaval, but also of self-conscious efforts at restoration and reconstruction. It highlights the legal status and political plight of the hereditary native leadership following the conquest, and explores early colonial disputes over lands and resources in which certain parties – not only native lords but also Spaniards who married prominent Nahua noblewomen – cited inheritance and genealogy to challenge claims predicated on conquest and its spoils. Appearing before Spanish tribunals, they quickly appropriated the medieval Iberian legal category of "natural lords" (*señores naturales*) – those whose authority and noble privileges derived from local history rather than recent events – and stressed the inviolability of rights inherited from antiquity.[4] Yet such claims rarely went

---

[3] Luis Reyes García, *Cómo te confundes? Acaso no somos conquistadores?: anales de Juan Bautista* (México, DF: Centro de Investigaciones y Estudios Superiores en Antropología Social, 2001), 144–47.

[4] For background on this concept, see Robert S. Chamberlain, "The Concept of the Señor Natural as Revealed by Castillian Law and Administrative Documents," *Hispanic American Historical Review* 19, no. 2 (1939); Charles Gibson, *The Aztecs Under Spanish*

uncontested, as the caciques' patrimonies were themselves the products of a long and contentious history. To substantiate their claims, then, native lords, their indigenous and Spanish rivals, and their sympathizers all proclaimed dueling versions of local history before colonial officials, legitimating their own rights while challenging those of others. In this way colonial politics developed a backward-looking dimension as early as the 1530s, ensuring that preconquest history would remain politically relevant, to be recounted, disputed, and arbitrated within colonial forums. In this sense, New Spain was indeed the heir to Anahuac, as some of the political conflicts of the latter resurfaced as disputes within the legal apparatus of the former.

As petitioners offered colonial jurists conflicting versions of Mexican history, two interrelated motifs emerged. The first was an emphasis on "restoration" – meaning the tribute rights or local sovereignty their ancestors had enjoyed – a logical concern of displaced elites. But demands for restoration also implied continuity, the sense that the Spanish newcomers had joined an already established political arena rather than forged a new one. This amounted to a tendency or willful inclination to deny, blur, or disregard any distinctions between the legal and political institutions of New Spain and the native structures that preceded them. The new regime in Mexico City, they insisted, was legitimate precisely to the extent that it embraced and guaranteed the primordial rights of Anahuac's natural lords. In this way, the patrimonial interests of the central Mexican nobility were grandfathered into the cacophony of colonial politics. Many aspects of the old identities, rivalries, and agendas survived, sublimated into appeals to colonial institutions and laws.

Colonizing the *Pipiltin*

In settled Mesoamerica as in Europe, there was a small group born into the top of society that dressed and ate better, spoke differently, and dominated positions of civil and religious authority. The nonlaboring Mesoamerican aristocrats, approximately 10 percent of the population, were known among the Nahuas as *pipiltin* (singular *pilli*). They were the primary beneficiaries of the central Mexican political economy, which included a sophisticated tributary system. Literally translated as "child," the word "pilli" referenced, like its Hispanic analog *hidalgo* ("son of

Rule: A History of the Indians of the Valley of Mexico, 1519–1810 (Stanford: Stanford University Press, 1964), 155.

something"), the hereditary essence of nobility.[5] While referring to the aristocracy in general, in regular usage a pilli was a minor nobleman, usually the relation of a more powerful lord, or *teuctli* (plural *teteuctin*), distinguished by his or her inheritance of an estate that included tribute-paying dependants. Both teteuctin and pipiltin were considered superior to the majority *macehualtin* (singular *macehualli*), the laboring commoners.

Political relationships defined the high nobility. Almost all teteuctin participated in the civil, military, and religious governing structures of an *altepetl* (plural *altepeme*), the ethnic city-state that was the primary sociopolitical unit of central Mexico. They typically lived in and managed a palace compound called a *tecpan* ("lord's place"), which housed their families while also serving as a site of administration and diplomacy.[6] The highest-ranking teuctli in an altepetl, almost always male, was revered as the "speaker," or *tlatoani* (plural *tlatoque*). The tlatoani embodied the political identity of an altepetl; indeed, a community without a tlatoani was not an altepetl, but rather a district or dependency of a more powerful polity. Although not a strict regime of primogeniture, most tlatoque were brothers, sons, or nephews of previous rulers who secured power with the consensus and support of a critical mass of local teteuctin. Noblewomen played an important role as mothers, as the dynastic legacy was generally transmitted to the sons of a tlatoani's highest-born wife.[7]

While they did perceive the heterogeneity of the Nahua aristocracy, the Spaniards tended to acknowledge only a simple duality consisting of an upper and lower group.[8] Those with major political or social influence they labeled "caciques," a word for a local chief or leader adopted from the Caribbean islanders. Those who were not heirs to a prominent estate, meanwhile, they termed *principales*, or "notables." (The macehualtin they called simply *macehuales* or "Indians.") When engaging colonial authorities, the pipiltin quickly found it necessary to master and deploy Spanish categories, and by the second postconquest generation

---

[5] Lockhart, *The Nahuas* 102, 506, n. 43; Pedro Carrasco, "Los linajes nobles del México antiguo," in *Estratificación social en la Mesoamérica prehispánica*, eds. Pedro Carrasco and Johanna Broda (México: Centro de Investigaciones Superiores, Instituto Nacional de Antropología e Historia, 1976), 21–23.

[6] Susan T. Evans, "Architecture and Authority in an Aztec Village: Form and Function of a Tecpan," in *Land and Politics in the Valley of Mexico: A Two-Thousand-Year Perspective*, ed. H.R. Harvey (Albuquerque, NM: University of New Mexico Press, 1991).

[7] Lockhart, *The Nahuas* 14–28, 109.

[8] Charles Gibson, "The Aztec Aristocracy in Colonial Mexico," *Comparative Studies in Society and History* 2 (1960): 175–76.

commonly referred to themselves as "caciques and principales" to signal both civic leadership as well as noble pedigree. Hispanic tradition
also granted caciques the most visible and iconic marker of their status:
Without exception, upon receiving Christian names, they adopted the
old Iberian honorific titles of *don* and *doña* (from the Latin *dominus* and
domina, master and mistress). Increasingly archaic and rare among early
modern Spaniards, the *don* became a defining feature of elite indigenous
self-representation in America, available only to those who controlled a
noble estate or who attained high civic offices in an altepetl. Indeed, they
policed it among themselves, denying it to those deemed unworthy.[9]

Culturally, central Mexican elites were cosmopolitan. Power in
Anahuac after 1428 revolved around the "Triple Alliance": a political
and military partnership between the region's three dominant ancestral
groups: the Mexica with their capital at Tenochtitlan, the Acolhuaque
of Tetzcoco in the east, and the Tepaneca of Tlacopan in the west. The
three *tlatoloyan* (seats of government) were autonomous entities with
their own royal dynasties, yet they aligned in matters of war and imperial
administration, dividing the spoils among themselves.[10] As the ruler of
the Alliance's senior partner, the tlatoani of Tenochtitlan was hailed as
huei tlatoani, the "great" or "supreme" speaker. Intermarriage between
elite families was common, as it was a powerful diplomatic tool, a means
for weaker lords to secure alliances and more powerful families to build
networks and project influence.[11] This, along with extensive polygamy –
the Tetzcoca tlatoani Nezahualpilli (1464–1515) is famed for having
fathered perhaps 145 children – meant that the top ranks of Anahuac
were intricately related.[12]

As civic and military authorities, the pipiltin determined local responses
to the Spanish invasion of 1519–21. For the Triple Alliance, this agenda
demanded resistance once the newcomers turned overtly violent. Yet
provincial lords, lacking clear and forceful leadership from Tenochtitlan,
did not mount a unified response, thereby allowing the conquistadors to

---

[9] Lockhart, *The Nahuas* 129–30; Haskett, *Indigenous Rulers*: 135–37. Especially in the
late-colonial period, caciques and principales were sometimes distinguished in that the
former could style themselves *don* and *doña* while the latter could not.

[10] Gibson, *The Aztecs*: 9–20.

[11] Pedro Carrasco, *The Tenochca Empire of Ancient Mexico: The Triple Alliance of
Tenochtitlán, Tetzcoco, and Tlacopan* (Norman: University of Oklahoma Press, 1999),
19, 100–02.

[12] Bradley Thomas Benton, "The Lords of Tetzcoco: Sixteenth-Century Transformations
of Indigenous Leadership in the Aztec Empire's Second City" (Ph.D. diss., UCLA, 2012),
39–43.

assemble an anti-Mexica coalition of multiple native partners, mostly by way of copious promises of autonomy and reciprocity to local leaders.[13] After the fall of Tenochtitlan, the conqueror Hernando Cortés consolidated his hold over the pipiltin with a program of targeted assassination, systematically terrorizing local leaders into acquiescence and replacing dissenters with puppets drawn from rival factions.[14] Most notoriously, in 1525, while safely away from Mexico and its throngs, Cortés executed the three surviving heirs to the Triple Alliance – Cuauhtemoc of Tenochtitlan, Coanacoch of Tetzcoco, and Tetlepanquetzal of Tlacopan – and replaced them with younger or more compliant successors.[15] In Tenochtitlan specifically, Cortés appointed a nondynastic "governor," and later brought many others to Spain.[16]

Over the next several decades, a codified and sanctioned space emerged for an elite indigenous class to mediate between the ruling Hispanic and subordinate Indian worlds. The heirs to the pipiltin were to leverage their inherited political capital to supply and provide for a Spanish conqueror overclass, their privileged status confirmed and protected by the Spanish king. Thus did the caciques become a lynchpin of what colonial jurists understood as the "Two Republics": A colonial political and legal ideal that envisioned two discrete and self-governing, yet parallel societies in New Spain – the first Indian and the other Spanish, with the former subordinated to the latter. While Cortés had begun naming native "governors" as early as 1521, other offices in the *república de indios* ("Indian republic") appeared soon thereafter. In 1530, the crown ordered each native town to empower "able Indians" to administer important mundane affairs such as tax collection, water management, road improvement, and peace enforcement.[17] In the 1540s, colonial officials began implementing

[13] See Laura E. Matthew, and Michel R. Oudijk, ed. *Indian Conquistadors: Indigenous Allies in the Conquest of Mesoamerica* (Norman: University of Oklahoma Press, 2007).

[14] Charles Gibson, "Llamamiento general, Repartimiento, and the Empire of Acolhuacán," *Hispanic American Historical Review* 36, no. 1 (1956): 1–2; Ruiz-Medrano, *Mexico's Indigenous Communities*: 17–18.

[15] Cortés denied hanging Coanacoch alongside the other two tlatoque, yet all sources agree that he died at the same time. The confusion might be explained by Cortés's alliance with don Fernando Cortés Ixtlilxochitl, Coanacoch's half-brother, who protested the punishment. Hernán Cortés, *Letters from Mexico*, trans. Anthony Pagden (New Haven: Yale University Press, 2001), 365–67, 518, n. 52.

[16] Chimalpahin Cuauhtlehuanitzin, *Codex Chimalpahin*: v. 1, 57–59; William F. Connell, *After Moctezuma: Indigenous Politics and Self-Government in Mexico City, 1524–1730* (Norman, OK: University of Oklahoma Press, 2011), 168; Gibson, *The Aztecs*: 168.

[17] Empress Juana to the Second Audiencia of New Spain, Madrid, July 12, 1530, in Vasco de Puga, *Provisiones, cédulas, instrucciones para el gobierno de la Nueva España*, facsimile ed. (Madrid: Ediciones Cultura Hispánica, 1945), v. 3, f. 40r.

the Iberian *cabildo* system of municipal government in native communities: An annually elected council consisting of first-instance magistrates, aldermen, and lesser officials such as notary and town crier.[18] To accommodate the still-relevant tlatoque, a biennial "governor" headed each cabildo, even though the position had no Iberian precedent. And although the viceroyalty frequently meddled in the Indian republics, the councils were active sites of local native politics for generations.[19]

The Indian republics had mixed effects on the traditional nobility. They initially facilitated their political preservation, as preconquest lineages dominated the early cabildos.[20] Yet cabildos were elected bodies, and therefore helped usher commoners into positions of authority, sometimes ennobling them. One result was an indigenous aristocracy in decline, one that traded in history and memories as much as real power and largesse. The transformation was gradual, but real; by 1600, administrative power in central Mexico's native towns was largely divorced from pedigree, and titles such as "cacique" and "principal" referred to cabildo officers as often as to men and women of lineage.[21] The overall enervation of central Mexico's traditional leadership contrasts somewhat with highland Peru, where the crown's reliance on silver production secured a position of relative prominence for local caciques as imperial liaisons outside and above the cabildos.[22]

[18] Charles Gibson, *Tlaxcala in the Sixteenth Century* (Stanford, CA: Stanford University Press, 1967), 62–63; James Lockhart, Frances Berdan, and Arthur J.O. Anderson, eds. *The Tlaxcalan Actas: A Compendium of the Records of the Cabildo of Tlaxcala, 1545–1627* (Provo, UT: University of Utah Press, 1986).

[19] On viceregal meddling and outsider governors, see Lockhart, *The Nahuas* 33–35; Gibson, *The Aztecs*: 181. For long-term studies of individual cabildos, see Connell, *After Moctezuma*; Haskett, *Indigenous Rulers*; Andrea Martínez Baracs, *Un gobierno de indios: Tlaxcala, 1519–1750* (México: Fondo de Cultura Económica, 2008).

[20] See Robert Haskett, "Indian Town Government in Colonial Cuernavaca: Persistance, Adaptation, Change," *Hispanic American Historical Review* 71, no. 3 (1987); Robert S. Haskett, "Living in Two Worlds: Continuity and Change among Cuernavaca's Colonial Indigenous Ruling Elite," *Ethnohistory* 35, no. 1 (1988); Haskett, *Indigenous Rulers*: 131–37; Kellogg, *Law and the Transformation of Aztec Culture*: 24; Lockhart, *The Nahuas* 28–41, 112; Lockhart, *The Tlaxcalan Actas: A Compendium of the Records of the Cabildo of Tlaxcala, 1545–1627*, 11–12; Arij Ouweneel, "From "tlatocayotl" to "gobernadoryotl": A Critical Examination of Indigenous Rule in 18th-Century Central Mexico," *American Ethnologist* 22, no. 4 (1995).

[21] See Margarita Menegus Bornemann, *Del señorío indígena a la república de indios: el caso de Toluca, 1500–1600* (México: Consejo Nacional para la Cultura y las Artes, 1991).

[22] Peruvian Viceroy Francisco de Toledo's reforms in the 1570s, designed to maximize silver production and route its profits to the royal treasury, required local Indian leaders to direct labor gangs and oversee tax collections. Andean nobles, while retaining few of their preconquest social roles, thus remained quite consequential in provincial affairs.

Mesoamerican landed patrimonies – which early imperial decrees explicitly respected – experienced parallel transformations.[23] Although the European notion of "property rights" had no true equivalent in Nahua society – estates were attached to the office as much as the person – Spaniards understood noble lands (*teuctlalli* or *pillalli*) as "Indian *mayorazgos*" or entailed estates, and institutionalized them as *cacicazgos*.[24] Meanwhile, as the native population collapsed over the sixteenth century, many lords were compelled to sell or rent unused community lands to Spaniards and mestizos – even though this was technically illegal.[25] As cacicazgos acquired the characteristics of private property, the residual loyalty of the macehualtin dissipated.

Yet most important for the current study were colonial efforts to secure the cultural allegiance of central Mexico's native leaders. While some ambitious Spaniards pursued marriages with native noblewomen due to inherit tributes or rents, education was the preferred tactic with regards to men.[26] Indeed, the evangelical enterprise that transformed the spiritual landscape of Mexico began with and depended heavily upon the nobility, especially the younger generation. As early as 1524, Cortés ordered noble children to be removed into the care of the Church.[27] Once educated in Spanish language and customs, they were to become teachers to their parents, both modeling and enforcing the indigenous reduction to

See David T. Garrett, *Shadows of Empire: The Indian Nobility of Cusco, 1750–1825* (Cambridge: Cambridge University Press, 2005), 34–44; Kenneth J. Andrien, *Andean Worlds: Indigenous History, Culture, and Consciousness under Spanish Rule, 1532–1825* (Albuquerque, NM: University of New Mexico Press, 2001), 50–53.

[23] Queen Juana to the Audiencia of Mexico, Valladolid, Dec 1, 1550, in Puga, *Provisiones, cédulas, instrucciones para el gobierno de la Nueva España*: v.3, f. 122r.

[24] RLI-VI, 7.1. Margarita Menegus Bornemann notes aspects of private landownership as well as Mesoamerican tributary practices in the Novohispanic cacicazgo, and describes it as "a complex institution blending rights both ancient and new." Margarita Menegus Bornemann, "El cacicazgo en Nueva España," in *El cacicazgo en Nueva España y Filipinas*, eds. Margarita Menegus Bornemann and Rodolfo Aguirre Salvador (México: Universidad Nacional Autónoma de México, Plaza y Valdés, 2005), 69.

[25] Lockhart, *The Nahuas* 133; Terraciano, *The Mixtecs*: 229; Gibson, *The Aztecs*: 106, 263–67; Reyes García, *Anales de Juan Bautista*: 42.

[26] Pedro Carrasco, "Indian–Spanish Marriages in the First Century of the Colony," in *Indian Women of Early Mexico*, eds. Susan Schroeder, Stephanie Wood, and Robert Haskett (Norman: University of Oklahoma Press, 1997).

[27] Hernando Cortés, "Ordenanzas de buen gobierno dadas por Hernando Cortés para la Nueva España," no. 10, in *Colección de documentos inéditos, relativos al descubrimiento, conquista y organización de las antiguas posesiones españolas de América y Oceanía, sacados de los archivos del reino, y muy especialmente del Indias*, 42 vols. (Madrid: Colección de documentos inéditos de Indias,1864–84), v. 26, 135–48.; Cortés, *Letters from Mexico*: 336, 511–12, n. 69.

colonial law and religion. The king quickly extended this policy – which echoed contemporary efforts to integrate the former Muslims of southern Castile – demanding in 1526 that twenty of the "most noble, able, and capable children" of Anahuac be placed in Castilian monasteries to learn "how to live politically according to order and reason" before returning home as vanguards of Hispanism.[28] By the mid 1530s, this policy was generalized; noble children were to be removed into the care of the friars "so that the children of caciques – who are to govern the Indians – are instructed while still young in our Holy Catholic Faith."[29] According to the seventeenth-century Franciscan chronicler Juan de Torquemada, the Indians of Mexico were converted "by way of their children."[30]

The most famous early initiative of this sort was the Franciscan College of Santa Cruz de Tlatelolco, established in 1536 under the joint sponsorship of the first viceroy and the first archbishop, don Antonio de Mendoza (r. 1535–50) and fray Juan de Zumárraga (r. 1528–48). For several decades at Santa Cruz, a substantial number of Anahuac's noble boys received a pre-Tridentine humanist education, learning to read, write, and speak Spanish and Latin. They also worked with the Franciscans to produce written grammars for Nahuatl, and became the first Amerindians to write their own language using the Roman alphabet.[31] In helping to translate Christian ideas and concepts into Nahuatl, and Nahua ideas and concepts into Spanish, the native intellectuals of Santa Cruz contributed to the complex and influential theological project that some have understood as "the Nahuatlization of Christianity."[32]

[28] Carlos V to the Governor or Acting Authority of New Spain, Granada, Nov 9, 1526, in Puga, *Provisiones, cédulas, instrucciones para el gobierno de la Nueva España*: v. 3 f. 21r.

[29] RLI-I, 23.11.

[30] Torquemada, *Monarquía indiana*: v. 5, 62.

[31] Francis Borgia Steck, "The First College in America: Santa Cruz de Tlatelolco," *The Catholic Educational Review* 34(1936); Silvermoon, "The Imperial College of Tlatelolco and the Emergence of a New Nahua Intellectual Elite in New Spain (1500–1760)" (Ph.D. diss., Duke University, 2007); Rocío Cortés, "The Colegio Imperial de Santa Cruz de Tlatelolco and Its Aftermath: Nahua Intellectuals and the Spiritual Conquest of Mexico," in *A Companion to Latin American Literature and Culture*, ed. Sarah Castro-Klaren (Malden, MA: Blackwell, 2008).

[32] Charles Dibble, "The Nahuatlization of Christianity," in *Sixteenth-Century Mexico: The Work of Sahagún*, ed. Munro Edmunson (Albuquerque: University of New Mexico Press, 1974), 225–33. See also Louise M. Burkhart, *The Slippery Earth: Nahua–Christian Moral Dialogue in Sixteenth-Century Mexico* (Tucson, AZ: University of Arizona Press, 1989); Mark Christensen, *Nahua and Maya Catholicisms: Texts and Religion in Colonial Central Mexico and Yucatan* (Stanford: Stanford University Press, 2013); David

Santa Cruz was always controversial, as many ecclesiastical and secular authorities disapproved of its objectives.[33] Political opposition, along with floods and epidemics, diminished the school considerably by 1570. Nonetheless, the project left a profound imprint on the Nahua upper class. Most significantly, it marked the first emergence of a *ladino* ("Latinized," or bilingual) vanguard among the most prominent central Mexican lineages. These bicultural *hijos de caciques* ("children of caciques"), dressing like Spaniards and citing Cicero in the original Latin, gained partial access to the exclusive and erudite realm of viceregal politics, which relied heavily upon the written word.[34] Colonial authorities valued educated ladinos highly, as intermediaries, translators, and envoys between the Hispanic and indigenous worlds, as well as "good Indians" to serve as examples to their compatriots.[35] As a result, they gained some access to the top circles of Spanish administration on both sides of the Atlantic, a phenomenon historians have only recently begun to fully assess.[36]

Crucially, although somewhat culturally estranged from their ancestral communities, ecclesiastical and secular officials alike understood Latinized caciques as trustworthy authorities on native history and culture.[37] For centuries, non-Indians interested in Mexican antiquity habitually turned to the ladino caciques, those who could and did "translate" indigenous oral traditions and pictorial records into alphabetic Nahuatl, Castilian, or Latin. Indeed, many of the most important sixteenth-century alphabetic texts on Mesoamerican history derive from a relatively tiny handful of central Mexican ladinos trained at Tlatelolco.[38]

Tavárez, "Nahua Intellectuals, Franciscan Scholars, and the *Devotio moderna* in Colonial Mexico," *The Americas* 70, no. 2 (2013).

[33] Torquemada, *Monarquía indiana*: v. 5, 176–78. "There is nothing in this world, however good and beneficial it may be, that does not face opposition," lamented Torquemada.

[34] Connell, *After Moctezuma*: 72–73; Silvermoon, "Imperial College of Tlatelolco," 281–91.

[35] Toribio de Benavente Motolinia, *Motolinía's History of the Indians of New Spain*, trans. Francis Borgia Steck (Washington, DC: Academy of American Franciscan History, 1951), 176. Motolinia was referring to don Francisco, the governor of Cuitlahuac after the conquest, who invited the friars and helped build the local church.

[36] See, for example, José Carlos de la Puente Luna, "The Many Tongues of the King: Indigenous Language Interpreters and the Making of the Spanish Empire," *Colonial Latin American Review* 23, no. 2 (2014).

[37] Manuel Aguilar Moreno calls them "cultural informants." Manuel Aguilar Moreno, "The *Indio Ladino* as Cultural Mediator in the Colonial Society," *Estudios de cultura nahuatl* 33(2002): 154; Gibson, *The Aztecs*: 156.

[38] See Pedro Carrasco, "The Territorial Structure of the Aztec Empire," in *Land and Politics in the Valley of Mexico: A Two-Thousand-Year Perspective*, ed. H.R. Harvey (Albuquerque, NM: University of New Mexico Press, 1991); Carrasco, *Tenochca Empire*:

The relationship between the Christian hijos de caciques and the Franciscans at Santa Cruz – in which the latter learned about Anahuac from the former – would both model and fuel the creole appropriation of native history, detailed in subsequent chapters.

Patrimony and *amparo:* the cacique agenda

Spanish rule set in motion a series of large-scale processes that inexorably marginalized the Indian elite. The incipient export system cut deeply into their income by diverting labor, while crown magistrates and cabildos rendered them politically superfluous from both above and below. Meanwhile, native communities devastated by epidemics could not support a nonlaboring aristocracy. A handful escaped penury by joining the Hispanic nobility; a grandson of Moctezuma in Spain, for example, married a Spanish heiress, their descendants recognized as the Counts of Moctezuma.[39] Others were not so fortunate; impoverished and disempowered, they succumbed to what Emma Pérez-Rocha and Rafael Tena have termed "macehualization."[40]

Yet as a group the caciques did not disappear, nor were they ever inconsequential.[41] Imperial administration in New Spain encouraged – and indeed was partially premised on – the survival of a semiprivileged

---

50–61; Kevin Terraciano, "Three Views of the Conquest of Mexico from the *Other Mexica*," in *The Conquest All Over Again: Nahuas and Zapotecs Thinking, Writing, and Painting Spanish Colonialism*, ed. Susan Schroeder (Portland, OR: Sussex Academic Press, 2011), 19–22.

[39] This was don Diego Luis Moctezuma, the son of don Pedro Moctezuma Tlacahuepantzin. Forbidden from returning to Mexico, he married Francisca de la Cueva, a daughter of the Duke of Alburquerque. See Francisco L. Jiménez Abollado, "Don Diego Luis Moctezuma, nieto de *Hueytlatoani*, padre de conde: un noble indígena entre dos mundos," *Anuario de Estudios Americanos* 65, no. 1 (2008); Francisco Luis Jiménez Abollado and Verenice Cipatli Ramírez Calva, *Pretensiones señoriales de don Pedro Moctezuma Tlacahuepantzin Yohualicahuacatzin: Desafíos y vicisitudes de un mayorazgo, 1528–1606. Estudio y fuentes documentales* (Pachuca: Universidad Nacional Autónoma del Estado de Hidalgo, 2011), 104–07.

[40] PRT, 65–72; Lockhart, *The Nahuas* 112–13.

[41] Regional variation was the rule; in some areas, caciques all but disappeared, while in others they remained quite influential into the nineteenth century. See, for example, John K. Chance, "Indian Elites in Late Colonial Mesoamerica," in *Caciques and Their People: A Volume in Honor of Ronald Spores*, eds. Joyce Marcus, and Judith Francis Zeitlin (Ann Arbor, MI: University of Michigan Museum of Anthropology, 1994); John Chance, "The Caciques of Tecali: Class and Ethnic Identity in Late Colonial Mexico," *Hispanic American Historical Review* 76, no. 3 (1996); William Taylor, "Cacicazgos coloniales en el valle de Oaxaca," *Historia mexicana* XX, no. 1 (1970); Margarita Menegus Bornemann and Rodolfo Aguirre Salvador, eds. *El cacicazgo en Nueva España y Filipinas* (México: Universidad Nacional Autónoma de México, Plaza y Valdés, 2005).

FIGURE 2 Viceroy Luis de Velasco recognizes the Nahua cabildo officers of central Mexico, from *Codex Osuna*. Spain, Archivo Histórico de la Nobleza, Ministry of Education, Culture, and Sport, OSUNA, C2230, D.1(4), f. 9v.

indigenous intermediary group. Hapsburg Spain was an indirect, confederated empire, in which governance occurred via informal and formal negotiations between crown agents and local leaders.[42] Ideally, caciques were to speak for native communities before the crown, and represent the crown before their communities (Figure 2). This scheme encouraged the natural lords to adorn their pre-Hispanic lineages with the visible privileges and symbols of Spanish-style nobility.

The consolidation of the caciques' intermediary roles occurred in stages. The first came in 1523, when Cortés disobeyed the crown and implemented the *encomienda* system in central Mexico, assigning to individual conquistadors the rights to regular in-kind tributes from specified native communities.[43] *Encomenderos* (the beneficiaries of encomiendas) negotiated the terms with local caciques, who then oversaw

[42] For the premodern dimension of viceregal government, see Alejandro Cañeque, *The King's Living Image: The Culture and Politics of Viceregal Power in Colonial Mexico* (New York: Routledge, 2004).

[43] Carlos V was afraid that encomiendas would wreak the same havoc in Mexico that they had in the Caribbean, where the indigenous population was collapsing rapidly. See Instructions of Carlos V to Hernando Cortés, Valladolid, June 26, 1523, in Richard Koneztke, ed. *Colección de documentos para la historia de la formación social de Hispanoamérica, 1493–1810, ser. 1,* 3 vols. (Madrid: Consejo Superior de Investigaciones Científicas, 1953–1958), v. 1, 74–77. See also Lesley Byrd Simpson, *The Encomienda in New Spain: The Beginning of Spanish Mexico* (Berkeley: University of California Press, 1966), 56–72.

tribute collection and delivery. They were also charged with ensuring the Christianization of those entrusted to them, and upon baptism many native lords adopted the Hispanic surnames of their encomenderos, who served as godparents. Perversely, encomiendas facilitated a certain convergence of interests between local leaders and encomenderos by transforming the former into tax farmers; one result, notoriously, was lawlessness and recurring violence. Yet a new era began in 1531, when a group of highly trained Spanish jurists called *oidores* ("hearers") arrived in Mexico City to establish the so-called Second Audiencia, a tribunal wielding supreme judicial and executive authority. The audiencia's primary objective was to finally yoke New Spain – and the encomenderos – to the king's law.[44] The oidores took seriously the oft-repeated royal insistence that nonbelligerent Indians were "free vassals" of the king of Spain.[45] Drawing upon Iberian legal traditions that afforded a measure of self-governance to different ethnic communities under the crown, the members of the Second Audiencia were inclined to see caciques as natural lords rather than the underlings of encomenderos.[46]

Caciques gained another secular advocate in early 1535 with the arrival of don Antonio de Mendoza, the first viceroy and president of the audiencia. Mendoza recognized the pragmatic benefits of a well-disposed native elite, and his early ordinances indicate a general inclination to seek convergences between the interests of indigenous lords and colonial administration.[47] This is perhaps best symbolized by his incomplete efforts to re-empower the noble lineages of Anahuac under his own authority (and, not coincidentally, bypassing or marginalizing the encomenderos). Most famously, in 1538, he appointed a nephew and son-in-law of Moctezuma, don Diego de Alvarado Huanitzin, as the governor of Tenochtitlan – an act that Nahua observers understood as a dynastic restoration thirteen years after the execution of Cuauhtemoc.[48]

---

[44] Ethelia Ruiz-Medrano, *Reshaping New Spain: Government and Private Interests in the Colonial Bureaucracy, 1531–1550*, trans. Julia Constantino and Pauline Marmasse (Boulder, CO: University Press of Colorado, 2006), 15; Simpson, *The Encomienda in New Spain: The Beginning of Spanish Mexico*, 84–110.

[45] RLI-VI, 2.1.

[46] See Woodrow Borah, *Justice By Insurance: The General Indian Court of Colonial Mexico and the Legal Aides of the Half-Real* (Berkeley and Los Angeles: University of California Press, 1983), 15–16.

[47] Ordinances of Viceroy Mendoza Regarding Indians, Mexico City, June 30, 1536, AGI, Patronato 180, R. 67; see also RLI-VI, 2.1; and Simpson, *The Encomienda in New Spain: The Beginning of Spanish Mexico*: 111–22.

[48] Huanitzin's wife was doña Francisca de Moctezuma, daughter of the former huei tlatoani. Connell, *After Moctezuma*: 11–13; María Castañeda de la Paz, "Historia de

Thus, under Mendoza no less than Cortés, a selective tolerance for indigenous customs in colonial administration allowed royal officials to assume control of an already intact and wealth-producing civilization. Yet it also made preconquest Anahuac politically and legally relevant to the new colonial government. Anchored by the audiencia, the incipient regime theoretically committed itself to accommodating what it considered Mexico's "natural" social and political organization.[49] Within several decades the attitude had become explicit and official, as a royal decree of 1555 ordered that "the laws and good customs that the Indians had in antiquity" were to be "respected and enforced, so long as they do not conflict with Our Sacred Religion" or any Spanish laws.[50] Such an approach held major implications for indigenous leaders, those whose authority was rooted in local customs. Accordingly, another decree of 1557 explicitly declared that the Christian descendants of those who were "during the time of their infidelity caciques and lords of pueblos" should conserve their rights, and that submission to the crown "should not worsen their condition."[51]

The oidores and Viceroy Mendoza also infuriated the encomenderos by opening their doors to native litigants. Given access to the audiencia, native subjects, and especially caciques, began rearticulating their grievances in ways accessible and persuasive to the oidores, their cases arranged by a *procurador* (solicitor) – who during the sixteenth century was a salaried *protector de indios*, or Indians' legal advocate appointed by the viceroy.[52] The role of procuradores is clear within the legal records, inasmuch as they articulate native grievances according to the expected protocols and rhetoric of the audiencia. Interpreters, known as *nahuatlatos* (Nahuatl-speakers), also answered to the tribunal rather than to the litigants (though this was not necessarily the case in first-instance hearings before provincial magistrates). Together, they received the petitioners, distilled their claims into simple appeals to imperial law

una casa real. Origen y ocaso del linaje gobernante en México-Tenochtitlan," *Nuevo Mundo, Mundos Nuevos* (2011), http://nuevomundo.revues.org/60624.

[49] Instructions of Carlos V to Hernando Cortés, Valladolid, June 26, 1523, in Koneztke, *Colección de documentos para la historia de la formación social de Hispanoamérica, 1493–1810*, ser. *1*, v. *1*, 76. See also *Colección de documentos inéditos relativos al descubrimiento, conquista, y organización de las antiguas posesiónes españolas de ultramar*. vol. 10 (Madrid: Real Academia de la Historia, 1897), v. 10, no. 3, 119.

[50] Decree of Felipe II, Valladolid, Aug 6, 1555, in Koneztke, *Colección de documentos para la historia de la formación social de Hispanoamérica, 1493–1810*, ser. *1*, v. *1*, 330–31.

[51] Decree of Felipe II, Valladolid, Feb 26, 1557, in ibid., v. 1, 360. See also RLI-VI, 7.1.

[52] Borah, *Justice by Insurance*: 65–75.

or the crown's Christian conscience, and read them aloud before the audiencia.[53]

While thematically and rhetorically consistent, cacique petitions and other legal documents are highly eclectic. Some were produced as part of regular colonial administrative procedures such as land titling or the *post hoc* audits of crown officials, while others were occasioned by disputes over lands and tributes. Unsurprisingly given their peculiar plight, however, cacique litigants almost invariably demanded official crown recognition of their noble quality. Their goal was *amparo*, official "protective" clarifications of their noble rights and privileges.[54] Successful litigants received notarized copies of favorable rulings as amparos, and preserved them as precious heirlooms for later generations.

Nothing in the Spanish legal or cultural apparatus prevented the recognition of noble distinctions among non-Christian peoples.[55] Nonetheless, a bevy of conflicting colonial policies under Viceroys Mendoza and don Luis de Velasco I (r. 1550–64) simultaneously prompted, facilitated, and frustrated the lords' ambitions. Both viceroys envisioned the native nobility as a vanguard of Hispanization, and worked to co-opt them while preserving their noble character. For example, Mendoza in 1537 proposed a new knightly order specifically for friendly teteuctin, the "*Tecle* Knights" (sic), to reward sincere religious and political fealty.[56] He also helped codify a new schedule of privileges largely analogous to that of Spanish hidalgos, such as the all-important right to possess land privately and therefore style themselves *don* and *doña*.[57] Like the mayorazgos of Spain, cacicazgos superseded the authority of provincial judges and corregidores. They were off-limits to debt collectors, and could only be revoked or adjusted by the audiencia itself.[58] Dominion over property

---

[53] Ibid., 235–39.

[54] Owensby, *Empire of Law*: 20.

[55] Mónica Domínguez Torres, "Emblazoning Identity: Indigenous Heraldry in Colonial Mexico and Peru," in *Contested Visions in the Spanish Colonial World*, ed. Ilona Katzew (Los Angeles: Los Angeles County Museum of Art, 2011), 100–02.

[56] Georges Baudot, *Utopia and History in Mexico: The First Chroniclers of Mexican Civilization (1520–1569)*, trans. Bernard R. Ortíz de Montellano and Thelma Ortíz de Montellano (Niwot, CO: University Press of Colorado, 1995), 190.

[57] Delfina Esmeralda López Sarrelangue, *La nobleza indígena de Pátzcuaro en la época virreinal* (Mexico: Universidad Nacional Autónoma de México, Instituto de Investigaciones Históricas, 1965), 111–44.

[58] Decree of Carlos V, Valladolid, Aug 26, 1547, AGI-I 427, L.30, f.40v-41r; Decree of Philip II, June 19, 1558, Valladolid, in Koneztke, *Colección de documentos para la historia de la formación social de Hispanoamérica, 1493–1810, ser. 1, v. 1*, 365. See also RLI-VI, 7.2.

also entailed the (theoretically) advantageous right to petition the king directly.[59]

Caciques also enjoyed a series of social and legal privileges. Crucially, they were exempt from labor and tribute obligations, corporal punishment and debtors' prison, and certain taxes (although the latter was controversial until 1572). These distinctions were visibly worn, as caciques were also exempt from the general restrictions on native dress and hairstyle.[60] Most importantly, they maintained the rights to heraldry, the most important signal of noble status in the Hispanic world.[61] Viceroy Velasco I was particularly liberal with such grants, and for centuries families throughout New Spain affixed crests originally acquired in the 1550s and 1560s above their doors.

Caciques were also allowed to ride horses and carry swords, the social and economic benefits of which were substantial.[62] Viceroy Mendoza began distributing such privileges to the high nobility of the Triple Alliance in the late 1530s, and granted many more to local leaders who contributed to his wars in western Mexico the following decade.[63] Towns or regions might send collective delegations in search of such licenses, with several self-proclaimed caciques receiving noble exemptions on the same day.[64] A royal investigation of 1547 listed no fewer than seventy-eight native lords with the explicit rights to ride horses and carry swords, including thirteen from Anahuac, thirteen from Michoacan, nine from Oaxaca, and eighteen from Tlaxcala.[65] After 1570, however, such licenses became increasingly widespread, and while they

---

[59] *Cedulario indiano recopilado por Diego de Encinas*, facsimile ed., 4 vols. (Madrid: Ediciones Cultura Hispánica, 1945), v. 4, 345–48.

[60] Puga, *Provisiones, cédulas, instrucciones para el gobierno de la Nueva España*: ff. 131r, 40v. See also Carlos V to Viceroy Mendoza, Valladolid, Feb 22, 1459, in Koneztke, *Colección de documentos para la historia de la formación social de Hispanoamérica, 1493–1810, ser. 1, v. 1, 255.*

[61] J. H. Elliott, *Imperial Spain, 1469–1716* (London: Penguin, 2002), 114–17.

[62] Decree of Prince Felipe Against Indian Ownership of Swords and Daggers; Decree of Prince Felipe Against Indian Ownership of Arquebuses and Horses, Madrid, Dec 17, 1551, in Koneztke, *Colección de documentos para la historia de la formación social de Hispanoamérica, 1493–1810, ser. 1, v. 1, 292–94.*

[63] See AGN-M 1, Exp. 24–25, f. 13v; Exp. 102, f. 51v; Exp. 266, f. 126; Exp. 279, f. 130; Exp. 315, f. 145v. In these cases, all from 1542, the viceroy licensed caciques from various provinces to own and ride horses.

[64] Examples are AGN-GP 1, Exp. 4, f. 2; and AGN-GP 4, Exp. 170–80, ff. 55–56.

[65] José-Juan López-Portillo reproduces the entire list, and indicates the specific privileges in each case. López-Portillo García-López, "Another Jerusalem: Political Legitimacy and Courtly Government in the Kingdom of New Spain (1535–1568)," 357–72.

remained honorable, eventually lost their rigid connection to pedigree and lineage.[66]

Yet contemporaneous policies restrained the power of the native elite even as they preserved it. Cacique rights were, of course, balanced against many other considerations, including the claims of encomenderos and the oidores' own hegemonic impulse to impose "good customs" on the Indians. For example, a decree of 1535 allowed the sale of Indian lands to Spaniards – a horribly detrimental practice that was subsequently revoked.[67] In 1538, the crown decreed that native governors were not to style themselves as the "lords" (*señores*) of pueblos, as that word hinted at their previous claim to sovereignty; instead, they were merely "caciques," local notables with cacicazgos specified and sanctioned by the king.[68] This reimagined caciques as property owners rather than rulers, and helped further shift real power at the local level to crown agents and elected cabildos. Other limitations followed logically. For example, in 1551 caciques were prohibited from applying capital punishment, a highly symbolic restraint on local sovereignty.[69] More consequential, however, were decrees that sharply restricted the caciques' aristocratic lifestyles, particularly in Tenochtitlan. Two in particular – one forbidding tributes in the form of personal services (1551) and another requiring tributes to be paid in specie (1564) – provoked loud cries of disinheritance, and were the immediate impetus for many of the petitions and testimonials examined below.[70]

In the end, this array of symbolic privileges afforded them with some means of resisting macehualization, yet only by adopting a diminished mode of eliteness quite distinct from that of their forebears. Accordingly, a substantial portion of the viceregal caseload during the sixteenth century involved local native leaders who sought the trappings of a Hispanic nobility. The heraldry that often resulted reflects the postconquest reinvention of the teteuctin as Indo-Hispanic noblemen, blending Mesoamerican aesthetic motifs and glyphic allusions with symbols of political incorporation into the Castilian crown, such as lion of Castile-León and

---

[66] Robert C. Schwaller, ""For Honor and Defence": Race and the Right to Bear Arms in Early Colonial Mexico," *Colonial Latin American Review* 21, no. 2 (2012).

[67] Decree of Carlos V, Mar 23, 1535, AGN RC Duplicadas 1, exp. 156, f. 147.

[68] Emperor Carlos V and Empress Juana, decree of Feb 26, 1538, RLI-VI, 7.5.

[69] Prince Felipe to the Audiencia of Peru, Madrid, Dec 17, 1551, in Koneztke, *Colección de documentos para la historia de la formación social de Hispanoamérica, 1493–1810*, ser. 1, v. 1, 295–96.

[70] Reyes García, *Anales de Juan Bautista*: 29–40.

the Christian cross.[71] For example, the blazon of don Antonio Cortés Totoquihuaztli (1564), a tlatoani of Tlacopan discussed at length below, incorporates representations of Nahua weaponry and elite architecture – signifying martial prowess and landed wealth, the essential components of nobility – along with invocations of Christian piety and loyalty to the crown.[72] While such "paper shields" were inert against the social and economic processes that undermined the natural lords, nobility was its own reward, a form of heritable prestige distinct from material wealth.[73] William Taylor and others have traced the emergence of a "dual hierarchy" in some colonial native communities, wherein material wealth and noble lineage overlapped but often functioned independently.[74] A not dissimilar situation existed in early modern Spain; like don Quixote and other pauper-hidalgos, even penniless caciques could assert noble prerogatives – and pass them to their descendants (Figure 3).

Despite their diversity, early cacique petitions typically fall into one of two categories: Those advocating the general rights of Indian nobles under colonial law, and those defending individual patrimonies against outsiders and rivals. While cacique petitioners typically represented themselves as individuals, during the early decades they sometimes formed a single corporate interest. A Nahuatl letter of 1556, for example, is signed by (among others) the dynastic tlatoque of Tenochtitlan, Tetzcoco, Tlacopan, Coyoacan, Iztapalapa, and Tlatelolco.[75] Such collaborations reflect both their shared plight as well as the long history of intermarriage among the nobility of Anahuac – a practice that continued well into the colonial era. In 1562, the sitting tlatoque of the defunct Triple Alliance – don

---

[71] Many of these were published in full color in *Nobiliario de conquistadores de Indias* (Madrid: Imprenta de M. Tello, 1892).

[72] Domínguez Torres, "Emblazoning Identity" 100.

[73] Robert Haskett, "Paper Shields: The Ideology of Coats of Arms in Colonial Mexican Primordial Titles," *Ethnohistory* 43, no. 1 (1996); María Castañeda de la Paz, "Central Mexican Indigenous Coats of Arms and the Conquest of Mesoamerica," *Ethnohistory* 56, no. 1 (2009); Domínguez Torres, "Emblazoning Identity."

[74] See Pedro Carrasco, "The Civil–Religious Hierarchy in Mesoamerican Communities: Pre-Spanish Background and Colonial Development," *American Anthropologist* 63(1961); Chance, "The Caciques of Tecali: Class and Ethnic Identity in Late Colonial Mexico."; William Taylor, *Landlord and Peasant in Colonial Oaxaca* (Stanford, CA: Stanford University Press, 1972), 52.

[75] Letter of the Lords and Principales of Mexico and Its Provinces, Mexico, May 2, 1556, in Martin Lienhard, ed. *Testimonios, cartas, y manifiestos indígenas desde la conquista hasta comienzos del siglo XX* (Caracas: Biblioteca Ayacucho, 1992), 40–42.

FIGURE 3 Arms of don Antonio Cortés Totoquihuaztli. Fundación Casa de Alba, Madrid, Spain.

Cristóbal de Guzmán Cecetzin of Tenochtitlan, don Hernando Pimentel Nezahualcoyotl of Tetzcoco, and don Antonio Cortés Totoquihuaztli of Tlacopan – petitioned for amparo; don Cristóbal was don Antonio's uncle, while don Antonio and don Hernando's children had recently married.[76]

Cacique self-fashioning: antiquity, fealty, and piety

Caciques seeking justice from the audiencia were compelled to represent themselves in ways persuasive to colonial officials and attuned to imperial laws. Thus, while the viceroy and the oidores were charged to recognize the legitimacy of inoffensive native customs, native litigants needed to accommodate the audiencia's own procedural and rhetorical expectations. The result was an intricate marriage of Western legalism and Mesoamerican history, in which native lords invoked medieval and early modern Iberian laws to defend patrimonies originating in Aztec Mexico. In doing so, the caciques implicitly and explicitly rechristened themselves as noble American vassals of the Spanish king. This new political identity presupposed and required their reinvention by way of an explanatory historical narrative, one that de-emphasized conflict in favor of allusions to cooperation and mutuality between crown and cacique, and that reimagined Mesoamerican altepeme as autonomous principalities within the confederated empire of Hapsburg Spain. The testimonies of the native lords are rich with such ideas.

To be concise, the reinvention of the caciques as Indo-Hispanic fuedal lords revolved around three distinct but self-reinforcing assertions: Petitioners emphasized the *primordiality* of their inherited legacies, their steadfast *fealty* to the Spanish monarch, and their impeccable Christian *orthodoxy*. In doing so, they self-consciously drew analogies between themselves and Spanish hidalgos, who likewise rooted their superiority in genealogy, services, and religious purity. Yet by applying such ideals to Mesoamerican lineages and the vagaries of Mesoamerican history, they pioneered a tradition of noble self-fashioning that blended neo-Aztec, Hispanic royalist, and Christian sympathies into one synthetic historical identity, anchored by testimonials that implicitly denied or ignored any historical tensions between the ruling lineages of Anahuac, the Spanish crown, and the Catholic Church.

[76] See PRT, 82–83; and Carrasco, *Tenochca Empire*: 52, 446, n. 13.

This blend was rife with contradictions. For example, it required the lords to proclaim both the greatness of their ancestral legacies as well as the justice of the colonial violence that ended them. Yet for all its ambiguities, it was politically advantageous, as well as legally astute. Its power lay in how it reconciled Mesoamerican traditions to Spanish rule. Assertions of antiquity, loyalty, and piety all indicated *volition* – the voluntary and willful incorporation of America's indigenous polities into the Spanish crown. This was initially necessary to prevent the enslavement of Indians – which remained controversial until 1537 – as Spanish law considered voluntary submission necessary for the status of "free vassalage" and its attendant rights to crown protection and support.[77] But assertions of volition could mask deeper political agendas. If central Mexico's rulers voluntarily embraced Spanish rule, what, exactly, did they agree to? Did they exchange political *subordination* in return for Christian salvation, as Hispanic jurists tended to argue? Or did they negotiate an *alliance* in which they integrated into the crown as autonomous lords? While the former subjected native communities to the whims of Spanish settlers and minor officials, the latter availed itself of the possibilities for suzerainty inherent in the composite monarchy of the Hapsburgs. The caciques, unsurprisingly, emphasized the latter, and thereby sought to shepherd the noble legacies of Anahuac largely intact into New Spain. By retrospectively envisioning harmony between native lineages and the colonial order, they granted the former a voice within the structures of the latter. This is the legal environment that encouraged stories of proto-Christian Aztecs, native conquistadors, Indian evangelizers, and other symbols attesting to the indispensability of Anahuac's lineages in New Spain.

The theme of primordiality, in which caciques rooted the origins of their claims in a remote and heroic antiquity, was attuned to a bias in the Spanish legal tradition toward "immemoriality" – the notion that a status quo demanded respect *ab initio* if it had been that way for a long time. Immemoriality was a potential source of rhetorical power for native litigants, as they could posture as the authoritative bearers of an historical knowledge no Spaniard could truly contest.[78] Recognizing, for

---

[77] Gibson, "Conquest, Capitulation, and Indian Treaties."

[78] "Pre-Hispanic memory," notes Frank Salomon, "was presumed to include a crucial point of knowledge no Spaniard could supply, namely, knowledge of 'immemorial' social facts that colonial law was charged to respect yet could not itself define." Frank Salomon, "Collquiri's Dam: The Colonial Re-Voicing of an Appeal to the Archaic," in *Native Traditions in the Postconquest World*, eds. Elizabeth Hill Boone, and Tom Cummins (Washington, DC: Dumbarton Oaks Research Library and Collection, 1998), 273.

example, that encomenderos enjoyed the rights to native tributes, but not the land itself, caciques elaborated upon on the extent of their ancestral domains – often drawing up maps for the occasion – and insisted that the oidores were morally and legally bound to respect their patrimonies. Their petitions frequently invoked "the time of Moctezuma" (*en tiempo de Moctezuma*) and "ancient times" (*tiempos antiguos*) – shorthand expressions for the immediate and more distant preconquest eras. Most common, however, was "time immemorial" – or, as commonly phrased in the 1530s, "a time so distant the memories of men cannot contradict it" (*de tanto tiempo aca que memoria de hombres no es en contrario*).[79] From the perspective of early New Spain, antiquity was a time and place without Spaniards and encomiendas, thereby affording opportunities to those caciques able to reframe their immediate troubles in terms of Mesoamerican history.

The caciques' second rhetorical emphasis was continuity, the postconquest legitimacy of their ancestral authority and prestige. The implementation of colonial institutions in America, they argued, neither dismantled nor obviated traditional systems of local governance and social differentiation. Instead, their patrimonies were complementary to, and indeed fundamentally necessary for, effective administration. Like primordiality, this agenda demanded a historical basis; in this case, detailed stories of collaboration with and support for the conquistadors and early colonial officials. And indeed, many central Mexican caciques did not hesitate to demand restitution for services rendered. Nor were they reluctant to superimpose considerations of fealty upon local political disputes, even those that predated the Spanish conquest, thereby portraying their rivals, both Spanish and non-Spanish, as enemies of the king, and themselves as the king's faithful partisans. By remembering themselves onto the winning side of the Spanish invasion and colonization of America, these accounts appealed to Castilian law while recasting native lords as the triumphant co-architects of New Spain, conferring upon them the moral and political standing to protest any disrespect or diminishment they experienced as illegal and unjust according to the Spaniards' own ideals.

A third recurring theme in cacique testimonials was the invocation of religious orthodoxy. Native elites seeking favors from colonial institutions were compelled to emphasize, not only the authenticity of their

---

[79] Probanza of the lords of Tlatelolco, July–Oct 1536, AGI, Justicia 159, N.5, f. 1331v. Regarding immemoriality as the fundamental native claim to rights and property within the hegemony of the state and its colonial precursors, see Richard J. Perry, *From Time Immemorial: Indigenous Peoples and State Systems* (Austin, TX: University of Texas Press, 1996), 8–17.

Christian convictions, but also – due to the Spanish belief that heresy and infidelity tainted bloodlines – the swiftness and enthusiasm of their ancestors' conversions. Any narrative recasting native peoples as Christian believers rather than hostile infidels upended the neo-Crusader moral justification for conquistador violence and colonial domination. According to Louise Burkhart, "by outdoing the Spaniards at their own religion," Nahuas challenged Spanish pretensions to unlimited rights-by-conquest.[80] It reminded them of the nontribal, universalist origins of their own Christian religion even as it elevated the caciques' status from barbarian chiefs to sympathetic co-religionists. Beyond the first postconquest generation, this trope grew increasingly elaborate, and tales of zealous Nahua crusaders and martyrs are not wholly uncommon in cacique testimonies. As we will see, some cacique voices even extended this idea into the distant past, and attributed providential, monotheistic, and proto-Christian beliefs to their pre-Hispanic ancestors.

Historical ventriloquism and the Spanish heirs of Moctezuma

The surviving nobles of Anahuac were not the only faction within early colonial politics concerned with the preservation of inherited rights. Indeed, counter-intuitively, certain conquistadors were among the first to demand the postconquest recognition of some central Mexican patrimonies. Their efforts were self-interested, and revolved around the memory of the deceased huei tlatoani Moctezuma, as several of them sought to benefit politically and materially by marrying his daughters. In doing so, they became invested in Mesoamerican history in ways both parallel to the indigenous nobility and in contrast to other conquistadors; while the former emphasized the rights of inheritance, the latter were more invested in the spoils of conquest. Thus, like the pipiltin, the Spanish sons-in-law of Moctezuma sought to ensure the postconquest survival of the preconquest noble claims they hoped to inherit. This made them, in a sense, the proto-creoles: They were the first non-natives to appropriate Mesoamerican history, understood as the legacy of caciques, and deploy it in support of their own colonial interests *vis a vis* other Spaniards.

Ironically, the notion of continuity between Anahuac and Spanish Mexico originated in the machinations of Hernando Cortés himself, who justified his attack on sovereign peoples by audaciously portraying himself

---

[80] Louise M. Burkhart, "Pious Performances: Christian Pageantry and Native Identity in Early Colonial Mexico," in *Native Traditions in the Postconquest World*, eds. Elizabeth Hill Boone and Tom Cummins (Washington, DC: Dumbarton Oaks, 1998), 369.

as Moctezuma's chosen successor. Writing in the autumn of 1520 – just after the death of Moctezuma but before the fall of Tenochtitlan – the conquistador famously recorded that the tlatoani, believing the Spaniards to be representatives of a legendary ruler long prophesied to return to central Mexico, had voluntarily turned over his domain to Holy Roman Emperor Carlos V (Carlos I of Castile) intact and in its entirety, in a lawful and peaceful *translatio imperii* (transfer of rule).[81] It was an early instance of what would become a feature of creole literature: A rhetorical strategy we might call "historical ventriloquism," wherein non-native authors legitimated their agendas by retroactively placing them on the lips of a deceased native authority. Cortés was in criminal violation of explicit orders to stay out of Mexico, and the supposed "donation" of Moctezuma obviated contemporary learned concerns that he had engaged in unwarranted aggression against a legitimate sovereign.[82] The donation story recast the violence as a rebellion against the Spanish crown, allowing Cortés to posture as a loyal champion of the king.

By itself, the story is a premier example of Cortesian hubris. But the conqueror went even further in his letter, implying that Moctezuma understood his concession not as the acceptance of a new, more powerful liege, but as the *restoration* of Anahuac to one with long-established

---

[81] The translatio imperii was a medieval legal principle that measured the legitimacy of a sovereign by linking it, via a series of intact "transfers," to classical antiquity. Cortés, *Letters From Mexico*: 85–86. The ancestral ruler of whom Moctezuma speaks is traditionally assumed to be Quetzalcoatl, associated in Mesoamerican lore with both the East – from where the Spaniards arrived – and the calendar year Ce-Acatl (1-Reed, or 1519), the date of their arrival. Cortés would certainly have known of the Quetzalcoatl legend; however, the extent to which such legends truly informed native responses to the invasion is unclear. See Camilla Townsend, "Burying the White Gods: New Perspectives on the Conquest of Mexico," *Hispanic American Historical Review* 108, no. 3 (2003). On *translatio imperii*, see also Brading, *The First America*: 27; Anthony Pagden, *Lords of All the World: Ideologies of Empire in Spain, Britain, and France, c. 1500–1800* (New Haven, CT: Yale University Press, 1995), 32.

[82] As Cortés was consolidating his conquests, the Dominican jurists of the "Salamanca School" (who held the ear of the king) were scouring natural and canon law for ways to confirm the legality of Spanish violence in America. As Anthony Pagden reports, they found precious few, much to their own consternation. Absent excessive tyranny over the innocent, they concluded, even the "barbarian" monarchs of America maintained sovereignty; Spanish authority, therefore, was only justified where local peoples actively and voluntarily requested it. Meanwhile, Beatríz Pastor argues that Cortés's letters from Mexico are essentially fictional, and defined entirely by his "need to legitimize his venture and consolidate his power." Pagden, *Spanish Imperialism and the Political Imagination*: 13–36. Beatríz Pastor, *The Armature of Conquest: Spanish Accounts of the Discovery of America, 1492–1589*, trans. Lydia Longstreth Hunt (Stanford: Stanford University Press, 1992), 99.

historical rights in Mexico, even invoking the Spanish legal concept of "natural lordship." Moctezuma's authority, in other words, was ultimately derived from Carlos V, even before the two sovereigns knew of one another's existence; the Mexica, wrote Cortés, welcomed the newcomers with "such good will and delight... that it seemed as if *ab initio* they had known [Carlos V] to be their king and rightful lord."[83] In this sense, to challenge Carlos was also to defy Moctezuma – whom he called the king's "captain" in Tenochtitlan – and vice versa, a twist that made Cortés the guarantor of Moctezuma's authority.[84] In other words, Cortés denied that any conquest had taken place. Rather than resistance, defeat, and displacement, he told of a political continuity legally indistinct from an uncontested dynastic succession, such as that between a father and son, in which the old order remained intact to be presided over by a new sovereign.

In the aftermath of the conquest, Cortés sought to preserve his pretense of stewardship over the late tlatoani's domains; in true Mesoamerican fashion, he did so by way of strategic marriage alliances with the most prominent daughters of the previous ruler. Moctezuma's most important female heir was Tecuichpochtzin (c. 1509 to c.1550).[85] Descended on both sides from the royal dynasty, her lineage was the most prestigious and her heirs maintained the most compelling claims to the *tlatocayotl* (speakership) of Tenochtitlan. Unsurprisingly, she was highly desired as a bride; and indeed she was said to have married (and survived) three of the most prominent noblemen of Tenochtitlan while still young, including the final two emperors, her uncles Cuitlahua and Cuauhtemoc. After the latter's execution in 1525, Cortés continued where the Tenochca nobility had left, and assumed responsibility for the thrice-widowed teenager, now baptized doña Isabel Moctezuma. After fathering his own child with her, in June of 1526 he arranged her marriage to a fellow conquistador, and granted her the important encomienda of Tlacopan.[86]

---

[83] Cortés, *Letters from Mexico*: 113.

[84] Ibid., 99.

[85] Tecuichpochtzin's mother's name is given as Tecalco ("In of the House of Stone") in sixteenth-century sources, yet this might have been a mistake of Spanish scribes who recorded her description by testators as if it were her name. She was Moctezuma's cousin, a daughter of huei tlatoani Ahuitzotl (r. 1486–1502). See PRT, 76.

[86] The natural-born child of doña Isabel Moctezuma and Cortés was doña Leonor Cortés Moctezuma, who later married the Spaniard Juan de Tolosa, co-founder of the silver-mining center of Zacatecas. See Donald E. Chipman, *Moctezuma's Children: Aztec Royalty Under Spanish Rule, 1520–1700* (Austin: University of Texas Press, 2005), 96–118.

In yet another act of historical ventriloquism, Cortés portrayed his guardianship over doña Isabel as the late tlatoani's own dying wish. In granting her the Tlacopan encomienda he told a story, rich in pathos, in which the mortally wounded Moctezuma invested Cortés with the care of his daughters:

Fearing he would die, [Moctezuma] prayed and charged me very earnestly, that, remembering how much he loved me and desired to please me, should he die of the wound I should take charge of his three daughters and have them baptized and taught our religion, for he knew that it was very good.... He also wished me to give account to his Majesty of his having left his daughters to my care, and to entreat them in his name, to be pleased to command me to look after them, and to keep them under my protection and administration, for he was a servant and subject of His Majesty, and had always been kindly disposed toward the Spaniards.[87]

The conquistador repeated the dubious story of Moctezuma's dying wishes the following year while granting the encomienda of Ecatepec to doña Isabel's half-sister, doña Leonor Moctezuma, upon her marriage to the conquistador Cristóbal de Valderrama.[88] As before, he postured as the legitimate guardian of doña Leonor by Moctezuma's own explicit authority, and described Moctezuma as a heroic and devoted ally of Spain. Indeed, he explicitly framed doña Leonor's encomienda as "remuneration" for the many services Moctezuma had rendered to Carlos V.[89] As for Moctezuma's other surviving children, he explained, they were mentally and physically unfit to inherit.[90] Illustrating their special usefulness to Cortés, doña Leonor and doña Isabel Moctezuma were the only two non-Spanish encomenderas in central Mexico. Unlike other encomiendas, moreover, which were to escheat after the second generation, theirs were perpetual holdings more akin

---

[87] "Grant of Cortés to doña Isabel Moctezuma," Mexico, June 27, 1526, in William Hickling Prescott, *Mexico, and the Life of the Conqueror Fernando Cortés*, 2 vols. (New York: Peter Fenelon Collier, 1898), v. 2, 441–42.

[88] Robert Himmerich y Valencia, *The Encomenderos of New Spain, 1521–1555* (Austin: University of Texas Press, 1996). 196; Peter Gerhard, *A Guide to the Historical Geography of New Spain* (London: Cambridge University Press, 1972), 226–27. According to Chimalpahin, doña Leonor's mother was Tzihuacxochitzin, a granddaughter of Tlacaeleltzin, the great *cihuacoatl* (prime minister) and architect of the Mexica empire. Chimalpahin Cuauhtlehuanitzin, *Codex Chimalpahin*: v. 1, 52–55.

[89] Grant of the Encomienda of Ecatepec to doña Marina (Leonor) Moctezuma, Mar 14, 1527, AGI-J 159, N. 5, f. 1088v-1090v.

[90] See Cortés, *Letters from Mexico*: 156; Prescott, *Mexico, and the Life of the Conqueror Fernando Cortés*: 437.

to feudal estates, greatly enhancing the value of marriage to their beneficiaries.[91]

In 1528 Cortes returned to Spain, where the king dubbed him *Marqués del Valle de Oaxaca*, lord of a vast and populous estate in central and southern Mexico. His fortunes thus secured, he was no longer invested in the preservation of natural lordship in Mexico. That task fell instead to the Spanish husbands, mestizo children, and creole descendants of doña Isabel and doña Leonor Moctezuma. (As for the women themselves, they are largely silent in the records, and it is difficult to parse their perspectives from the machinations of the many Spanish men who controlled their fates.) Part of this agenda involved strategically representing Moctezuma's patrimony as legally equivalent to landed property while repeating stories of his wise and firm support for the Spaniards. Given his virtue and his courageous services to Carlos V, they argued, his lands and tributes could not be forfeit after the fall of Tenochtitlan, but should by rights belong to his surviving heirs. Cuitlahua (r. 1520) and Cuauhtemoc (r. 1520–25) – Moctezuma's successors – were interim stewards of Tenochtitlan at best, and in any event had no claims to Moctezuma's lands, which remained the exclusive domain of his beloved daughters, their wives. By way of consistent legal action adorned with frequent appeals to historical legitimacy, the Spanish sons-in-law of Moctezuma ensured that the Moctezuma name would retain a considerable residual power for generations, among Spanish-speaking mestizos and creoles as well as natives.

Doña Isabel's sixth and final husband was the conquistador Juan Cano de Saavedra, with whom she had five children before her death circa 1550. Predictably, Cano was an energetic advocate for doña Isabel's inheritance, which he consistently portrayed as derived from the deep royal tradition of imperial Tenochtitlan embodied by Moctezuma, the wise and "obedient" vassal of Carlos V.[92] Soon after marrying doña Isabel in 1531, Cano commissioned the Franciscans to investigate and articulate her genealogical claims. The result was an invaluable pair of Spanish-language interpretations of now-unknown Tenochca pictorial histories.[93]

---

[91] Gibson, *The Aztecs*: 423–26.

[92] For the story of Cano's legal battle – which began in 1546 and lasted ten years, well after doña Isabel's death – see Chipman, *Moctezuma's Children*: 58–74. His heirs continued to squabble into the next generation and beyond.

[93] The first is the *Relación de la genealogía y linaje de los señores que han señoreado esta tierra* (*Account of the Genealogy and Lineage of the Lords Who Have Governed This Land*), while the second is titled simply *Origin of the Mexicans*.

They map the Culhua-Tolteca ancestry of the Tenochca dynasty and trace the rise of imperial Tenochtitlan according to the successive victories of its nine preconquest tlatoque, and conclude by delineating the late Moctezuma's patrimonial estates and doña Isabel's rights thereto.[94] Thus were Spaniards citing Aztec history for their own purposes as early as 1532, and the Cano relations are early examples of the non-native colonial repurposing of native history.

Cano continued to invoke natural lordship in subsequent efforts to secure doña Isabel's encomienda for himself and his heirs. The conquistador eulogized Moctezuma in a series of interviews with the chronicler Gonzalo Fernández de Oviedo in 1544, representing his late father-in-law as exceedingly generous and hospitable to "the Christians." "As soon as [the Spaniards] disembarked in the port of San Juan de Ulúa," Cano insisted, Moctezuma had "sent his messengers to welcome them and he sent great gifts of gold and silver and precious stones," providing generously for them during their arduous trek to Tenochtitlan.[95] When the Spaniards massacred unarmed Tenochca nobles in May of 1520 – the event that touched off open warfare – Moctezuma was understandably "wrathful," yet his loyalty to Carlos V was solid, such that he rejected popular demands to expel the foreigners. In this way, what the Mexica perceived as weakness, Cano reinterpreted as an act of courage, loyalty, and resolve.[96] In a subsequent letter to Carlos V rife with historical ventriloquism, Cano even retroactively Christianized the huei tlatoani, arguing that Moctezuma's hospitality derived entirely from his sincere commitment to the Church. Immediately upon hearing of the arrival of the Christians, Cano wrote, Moctezuma "desired to learn our holy Catholic faith and receive it." Once given the chance, he converted and was baptized "without offering resistance." This is highly dubious; despite its widespread acceptance in later generations, contemporary eyewitnesses recorded no such episode, and indeed lamented that Moctezuma died

---

[94] See "Relación de la genealogía y linaje de los señores que han señoreado..." and "Origen de los mexicanos" in García Icazbalceta, *Nueva colección de documentos para la historia de México: Pomar-Zurita, relaciones antiguas (Siglo XVI)*, 240–80.

[95] Probanza of Juan Cano, Mexico, 1546, in Emma Pérez-Rocha, ed. *Privilegios en lucha: La información de doña Isabel Moctezuma* (Mexico: Instituto Nacional de Antropología e Historia, 1998), 61–62.

[96] Oviedo's *Quincuagenas* are semi-fictionalized dialogues between Oviedo and consequential contemporary figures in Spanish America. In 1544, Cano traveled to Santo Domingo, and met Oviedo while preparing his case on behalf of the Tlacopan encomienda. See "Dialogue of Oviedo with don Juan Cano," in Prescott, *Mexico, and the Life of the Conqueror Fernando Cortés*: v. 2, 437–38.

unbaptized.[97] Yet the myth of a Christian huei tlatoani supported the defense of doña Isabel's inheritance. According to Cano, not only was Moctezuma faithful to both his new creed and his new liege, he even died a martyr; "for this the Indians killed him, and he died in your service."[98]

Cano's efforts on behalf of the Tlacopan encomienda were largely successful – much to the chagrin of its dynastic tlatoani, as we will see in Chapter 3. As other encomiendas began to disappear during the 1540s and after, doña Isabel's continued to accumulate further rights, and when she died it was the single largest encomienda remaining in central Mexico.[99] The contemporaneous experience of doña Leonor Moctezuma resembled that of her half-sister doña Isabel. Immediately after receiving the encomienda of Ecatepec, she married two Spanish conquistadors in succession, bearing a daughter with the second, Cristóbal de Valderrama. Like Juan Cano, Valderrama defended his wife's claims by rooting them in Moctezuma's legacy rather than the conquest.[100] For example, in 1531 Valderrama complained to the new audiencia that the natural lords of Tlatelolco – the Mexica sister-city of Tenochtitlan – were extracting tributes illegally from a pair of fishing settlements on the northwestern shore of Lake Texcoco, within his wife's encomienda. The villages, he argued, were part of Moctezuma's private estate, and therefore belonged to doña Leonor as his daughter and heir.

Ultimately, the case reflected conflicting interpretations of encomienda rights, with Valderrama taking the expansive view. Yet in pursuing his claims Valderrama, probably knowingly, revived a long-standing controversy of Anahuac – the precise status of Tlatelolco *vis a vis* Tenochtitlan and the Triple Alliance. While ancestrally related to the Tenochca who shared their island, the two Mexica polities had a complex relationship, and despite its subjugation to and partial assimilation with Tenochtitlan, Tlatelolco retained a stubbornly independent identity.[101]

---

[97] The great seventeenth-century chronicler fray Juan de Torquemada explicitly cast doubt upon accounts of a Christian Moctezuma, precisely because they only arose well after the conquest. See Cortés, *Letters from Mexico*: 132–33; Bernal Díaz del Castillo, *The Conquest of New Spain*, trans. J.M. Cohen (London and New York: Penguin, 1963), 294. Torquemada, *Monarquía indiana*: v. 4, 213–14.

[98] Juan Cano to the Royal Audiencia of Mexico City, Mexico, Oct 26, 1546, in Pérez-Rocha, *Privilegios en lucha: La información de doña Isabel Moctezuma*, 50.

[99] See Chipman, *Moctezuma's Children*: 65; Gibson, *The Aztecs*: 423–26.

[100] Chimalpahin charted the descendants of the Valderrama de Moctezumas. See Chimalpahin Cuauhtlehuanitzin, *Codex Chimalpahin*: v. 2, 109.

[101] See Ana Garduño, *Conflictos y alianzas entre Tlatelolco y Tenochtitlan, siglos XII a XV* (México, D.F.: Instituto Nacional de Antropología e Historia, 1997).

The old Tenochca-Tlatelolca rivalry, then, became an undercurrent in the colonial dispute between Tlatelolco's leaders and Cristóbal de Valderrama, a Spanish son-in-law of Moctezuma, ninth emperor of Tenochtitlan. In elevating his wife's claims to Moctezuma's patrimony, Valderrama articulated the Tenochca view of Tlatelolco's historic rights, challenging Tlatelolco's identity as an independent altepetl and denying its autonomous rights to any extramural tributes. The inhabitants of the disputed settlements "were all [Moctezuma's] slaves and maceguales," he insisted, "and as such in the name of Moctezuma they labored in those lands at his command," delivering the subsequent rents to his private purse.[102] Valderrama's native witnesses supported his allegations, contending that "before the Spaniards came to this New Spain" the disputed settlements held no esteem for Tlatelolco, and paid tribute only to Moctezuma himself.[103]

Valderrama also echoed both Cortés and Cano in invoking the hagiographic memory of Moctezuma, remembering him as a dedicated friend of Castile. But his own account of the huei tlatoani's death differed in a highly revealing way. Valderrama alleged that the true rebels and enemies of Moctezuma and Carlos V were the same Tlatelolca who happened to be challenging his wife's encomienda rights. "After Moctezuma gave the obedience of Tenochtitlan and its provinces to Your Majesty," he argued in 1536, "the Tlatelolca rose in rebellion and made war on Your Majesty." It was the Tlatelolca, moreoever, who had heinously and shamefully assassinated Moctezuma, their rightful sovereign and the sworn vassal of Carlos V. With their treason, he concluded, the lords of Tlatelolco had relinquished all rights to lands and tributes outside of their own boundaries, especially those that conflicted with the inheritance of doña Leonor, whose father they had most viciously murdered.[104]

Like the Cano-Moctezumas, the heirs of doña Leonor Moctezuma continued to promote family interests via references to the immemorial rights of Moctezuma and the illegitimacy of Tlatelolco. In this way, the intra-Mexica rivalry, centuries old, underlay colonial-era disputes between non-Indians for decades following the conquest. In 1558, doña Leonor's Spanish son-in-law, Diego Arias de Sotelo, defended the encomienda by repeating Valderrama's contention that Tlatelolco boasted of no

---

[102] Petition of Cristóbal de Valderrama, Oct 26, 1531, AGI-J 124, N.5, f. 1268v-69r.
[103] Probanza of Ecatepec, Mar 17, 1553, AGI-J 159, N.5, f. 1067r.
[104] Examination and probanza of Cristóbal de Valderrama, June 20, 1536, AGI-J 124, N.5, f. 1294r-94v.

independent tlatocayotl before 1521, but rather was a mere "district" of Tenochtitlan with no standing to contest Moctezuma's inheritance.[105] The creole descendants of doña Leonor Moctezuma even tried to appropriate the legacies of other long-deceased Tenochca notables; in 1555, for example, Sotelo's attorney argued that beyond the many "pueblos and hereditary lands, houses, and other properties" that had belonged to Moctezuma, doña Leonor should have also inherited the estates of her mother, a granddaughter of the revered Tenochca *cihuacoatl* (prime minister) and war strategist Tlacaeleltzin (1397–1487).[106] In 1562, the Spaniard Sotelo continued to demand the perpetuity of his encomienda via references to the ancient rights of the Tenochca royalty.[107]

Few in the early postconquest arena were greater champions of Moctezuma's patrimony than the Spaniards who married his daughters and claimed it for themselves. Despite the colonial ideology of social and ethnic hierarchy, as "elite mestizos" with conquering Spanish and noble indigenous ancestors, the Cano-Moctezumas and Sotelo-Moctezumas leveraged their mothers' heritage to achieve power and wealth in colonial politics and society.[108] In doing so – by demanding the survival and "restoration" of indigenous patrimonies – they necessarily invoked and contributed to the emerging argument for Mexican natural lordship under Spanish rule. The premise of *translatio* and the inheritance of Moctezuma's daughters were early attempts to ennoble and secure colonial-era fortunes by rooting them in a precolonial heritage.

Yet on a deeper, more sentimental level, for Spanish conquistadors to posture as the successors to indigenous lineages was rife with subversive potential, as it implied or asserted an America-based power and authority derived independently from the Spanish crown. Indeed, the king's worst fears were realized in Peru in the 1540s when some conquistadors, angry over laws restricting the heritability of encomiendas, killed the viceroy and almost proclaimed an independent Hispano-American kingdom under Gonzalo Pizarro, whom they encouraged to marry an Andean princess and become the new "Inca." In Mexico, where the first viceroys were more cautious and refused to restrict encomiendas by outright fiat, no

---

[105] Examination and probanza of Diego Arias de Sotelo, Feb 21, 1558, AGI-J 124, N.5, f. 1120r-1149v.

[106] Carlos V to the Audiencia of Mexico City, Oct 26, 1555, AGI-J 124, N.5, f. 1110v-1111r; PRT, 77.

[107] Diego Arias de Sotelo to King Felipe II, Apr 30, 1562, in PRT, 259–60.

[108] On "elite mestizos," see Robert C. Schwaller, "Defining Difference in Early New Spain" (Ph.D. diss., Pennsylvania State University, 2010), 153–78.

such uprising occurred, yet analogous dreams of an encomenderos' independence under a creole "tlatoani" existed nonetheless. Most famously, in June of 1566 a handful of second-generation encomenderos in Mexico City theatrically recreated the donation of Moctezuma in a way that recast them as the heirs to the Mexican "throne" in a bold, if symbolic, rebuke to the crown.

Alonso de Ávila Alvarado was the encomendero of Cuauhtitlan and Xaltocan, north of Mexico City; his younger brother was Gil González de Ávila, encomendero of Ixmiquilpan (Hidalgo). Both were sons of the conquistador and companion of Cortés, Gil González de Benavides, and were, like many of their peers, upset over the crown's hostility to the perpetuation of encomiendas.[109] They were also dependents of Hernando Cortés's Spanish son and heir, Martín Cortés, who had recently returned to Mexico with great fanfare.[110] During elaborate weeklong celebrations marking the baptism of Cortés's sons, Alonso de Ávila commissioned native craftsmen in Cuauhtitlan to produce costumes and accessories in the traditional style of Anahuac. At a banquet one night, he organized a farce in which he and twenty-two like-minded companions – one of whom was Diego Arias de Sotelo, widower of the late doña Leonor de Valderrama y Moctezuma – appeared before Cortés dressed like "cacique Indians," regaling him and his wife with food and drink in the manner "that the Indians used to celebrate their fiestas." With Alonso impersonating the late huei tlatoani Moctezuma, dressed in royal Aztec garb and adorned with feathers, jewels, and flowers, he embraced Martín Cortés in an overt allusion to the original reception of his father in Tenochtitlan. Most intriguingly, the conspirators laid a crown of feathers "in the customary style of the Indians" on the head of their "queen," Cortés's wife; later accounts also told that they crowned Martín as well.[111]

There was nothing secret about these subversive festivities; they took place with the knowledge of a crown representative (*visitador*) and the other notables of contemporary Mexico City – including the native nobility, who recorded it in their annals.[112] The following month, the

[109] Orozco y Berra, *Noticia histórica de la conjuración del Marqués del Valle*, 28–29.

[110] "Memorial de los conquistadores de esta Nueva España," in Baltasar Dorantes de Carranza, *Sumaria relación de las cosas de la Nueva España* (Mexico: Editorial Porrúa, 1987), 388–90.

[111] "Process against Alonso de Ávila Alvarado and Gil Gonzalez, his brother," July 16, 1566, in Orozco y Berra, *Noticia histórica de la conjuración del Marqués del Valle*, 6–9; Torquemada, *Monarquía indiana*: v. 1, 390–91.

[112] The *Annals of Juan Bautista* notes the sentencing and execution of the Ávila brothers. See Reyes García, *Anales de Juan Bautista*: 148–51.

Ávila brothers and their companions were placed under house arrest and accused of conspiracy to commit treason, raid the viceregal treasury, and make themselves the absolute masters of the Indians. While Cortés escaped with only minor censure, the Ávila brothers received the ultimate punishment, and their severed heads were displayed for six days before the viceregal palace.[113]

Although the "conspiracy of the marqués" came to naught, a more richly symbolic expression of the creole fantasy of "inheriting" the ruling traditions of Anahuac would be difficult to imagine. It was a particularly striking example of historical ventriloquism, as by dressing as Nahua noblemen the conspirators visually reframed the creole-encomendero agenda as that of the native "Mexican" leadership. As early as the first and second postconquest generations, discontented conquistadors and their creole sons were mining native Mexican history and culture for the words and symbols by which they could differentiate themselves from their Spanish parents and ancestors.

Defending immemorial rights: early cacique legal engagements

If the premise of continuity and inheritance between Anahuac and New Spain served the interests of a small faction of Spanish conquerors and their creole and elite mestizo children, it was central to the strategies of just about every indigenous noble family. A brief exploration of the kinds of disputes handled before the audiencia after 1531 demonstrates the frequency with which caciques defended their interests via references to ancestral rights. As legacy elites, genealogy and custom anchored the caciques' pretensions to authority and resources, while Spanish ascendancy and the encomienda system compelled them to substantiate their claims by rooting them deeply in Mexican history. However, such arguments opened the caciques to challenges from rivals, both native and Spanish, who gave contrasting accounts.

Naturally, the highest-profile audiencia cases in the 1530s and after involved the survivors and heirs of the Triple Alliance who, after accepting baptism and Spanish vassalage, expected to inherit the positions held by their fathers and grandfathers. While we might intuitively expect the grand lineages of Tenochtitlan to assert the clearest and most compelling claims in the postconquest world, they were, in practice, the first to lose grasp of their preconquest status and its attendant privileges. As the primary seat of Spanish power and the only official *ciudad de españoles*

---

[113] See Torquemada, *Monarquía indiana*: 390–95.

("Spanish City") in the basin of Mexico, the city escheated permanently to the crown after the death of Cuauhtemoc in 1525. However, the rise of encomiendas elsewhere stripped the incomes of the Tenochca elite, previously accustomed to imperial tributes. Thus, while it maintained a large indigenous population and its own structures of municipal administration, the Indian government of Tenochtitlan – now a network of satellite neighborhoods on the outskirts of the Spanish capital – was largely disabused of any pretensions toward restoration.[114] Even don Diego de Alvarado Huanitzin eventually relinquished his rights to imperial tributes upon becoming governor in 1538.[115]

As for the surviving heirs to Moctezuma, they were neutralized in other ways.[116] As we have seen, doña Isabel Tecuichpochtzin and doña Leonor Moctezuma were given encomiendas upon their marriages to conquistadors, their mestizo children becoming leaders in the emerging creole world of Mexico City. Only a handful of Moctezuma's sons survived the conquest. Nezahualtecolotl, baptized don Martín Cortés, made three journeys to Spain to represent Tenochtitlan before the crown; there he trained with the Franciscans and married a Spanish noblewoman. However, a Tenochca rival poisoned him to death before he could return triumphantly as an encomendero.[117] As it happened, then, Moctezuma's most prominent son after the conquest was don Pedro Moctezuma Tlacahuepantzin. Due to his alliance with Cortés – and unlike most of his kinsmen and peers – don Pedro was granted what were officially portrayed as ancestral rights to the encomienda of Tula (Hidalgo), where his mother, doña María Miahuaxochitzin, belonged to the royal line.[118]

---

[114] Gibson, *The Aztecs*: 368–95, 438.

[115] José Rubén Romero Galván, *Los privilegios perdidos: Hernando Alvarado Tezozomoc, su tiempo, su nobleza, y su Crónica mexicana* (Mexico City: Universidad Nacional Autónoma de México, 2003), 84–85.

[116] The Nahua historian Chimalpahin lists nineteen children of Moctezuma. At least five died before the fall of Tenochtitlan, three of whom were killed by the Mexica during the Spaniards' nighttime escape from the city on June 30, 1520, known as the *noche triste*. Chimalpahin also hints that Cuauhtemoc may have murdered several children who remained so as to secure his ascension. Chimalpahin Cuauhtlehuanitzin, *Codex Chimalpahin*: v. 1, 159–65.

[117] María Castañeda de la Paz, *Conflictos y alianzas en tiempos de cambio: Azcapotzalco, Tlacopan, Tenochtitlan, y Tlatelolco (siglos XII-XVI)* (México: Universidad Nacional Autónoma de México, Instituto de Investigaciones Antropológicas, 2013), 254. Don Martín's assassin was don Hernando de Tapia Motelchiuhtzin, the ladino son of don Andrés de Tapia Motelchiuhtzin, a former captain under Cuauhtemoc and later non-dynastic governor of Tenochtitlan between 1526 and 1530.

[118] PRT, 75, 141–44.

While he always retained a position of prominence and influence among the native sector of Mexico City, as an encomendero it is unlikely that he was ever considered eligible for the tlatocayotl of Tenochtitlan, among Spaniards and the Tenochca alike. Yet even don Pedro still found it necessary to litigate in defense of his interests, an effort that lasted his entire life, and which brought him into frequent conflict with the local nobility of Tula. While not technically an agenda of restoration – his encomienda, while built atop a pre-Hispanic patrimony, was in reality a postconquest innovation – his case nonetheless rested on historical legitimation, and he emphasized his mother's inheritance before colonial officials. Therefore, like Cano and Valderrama – and unlike most other encomenderos – don Pedro perceived his encomienda rights as part of his inheritance, derived from ancestry rather than conquest.[119] The many descendants of don Pedro, bearing the Moctezuma surname, remained prominent in and around Tula for generations.

The Tenochca royal line having been largely incorporated and co-opted, the leaders of Tlatelolco were somewhat more assertive in pressing a restorationist agenda during the first postconquest decades. The Tlatelolca nobility was ancestrally related to yet politically distinct from their Tenochca cousins. In 1473, the last independent tlatoani of Tlatelolco had perished while challenging Tenochtitlan's hegemony, and was replaced with a Tenochca-appointed *quauhtlatoani*, or nondynastic ruler.[120] Nonetheless, Tlatelolco's leaders continued to understand themselves as the heirs to a distinct imperial legacy – an identity of pride entwined with a sense of grievance typically expressed as anti-Tenochca resentment.[121] Indeed, there is evidence that Tlatelolco had already been seeking to reestablish some influence in the northern end of the lake basin prior to the Spaniards' arrival, under none other than the future huei tlatoani, Cuauhtemoc, whose mother was Tlatelolca and who maintained properties there.[122] Thus, in a strange way, Spanish power initially

---

[119] For the story of don Pedro Tlacahuepantzin's lifelong efforts to consolidate his noble privileges, see Jiménez Abollado, *Pretensiones señoriales de don Pedro Moctezuma.*

[120] See Castañeda de la Paz, *Conflictos y alianzas*: 158–65; *Anales de Tlatelolco*, trans. Rafael Tena (México, DF: CONACULTA, 2004), 22–25.

[121] See Terraciano, "Three Views of the Conquest of Mexico from the *Other* Mexica."

[122] Cuauhtemoc was the son of the Mexica emperor Ahuizotl (r. 1486–1502) and a Tlatelolca noblewoman. While Acolhua sources identify his mother as Tiyacapatzin, a daughter of the last independent Tlatelolca tlatoani Moquihuix and granddaughter of Nezahualcoyotl of Tetzcoco, Chimalpahin names her as Tecapantzin, a niece of Tlacateotl (d. 1427), a former tlatoani of Tlatelolco. See Castañeda de la Paz, *Conflictos y alianzas*; *Anales de Tlatelolco*: 79–84; Chimalpahin Cuauhtlehuanitzin, *Codex*

promised to restore a measure of autonomy to Tlatelolco, inasmuch as it was no longer directly subject to Tenochtitlan, its more powerful neighbor. By 1526, Tlatelolco had received its own *doctrina* (Franciscan spiritual district), and like Tenochtitlan was declared a direct crown holding exempt from encomiendas.[123] Yet most importantly from the perspective of the local nobility, the Spanish conquest occasioned the restoration of its tlatocayotl. In the person of don Pedro Temilotzin (r. 1521–23), a lieutenant of Cuauhtemoc and a descendant of the dispossessed dynasty, Tlatelolco once again boasted of its own tlatoani, the clearest symbol of autonomy in the Nahua world. Indeed, the *Florentine Codex*, compiled in Tlatelolco with much Tlatelolca input, records that the conquering Spaniards "gave back and restored (*oquinmacaque oquincuepilique*)" to Tlatelolco its independence.[124]

Seeing themselves as once again an autonomous altepetl, Tlatelolco's newly emboldened leadership initiated several unsuccessful attempts to "reclaim" the rights to lands and resources that they believed stolen following their 1473 conquest by Tenochtitlan. Under the tlatoani don Juan Quauiconoc (1530–37), the Tlatelolca moved to assert tribute rights among a series of small settlements along the northern end of the lake basin. This inevitably brought them into conflict with both encomenderos as well as other caciques, both of whom challenged Tlatelolco's ability to access resources they had lost fifty years prior to the conquest. In the subsequent audiencia proceedings, don Juan portrayed his actions as the restoration of immemorial rights; the encomenderos and their allies, by contrast, argued that the Spanish conquest had unmade the Mexica tyranny of the previous era, thereby rendering all such Tlatelolca claims invalid.

In Ecatepec, along the lake shore north of Tlatelolco, don Juan Quauiconoc faced Cristóbal de Valderrama, the husband of the

---

Chimalpahin: v. 2, 99. On Tlatelolco's status in Anahuac, see Castañeda de la Paz, *Conflictos y alianzas*: 135–57; Robert Barlow, *Tlatelolco: Rival de Tenochtitlan*, Obras de Robert Barlow (México: Instituto Nacional de Antropología e Historia, 1987), 133; Frederic Hicks, "Xaltocan under Mexica Domination, 1435–1520," in *The Caciques and Their People: A Volume in Honor of Ronald Spores*, ed. Joyce Marcus, and Judith Francis Zeitlin (Ann Arbor, MI: University of Michigan Museum of Anthropology, 1994), 69.

[123] Gibson, *The Aztecs*: 372–73.

[124] Bernardino de Sahagún, *General History of the Things of New Spain*, trans. Arthur J.O. Anderson, and Charles E. Dibble, 13 vols. (Santa Fe, NM: School of American Research, 1950–82), v. 8, 7–8. See also James Lockhart, ed. *We People Here: Nahuatl Accounts of the Conquest of Mexico* (Eugene, OR: Wipf & Stock, 2004), 29–30; *Anales de Tlatelolco*: 36–39.

encomendera doña Leonor Moctezuma. He insisted that Cortés had exceeded his authority by including several extramural Tlatelolca colonies in doña Leonor's encomienda.[125] An inquiry of 1536 held that the lords of Tlatelolco "were the first founders and settlers of the aforementioned villages" who had first cultivated the lands with their own macehuales and on their own authority. Thus, the settlements were indivisible units within a greater Tlatelolca ethnic realm, and therefore likewise exempt from encomiendas.[126] Its inhabitants even attended mass, not in Ecatepec, but in Tlatelolco.[127]

Don Juan Quauiconoc's efforts to restore the historic scope of Tlatelolco's domains also brought him into conflict with the island-altepetl Xaltocan, in the northern end of the basin, along with its encomendero, Gil González de Benavides (father of the Ávila brothers that later led the conspiracy of the marqués). In 1534, the cacique of Xaltocan, don Francisco, alleged that the lords of Tlatelolco had recently subdued and usurped resources from several nearby settlements within his own domain. The ensuing litigation revolved around contrasting histories of the so-called Tepaneca War of 1427-28, which marked the beginning of Mexica hegemony over Xaltocan.[128] Whereas the Xaltocameca asserted sovereignty over surrounding lands, don Juan again cited ancestral ties.[129] Despite their proximity to Xaltocan, he argued, the estancias consisted of Tlatelolca settlers who had paid tributes to the lords of Tlatelolco since "the time of Moctezuma and before."[130]

---

[125] The story of this dispute in the 1530s is in Margarita Vargas Betancourt, "Caciques tlatelolcas y tenencia de la tierra en el siglo XVI," *Nuevo Mundo, Mundos Nuevos* (2011), http://nuevomundo.revues.org/60635. The documents list a "Petecalco" along-side don Juan Quauiconoc as a co-defendant in the case; this is a corruption of the Nahua civic title *petlacalcatl*, or provincial treasurer and tribute-collector. Presumably this was the man whom don Juan had sent to gather tributes from the two disputed settlements.

[126] Statement of the lords of Tlatelolco, n.d. (Oct 1531), AGI, Seville, Spain, Justicia 159, N.5, f. 1265v-1266r. Note: this file has a pagination error, and these folio numbers are repeated twice.

[127] Probanza of the Lords of Tlatelolco, July–Oct 1536, AGI-J 159, N.5, ff. 1331r-1333v.

[128] Archeological and historical evidence suggests that later generations of Xaltocameca saw Tenochtitlan as having usurped their rightful preeminence in the northern Valley of Mexico, and that echoes of such resentment are still perceptible today. See Christopher T. Morehart, "What If the Aztec Empire Never Existed? The Prerequisites of Empire and the Politics of Plausible Alternative Histories," *American Anthropologist* 114, no. 2 (2012).

[129] Process between Gil Gonzales de Benavides and the Governor and Principales of Saltoca with the pueblo of Tateluco, 1536, AGI, Justicia 123, N.2.

[130] Don Francisco of Xaltocan against don Juan and don Pablo, governors of Tlatelolco, Mexico City, AGI-J 123, N.2. A thorough ethnographic analysis of the case is in Hicks, "Xaltocan under Mexica Domination, 1435-1520."

The region did indeed have ancestral links to Tlatelolco, a fact don Francisco conceded in a second statement to the audiencia.[131] Yet he considered this irrelevant, accusing the Tlatelolca of "wag[ing] war upon Saltoca during a time of tyranny." "The caciques of Saltoca," meanwhile, were unable to resist, and obeyed only "because they were poor, and of few privileges and means."[132] One of don Francisco's witnesses placed his case into a broader historical context.

> In ancient times, the Mexicans tyrannically usurped this whole region by force and war, taking many lands and domains and estancias and compelling them to serve and contribute to them . . . until the Spaniards came and unmade (*deshizo*) the aforementioned occupation and tyranny that the Mexicans had imposed, and everyone went back to having and possessing that which their ancestors had before the said violence.[133]

Thus did don Francisco of Xaltocan portray the era of Mexica hegemony as an unfortunate historical aberration. By defeating the Mexica and confirming the estancias as subject to Xaltocan, Cortés had not so much upended Anahuac's tributary relationships, but rather "restored" an organic and legitimate *status quo ante* rooted in a distant past "so long ago that the memories of men do not contradict it."[134]

Don Juan Quauiconoc's rebuttal began with an account of the reign of the early fifteenth-century tlatoani Tlacateotl of Tlatelolco. Citing "paintings and figures," he and his witnesses told that the disputed lands had been "calm," uninhabited territory, consisting only of "mountains and fields" within the domain of tlatoani Nezahualcoyotl of Tetzcoco. Seeking to secure food and other resources for his island-bound community, Tlacateotl acquired a concession from Nezahualcoyotl and sent colonists to expand into the region and make it flourish. The chronology here is confused, as Tlacateotl died before Nezahualcoyotl had secured his power, and other date these events to a later era.[135] Nonetheless, the story gave don Juan the standing to emphasize Tlatelolco's historic rights in the

---

[131] After an era of prominence during the fourteenth century, the original Otomí rulers of Xaltocan were defeated by Azcapotzalco in 1395; after a period of depopulation, the region was resettled by Mexica colonists from Tlatelolco. Ibid., 67; Carrasco, *Tenochca Empire*: 106.

[132] Examination of Don Francisco of Xaltocan, Mar 5, 1535, Mexico City, AGI-J 123, N.2, unnumbered.

[133] Testimony of Juan indio of Tecama, Probanza of don Francisco of Xaltocan, Nov 4–23, 1534, AGI, Justicia 123, N.2, unnumbered.

[134] Examination of don Francisco of Xaltocan, Mar 5, 135, AGI-J 123, N.2, unnumbered.

[135] Nezahualcoyotl was not in a position to distribute lands until after 1431, whereas Tlacateotl died in the late 1420s. See Barlow, *Tlatelolco: Rival de Tenochtitlan*: 77–81; Perla Valle, ed. *Ordenanza del señor Cuauhtémoc* (México: Gobierno del Distrito

area: For "so much time that the memories of men [could] not contradict it," the inhabitants of the settlements had given annual tributes of maize, seeds, blankets, lime, and personal labor to the lords of Tlatelolco. The cacique of Xaltocan, meanwhile, had no legitimate rights to the settlements, and indeed was only acting at the behest of a mendacious Spanish encomendero.[136] This version of history portrayed the cacique of Xaltocan and the encomendero González as ambitious usurpers acting against the long-established domains of Tlatelolco.

Don Juan's legal strategy was ultimately successful, as the Council of the Indies confirmed Tlatelolco's tributary rights in 1537. However, long-term colonial processes achieved what concerted legal effort could not, and Tlatelolco eventually lost control over the majority of its extramural tributaries.[137] Those efforts, however, confirm the survival and relevance of many of Anahuac's ancestral relationships, retrofitted to the legal and political apparatus of Hispanic New Spain.

Tlacopan, the Tepaneca capital of the Triple Alliance, suffered a power vacuum in the first decades of the colonial era. Its tlatoani, Totoquihuaztli, had died during the smallpox epidemoc of 1520, and Cortés executed his successor Tetlepanquetzal alongside Cuauhtemoc in 1525. Totoquihuaztli's eldest surviving son, baptized don Gabriel, died soon thereafter during Cortés's expedition to Honduras. The tlatocayotl passed then to don Antonio Cortés Totoquihuaztli, yet as he was merely a child living with the Franciscan friars, a series of nondynastic leaders commandeered the altepetl.[138] In the meantime, Cortés gave Tlacopan – a proud capital of the Triple Alliance – in encomienda to doña Isabel Moctezuma, diminishing its status considerably. Upon her death circa 1550, however, the refined and Latin-speaking don Antonio Cortés took his place as tlatoani, and launched a campaign to restore Tlacopan's suzerainty. We will examine his efforts in Chapter 3.

Meanwhile, the leaders of Acolhuacan (the Acolhua realm) were embroiled in their own struggles to grandfather preconquest rights into the new era. Most sixteenth-century Acolhua lords traced their rights to the reign of the tlatoani Nezahualcoyotl (r. 1431–72), and almost invariably cited his legacy when pressing claims before Spanish officials. As a

Federal, 2000), 108–09, 56–57; Chimalpahin Cuauhtlehuanitzin, *Codex Chimalpahin*: v. 1, 130–33; *Anales de Tlatelolco*: 25, 88–91.

[136] Examination and probanza of don Juan of Tlatelolco, May 7, 1535, AGI, Justicia 123, N.2, unnumbered; Probanza of Tlatelolco regarding the value of the settlements, May 7, 1535, AGI, Justicia 123, N.2, unnumbered.

[137] See Gibson, *The Aztecs*: 372–73.

[138] Castañeda de la Paz, *Conflictos y alianzas*: 206–08.

young prince, Nezahualcoyotl had allied with the Mexica of Tenochtitlan to overthrow the Tepaneca empire headquartered at Azcapotzalco, and in 1431 became the supreme authority of the Acolhuaque, who dominated the eastern end of the lake basin. During his reign, he partitioned the various Acolhua provinces and confirmed their tlatoque; some were his sons, while others married his daughters.[139] Of course, for every new lineage, there was one that felt dispossessed. Postconquest disputes in that region, then, tended to pit the powerful descendants of Nezahualcoyotl against provincial lords with historic grievances.

In the 1530s and 1540s, Acolhuacan was still dominated by the many sons of Nezahualpilli (r. 1472–1515), the son and successor to Nezahualcoyotl.[140] While intrigue and factionalism among the many brothers and half-brothers had fueled instability and upheaval in Acolhua politics as successive tlatoque died without indicating their chosen heirs, they typically formed a united front when dealing with rebellious tributaries, citing the authority of Nezahualcoyotl and the eternal rights of his descendants.[141] In the 1530s, for example, the cacique of Axapusco and its encomendero challenged the sons of Nezahualpilli over the rights to tributes from a pair of villages near Otumba. The case was murky; while Axapusco had previously been a non-tlatoani satellite of Otumba, it had its own encomendero.[142] Yet a son of Nezahualpilli named don Francisco challenged Axapusco's pretensions to the settlements with a detailed genealogy indicating that they had customarily paid tributes to the lords of Otumba since the reign of Nezahualcoyotl's father, the supreme Acolhua leader Ixtlilxochitl I (r. 1409–18). Thus, don Francisco concluded, the lands at question had always paid tributes to the lords of Otumba, "for so long that the memories of man cannot contradict it."[143] Reflecting the clout of the Tetzcoca ruling family, in 1541 the audiencia ruled against Axapusco, despite the fact that its encomendero, Francisco

---

[139] Carrasco, *Tenochca Empire*: 31, 136–41.

[140] For the early colonial political history of the Tetzcoco tlatocayotl, see Bradley Benton, "Beyond the Burned Stake: The Rule of Don Antonio Pimentel Tlahuitoltzin in Tetzcoco, 1540–45," in *Texcoco: Prehispanic and Colonial Perspectives*, eds. Jongsoo Lee and Galen Brokaw (Boulder: University Press of Colorado, 2014).

[141] See the "Letter of Juan de San Antonio," a 1564 Nahuatl account by a noninheriting grandson of Nezahualpilli, for examples of discontent and conflict between and among the royal family. "Letter of Juan de San Antonio," in Chimalpahin Cuauhtlehuanitzin, *Codex Chimalpahin*: v. 2, 206–39.

[142] Gerhard, *Guide to Historical Geography*: 208.

[143] Probanza of don Francisco of Otumba, June 10–23, 1534, AGI-J 134, N.1, unnumbered.

de Santa Cruz, sat with Mexico City's Spanish cabildo. However, the jurisdictional disputes between the two pueblos would survive deep into the colonial era, with Otumba repeatedly asserting historical dominion and Axapusco insisting it had always been independent.[144]

In another contemporaneous episode, in 1530 the tlatoani of Tetz-coco, don Fernando Cortés Ixtlilxochitl (r. 1526–31) – another son of Nezahualpilli – subjugated and extracted tributes from a pair of set-tlements historically beholden to the autonomous altepetl of Tequesist-lan. Several years later, the local lord, don Juan, petitioned the audien-cia for restitution. Interestingly, don Juan's case was a defense of the encomienda system established by Cortés. Tequesistlan's encomienda, he argued, was simply a colonial reiteration of its historic autonomy, and Ixtlilxochitl's actions, by violating the encomienda, was also a violation of a long-established sovereignty. "When the Marqués conquered and won this New Spain," declared don Juan's examination, "[he promised that] all those who had had lands and estancias stolen would have them returned, and they would serve again how they had customarily served before." In carving out the Tequesistlan encomienda, therefore, Cortés had restored the pueblo's traditional independence.[145] As one witness explained: "In the time of Moctezuma and the other ancient lords," the disputed estancias had supported the lords of Tequesistlan; Tequesistlan, meanwhile, had paid tributes to the lords of Tetzcoco, but only "until the Marqués del Valle came to this land and divided off Tequecistlan from the domain of Tezcuco." Don Fernando Ixtlilxochitl, then, had no right to "intrude" (*entremeter*) into the rightful possessions of Tequesistlan and kill its lord.[146] Following this unprovoked attack, therefore, Tetz-coco had maintained its control only through "tyranny and war... and not through legitimate title."[147] Once again, a native litigant backed by a Spanish encomendero cited remote history to imbue an encomienda with an ancient foundation, thereby obligating the authorities of New Spain to wield their colonially derived power to secure the ancient relationships of Anahuac.

The caciques of Tetzcoco responded with a counter-history revolving around the legacy of Nezahualcoyotl and challenging the historic basis for the Tequesistlan encomienda. The tlatoani at the time was Ixtlilxochitl's

---

[144] See Gibson, *The Aztecs*: 71.
[145] Examination of the caciques of Tequecistlan, Dec 13, 1537, AGI-J 128, N.1, f. 85v-86r.
[146] Probanza of don Juan of Tequecistlan, Apr 20, 1537, AGI-J 128, N.1, p.2 f. 19r.
[147] Petition of don Juan of Tequesistlan, Mar 6, 1537, AGI-J 128, N.1, p. 2, f. 9v.

half-brother, don Pedro Tetlahuehuetzquititzin (r. 1534–39); in his testimony, he represented Tequesistlan as part of the inheritance of his revered grandfather. One elderly witness reported that Nezahualcoyotl had given the lands surrounding Tequesistlan to his many sons and daughters as their personal domains, and thus the lords of Tetzcoco possessed the rights to all their tributes. As for Tequesistlan itself, he described it as a mere "district" (*barrio*) of the city of Tetzcoco "since a very ancient time." All had been peaceful until Cortés gave it in encomienda, thereby severing it from its rightful place subject to the Acolhua royal family.[148] Its cacique, therefore, was no true tlatoani of lineage, and therefore could not presume tribute rights over other communities within Acolhuacan. Finally, don Pedro Tetlahuehuetzquititzin and his witnesses reminded the oidores that the sons of Nezahualpilli had been among Cortés's most useful allies, having "given peace [to the Spaniards] and going out to receive them with charity and service and food to eat."[149] This severely oversimplified the history of the Tetzcoco-Castile alliance, yet the fiction of unity was useful to both the audiencia and the surviving children of Nezahualpilli, as it allowed the former to cite natural lordship in order to restrict an encomienda, and the latter to garner viceregal support for their own patrimonial claims over local rivals.[150]

By 1540, the heirs to Nezahualcoyotl had successfully established themselves as the crown's most important vassals in Acolhuacan. Yet the prominence of Nezahualpilli's children and grandchildren was hardly an inevitable outcome of conquest-era alliances; it was also, in part, a result of postconquest litigation and political maneuvering. Nezahualcoyotl himself had spent much of his life fighting to secure and consolidate his tlatocayotl; his descendants did likewise before the scribes of Spanish colonial justice. Partially by their efforts, nobility and privilege in colonial Tetzcoco and Acolhuacan derived from Nezahualcoyotl, in the sixteenth century no less than in the fifteenth, and Nezahualcoyotl's legacy would remain a cornerstone of Acolhua legal and political rhetoric

---

[148] The encomienda was that of the Spaniard Juan de Tovar. Gerhard, *Guide to Historical Geography*: 274.

[149] Testimony of Miguel Tescuxulaltecle, Probanza of don Pedro of Tezcuco, May 16, 1537, AGI 128, N.1, f. 62r-64r.

[150] The audiencia ruled in favor of don Pedro Tetlahuehuetzquititzin in both its first and second pronouncements, on Oct 30, 1537 and again on Mar 1, 1538. Case summary of don Juan of Tequesistlan and Totolcingo vs. don Pedro of Tezcoco, Apr 22, 1542, Valladolid, AGI-J 128, N.1, f. 1v-2r.

for centuries.[151] As Juan Bautista de Pomar – a mestizo grandson of Nezahualpilli and ally to his cacique descendants, the Pimentels and Alvarados – insisted in 1593, "those who are not descended from Nezahualpilli are excluded [from positions of authority in Tetzcoco] by rights both divine and human."[152]

Conclusion

Painfully aware of their precarious position and motivated by dreams of lordship restored, resentful over broken promises, nostalgic for lost glory, and jealous of their social distinction, by the 1530s the surviving pipiltin of Anahuac were regularly imploring colonial officials to acknowledge their rights and enforce promises of autonomy and confederation. Caciques could litigate defensively or offensively – either protesting the diminishment or seeking the expansion of their prerogatives – but in either case their plight required a delicate rhetorical balance of subversion and supplication in which they accepted the essential premise of Spanish hegemony while grandfathering in as much of their pre-Hispanic prestige as possible. By invoking and engaging Hispano-Catholic values and legal traditions and applying them to their own ancestries, they grafted the ruling lineages of the past onto the new colonial reality. Due in part to the legal campaigns of the early native nobility, Mesoamerican history never became the esoteric interest of antiquarians; rather, it remained a vital and contested ground upon which colonial-era disputes continued to be waged. New Spain, the lords implied, was not so new at all; it had its own long and momentous history, one that no conquest or conversion could render irrelevant.

Thus do we sense, in the early rhetoric of caciques as well as the historical ventriloquism of Spaniards invested in the notion of inherited rights, an expectation and insistence on continuity, on both the ancient and contemporary legitimacy of the patrimonies of Anahuac, once recodified as colonial cacicazgos or encomiendas. In this way, the sense that the history of New Spain predated the conquest of Tenochtitlan – that Spanish Mexico included rather than replaced native Anahuac – permeated colonial politics as early as the 1530s. Like Cortés himself, the protagonists of

---

[151] Fernando Horcasitas, "Los descendientes de Nezahualpilli: Documentos del cacicazgo de Tetzcoco (1545–1855)," *Estudios de cultura nahuatl* 6 (1978).

[152] Petition of Juan de Pomar, Tetzcoco, Apr 13, 1593, AGN-T 1740, Exp. 1, f. 141v. I am grateful to Brad Benton for the transcription of this document.

these disputes did not so much acknowledge a conquest but a transfer of rule; indeed, postconquest Nahua petitioners sometimes addressed the king as "huei tlatoani."[153]

Going further, the politically useful fiction of continuity aligned the agendas of the natural lords and the Spanish conquistadors who married into their ranks, installed themselves as encomenderos, or otherwise hoped to take their place. We can thus view Juan Cano de Saavedra, the conspirators of 1566, and the encomenderos who opportunistically championed the historic sovereignty of their domains as forerunners to Mexican creolism, inasmuch as they envisioned themselves as heirs to Anahuac. It was a characteristic of creole historiography and self-representation to dignify, validate, and consolidate colonial fortunes by reimagining them as the fruits of Mexican antiquity, and themselves as the heirs to caciques.

[153] The authors of the *Annals of Tlatelolco* (~1545), one of the earliest Nahuatl-language documents, refer to Carlos V as "huei teoutl tlatohuani Castilla moyetztica" ("great [Spanish] emperor there in Castile"). By the second generation, however, many Nahua authors had adopted the Spanish loanword "rey," or king. Nonetheless, educated Nahuas in later generations, interested in retaining and showcasing a high Nahuatl style, often preferred to revert to the original "huei tlatoani." See "Letter of the Cabildo of Huejotzingo to the King, 1560," in Lockhart, *We People Here*, 288; Castañeda de la Paz, *Anales de Tlatelolco*: 37.

3

Cacique informants and early Spanish texts, 1535–80

Your Majesty is forever pledged to combat the barbarous nations, infidels, and devil-worshippers, in sum, all the enemies of God; and to draw them away from the darkness and into the resplendent light of Christianity... all of which Your Majesty has happily worked among us, as by combating the horrible army of demons by way of your Spaniards, and by introducing Christianity... you have wrought a sublime tranquility in our province – such that, although we are pained by the slaughter of our forebears and the not-insignificant loss of our worldly goods, we nonetheless humbly recognize the immortal benefit of Your Majesty['s rule].

Don Antonio Cortés Totoquihuaztli, tlatoani of Tlacopan, 1552[1]

I also have [a history] given to me by a noble Indian of... Xaltocan named don Pablo Nazareo, who was raised since boyhood with the first twelve friars... and was very virtuous and a very good Christian.... He had some ancient paintings [from the College of Santa Cruz de Tlatelolco] from which he derived the [historical accounts] he gave me. He was married to the daughter of a brother of Moctezuma named don Juan Axayac, whom I met when he was very old. He had great knowledge of all things pertaining to that land, and [although] he helped the Spaniards in the conquest... don Pablo cared for him at home, because he was very poor and had nothing more than the [small pension] granted by a royal order.

Alonso de Zorita, c. 1580[2]

This chapter examines the historical reconstructions of indigenous lords from central Mexico and Querétaro during the mid sixteenth century,

[1] Don Antonio Cortés Totoquihuaztli to Emperor Carlos V, Dec 1, 1552, in PRT, 167–68.
[2] Alonso de Zorita, *Relación de la Nueva España*, 2 edn., 2 vols. (Mexico: CONACULTA, 2011), v. 1, 103–04.

identifies their most pressing rhetorical concerns, and explores how these influenced contemporary Spanish perceptions and portrayals of native culture and history. This was the golden age of Nahua literacy. Educated and multilingual, many sons of Anahuac's elite lineages engaged the viceregal regime to secure the promised array of colonial privileges. In negotiations with the viceroy and his agents, they detailed ancestral rights and domains, the blood and treasure their fathers had risked on behalf of the Spaniards and their Church, and their contemporary penury. Among other genres, their efforts resulted in an extensive corpus of native- or partially native-authored ethnohistorical material such as genealogies and estate maps. The result was a characteristic, if emotionally ambivalent blend of ethnic patriotism and Hispano-Catholic triumphalism, in which bittersweet memories of preconquest glory coexisted with and informed fervent expressions of loyalty to Spain, its conquest, and its Church.

Meanwhile, these same native lords, bilingual and bicultural, served as informants for contemporary Spaniards and creoles concerned, for a variety of reasons, with inquiries into Mexican history and culture. By far the most prominent of such collaborations was the monumental evangelical-ethnographic project of the early Franciscan friars. Others stemmed from secular investigations relating to colonial administration. In both cases, the influence of cacique informants is pervasive and readily evident, as they combined an obsession with pre-Hispanic dynastic successions with an emphasis on the preservation of cacique power as indispensable to peace and stability in New Spain. In this way, the cacique agenda informed some of the earliest and most influential texts within what would become the creole historiographical tradition.

"In ancient times they were great lords": detailing decline and merit in cacique self-representation

In 1528, Hernando Cortés returned to Spain to solidify his favor with Carlos V. To impress the king – and to discourage rebellion – his retinue included about forty Nahua noblemen, mostly younger relatives of the old ruling triumvirate.[3] While in Spain, they received an education in Catholic doctrine and the Castilian language; a handful also married Spanish women.[4] Yet when they returned to Mexico they confronted a transformed political landscape, one in which they were superfluous

---

[3] Prescott, *Mexico, and the Life of the Conqueror Fernando Cortés*: v. 2, 345.
[4] Carrasco, "Indian–Spanish Marriages in the First Century of the Colony," 90, 102.

and the encomenderos ascendant. Frustrated and humiliated, in 1532 the Tenochca nobility appealed to the king's conscience, via the new Second Audiencia:

> Holy, Catholic, Caesarean Majesty...we inform you of the penury, necessity, and opprobrium which we suffer...because [although] being the sons of whom we are, our fathers and grandfathers having been those lords that reigned over and governed this land, we are now its poorest, having no bread of our own to eat. We beg Your Grace that, understanding the services that we and our fathers have performed and expect to perform for you, you will pity us our misery, look to your royal conscience, and grant us favors like those of your Spanish vassals in these lands – favors without subjection to any Spaniard beside Your Grace.[5]

Individually, the petitioners requested the restoration of a series of patrimonial lands and tributes swallowed by the encomiendas. They framed their grievances as insults to noble dignity. "Because [Tenochtitlan] is populated with Spaniards," they complained, "we are poorer than the gentlemen (*vecinos*) of other pueblos and cities where there are none; being as it was the noblest city, served by all, it is unjust...that we be their subjects and vassals."[6] The crown responded the following year, ordering the oidores to investigate the lords' claims and make amends.[7] Although they saw little in the way of restitution, it was the beginning of a decades-long epistolary campaign among the descendants of the old Triple Alliance: Citing ancestral grandeur alongside proclamations of steadfast loyalty and piety, the caciques of Anahuac repeatedly exhorted the king to defend their noble prerogatives as the natural lords of New Spain (Figure 4).

In Tenochtitlan specifically it was a losing battle, however. The rise of Spanish Mexico City placed the traditional nobility in an impossible position. Beyond the loss of imperial tributes, the indigenous population of Tenochtitlan became heavily involved in the urban service economy as artisans, vendors, and builders, which aligned their interests with the emergent mercantile class and against the natural lords, whom they accused of levying excessive tribute burdens. The final dynastic governor,

---

[5] "Parecer de la Segunda Audiencia sobre una petición de varios principales de la Ciudad de México," June 18 1532, in PRT, 99.

[6] "Parecer de la Segunda Audiencia sobre una petición de varios principales de la Ciudad de México," June 18, 1532, in PRT, 102.

[7] Decree of Queen Juana in favor of don Pablo, don Diego, and don Pedro of Tenochtitlan, Valladolid, July 7, 1533, in Puga, *Provisiones, cédulas, instrucciones para el gobierno de la Nueva España*: f. 111.

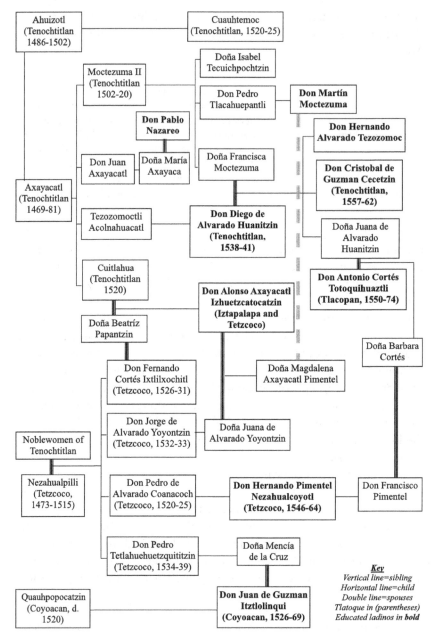

FIGURE 4 Intermarriage among the high nobility of central Mexico, sixteenth century

don Luís de Santamaría Cipac, died in 1565, resentful at his own irrelevance and reviled by commoners who named him "Nanacatl" (toadstool) due to his perceived inability to defend their interests.[8] Future governors of Tenochtitlan were at best only obliquely related to the preconquest tlatoque, and focused on idiosyncratic concerns relating to municipal administration rather than the restoration of pre-Hispanic patrimonies.[9]

Elsewhere in Anahuac, however, dynastic successors remained heavily engaged in the quest for the restoration of traditional tributes and guarantees of noble privileges. The Acolhua lords of Tetzcoco and its satellites – the self-proclaimed heirs to Nezahualcoyotl – were pioneers in this effort. Their most prominent representative was don Hernando Pimentel Nezahualcoyotl, the son of Coanacoch, who assumed the tlatocayotl in 1546 upon the death of his uncle, don Antonio Pimentel Tlahuitoltzin (r. 1539–46). His was a watershed moment in Tetzcoca politics, as don Hernando was the first tlatoani since 1515 that was not a son of Nezahualpilli. He was also the first Tetzcoca leader to have been educated by the Franciscan friars. Adept at navigating the colonial system, don Hernando's time as tlatoani-governor (1546–64) was a brief era of stability in a Tetzcoco that had suffered almost unceasing political crises since the death of Nezahualpilli. With the friars' aid, he cultivated alliances with powerful patrons in the Hispanic world, and leveraged them to elevate Tetzcoco to the coveted crown status of "city," which conferred greater autonomy.[10]

Don Hernando's pursuit of favors and privileges relied heavily upon elaborate descriptions of Tetzcoco's preconquest magnificence, which he had never seen himself. In 1554, he solicited a personal audience with the king by representing himself as the lord of an ancient house nine centuries old.[11] Several years later, he requested the partial restoration of Nezahualpilli's estate. The occasion called for a precise accounting of his father's lost patrimony: The tributes of Tetzcoco's 123 former dependencies, he reasoned, would be worth 340,000 pesos annually, "more or less."[12]

[8] Reyes García, *Anales de Juan Bautista*: 31–37; Castañeda de la Paz, *Conflictos y alianzas*: 250–69.

[9] See Connell, *After Moctezuma*.

[10] Benton, "Beyond the Burned Stake."

[11] "Carta de don Hernando Pimentel Nezahualcóyotl al emperador Carlos V," Nov 25, 1554, in PRT, 189. There is no record of don Hernando ever traveling to Spain.

[12] Fernando de Alva Ixtlilxochitl, *Obras históricas*, ed. Edmundo O'Gorman, 2 vols. (Mexico: Universidad Nacional Autónoma de México, 1975), v. 1, 13.

Don Hernando also emphasized the Tetzcoco-Castile alliance. Acknowledging that the conquest had largely dispossessed the Acolhua ruling family, he nonetheless insisted that baptism and integration with Castile were "the greatest boon[s] I could have ever imagined."[13] In 1551, the tlatoani requested and received a coat of arms by referencing Tetzcoco's services to the conquistadors. The altepetl had joined the Spaniards immediately, he wrote, supplying them the thirteen brigantines with which they besieged the Mexica capital. The Tetzcoca lords had also accepted baptism voluntarily, and had "persevered" in the faith ever since.[14] By casting Tetzcoco as an unambiguous champion of Spanish rule, don Hernando's account strategically simplified a rather more ambiguous history in which the Acolhuaque had split into warring pro- and anti-Tenochca factions, and in which Cortés had kidnapped Coanacoch, his own father.

In the Tepaneca realm to the west, an important dynasty invoked similar themes, albeit under distinct conditions, and far less successfully. Don Antonio Cortés Totoquihuaztli the Elder (1516–74) was a son of the conquest-era tlatoani of Tlacopan as well as a grandson of the Tenochca governor don Diego de Alvarado Huanitzin.[15] As we have seen, Tlacopan was part of the encomienda of doña Isabel Moctezuma after 1526, and went mostly leaderless while the young don Antonio received a Franciscan education. After dona Isabel's death circa 1550, don Antonio finally took his place as tlatoani and governor, and had become a master Latinist and a powerful writer. As such, like his peer and relative by marriage, don Hernando Pimentel of Tetzcoco, he was a formidable advocate for his own patrimony as well as the Tlacopaneca nobility in general. Drawing upon his Franciscan connections – which included friar Alonso de Molina, a pioneer in alphabetic Nahuatl – and his intimate knowledge of the colonizer's language, customs, and laws, don Antonio labored for decades to salvage his family's slowly disintegrating legacy.[16] His mostly

---

[13] "Carta de don Hernando Pimentel Nezahualcóyotl al emperador Carlos V," Nov 25, 1554, in PRT, 189.

[14] Ignacio de Villar Villamil, "Armas para don Hernando Pimentel," in *Cedulario heráldico de conquistadores de Nueva España* (Mexico: Publicaciones del Museo Nacional, 1933), no. 128.

[15] While several sources have called the tlatoani of Tlacopan between 1550 and 1574, "the Younger," María Castañeda de la Paz has recently proven that he was, in fact, "the Elder," and that one of his sons was known during his own time as "the Younger." See Castañeda de la Paz, *Conflictos y alianzas*: 302–06.

[16] See Probanza of don Antonio Cortés Totoquihuaztli, Mexico, Mar 15, 1566, in PRT, 328–29.

unsuccessful struggle is one of the most sophisticated examples of cacique political and legal engagement in early New Spain.

Don Antonio's primary concerns were the preservation of his inherited cacicazgo – which he interpreted as the landed domains of the tlatoque of historic Tlacopan – as well as the economic integrity of his altepetl. Unlike don Hernando of Tetzcoco, however, don Antonio had to contend with the encomienda of doña Isabel Moctezuma. And while many central Mexican encomiendas were escheating to the crown during the 1550s and 1560s, Tlacopan was explicitly a perpetual holding, and stood to pass to the Cano-Moctezumas. Upon assuming the tlatocayotl, don Antonio sought to inform the king of the injustice of this situation. He argued that Tlacopan, as one of the three *tlatoloyan catca* (former capitals) of the Triple Alliance, had never known subjugation to another lord; it was co-equal to Tenochtitlan and Tetzcoco and deserved, like its counterparts, to be exempt from encomiendas. "Our pueblo never served; rather, it used to be served by many others," he lamented; "thus it is to us extremely burdensome to have to pay each year such immoderate tributes, and what is worse, to see ourselves deprived of our lands and other possessions."[17] He also reminded the king that when the Spaniards, "wounded and demoralized," had fled through Tlacopan upon their escape from Tenochtitlan, they were allowed to pass through unharmed. This was a very great service indeed, he insisted ominously, because "if we had made war ... not a man among them would have remained."[18] Unsurprisingly, the cacique's repeated petitions portrayed Cano and the late doña Isabel as cruel and greedy, and the encomienda itself as an affront to the dignity of an ancient lineage. In elegant Latin, don Antonio wrote that

... [our poverty has] been aggravated by the encomendero Juan Cano, with the excessive tributes that we give him every year; and not only by him, but also by the daughter of Montezoma that was his wife – who, although she was of our blood and nation [did not demonstrate] the piety and love that men naturally have for their own land and people, instead exercising a tyranny; as for us, born to noble and illustrious parents, she treated us like slaves.[19]

[17] Don Antonio Cortés to Emperor Carlos V, Tlacopan, Dec 1, 1552, in PRT, 174–75.

[18] Don Antonio Cortés to Emperor Carlos V, Tlacopan, Jan 6, 1552, in PRT, 161. Hernando Cortés himself does not report resistance in Tlacopan during the noche triste, but neither does he note receiving aid. Moreover, Tlacopan was the site of a major battle during the subsequent siege of Tenochtitlan the following year, as the resistance had set up barricades there. Cortés, *Letters from Mexico*: 138–39, 87–88.

[19] Don Antonio Cortés to Emperor Carlos V, Tlacopan, Dec 1, 1552, in PRT, 169.

Don Antonio's pleas were unsuccessful, and the encomienda passed to Juan Cano and his children. Yet he did not relent, and in the 1560s once again demanded that Tlacopan be extracted from the encomienda and placed within the royal estate. In this effort, he saw a small symbolic success, as Felipe II conceded a coat of arms to don Antonio in 1564.[20] Yet so long as the encomienda continued to siphon Tlacopan's wealth, he remained noble in theory only. A poignant petition of 1566 reveals the heartbreak and frustration of an aging aristocrat denied his patrimony. "Of the entire domain (*señorio*) of my father and grandfathers, who were caciques and lords of this *cabecera* (autonomous municipality) and its subjects, I do not possess a single pueblo," he declared. But with or without real wealth and power, pedigree remained central to don Antonio's sense of himself and his place in the world. Despite the indifference of the colonial regime, he requested that his oldest son, grandson, and descendents be confirmed as caciques and governors in perpetuity.[21] His Nahuatl testament, drawn up before his death in 1574, reveals a man who commanded great reverence and respect as tlatoani, but only a comparatively modest handful of lands and properties scattered throughout the area. "He also left two silver cups," reported the Nahua scribe, "and a mass was said [in his honor]; and this is all, because he left nothing else."[22] As we will see in subsequent chapters, however, don Antonio's legacy survived in other ways. His descendants continued to dominate Tlacopan's cabildo, while his support was central to the early establishment of a Jesuit presence in Mexico City, for almost two centuries a locus of collaboration and communication between the native elite and sympathetic creoles.[23]

Along with his Tetzcoca kinsman don Hernando Pimentel, don Antonio was also a leading voice among the Nahua nobility in general. In the early 1560s, the Tlacopaneca tlatoani penned their collective response to the new laws demanding tributes in specie, arguing that they were "defrauding" and threatening the dignity of an ancient aristocracy.[24] In a subtle rebuke, he implied that the king's failure to protect the caciques

---

[20] "Armas para d. Antonio Cortés," Barcelona, Mar 3, 1564, in Villar Villamil, *Cedulario heráldico*: no. 140.

[21] Representation of don Antonio Cortés to the King, Mexico, Tlacopan, Mar 15, 1566, AGI-J 1029, N.10, n.p.

[22] Testament of don Antonio Cortés Totoquihuaztli, Tlacopan, May 1, 1574, in PRT, 377–76.

[23] Castañeda de la Paz, *Conflictos y alianzas*: 306–13.

[24] See the Letter of the Lords and Principales of New Spain to Emperor Carlos V, Tlacopan, May 2, 1556, in PRT, 199–200.

was no fault of his own, but merely a result of his ignorance regarding the proper state of affairs in Anahuac, generously allowing that "Your Majesty was never informed of how things used to be." To rectify this situation, he assumed the role of a political and social historian, offering the king "some information regarding our ancient state": a list of all the settlements and lands previously subject to Tlacopan.[25] A related list, produced or commissioned by don Antonio, is known today as the *Memorial de Tlacopan*, and is an important source of information about the structure of the Triple Alliance.[26] Meanwhile, don Antonio contributed to the compilation of the *Codex Osuna* (1565), in which the central Mexican nobility collectively detailed their many unremunerated services to Spaniards during an official crown inquest into the viceroy's performance (*visita*). An appendix to the codex is a pictorial-Nahuatl political history of Tlacopan that partially reproduces the information in don Antonio's letters and the *Memorial de Tlacopan*. Although there is no signature, the alphabetic text, dated January 1565, matches don Antonio's elegant script.[27]

Attaching accounts of colonial-era services to invocations of ancestral greatness also defined the tactics of native lords from lesser altepeme in central Mexico. Don Pablo Nazareo, the son of the tlatoani of Xaltocan, was one of the more accomplished prodigies of the College of Santa Cruz de Tlatelolco, where he also served as rector and teacher of Latin.[28] During the 1560s, he performed duties with the Mexico City audiencia as a *fiscal* (legal aide) and interpreter.[29] Continuing local tradition, he married a Mexica noblewoman, doña María Axayaca Oceloxochitzin, a granddaughter of the fifteenth-century emperor Axayacatl and a niece to Moctezuma II. As an educated cacique with personal and professional ties to the highborn of Anahuac, the Franciscan mission, and the viceregal apparatus, don Pablo was intimately acquainted with both the elite native and elite Hispanic realms.

---

[25] Don Antonio Cortés and the Cabildo of Tlacopan to Felipe II, Tlacopan, Feb 20, 1561, in PRT, 245.

[26] Memorial of the Pueblos of Tlacopan, n.d. (probably 1561), in PRT, 249–51.

[27] Compare the Tlacopaneca section of the codex to don Antonio's letter of 1566. Representation of don Antonio Cortés to the King, Mexico, Tlacopan, Mar 15, 1566, AGI-J 1029, N.10, n.p.; *Pintura del gobernador, alcaldes y regidores de México: Códice Osuna*, 2 vols. (Madrid: Ministerio de Educación y Ciencia, Dirección General de Archivos y Bibliotecas, 1973), f. 34r-36v.

[28] Zorita, *Relación*: v. 1, 104.

[29] Don Pablo is mentioned in the *Anales de Juan Bautista* in this capacity several times. See Reyes García, *Anales de Juan Bautista*: 272–73, 84–85.

Don Pablo's case for royal favor, articulated within a series of Latin letters and petitions during the 1560s, revolved around both genealogical merit and services to the crown, punctuated with claims of dispossession and poverty. His petitions are remarkable for their rich genealogical detail, which linked him to the royal dynasties not only of Xaltocan, but also of Tenochtitlan, Azcapotzalco, Tlacopan, Tlatelolco, Cuernavaca, and other prominent altepeme. The result is a political history of Anahuac charting the lands and domains of numerous tlatoque over three centuries, with an emphasis on the Tolteca-Culhua heritage of the Tenochca ruling dynasty and the imperial Tepaneca-Azcapotzalca legacy of Xaltocan. These accounts gave don Pablo the leverage to request, as the heir to Xaltocan's immemorial natural lords, the restoration of its cacicazgo, which had recently been stripped from its encomendero, the alleged traitor Alonso de Ávila Alvarado.[30]

Don Pablo's letters also reflect his status as a go-between in the colonial world, and indeed he requested support based precisely upon this role. Don Pablo revived the idea of Moctezuma's donation to Cortés, adding that its mastermind had been none other than his father-in-law don Juan Axayacatl, the huei tlatoani's brother. Due to these overtures of peace, however, don Juan had been forced to flee Tenochtitlan following the emperor's death, despite being the rightful successor to Moctezuma; Cuauhtemoc was chosen in his absence. From that point on don Juan became a kind of mediator and peace emissary between the Mexica and the Spanish-led coalition – mirroring don Pablo's own position in colonial society – speaking on behalf of the hungry, the orphaned, and the homeless. After the hostilities had ceased, the dutiful don Juan joined Cuauhtemoc in the reconstruction of Tenochtitlan, and assisted the conquerors in securing warriors for secondary conquests further abroad.

By his own account, don Pablo had continued don Juan's tradition of peacemaking. Together, their services involved a long record of support for the evangelical mission, particularly in the foundation and administration of the College of Santa Cruz de Tlatelolco. Reflecting his Franciscan influences, he wrote that, in contrast to the Spaniards who conquered new populations by force, he and his colleagues had done so with nothing but good doctrine and exemplary virtue. "After extirpating many idolatrous evils at a not-insignificant cost," he explained, "for over 42 years and before... I pacified these Mexican provinces, instructing the children of the Indians in Christian doctrine [and] inculcating Christian customs."

[30] Don Pablo Nazareo to King Felipe II, Mar 17, 1566, in PRT, 348–64.

"By assimilating Christian customs," he explained, "they seem almost new men."

Allegations of penury rounded out don Pablo Nazareo's case. Despite their great services to the crown and the Church, don Pablo and don Juan Axayacatl endured a most ignoble poverty. His father-in-law "suffered an enormous injustice" after the conquest, as he received neither cacicazgo nor encomienda, insulting his ancestral rights and violating the promises of the early Spaniards whom he had supported. Meanwhile, the salaries and pensions resulting from don Pablo's labors at Santa Cruz were wholly insufficient to sustain his wife and children, placing them in an "extreme misery" unbecoming of one of the king's most loyal and useful vassals.[31]

Don Juan de Guzmán Itztlolinqui was the most important governor and tlatoani of postconquest Coyoacan. He was a true teuctli of Anahuac, with close ties to the Tenochca ruling dynasty; his father was Quauhpopocatzin, a Mexica nobleman, and his mother was the great-granddaughter of the second tlatoani of Tenochtitlan, Huitzilihuitl (r. 1391–1415).[32] Don Juan was a young boy at the time of the Spanish conquest; after his father died during the battle for Tenochtitlan, his brother assumed the tlatocayotl but died soon thereafter as Cortés's hostage. Don Juan himself became tlatoani in 1526, and remained so until his death in 1569 (although regents governed during his minority). He married doña Mencía de la Cruz, the daughter of don Pedro Tetlahuehuetzquititzin of Tetzcoco and cousin of don Hernando Pimentel Nezahualcoyotl.[33] He was thus a peer to both don Hernando and don Antonio Cortés Totoquihuaztli of Tlacopan, and he sometimes signed his name to their petitions.

In 1536, encouraged by the prodynastic inclinations of his new Viceroy Mendoza, don Juan initiated a process to liberate his domains from the marquisate of Cortés – who, he complained, had been "treating [the people of Coyoacan] like slaves," beating and imprisoning them, and levying tributes so excessive that many macehualtin had fled to the mountains.[34] He built his case around the services of his late father during the conquest of Tenochtitlan, who, he claimed, "died while protecting [the Spaniards from] the people of Monteçuma." "At the time when the Marqués del Valle and the Christians came to conquer and win this

---

[31] Don Pablo Nazareo to King Felipe II, Mar 17, 1566, in PRT, 344–46.

[32] Chimalpahin Cuauhtlehuanitzin, *Codex Chimalpahin*: v. 1, 39.

[33] See PRT, 84; ibid., v. 1, 39, 147–49; Horn, *Postconquest Coyoacan: Nahua–Spanish Relations in Central Mexico, 1519–1650*: 46–69.

[34] Statement of Merits of don Juan de Guzmán Itztlolinqui, Mexico, June 15, 1536, in PRT, 104.

New Spain," he told, his father had been a "captain" of Moctezuma, and was sent to meet the strangers at Veracruz and usher them safely to Mexico. This he did, "and he guided and protected them . . . with much cunning and stealth so that the pueblos along the way would not kill them, as they were uneasy with the arrival of the Christians." Quauhpopocatzin did this, moreover, "willingly and with much love, as if [he] were a Christian like each of them." According to don Juan, his father even gave his life to ensure the success of the conquest. During their nighttime escape from Tenochtitlan in June 1520, Quauhpopocatzin guided the Spaniards through the city to the bridges, securing their passage off the island. As they fled, he remained behind, "helping and favoring all of them with his vassals, friends, and relatives, fighting like a valiant captain," holding the bridges until the Tenochca killed them all. Without his father, don Juan concluded, "all the Christians would have died and the city of Mexico would not have been won."[35]

Due to his youth and position within Anahuac's politics, don Juan Itztlolinqui became a close ally to the colonial regime – "treated as a Christian in dress and in practice" – and partially by his efforts his descendants fared relatively well.[36] He participated in Viceroy Mendoza's pacification wars in western Mexico in the early 1540s, and was one of only three Indian lords allowed the honor of riding alongside the viceroy.[37] During a 1550 investigation by oidor Gómez de Santillán, don Juan requested that his governorship be made hereditary, that the local councilmen be appointed for life from the local nobility, and that Coyoacan receive a municipal coat of arms.[38] The crown accepted his bid for nobility (but not his other requests), and his family motto became *credo in Deum patrem*.[39]

---

[35] Examination of don Juan de Guzmán Itztlolinqui, Mexico, June 10, 1536, in PRT, 108–09.

[36] Examination of don Juan de Guzmán Itztlolinqui, Mexico, June 10, 1536, in PRT, 109. Don Juan made substantial legal preparations to ensure that his children and descendants would inherit the same array of privileges that he himself enjoyed. See Petition of don Juan de Guzmán Itztlolinqui, Mexico, June 8, 1536, in PRT, 105.

[37] Francisco de Sandoval Acazitli, "Relación de la jornada que hizo don Francisco de Sandoval Acazitli, cacique y señor natural que fue del pueblo de Tlalmanalco," in *Colección de documentos para la historia de México*, ed. Joaquín García Icazbalceta, vol. 2 (México: Antigua Librería, 1866), 311.

[38] Petition of don Juan of Coyoacan, 1554, in Pedro Carrasco and Jesús Monjarás-Ruiz, eds. *Colección de documentos sobre Coyoacán*, 2 vols. (México: Centro de Investigaciones Superiores, 1976), 10.

[39] Concession of Arms to don Juan de Guzmán of Coyoacan, Valladolid, Sept 4, 1551, in *Cacicazgos y nobiliario indígena de la Nueva España*, ed. Guillermo S. Fernández de Recas (México, D.F.: Instituto Bibliográfico Mexicano, 1961), 53–54.

In citing ancestry alongside conquest-era services, don Juan Itztlolinqui and don Pablo Nazareo echoed the same formula as their relatives from Tetzcoco and Tlacopan. Yet other midcentury caciques asserted different merits according to the particulars of local history. One remarkable example comes from Azcapotzalco – a relatively minor altepetl which nonetheless boasted of a splendid imperial heritage predating that of Tenochtitlan. Its most famous postconquest son was don Antonio Valeriano (d. 1605). Although not of high noble birth, he won lasting fame as a prodigy at the College of Santa Cruz de Tlatelolco, where he taught Latin alongside don Pablo Nazareo, and helped lead the Franciscans' midcentury efforts to compile native artifacts and detail Nahua history and culture.[40] He married up, to the daughter of don Diego de Alvarado Huanitzin, thus securing a place among the Tenochca elite.[41] Indeed, he even became the first nondynastic governor of Tenochtitlan, where between 1573 and 1599 he skillfully oversaw the Indian republic. Yet earlier, during the 1550s and 1560s, Antonio Valeriano (not yet addressed as *don*) sat with the cabildo of his native Azcapotzalco, a majority Tepaneca community. While there, he deployed his erudition on its behalf.

In 1561, the Azcapotzalca cabildo petitioned for labor and tribute exemptions, the restitution of lost lands, the right to a weekly market, and elevation to the status of city. Written in elegant Latin, Valeriano clearly authored the letter, which explicitly holds its own scholarly erudition forward as evidence of Azcapotzalco's innate worthiness.[42] The petition consisted largely of a patriotic account of local history, yet in contrast to the accounts from the heirs to the Triple Alliance, Valeriano reached to an even more distant era – the thirteenth century – to frame his appeal for favors. This reflected Azcapotzalco's unique history; although the Spaniards had found it a mere tributary of Tlacopan, the altepetl had dominated Anahuac prior to the 1420s. Valeriano's account was one of

[40] Zorita, *Relación*: v.1, 291.

[41] Huanitzin's son, don Hernando Alvarado Tezozomoc, had a much greater claim than Valeriano to the governorship by the logic of dynastic succession, but his own position as a scholar and interpreter to the audiencia (as well as widespread support for Valeriano) kept him from following his father and brother. Chimalpahin later noted that Valeriano was "not a nobleman" in his political history of Tenochtitlan. See Chimalpahin Cuauhtlehuanitzin, *Codex Chimalpahin*: v. 1, 172–73; Susan Schroeder, "The Truth about the *Crónica mexicayotl*," *Colonial Latin American Review* 20, no. 2 (2011): 235–36.

[42] Letter of the governors and officers of Azcapotzalco to Felipe II, Azcapotzalco, Feb 10, 1561, in PRT, 213–225.

decline and diminishment, contrasting his town's ancient greatness with its contemporary poverty.[43]

"Although at the present our pueblo is small," he began, "in the past . . . it surpassed [the other provinces] in antiquity and nobility." The elders told that Azcapotzalco had been founded fifteen centuries earlier, and that all the noble lineages of Anahuac had their origins there. At the height of its empire, Azcapotzalco maintained tributaries throughout central Mexico, from Cuernavaca in the south to Xilotepec (today Jilótepec) in the north. The Mexica, insisted Valeriano, had been mere squatters in lands controlled by Azcapotzalco, and it was only out of pity that its lord had allowed them to settle Tenochtitlan and sustain themselves from the lake.[44] The imperial order collapsed, however, when the ungrateful Mexica attacked Azcapotzalco, repaying this benevolence with betrayal and violence. Valeriano concluded by stating the purpose of his history: "So that our pueblo, which as we have shown was historically a *provincia* (independent province), should be named a city by Your Clemency." On the municipal coat of arms it proposed, the cabildo placed the image of a heart, to symbolize how, just as the heart is the origin of all life, Azcapotzalco was the origin of all nobility in "New Spain."[45] The implications were subtle, yet powerful: Justice and reason demanded that Spanish officials acknowledge and embrace the Azcapotzalca legacy, the most ancient in all the land.

Other Nahua lords were likewise inclined to emphasize postconquest penury, especially those communities with a Franciscan presence, often misrepresenting the true scope of their ancestors' traditional privileges and sovereignty.[46] The result was a pathos aimed directly at the king's sense of charity. "We declare to you that it will not be long before your city of Huejotzingo completely disappears and perishes," wrote the assembled leadership of that town in 1560, "because our fathers, grandfathers and ancestors knew no tribute and gave tribute to no one, but were

---

[43] For the postconquest political history of Azcapotzalco, see Castañeda de la Paz, *Conflictos y alianzas*: 322–37.

[44] Letter of the governors and officers of Azcapotzalco to Felipe II, Azcapotzalco, Feb 10, 1561, in PRT, 218–21, quote from 218.

[45] Letter of the governors and officers of Azcapotzalco to Felipe II, Azcapotzalco, Feb 10, 1561, in PRT, 221.

[46] According to Lockhart, the "propaganda" of the native lords and their Franciscan sympathizers falsely portrayed the teteuctin and pipiltin as having previously enjoyed tribute exemptions. Lockhart, *The Nahuas*: 106.

independent." As restrictions were placed on their ability to extract tributes, they complained, the aristocracy was disintegrating: "Nobility is
seen among us no longer; now we resemble the commoners. As they eat
and dress, so do we; we have been very greatly afflicted, and our poverty
has reached its culmination."[47] A 1563 letter from Xochimilco expressed
the same status anxiety, waxing nostalgic about an era when their ancestors enjoyed unrestricted authority and prestige. "From time immemorial, when the Spaniards came and before," they wrote, the nobles lived in
harmony with compliant and respectful macehualtin, who "held them in
high recognition, giving them tokens of respect." The common folk had
grown rebellious, however, stripping their lords of income and leaving
them abject and miserable:

[Nowadays the caciques] are dying of hunger. In pagan times they were great
lords and the said Indians and macehuales served in their houses, building adobe
walls and performing other personal services, but now the caciques are as beaten
down as the macehuales, and all are equal. We implore your majesty to decree
and order that our lordship and patrimony be honored...and that upon our
verifying the above-said we be restored in our rights and sustained.[48]

Another example from the Puebla region illustrates the subtle ways that
postconquest concerns affected how native lords reframed local history.
Don Juan de Mendoza Tuzancotztli (d. 1556) was a Nahua cacique-
governor of Tecamachalco and a relative of the late Moctezuma. In 1553,
the aging don Juan complained that, due to the 1551 regulations restricting cacique tributes, local macehualtin were ignoring their obligations to
him as their natural lord. Bereft of income, he could no longer support
himself and his Spanish wife, doña Catalina de Escalona.[49] By way of an
interpreter and a procurador, his petition invoked the familiar themes of
pedigree, fealty, and Christian piety.

Don Juan argued that he "embod[ied] many merits" due to his "ancient
nobility," to say nothing of the great services he and his relatives had performed on behalf of the Spanish conquest, or his marriage to a Spanish

[47] "Letter of the Cabildo of Huejotzingo to the King, 1560," in Lockhart, *We People Here,*
     295.
[48] "Letter from the Nahua Nobles of Xochimilco," in Matthew Restall, Lisa Sousa, and
     Kevin Terraciano, eds. *Mesoamerican Voices: Native-language Writings from Colonial
     Mexico, Oaxaca, Yucatan, and Guatemala* (New York: Cambridge University Press,
     2005), 68.
[49] *Anales de Tecamachalco, 1398–1590,* trans. Eustaquio Celestino Solís, and Luis Reyes
     García (Mexico: CIESAS, 1992), 34–35.

woman.[50] With the aid of doña Catalina, the tlatoani assembled his case in Puebla over the next year and a half; she presented Spanish witnesses, while he provided native ones. Together, they produced a detailed account of his immemorial lineage and his services to the Spanish cause. Citing "memories and paintings," they traced his paternal ancestry to five generations, declaring him the sole heir to a ruling legacy over 800 years old.[51] During the conquest, Tecamachalco played a crucial role simply by omission: Lying along the road between Tenochtitlan and Veracruz, it could have – but did not – strangle the Spaniards' lifeline to the coast. "Any resistance by don Juan, however small," insisted his petition, "would have been a great impediment to the Spaniards' success, so don Juan's service was very great indeed." Meanwhile, as tlatoani of Tecamachalco, don Juan was a model of Christian virtue who always maintained good relations between Spaniards and Indians.[52] Don Juan's witnesses embellished his case, lauding his character while arguing that doña Catalina, being Spanish, required more income concordant with her elevated status.[53]

Don Juan's case, however, required more than the usual assertions of merit and services, as several nephews were also laying claim to the tlatocayotl and cacicazgo, compelling him to erase certain cultural incongruencies with clever locutions. In the Christian tradition, only "legitimate" children born within the confines of Christian matrimony could typically inherit noble titles. Yet what was "legitimacy" among the polygamous aristocracy of pre-Hispanic Mexico, where household as well as blood defined status? Typical among his cohort, don Juan advanced a self-legitimating solution: He reversed the logic of legitimacy to obviate its Christian element – one did not inherit because one was legitimate, one was legitimate because one inherited. This aligned the Christian concept with the Nahua distinction between the "treasured children" (*tlazopilli*) of high-ranking wives who inherited estates and tributes, and

[50] Petition of don Juan de Mendoza Tuçancoztli, Dec 5, 1553, Mexico City, AGI-J 1013, N.1, R.1, unnumbered.

[51] The document lists his father as Acoachitzin; his grandfather and grandmother as Quechultepantzin and Matlaxochitl; his great-grandparents as Omequiahuiztin and Cespanqui; and his great-great grandparents as Çeolintet and Malinaxochitl. Meanwhile, several witnesses mentioned that he was the grandson of Moctezuma on his mother's side, although she goes unnamed.

[52] Examination of don Juan de Mendoza Tuçancoztli, Feb 21, 1554, Puebla, AGI-J 1013, N.1, R.1, unnumbered.

[53] Prueba of don Juan de Mendoza Tuçancoztli, April-May 1555, Puebla, AGI-J 1013, N.1, R.1, unnumbered. See also Gerhard, *Guide to Historical Geography*: 280.

the noninheriting "household children" (*calpanpilli*) of secondary wives and concubines.[54] Deploying this logic, he disqualified rival half-brothers to Spanish officials. "Although there were other [women in the household] that were concubines (*mancebas*)," he testified, "the children of the latter were bastards, distinct from the [legitimate heirs]."[55] Don Juan's case highlights the legal creativity by which native lords might imagine or presume commensurability between Mesoamerican and Hispanic institutions.

Frontier violence and services to the king

The armed "pacifications" of western, northern, and southern Mesoamerica began in the mid 1520s and continued for decades. This process involved tens of thousands of indigenous allies drafted and coerced into fighting, drawn primarily from central Mexico.[56] For some native lords, expanding frontiers represented opportunities to elicit favors as victorious war captains. The genre emphasized "services": Individual heroism as well as suffering endured in the name of the king. Petitioners argued that their blood and sweat had enabled the Christians' triumph against the savage peoples of the American backcountry.

As the largest contingent in Cortés's anti-Mexica coalition, the independent confederation of Tlaxcala was the archetypal community of what the Spaniards called *indios amigos,* or "friendly Indians." Not only did they provide the bulk of Cortés's fighters against Tenochtitlan, they also contributed greatly to the secondary conquests that followed. Its leaders' initial investment in Spanish colonialism paid many long-term dividends in the form of privileges mostly unavailable to other groups, such as exemption from encomiendas and certain taxes. In 1535, Tlaxcala became the first native realm in America to achieve the status of city – "The Very Noble and Loyal City of Tlaxcala," complete with its own diocese – and in 1545 it received the first official Indian republic. A royal decree of 1545, prompted by the personal intervention of Cortés, confirmed Tlaxcala's extraordinary status: "At no time in the future of the world will the city of Tlaxcala be severed or released from our royal

---

54 Camilla Townsend, *Malintzin's Choices: An Indian Woman in the Conquest of Mexico* (Albuquerque, NM: University of New Mexico Press, 2006), 21.

55 Probanza of don Juan de Mendoza, Puebla, Feb 1554–May 1555, AGI-J 1013, N.1, R.1, n.p.

56 See Matthew and Oudijk, *Indian Conquistadors*; and Ida Altman, *The War for Mexico's West: Indians and Spaniards in New Galicia, 1524–1550* (Albuquerque: University of New Mexico Press, 2010).

crown . . . we will instead preserve it, forever incorporated into it."[57] Yet Tlaxcala's extraordinary privileges did not accrue without consistent and sustained advocacy; between 1526 and 1585, for example, Tlaxcala sent six separate delegations to Spain.[58] At the core of Tlaxcalteca distinction was a historical narrative casting the altepetl as the premier Indo-Christian republic within the composite monarchy of Spain: the most pious, the most loyal, and the most beloved of the king. This sentiment would, as we will see in subsequent chapters, occupy a central place in greater Novohispanic lore. Whether as the pioneers of Nahua Catholicism or as native guardians of colonial institutions, the Tlaxcalteca were co-founders of New Spain; indeed, this was their identity, a source of both pride and privilege.

One of the earliest and most iconic expressions of Tlaxcalteca exceptionalism is the *Lienzo de Tlaxcala*, a famous cloth painting commissioned by the cabildo in the 1550s that pictorially narrated Tlaxcala's role in the fall of Tenochtitlan and the pacification of New Spain and Central America.[59] While one copy hung prominently in the cabildo chamber, another was sent to the viceroy, and a third to the king himself. Like other native records of the era, the document was intended to solidify the Tlaxcalteca claim to royal privileges and exemptions. As an account of history, the *Lienzo* portrayed the Castile-Tlaxcala partnership as natural, complete, and steadfast. It also strategically forgot a number of real conflicts and challenges arising from the alliance. Spanish accounts tell that the Tlaxcalteca fiercely resisted their presence for several weeks, and that some anti-Spanish dissidents – including Xicotencatl the Younger, son of one of the four tlatoque of the Tlaxcalteca confederation – continued to operate for over a year. The *Lienzo*, by contrast, mentioned none of this, featuring instead a sublimely peaceful representation of the four tlatoque receiving the Eucharist for the first time.

---

[57] Carlos Sempat Assadourian and Andrea Martínez Baracs, eds. *Tlaxcala: textos de su historia, siglo XVI* (Tlaxcala: Gobierno del Estado de Tlaxcala, 1991), 256. Gibson notes evidence, however, that Cortés may have exploited Tlaxcala's privileges, enriching himself by skimming their tributes – acting in practice as an unofficial encomendero. See Gibson, *Tlaxcala in the Sixteenth Century*: 62–64.

[58] Gibson, *Tlaxcala in the Sixteenth Century*: 158–94. See also Borah, *Justice by Insurance*: 302–04.

[59] A modern facsimile of the *Lienzo* is in Diego Muñoz Camargo, *Descripción de la ciudad y provincia de Tlaxcala de las Indias y del Mar Océano para el buen gobierno y ennoblecimiento dellas*, ed. René Acuña (México: Instituto de Investigaciones Filológicas, Universidad Nacional Autónoma de México, 1981).

The Tlaxcalteca effort to brand their city exceptional met with some success. While the bulk of its services to the crown occurred prior to 1531 in the conquests of Anahuac, Nueva Galicia, Yucatán, and Guatemala, most of the city's extraordinary privileges – the seeds of the legend of Tlaxcalteca exceptionalism – were granted between 1535 and 1589, securing Tlaxcala's reputation for steadfast loyalty.[60] In 1552, Viceroy Velasco I lavished gratitude on the city for its "goodness, Christianity, and loyalty."[61] On a single day, August 16, 1563, a group of at least eight Tlaxcalteca noblemen in Madrid – the children of the original allies of Castile – received coats of arms. The son of don Francisco Aquiyahualcatltechutel was honored for his father's heroism in both Tenochtitlan and Nueva Galicia.[62] Don Antonio de la Cadena's father had performed "great feats" in Central America "at significant personal cost."[63] Don Gerónimo de Águila's heraldry likewise recognized the "great risks," his father had undertaken for the king, in which he "hazard[ed] his person and life, and with much cost to [his] estate."[64] Don Juan de la Cerda (Xicotencatl) told a rather dubious tale: His father had greeted Cortés upon his first landing on the coast, and had sworn allegiance to Carlos V on the spot.[65] The concession to don Juan Manrique de Lara Maxixcatzi spun a succinct version of the Tlaxcalteca legend; his father, seeking baptism, had "subjected himself peacefully to our service out of

---

[60] A list of Tlaxcala's sixteenth-century favors and exemptions is in Gibson, *Tlaxcala in the Sixteenth Century*: 229–34. See also R. Jovita Baber, "Empire, Indians, and the Negotiation for the Status of City in Tlaxcala," in *Negotiation within Domination: New Spain's Indian Pueblos Confront the Spanish State*, eds. Ethelia Ruiz-Medrano and Susan Kellogg (Boulder: University Press of Colorado, 2010).

[61] Nicolás Faustino Mazihcahtzin y Calmecahua, "Descripción del Lienzo de Tlaxcala," *Revista Mexicana de Estudios Históricos* 1, no. 2 (1927): 65.

[62] Concession of Arms of don Pablo de Castilla of Tlaxcala, Madrid, Aug 16, 1563, in Villar Villamil, *Cedulario heráldico*: no. 132. In regularized Nahuatl, the name would be *Aquiahualcatecutli*.

[63] Concession of Arms of Antonio de la Cadena of Tlaxcala, Madrid, Aug 16, 1563, in ibid., no. 131. His father's name is given as "Tlacuzcalcate"; this is presumably a corruption of the Nahuatl military title *tlacochcalcatl*, or "Person at the Armory." See Lockhart, *The Nahuas* 42, 487, n. 109.

[64] Concession of Arms of Gerónima del Águila of Tlaxcala, Madrid, Aug 16, 1563, in Villar Villamil, *Cedulario heráldico*: no. 139.

[65] Concession of Arms of don Juan de la Cerda of Tlaxcala, Madrid, Aug 16, 1563, in ibid., no. 133. The name Xicotencatl does not appear on the concession, but later Tlaxcalteca historians applied this name to don Juan. See Manuel de los Santos y Salazar (unattributed), "Computo cronológico de los indios mexicanos," in *Documentos para la historia de México, 3a serie*, vol. 1 (Mexico: Vicente García Torres, 1856), 243.

sincere love," and had proven indispensable to the Castilian cause ever since.[66]

As the frontier continued to expand, so did the list of services provided by the ever-loyal Tlaxcalteca. Most famously, in 1591 Viceroy Luis de Velasco II contracted with Tlaxcala to send 400 families to settle, plant, and secure new areas in today's states of Coahuila, Durango, and Chihuahua. The settlers received considerable privileges in return, such as a thirty-year exemption from certain taxes; meanwhile, their leaders – and their descendants – retained the permanent rights to bear arms, ride horses, and dress as Spaniards. While Tlaxcala was not the only central Mexican community to contribute to the project, it provided by far the most settlers, such that in later years "Tlaxcalan" became synonymous in the north with indigenous frontiersmen and women, regardless of ancestry.[67] Tlaxcalteca political and legal advocates both in central Mexico as well as in the north cited this episode for the rest of the colonial era.[68] Indeed, this was their identity. Sean F. McEnroe argues that, by exporting the unique Tlaxcalteca brand of indigenous vassalage to the north and northeast, "Greater Tlaxcala" played a key role in the spread and consolidation of a unified Mexican political culture into vast and diverse new areas. Far more than other native corporate identities, Tlaxcala's was premised on memories of alliance and reciprocity with the crown. Therefore, according to McEnroe, the "Tlaxcalan model" provided the Chichimeca peoples of the north with a more direct and potentially less contentious path to Spanish vassalage (and later Mexican citizenship) by facilitating the cooptation, rather than eradication, of already established social and political categories.[69]

While no other community as a whole matched Tlaxcala, many individual lords from other altepeme likewise represented themselves as indios amigos, following a similar rhetorical script. One such indio amigo was the Nahua lord don Diego Ximenes Cortés Chimalpopoca of Almoloya (México), a heir to the Mexica lineage that had previously subjugated

[66] Concession of Arms of don Juan Manrique de Lara Maxizcatzin, Madrid, Aug 16, 1563, in Villar Villamil, *Cedulario heráldico*: no. 136.

[67] See Philip Wayne Powell, "North America's First Frontier, 1546–1603," in *Essays on Frontiers in World History*, eds. George Wolfskill and Stanley Palmer (College Station, TX: Texas A&M University Press, 1983).

[68] See Testimony of the Caciques of Nuestra Señora de la Concepción Almoloya, Mexico, 1752, AGN-VM 234, Exp. 3, ff. 30–31.

[69] Sean F. McEnroe, *From Colony to Nationhood in Mexico: Laying the Foundations, 1560–1840* (New York: Cambridge University Press, 2012).

the area.[70] Following Mexica precedent, for his violent subjugation of Michoacan (1529–30) the conquistador-oidor Nuño de Guzmán relied heavily on the peoples living west of Anahuac, including Almoloya. Don Diego's account models the genre. Soon after returning from war, he successfully petitioned for a title of nobility, which he received in 1534. The title details don Diego's great heroism against the "barbarous" peoples "scattered in the mountains [of Nueva Galicia] and severed from the religion of our Holy Catholic Faith." Stoically and willingly suffering deprivation and hunger, don Diego "put [his] life in great risk and danger" to ensure the success of the mission. One feat in particular stood out; one day in Michoacan

a large number of [Chichimecas] fell upon the Spaniards, surrounding them violently, taking them at will without parley (*sin concierto*), until [don Diego], with the aid of Our Lord, made raw war against them, wherein a number of them immediately fell dead upon the ground. And seeing this, the rest retreated, and the war ceased, and the Spaniards recovered.[71]

Ten years after Guzmán's rampage, Viceroy Mendoza embarked on yet another campaign to pacify Nueva Galicia, remembered today as the pyrrhic Mixton War (1540–41).[72] As before, it provided numerous central Mexican lords with opportunities to prove their fealty and demand reciprocity. A most elaborate account of heroic services comes from don Francisco de Sandoval Acazitli, a cacique of Tlalmanalco in the realm of Chalco, who in a Nahuatl memoir recorded his and his brothers' exploits on behalf of the viceroy. Like a medieval chronicle, it lingers on the intricate rituals of battle – donning armor, brandishing weapons, hand-to-hand combat – as well as on the hardships endured by the protagonist.

---

[70] Almoloya was a tributary of nearby Sultepec, which had been conquered in the early sixteenth century by Moctezuma II. Although its linguistic majority was Mazahua, its rulers were Nahuas. Gerhard, *Guide to Historical Geography*: 267–68.

[71] Concession of Arms to don Diego Ximenes Cortés Chimalpopoca of Almoloya, Zaragoza, Jan 6 1534, AGN-VM 241, Exp. 1, f. 23.

[72] Francisco de Sandoval Acazitli, "Relación de la jornada que hizo don Francisco de Sandoval Acazitli, cacique y señor natural que fue del pueblo de Tlalmanalco," in García Icazbalceta, *Colección de documentos para la historia de México*, 307–32. The chronicle was written by the literate Chalca nobleman Gabriel de Castañeda, an attendant of don Francisco who kept a daily journal of the expedition (although the narrative leaps sporadically between first- and third-person perspectives). The original Nahuatl version is unknown; only a 1641 Spanish translation remains. See Ida Altman, "Conquest, Coercion, and Collaboration: Indian Allies and the Campaigns in Nueva Galicia," in *Indian Conquistadors: Indigenous Allies in the Conquest of Mesoamerica*, eds. Laura E. Matthew, and Michel R. Oudijk (Norman, OK: University of Oklahoma Press, 2007).

In one episode, the hero and his warriors, poorly supplied in hostile territory, are forced to sleep fully armed, wear dirty clothes, and subsist solely on toasted maize for three days.[73] In another, the Chalca are ambushed by "barbarian" Chichimecas. Although unarmed and unready, don Francisco regroups, bravely dons his *ichcahuipilli* (a hard cotton vest), and responds with such ferocity that he captured two and slew no fewer than seven enemies in a matter of minutes. "So strongly did he attack the Chichimecos that they did not dare return."[74]

The account contextualizes don Francisco's endeavors in terms of his reciprocal devotion to Viceroy Mendoza, who addresses the cacique almost as an equal. It proudly recalls that don Francisco was, along with don Juan de Guzmán Iztlolinqui of Coyoacan and the future governor of Tlatelolco, don Diego de Mendoza Imauhyantzin (r. 1549-62), one of only three natural lords honored to ride beside the viceroy.[75] In one scene, the Chalca warriors find Mendoza besieged by enemies, and rush in to turn the tide. Afterwards, Mendoza summons don Francisco and thanks him personally, declaring "very good people are those from Chalco."[76] Following the war, upon the company's triumphant return to Mexico City, the viceroy honors don Francisco by promising to favor him in all matters henceforth.[77]

Yet perhaps none in colonial Mexico relied more upon a record of frontier services than the Otomí caciques of Querétaro and the surrounding towns. While the Tlaxcalteca and others could boast of preconquest lineages, the Otomí leaders of the Bajío (parts of Querétaro, Michoacan, and Guanajuato) built an entire noble identity out of their role in the pacification of the region. Following the 1546 discovery of silver in Zacatecas, large numbers of Spaniards, natives, and Africans flowed northward to exploit the riches. The huge swaths of land that lay between Mexico and the mines, however, remained semihostile, inspiring diverse efforts under Viceroys Velasco I and Martín Enríquez (r. 1568-80) to repel Chichimeca raids and secure the road. One of their solutions was the defensive colonization of frontier zones and the foundation of new towns along the main travel routes.[78] The latter policy usually followed

---

73 Ibid., 316–17.
74 Acazitli, "Relación," 313.
75 Ibid., 311.
76 Ibid., 309.
77 Ibid., 331.
78 This echoed the frontier policies that Castilians had relied upon during their long confrontation with Muslim kingdoms in medieval Iberia. See Luis García de Valdeavellano y Arcimis, *Orígenes de la burguesía en la España medieval* (Madrid: Espasa-Calpe, 1969).

the former, as many of the first settlers were often the same allies who had previously fought on behalf of the viceroy.[79] As part of these efforts, they contracted Otomí groups from Xilotepec and Tula (Hidalgo) to enter the area as frontier captains and intermediaries on behalf of the colonial regime.[80] The most famous of these Otomí conquistadors was Connin (baptized don Fernando de Tapia), who, with a mix of his own kin and local Pames, settled the town of Querétaro and became its first cacique and governor as early as the 1530s.

Due to the fertile climate, the absence of major established settlements, and the silver strikes in Zacatecas, Querétaro was one of the few places in New Spain with a growing population during the mid sixteenth century, and as a local landowner and warlord don Fernando was well-placed to benefit. Conquest was as much an economic as a political enterprise, and don Fernando – whom John Tutino calls "an entrepreneurial frontiersman" – profited from the frontier because of, not despite, its relative lawlessness and instability.[81] Like his Spanish counterparts, he built his empire through a combination of ruthlessness and political savvy, leveraging conquests for viceregal reward, and viceregal rewards for further conquests.[82] Don Fernando won a land grant (*merced*) as early as 1547 from Viceroy Mendoza, and received several more during the 1550s and 1560s from Viceroy Velasco, including at least six sites for sheep and one for cattle.[83] In the end, he dominated Querétaro and the surrounding area for two decades, and his children continued to amass assets following his death circa 1571.

Although he could not boast of a noble ancestry, as an Indian conquistador and governor don Fernando nonetheless adopted the identity

---

[79] Philip Wayne Powell, "Presidios and Towns on the Silver Frontier of New Spain, 1550–1580," *Hispanic American Historical Review* 24, no. 2 (1944): 180–81.

[80] Captaincy of don Nicolás de San Luis, Tenochtitlan, May 1, 1557, in Fernández de Recas, *Cacicazgos*, 314–15, quote from 15. The frontier captains he named were: don Nicolás de San Luis, don Antonio de Luna, don Juan de la Cueva, Pedro de Granada, don Diego de Tapia, Lucás de León, Pedro Martín, Gabriel de San Miguel, Pedro López y Martín y Olua, Juan Sánchez, and Pedro de Aguilar. See also David Wright, ed. *Conquistadores otomíes en la guerra chichimeca* (Querétaro: Gobierno del Estado de Querétaro, 1988), 21; José Antonio Cruz Rangel, *Chichimecas, Misioneros, Soldados, y Terratenientes: Estrátegias de colonización, control, y poder en Querétaro y la Sierra Gorda, siglos XVI–XVIII* (Mexico: Archivo General de la Nación, 2003), 98–100.

[81] John Tutino, *Making a New World: Founding Capitalism in the Bajío and Spanish North America* (Durham: Duke University Press, 2011), 72–73. See also Cruz Rangel, *Chichimecas*: 75.

[82] See David Wright, ed. *Querétaro en el siglo XVI: Fuentes documentales primarias* (Querétaro: Gobierno del Estado de Querétaro, 1989), 370–76.

[83] Inventory of the Estate of don Diego de Tapia, Querétaro, 1614, AGI-ECJ 199A, ff. 243–251.

of a cacique and natural lord. He invoked the indio amigo trope with images of loyalty proven through adversity endured. In his 1561 statement of merits, he recalled that in settling the frontier he had gone "many years dressed only in animal skins and suffering many hardships, hungry and lacking many necessities." He also represented himself as the king's diligent captain, governing the region "with fairness and justice" while protecting the poor and the weak, and he had always secured the king's rightful tribute in full and on time. He was also committed to extending the king's domains, pacifying hostile peoples and founding new towns "with industry, good doctrine, and diligence."[84] He was, finally, a sincere Christian who had worked to pacify those living "in [barbarous] disservice to Our Lord God," and who supported the Franciscans in Querétaro and elsewhere.[85]

Due to its unique origins, sixteenth-century Querétaro was an Indian pueblo, but it was also a new colonial town without a preexisting political structure. Thus, unlike the lords of Anahuac, the Otomís of the Bajío always remembered the conquest as a time of foundations, the formation of a new society with new noble bloodlines. In this sense, the Otomí conquistadors resembled the creole descendants of Spanish conquistadors more than the nobility of Anahuac. We will encounter the reverberations of this unique legacy in subsequent chapters.

Caciques and friars in the sixteenth century

Spanish investigations into Mesoamerican history began almost immediately after the fall of Tenochtitlan. In 1524, the first Franciscan friars arrived into central Mexico, and began to learn about the peoples and cultures they sought to transform, considering this integral to their evangelical mission. Fray Bernardino de Sahagún, the primary compiler of the *Florentine Codex* (1550s–1560s) – by far the most comprehensive early account of Nahua culture and history – memorably likened himself to a doctor seeking to understand an illness so as to develop a cure.[86] Yet while the most widely circulated contemporary accounts of America and its peoples were learned interpretations of the reports of conquerors and explorers, the Franciscans interrogated local peoples and their leaders directly. Until the late 1570s, when a new generation of crown

---

[84] Examination of don Fernando de Tapia, Querétaro, Aug 11, 1561, in *Boletín del Archivo General de la Nación* V, no. 1 (1939): 38–40.

[85] Ibid., 37–38.

[86] Miguel León-Portilla, *Bernardino de Sahagún: First Anthropologist*, trans. Mauricio J. Mixco (Norman, OK: University of Oklahoma Press, 2002), 4–5.

administrators officially discouraged such investigations, the friars and a notable handful of other Spaniards engaged in the first systematic inquiries into pre-Columbian history derived from indigenous memories rather than the reports of outsiders.[87]

The role of indigenous partners in the production of Spanish-authored texts on Mesoamerica, however, is less well-known. The Franciscans relied heavily on painted manuscripts, on interviews with elderly Indians – and, crucially, on those whom they had educated, the ladino caciques of the second postconquest generation, men such as don Hernando Pimentel Nezahualcoyotl and don Antonio Cortés Totoquihuaztli. They assisted in the translation and interpretation of pictorial texts, and introduced the friars to the oral traditions and songs that were central to Mesoamerican historical knowledge. Indeed, native antiquarians and collaborators were present at every stage within the friars' investigations. For example, the earliest Franciscan works, such as the *Historia de los mexicanos por sus pinturas (History of the Mexicans According to their Paintings)*, compiled before 1536 by fray Andrés de Olmos – a consistent advocate for the pipiltin – explicitly acknowledged the contributions of native leaders. The history, it begins, derived from "the characters and writings that they used, and by the accounts of the elders and those who in pagan times were the priests and [religious authorities], and according to the lords and principales who were taught the law."[88] Not surprisingly, then, it reproduces the memories and dynastic concerns of that faction of the Mexica ruling class that traced itself to the Tolteca ancestors of Culhuacan. Tellingly, the account's chronology does not follow the Julian calendar; reflecting Mexica royal tradition, it counts the years since the foundation of Tenochtitlan, which was subsequently calculated to be 1325; the year of Cuauhtemoc's death (1525), for example, is given as 200.[89]

Indeed, historians today reference the "Nahua intellectuals" and "collaborators" of Sahagún as much as his "students" and "assistants."[90]

[87] Reformers influenced by the Council of Trent were hostile to the written preservation of non-Christian practices and history, fearing that it might obstruct evangelization by memorializing pagan "superstitions" and customs. See Rolena Adorno, "The 'indio ladino' as historian," in *Implicit Understandings: Observing, Reporting, and Reflecting on the Encounters Between Europeans and Other Peoples in the Early Modern Era*, ed. Stuart B. Schwartz (Cambridge: Cambridge University Press, 1994), 395.

[88] "Historia de los mexicanos por sus pinturas," in García Icazbalceta, *Nueva colección de documentos para la historia de México: Pomar-Zurita, relaciones antiguas (Siglo XVI)*, 209.

[89] Ibid., 232–33.

[90] See Silvermoon, "Imperial College of Tlatelolco."; Tavárez, "Nahua Intellectuals, Franciscan Scholars, and the *Devotio moderna* in Colonial Mexico."

Their names are often difficult to come by, but some can be pieced together from other sources. Most prominently, fray Juan Bautista Viseo in 1606 expressed his gratitude to a number of Nahua colleagues – teachers, scholars, and authors – without whom the Franciscans' projects could not have succeeded. Hernando de Rivas of Tetzcoco (d. 1597) was a superb Latinist and translator who had worked with fray Alonso de Molina in the production of the first Nahuatl dictionary and grammar. Don Francisco Contreras de Baptista of Cuernavaca was another accomplished Latinist who later served as governor of Xochimilco. Don Juan Berardo of Huejotzingo taught Latin, while Diego Adriano of Tlatelolco – whom Bautista cites as a good friend – assisted with the editing and copying of Sahagún's materials. Don Antonio Valeriano, meanwhile, Bautista described as a latter-day Cicero or Quintilian, such was his mastery of Latin eloquence and rhetoric.[91]

This is not to say that the Franciscan *interpretation* of Mesoamerican history originated with the caciques – it did not. Rather, the Franciscan texts echo the caciques' obsession with noble genealogy and their emphasis on certain iconic historical episodes, and incorporate such details into the Franciscans' own strains of eschatology and theology. The result was a unique marriage of mendicant millennialism and Mesoamerican memory, in which the Aztec epic was revealed as America's Old Testament, rich with portents and omens heralding an inevitable Christian future. If the early natural lords alluded to an ideal of political continuity between Anahuac and New Spain, the Franciscans and the ladino caciques envisioned a spiritual continuity: Like St. Augustine's conception of ancient Rome, the Mexica Empire was a means by which God had prepared for the spread of the gospel in America.

Fray Toribio de Benavente (1482–1568) – called *Motolinia*, or "suffering one," by Nahuas affected by his extreme display of Franciscan asceticism – was one of the twelve friars to arrive in 1524, and was the most prolific chronicler of his cohort. Motolinia's accounts synthesized, elaborated upon, and disseminated those of his coreligionists, while also incorporating original material based on his own contacts among the Indian elite. He was a great friend to the native nobility of central Mexico – particularly in those altepeme – Tetzcoco, Tlaxcala, and Tlatelolco – where he was involved in establishing Franciscan communities. He was particularly close to don Hernando Pimentel Nezahualcoyotl

---

[91] Introduction to Juan Baptista Viseo, *Sermonario en lengua mexicana* (Mexico: Diego López Dávalos, 1606). n.p.

of Tetzcoco, to whom he was a mentor and advocate before the Spanish establishment. It was Motolinia, for example, whereby the Pimentels chose their Hispanic surname and coat of arms; Motolinia's patron in Spain was don Antonio Pimentel, the sixth count of Benavente (León), his hometown.[92] Motolinia also assisted personally in the restorationist agenda of don Antonio Cortés Totoquihuaztli of Tlacopan during the 1550s. Accordingly, Motolinia's *Memorial tetzcocano* is a political history of Tetzcoco clearly related to don Hernando Pimentel's own, a defense of the heirs of Nezahualcoyotl. It is also a companion to don Antonio Cortés's account of Tlacopaneca history.[93]

Motolinia's links to the high nobility of Anahuac are also apparent within the content of his histories. He acknowledges many by name, citing them as friends, as exemplars of Indian Christianity, and as authorities on local history and culture.[94] Most importantly, Motolinia always attributed the rapid spread of Christianity to the converted lords with whom he was acquainted, as their exemplary piety inspired the commoners, who had, until recently, "been very asleep," living in ignorance.[95] Unsurprisingly, then, he was an outspoken and consistent advocate for the education of cacique children, and his work is peppered with anecdotes detailing their religious zeal and intellectual achievements.[96] Most famously, he reported that in Tlaxcala in 1527, three years before his arrival into that town, three young boys – the noble children Cristóbal Acxotecatl and Antonio Xicotencatl, and their serving-boy Juan – were martyred by their own parents after helping the friars uncover and destroy their religious images. According to Motolinia, the proud family of "Cristobalito" was the source of his information.[97] As we will see in subsequent chapters, Motolinia's story of the three boy-martyrs became a staple of Tlaxcalteca and creole patriotism for centuries, cited repeatedly as proof of Tlaxcala's exceptional virtue as well as the

---

[92] Motolinía's 1541 *History of the Indians of New Spain* was dedicated to the Count of Benavente. Motolinia, *History of the Indians of New Spain*: 73–84; Benton, "The Lords of Tetzcoco" 95.

[93] See Carrasco, *Tenochca Empire*: 50–53.

[94] For example, Motolinia proudly relates the conversion stories of the lords of Cuitlahuac, Cuernavaca, Huaquechula (Puebla), and Michoacan. Motolinia, *History of the Indians of New Spain*: 175–76, 94–95, 208–09.

[95] Toribio de Benavente Motolinia, *Memoriales* (Madrid: Ediciones Atlas, 1970), 58.

[96] Motolinia, *History of the Indians of New Spain*: 295–98.

[97] See Toribio de Benavente Motolinía, "Historia de los indios de la Nueva España," in Joaquín García Icazbalceta, *Colección de documentos para la historia de México, tomo primero* (Mexico: Librería de J. M. Andrade, 1858), 214–24.

potential of native Christians more generally.[98] Ultimately, Motolinia's fervent belief in the ardor of native Christianity fueled a proto-patriotic sentiment most closely associated with later generations of creoles: Overt resentment toward Spaniards who disdained native culture and history. "Let no one think that I have gone too far in sounding the praises of Mexico," he wrote: "The truth is, I have touched very briefly on only a small part of the many things that could be said of it."[99]

The 1550s and 1560s, when the ladino caciques were also tlatoque in their ancestral communities, marked the most active phase of Nahua–Franciscan collaboration, headquartered at Tlatelolco under the guidance of Sahagún and his colleagues. Historians continue to delve into the *Florentine Codex* and other materials – Nahuatl, Spanish, and Latin, mixed-pictorial and purely alphabetic – that derived from the Tlatelolco investigations. While Sahagún's presence is clear and pervasive, an emerging consensus suggests that the cacique scholars had a broad influence over both the content of the histories as well as the political and ethnic perspectives represented therein. They were integral, for example, to the process by which the Franciscans encountered Christian portents in Mesoamerican history; as Pablo Escalante Gonzalbo has demonstrated, the Nahua painters wove Christian artistic motifs into their accounts of mythical and historic events from Anahuac, thereby representing them as Mexican iterations of universal Christian history – a theme that lay at the heart of the Franciscan vision.[100]

Beyond the Franciscans, the other major religiously inspired investigation into Mesoamerican history was that of fray Diego Durán (d. 1588), a Dominican who arrived in Mexico as a young child and identified it as his patria. Unlike the Franciscans' Christian providentialism, Durán's *History of the Indies of New Spain* (1565–81) understands preconquest history on its own terms – an intellectual enterprise that Georges Baudot characterized as "a kind of national revindication."[101] It is essentially a Spanish translation of materials previously compiled by the caciques at

---

[98] See Torquemada, *Monarquía indiana*, v. 5, 132–57; and Robert Haskett, "Dying for Conversion: Faith, Obedience, and the Tlaxcalan Boy Martyrs in New Spain," *Colonial Latin American Review* 17, no. 2 (2008): 186–87.

[99] Motolinia, *History of the Indians of New Spain*: 266.

[100] See Pablo Escalante Gonzalbo, "The Painters of Sahagún's Manuscripts: Mediators between Two Worlds," in *Sahagún at 500: Essays on the Quincentenary of the Birth of Fr. Bernardino de Sahagún*, ed. John F. Schwaller (Berkeley, CA: Academy of American Franciscan History, 2003).

[101] Baudot, *Utopia and History in Mexico*, 72, n. 1.

Tlatelolco. María Castañeda de la Paz has inferred the existence in the library at Santa Cruz of a collection of alphabetic and pictorial materials associated with and based upon the *Tira de la peregrinación* (also called *Codex Boturini*), a pictographic account of the legendary pilgrimage from Aztlan dating to the early 1530s. This collection served as a major basis not only for Durán's history but also those of his contemporaries: his cousin, the Jesuit Juan de Tovar (addressed in Chapter 5), and the Tenochca chronicler don Hernando Alvarado Tezozomoc (examined in Chapter 4).[102] Collectively, these three texts would, along with the Franciscan materials, serve as a primary vector by which the Mexica origins story as we know it today – the exodus from Aztlan, the arrival in Anahuac and subordination to Azcapotzalco, and the providential foundation of Tenochtitlan on the island of Mexico – would become known to later generations of creoles. The creole advocate Baltasar Dorantes de Carranza, for example – one of the first to explicitly speak as a creole on behalf of creoles – derived much of his 1604 account from Durán's history.[103] This marked an important moment in the emergence of creole consciousness, as rather than rely entirely on conquistador accounts, Dorantes de Carranza looked to the native-derived texts as well.

Like Sahagún and the Franciscans, Durán relied not only on the caciques' materials, but also upon their active contributions as translators, interpreters, and painters. While Durán was not fastidious in crediting his sources, he explicitly acknowledged his reliance on local elders and their painted texts.[104] He also lamented the high morbidity of his era, as many of those who could have informed his chronicle had already died. The result, unsurprisingly, was a proto-patriotic account of central Mexican history that aligned, both in content and tone, with those of contemporary caciques: Anahuac was a noble civilization, and its disappearance should be lamented rather than celebrated. Durán wrote that his "special purpose" was to preserve knowledge of "the Aztec nation" which, despite its egregious religious errors, was a place of unsurpassed "government and good order, submission and reverence, majesty and authority, courage, and fortitude." Once informed of the "ancient glories" and "ancient splendor" of Anahuac, Durán hoped, newcomers

---

[102] María Castañeda de la Paz, "El Códice X o los anales del "Grupo de la Tira de la Peregrinación." Copias, duplicaciones, y su uso por parte de los cronistas," *Tlalocan* XV (2008).

[103] Dorantes de Carranza, *Sumaria relación*: xxix.

[104] Diego Durán, *History of the Indies of New Spain*, trans. Doris Heyden (Norman, OK: University of Oklahoma Press, 1994), 3.

to Mexico – meaning peninsular Spaniards – would "lose the bad and false opinion that these Aztec people were barbarian and uncivilized."[105]

Cacique declinism in Spanish secular texts

For different reasons, secular Spaniards also contributed to sixteenth-century investigations into local history and culture. As we have seen, some of the earliest nonreligious inquiries into Anahuac were commissioned by Juan Cano de Saavedra as part of his efforts to consolidate his wife's claims to the Moctezuma patrimony. Yet among the most comprehensive secular accounts of preconquest Mexico in the sixteenth century were those of Alonso de Zorita (1512–85), an oidor in Mexico City between 1556 and 1565. Upon his return to Spain, he answered the king's call for information on pre-Hispanic tributary practices with an extensive account titled *Breve y sumaria relación de los señores... que había en la Nueva España* (*Brief and Summary Relation of the Lords... of New Spain*) – a quickly forgotten text that nonetheless reemerged as a foundation of the creole archive of the late-seventeenth and eighteenth centuries.

Outside of the Franciscans, the caciques of New Spain had no greater friend than Zorita, and as its title suggests, his account closely replicates the perspectives of his cacique contemporaries. Hearkening to an earlier era of order and prosperity, it laments the decline of the native nobility, and indeed blames the social and economic ills of colonial Mexico on the dispossession of its natural lords. Zorita believed that Mexico's peoples were best served by their own leaders executing their own laws and customs. Great lawgivers such as Nezahualcoyotl of Tetzcoco and Maxixcatzin of Tlaxcala had promoted virtue and prevented vice with legal codes carefully attuned to the particular follies and weaknesses of their vassals. Spanish rule had dismantled this ingenious system, and the price was paid in blood, lawlessness, and misery.[106]

Under the old system of government, wrote Zorita, "the whole land was at peace. Spaniards and Indians alike were content, and more tribute was paid, and with less hardship, because government was in the hands of the natural lords." Yet as commoner-dominated cabildos increasingly

[105] Ibid., 20–21.

[106] Alonso de Zorita, *Life and Labor in Ancient Mexico: The Brief and Summary Relation of the Lords of New Spain by Alonso de Zorita*, trans. Benjamin Keen, 2nd edn. (Norman: University of Oklahoma Press, 1994), 127–33.

siphoned power away from the caciques, native pueblos had descended into chaos and decadence. "No harmony remains among the Indians of New Spain," he lamented, "because the commoners have lost all feeling of shame as concerns their lords and principales, [and] they have risen up . . . and lost the respect they once had for them."[107] Like the caciques, Zorita's solution involved the restoration of the lords' inherited authority, and a renewed emphasis on cacique autonomy within the Spanish crown. "The benefits that the subjects derived from the rule of their lords were very great," he explained, and "they would be as great today if the same order existed. The lords looked after everything and saw that the Indians lived a proper life."[108]

Zorita was widely read, and derived much information from the Franciscans as well as the conquest-era chroniclers. Yet he also explicitly relied upon the ladino caciques with whom he was acquainted. As oidor, he was familiar with the leaders of the old Triple Alliance, including the cabildos of Tenochtitlan and Tlatelolco, don Hernando Pimentel of Tetzcoco, and don Antonio Cortés of Tlacopan. He was especially close to don Pablo Nazareo of Xaltocan, the Latinist and interpreter whom he had known from their shared time with the audiencia in the early 1560s. Before his death in 1585, Zorita authored a sprawling *Relación de la Nueva España* (*History of New Spain*), which incorporated genealogical information from two now-unknown texts that don Pablo authored and gifted to Zorita.[109] His source, Zorita insisted, was a "very virtuous and very good Christian, well-versed in doctrine and a good Latinist, rhetorician, logician, and philosopher, and not a bad poet" as well. Perfectly replicating don Pablo's own self-representation, Zorita lamented how don Pablo and his father-in-law, don Juan Axayacatl, were languishing in poverty, despite their pedigree and their services to the viceroyalty.[110]

Although they were far less connected to the nucleus of Spanish power in Mexico City, the native leadership from less-prominent pueblos also had opportunities to communicate their historical visions to Spaniards and creoles. One important episode of creole-cacique collaboration occurred in 1579–85, the period of the *relaciones geográficas* ("geographical relations"): A crown-driven questionnaire of fifty items bearing on local history, culture, and society, sent to every corner of the

---

[107] Ibid., 116–17.
[108] Ibid., 123.
[109] The texts were titled, simply, *Relación* and *Memoriales*. See Zorita, *Relación*: v. 1, 317–20.
[110] Ibid., v. 1, 103–04.

Spanish world as a means of imperial self-discovery and consolidation.[111] While most relaciones were compiled by creole and Spanish functionaries, many of its authors consulted native informants, generally caciques and officials in the local Indian republics, some named and some anonymous. The indigenous influence on the final product is often quite clear, particularly in their graphic and cartographic elements.[112] While the questionnaire did not require it, many authors provided narrative or quasi-narrative responses. The accounts that resulted often evince the caciques' characteristic blend of identification with Anahuac and overt Hispano-Catholic commitments. There is also evidence that provincial officials, mostly creoles, were quite familiar with the pre-Hispanic histories of their assigned regions, and sometimes considered them their own. Reflecting the influence of the local caciques with whom they were acquainted, creole administrators were likely to locate the origins of their towns deep in the preconquest past.

There were three items in the questionnaire specifically pertaining to native history.[113] While conceived for primarily imperialistic reasons, they represented opportunities for native informants to contribute their own versions of local history to the written record, and to express dissatisfaction with contemporary society and culture. Accordingly, many responses express the sense of historical decline most commonly associated with the caciques, for example, by drawing an implicit contrast between the order and stability of the pre-Hispanic era, and the disorder, corruption, and vice that followed it. Like the midcentury caciques and sympathizers such as Zorita, several relaciones overtly mourn a time when Mexico's natural lords enjoyed the respect and deference they deserved.

Such sentiments permeate the relación of Coatepec (Mexico), written in 1579. Citing the "ancient paintings" of elderly informants among the local nobility, its Nahuatl-speaking Spanish author chronicled a proudly independent people who traced their origins to 1174.[114] Coatepec's lords were enormously valiant and successful both politically and militarily, especially in their frequent wars with Chalco. Such was their prominence that passers-by always "lowered their heads with much humility, doing

---

[111] Howard F. Cline, "The Relaciones Geográficas of the Spanish Indies, 1577–1586," *Hispanic American Historical Review* 44, no. 3 (1964).

[112] Barbara Mundy, *The Mapping of New Spain: Indigenous Cartography and the Maps of the Relaciones geográficas* (Chicago: University of Chicago Press, 1996).

[113] Howard Cline translated and published the entire questionnaire. Cline, "The Relaciones Geográficas of the Spanish Indies, 1577–1586," 364–71.

[114] "Relación de Coatepec y su partido," 125–27, 133–34.

them great reverence and respect."[115] Obeyed promptly by their vassals and feared by criminals, they nurtured Coatepec's independence for centuries despite the best efforts of their foreign enemies. Unfortunately, in the mid fifteenth century Moctezuma I and Nezahualcoyotl of the Triple Alliance exploited the weakness and inexperience of the boy-tlatoani Tlacoquetzin, bringing Coatepec's treasured autonomy to an end. The ruling line soon faded with the arrival of Cortés.[116]

Meanwhile, in 1580 in Tepeaca (Puebla), an elderly nobleman named don Tomás de Aquino told a similar story to the local crown magistrate. He told that the pueblo was founded in 1270 and became the site of a sublimely well-ordered society.[117] "The noble people sought to nurture good customs in their children, and trained them in the arts of war and other good exercises," he remembered.[118] Their prosperity, according to don Tomás, was in part a result of proper deference for the hereditary aristocracy. "[The nobles] were very revered and respected by the plebeians, [who] would not even look them in the eyes. The noble people lived very respected and enjoyed much freedom."[119]

The questionnaire was distributed in the immediate wake of one of the worst epidemics of colonial Mexico, the devastating *cocoliztli* of 1576. Probably typhus combined with other ailments, locals described the sickness as *eztli toyacacpa,* "blood came from our noses."[120] The morbidity and fear it left in its wake is perceptible in the relaciones, as some of the informants contrasted contemporary sufferings to what they perceived as a far more healthful pre-Hispanic era. In 1580, the governor and councilmen of Ocopetlayucan (Puebla) told the alcalde mayor that, in previous eras, the people "lived for a very long time, and they did not die until they were old; and that now, ever since the Marqués entered this land, they suffer from many serious diseases of *cocolizte,* in which a great quantity of them die."[121] The informants in Coatepec similarly noted that in the past people typically lived 110 years and more due to a beneficial combination of good stewardship and good lifestyle. There

---

[115] Ibid., 145.

[116] Ibid., 141–45, quote from 144.

[117] "Relación de Tepeaca y su partido," in Acuña, *Relaciones geográficas del siglo XVI,* v. 5, 217–18.

[118] Ibid., 244.

[119] Ibid., 245.

[120] Noble David Cook, *Born to Die: Disease and New World Conquest, 1492–1650* (New York: Cambridge University Press, 1998), 121.

[121] "Relación de Ocopetlayucan," in Acuña, *Relaciones geográficas del siglo XVI,* v. 7, 81, quote from 87.

was no drunkenness, sloth, or vice before the Spaniards arrived, as their leaders kept them healthily occupied by training constantly for war.[122] Don Tomás in Tepeaca was rather blunt: The reason the people were dying was because of the Spaniards' excessive demands for labor.[123]

Yet even as they lamented their colonial-era decline and impoverishment, some cacique informants took the opportunity to advertise their ancestors' services during the conquest. In 1580 in Cozcatlan (Puebla), the local nobility reported that "neither they nor their ancestors were ever conquered by the Marqués del Valle." Instead, wrote the Spanish author, they had voluntarily welcomed and pledged their allegiance to Cortés with gifts of gold, jewels, and precious stones in a carved wooden chest.[124] The governor of the coastal community of Mizantla (Veracruz) told a similar tale that same year. In 1519, he recalled, all the local people learned of the arrival of "some gods, children of the sun." Curious, the local ruler offered his friendship to Cortés along with gifts of turkeys, maize, blankets, honey, and gold. From then on, Mizantla had provisioned the critical Spanish port of Veracruz with food and labor.[125] The officers of Ocopetlayucan likewise reported that their leader, Cuixcocatl, had forged an alliance with Cortés, thus avoiding bloodshed.[126]

Some relaciones – particularly those indicative of a close relationship between the Hispanic author and the local nobility – also sought to redeem native religiosity to a Spanish audience. In Iztapalapa (DF), for example, the Nahuatl-speaking Spanish magistrate Francisco de Loya attested to the depth and sincerity of local Christian devotion, which he argued stemmed from the example set by his friend and informant, don Alonso Axayacatl Ixhuetzcatocatzin (~1520–83), a son of the penultimate huei tlatoani Cuitlahua and an educated and ladino scholar and antiquarian. Due to his elite parentage as well as his Hispanic upbringing, don Alonso was a well-connected and influential exemplar

---

[122] "Relación de Coatepec," 147–66, quote from 166.

[123] "Relación de Tepeaca," 246.

[124] "Relación de Cuzcatlan," in Acuña, *Relaciones geográficas del siglo XVI*, v. 5, 89–90, 96 quote from 96.

[125] "Relación de Misantla," in ibid., v. 5, 183–84, 88, quote from 88. It should be noted that, overall, this relación is rather scornful and ignorant of native history and culture, indicating more subjective distance from the local nobility. Rather than a mendicant community, Mizantla was served by secular priests, who had more worldly concerns than the mendicants and tended not to concern themselves as deeply with their native congregations. Mundy, *The Mapping of New Spain*: 83–84.

[126] "Relación de Ocopetlayucan," 82.

of the ladino cacique ideal of the sixteenth century.[127] According to Loya, the people of Iztapalapa were very devout and civil, a happy result of don Alonso's effective and "very Christian" guidance and latinity.[128]

Creole sentiments are also evident in other relaciones that seek to redeem local religiosity by blaming unsavory preconquest practices on Mexica tyranny. The author from Coatepec, for example, reported that idolatry was unheard of until the Mexica had forcibly displaced a rather benign local form of sun-worship. "They did not worship the devil until the upstart (*advenedizos*) Indians [from Mexico] arrived, [bringing] with them the idol they call Huichilobos" and requiring sacrifices of human blood.[129] Don Tomás de Aquino recalled that, while the people of Tepeaca had venerated a stone figure named Camaxtli, they were nonetheless essentially monotheistic, lacking only Christian revelation for a full understanding of God's true nature. They "understood that there was some great and supreme god that had created the sky, sun, moon, stars, the earth, and everything else"; yet because they were "rustic and unenlightened by the faith," they did not know where or how to direct their veneration.[130]

Another relación highly reflective of ties between provincial creoles and native leaders comes from the Otomí conquistador culture of the Bajío. The author of Querétaro's 1582 relación was Francisco Ramos de Córdoba, a scribe commissioned by Hernando de Vargas, an alcalde mayor who had befriended both don Fernando de Tapia Connin (who died circa 1572) and his five children, including the then-governor don Diego de Tapia. The account betrays the influence of the Tapias on local creole lore, as much of it is simply a paean to don Fernando and don Diego, crediting them with all that was good and prosperous in the area. Both its historical omissions and rhetorical flourishes align precisely with how the Tapias, as indios amigos and natural lords, preferred to represent themselves before the colonial regime.

As Connin was not a nobleman of lineage – he had been an independent merchant, or *pochtecatl*, prior to his alliance with Spain –

---

[127] Castañeda de la Paz, *Conflictos y alianzas*: 252, 383.
[128] "Relación de Mexicaltzingo y su partido," in René Acuña, ed. *Relaciones geográficas del siglo XVI*, 10 vols. (Mexico: UNAM, Instituto de Investigaciones Antropológicas, 1981–88), v. 7, 38. See also Chaplaincy of don Alonso Axayacatl, Mexico, 1618, AGN-BN 185, Exp. 90. In his testament, don Alonso appointed Francisco de Loya as the executor of his estate.
[129] "Relación de Coatepec," 144–45, 172–73, quote from 144.
[130] "Relación de Tepeaca," 243.

Ramos writes little about the pre-Hispanic era, implying that nothing important existed in the Bajío prior to the arrival of Connin.[131] In 1521, he records, the future conqueror was trading cloth and salt for animal skins destined for resale in Tenochtitlan. This is how he first witnessed the Spanish presence. Fleeing the destruction, Connin and his family settled among his Chichimeca associates, living peacefully for several years in caves near the future site of Querétaro.[132] His exile ended when Hernando Pérez de Bocanegra, the Spanish encomendero of Acámbaro, befriended Connin and convinced him to convert and join colonial society.[133] However, Connin's collaboration with Spaniards angered his Chichimeca hosts, who tried to kill him and the other Otomís. "But the Indian Conni was so discreet," wrote Ramos, "that upon learning of the [planned] rebellion, he pacified them by giving them from what he had, and with good reasoning not only did he dissuade them from killing him, he convinced them to receive the law of the Spaniards, [which] he found to be very good." Thus did Connin become don Fernando de Tapia.[134]

Ramos hailed the Tapias not only as model Indians, but as model Christians whose endeavors sustained the entire community. "Such was [don Fernando's] virtue and Christianity," gushed Ramos, "that it would require a great volume to record the many virtues embodied in this barbarian only newly arrived into the faith." But, he continued, it would be unjust for Querétaro's "Old Christians" (that is, Spaniards) to be ignorant of don Fernando's sublime goodness.[135] Together with the future priest Juan Sánchez de Alanís, don Fernando labored to realize the full potential of Querétaro's fertility with irrigation and settlers. Inspired by his Christian example, the scattered Chichimecas flocked to the new town and prospered under his benign leadership. In a long aside, Ramos wrote that he personally considered don Fernando a man of wisdom and virtue, because he lived like a Spanish gentleman.[136] "Regardless of the topic, he always responded with such good and lively reasoning, that I was amazed, because he was certainly an Indian of very good understanding." The cacique also led a sophisticated and cultivated personal life. He

---

[131] "Relación de Querétaro," in Acuña, *Relaciones geográficas del siglo XVI*, v. 10, 235–39. Acuña gives the scribe's name as Francisco Ramos de Cárdenas, but more recent histories record it as Córdoba. See Tutino, *Making a New World*: 91–94.
[132] "Relación de Querétaro," 217–18.
[133] Ibid., 219.
[134] Ibid., 220.
[135] Ibid., 220.
[136] John C. Super describes the Tapias as "completely Hispanized." See John C. Super, *La vida en Querétaro durante la colonia, 1531–1810* (Mexico: Fondo de Cultura Economica, 1983), 210.

ate in the Spanish style, at a table with chairs, tablecloth, and napkins, with covered food. Although he appreciated wine, no one ever saw him intoxicated.[137]

Don Fernando also took special responsibility for the spiritual development of the town. Seeing the need for more friars, he built living quarters and donated an orchard. As governor, he commissioned the altarpiece for the church, punished vagabonds and those who avoided mass, and he founded a hospital for Indians and poor Spaniards, sustained by proceeds from his ranches and orchards. "He ennobled this pueblo," wrote Ramos, "which is one of the most beautiful and lovely and blessed with abundance in all of New Spain." The previously barren land had blossomed, and don Fernando became "a very rich man." Yet although his wealth aroused envy, "he was a man of much integrity in all his dealings and contracts."[138]

The influence of don Diego de Tapia, don Fernando's son and the governor of Querétaro when Ramos wrote the relación, is clear in the remainder of the account.[139] The author sharply distinguished between the "reasonable" Tapias and the rest of the indigenous population, whom he slurred in the worst terms possible – as liars and thieves, "very dirty in their ways of dressing and eating," cruel, vulgar, cowardly, and inclined to "all manner of vices." Yet Ramos was careful to exempt the Tapias from such negative assessments, calling it "miraculous" the degree to which they had avoided the rusticity of their compatriots.[140] "I have probably gone a bit too far in singing the praises of a barbarian," he concluded, yet "I will simply say that he lived very well and, in my simple judgment, as a very good Christian." Referring to don Diego, he added: "His son currently governs this pueblo, and is of much ability," adding, "the children of such a good man deserve the grace of Your Majesty."[141]

Conclusion

The Latin eloquence of don Antonio Cortés Totoquihuaztli – exemplified in the tragic tone of the 1552 letter excerpted at the beginning of this

---

[137] "Relación de Querétaro," 222.
[138] Ibid., 221–23, 247–48.
[139] The Viceroy Count of Coruña confirmed don Diego as governor in 1581. Merits and Services of don Diego de Tapia, Mexico City, Feb 4, 1581, in *Boletín del Archivo General de la Nación* V (1939): 46–47.
[140] "Relación de Querétaro," 226–28.
[141] Ibid., 222.

chapter – captured the *geist* of the native nobility at midcentury. Don Antonio powerfully compared the caciques' plight to that of Job, whose pious endurance of divine afflictions was a badge of his own faithfulness; it was precisely the caciques' suffering, he wrote, that demonstrated their worthiness. The conquest-era deaths of his father and brother, and the usurpation of his patrimony by the Cano-Moctezumas, were his crosses to bear – and he had risen to the challenge. It was, ironically, his overt embrace of the conquest that enabled him to request the partial restoration of the patrimony it had erased.[142]

The efforts of don Antonio Cortés and the other cacique-governors of the sixteenth century to preserve and re-root their lineages in the new colonial order encountered meager results. Their successes were largely symbolic – grandiose heraldry and modest privileges – yet such symbols were impotent against the many social and economic threats facing the native elite. And indeed the crown's tolerance for the caciques' visions of restoration was both scarce and short-lived; in 1572, Felipe II advised the audiencia to be skeptical toward demands for the restitution of ancestral lands, noting that such claims, if successful, could "open the door for all the caciques and their successors to come before you and ask for the entire land, saying that they possessed it during the time of infidelity and begging [us to remedy their loss]."[143] Future efforts by native elites, as we will see, were far less ambitious, revolving largely around the preservation of tax exemptions and other social privileges rather than the restoration of pre-Hispanic patrimonies. Thus, we might consider the testimonials of such luminaries as don Antonio Cortés Totoquihuaztli and don Hernando Pimentel Nezahualcoyotl as the last cry of the teteuctin; an Indian elite survived, but was utterly transformed in the process. While their children and descendants continued to call themselves caciques and enjoy status and prestige derived from Mesoamerican history, they did so primarily as cabildo officers, landowners, and Indian hidalgos rather than as ruling tlatoque and lords of vassals.

Nonetheless, the caciques' stories of preconquest grandeur, heroic conquest-era services, and pious devotion survived the disintegration of their local authority and landed patrimonies. Absorbed and transmitted by their Spanish and creole sympathizers and collaborators, they – and their characteristic sense of pride entwined with loss – resonated with those in colonial society who felt compelled, for religious or patriotic

---

[142] Don Antonio Cortés Totoquihuaztli to King Charles V, Dec 1, 1552, in PRT, 167–68.
[143] Royal Cédula of Felipe II, Madrid, May 18, 1572, AGN-RCD 47, Exp. 363, f. 235v.

reasons, to locate New Spain's origins in Anahuac rather than its conquest. The documentary record attests to the close association during the sixteenth century between the highborn of Anahuac, the viceregal apparatus, and the regular clergy, especially in planning and executing the many religious festivals and secular celebrations that required the participation of all social castes. Don Antonio Cortés and don Pedro Moctezuma Tlacahuepantli, for example, helped inaugurate new churches and observe feast days alongside viceregal and ecclesiastical officials, contributing both their authority and their finances to enrich and solemnize the ceremonies.[144] There was, in short, no clear and sharp line separating the elite native and Hispanic realms during that era, and these interactions influenced contemporary historical writings.

This intellectual and thematic nexus is perceptible in the ways that some Spanish authors echoed the agenda of the natural lords and their sense of historical decline and decay. Like the caciques, Motolinia, Durán, and Zorita argued for the preservation of Anahuac's "natural" hierarchies, grandfathered intact into the composite Spanish crown. Like the caciques, they argued for native corporate autonomy, and the strict segregation between natives and non-natives. Like the caciques, they blamed postconquest upheavals for the myriad social vices and maladies that scornful Spaniards cited as evidence of the innate inferiority of Indians. And like the caciques, they insisted that the solution to such ills was the re-empowerment of the natural lords, loyal and devout Christians all.[145] To Zorita, the dispossession of the natural lords had ruined civic and moral virtue. Contemporary caciques, anxious, frustrated, and resentful of their own disinheritance, did not disagree.

[144] Reyes García, *Anales de Juan Bautista*: 150–51, 312–15, 184–85, 66–67.
[145] David Brading explores such aspects of these authors' works. Brading, *The First America*: 111–12, 19–22, 283–84.

4

Cacique-chroniclers and the origins of creole historiography, 1580–1640

This history [by don Fernando de Alva Ixtlilxochitl] is very correct and true as we know from the memories we inherited from our parents and grandparents, [and] as painted and written in the little that survives from our ancient histories and chronicles; and we recommend highly that this history be shown to the king, so that he may learn of everything and that the memory of the greatness and the deeds of our ancestors, the ancient kings and lords and other natives (naturales) of New Spain, will not be lost.

Cabildo of Cuauhtlancingo (Tetzcoco), 1608[1]

The labor I have put into [my account] has been immense; beyond the many hours I spent searching for these materials, which took more than fourteen years, it took seven more years to [write, as I continued to fulfill my duties in the convent of Santiago Tlatelolco].... Many things compelled me in the beginning to pen this history, one of which was to [put in chronological order the things recorded] by the friars of the order of my seraphic father San Francisco.... Another was the great affection I have for this poor Indian people and the desire to absolve them – not to [excuse] their errors and blindness, [but] to bring to light all the things they achieved in their pagan republics, which will liberate them from the bestial category to which our Spaniards have assigned them.

Fray Juan de Torquemada, 1615[2]

If the first half of the sixteenth century was the era of colonial expansion and administrative innovation in Mexico, the second half was a time

---

[1] The Governor and Cabildo of Quatlacinco (Cuautlancingo), Approbation of the History of don Fernando de Alva Cortés (Ixtlilxochitl), Otumba, Nov 18, 1608, in Fernando de Alva Ixtlilxochitl, *Obras históricas*, 2 vols. (México: Oficina tip. del Secretario de Fomento, 1892), v. 1, 463–44.

[2] Torquemada, *Monarquía indiana*: v. 1, xxix, xxxi.

of consolidation, as frontiers stabilized and governance routinized. With encomiendas escheating and without additional wealthy and populous Anahuacs to inspire further conquests, Spanish capital after 1550 turned increasingly to silver mining, and the incorporation of additional lands slowed to a trickle. The native population, moreover, continued to plummet; the epidemic of 1576 was the most catastrophic of the era, leaving many lands unoccupied even in the central areas, which both incentivized and facilitated the Spanish acquisition of large private estates.[3] Meanwhile, the crown's bottomless thirst for coin as well as the temperament of King Felipe II favored bureaucratization in imperial government, oriented less toward overt plunder and more to systematized, precapitalist forms of resource extraction and exports.[4]

The export economy and population loss also undermined the caciques' intermediary role as originally envisioned under the first two viceroys, mainly by destabilizing the integrity of the altepeme-pueblos. For all their visions of (partial) restoration, the children of such prominent midcentury tlatoque as don Hernando Pimentel Nezahualcoyotl and don Antonio Cortés Totoquihuaztli never attained the stature of their fathers. Many daughters of caciques, meanwhile, married Spaniards, resulting in mestizaje, cultural Hispanization, and in many cases alienation from commoners. The caciques' plight exacerbated their sense of decline and decay – the natural disposition of displaced aristocracies – as the rapid loss of authority, wealth, and prestige contrasted painfully with memories of splendor.

The powerful wield power; the powerless, on the other hand, wield words. Around the turn of the seventeenth century, a handful of writers affiliated with the indigenous nobility turned to the realm of letters to promote their patrimonies and the cacique agenda of noble distinctions and privileges. Both individually and in collaboration, in alphabetic and narrative texts they set down the history of their ancestors and the communities they governed, giving voice to the aristocratic and patriotic dignity they inherited but could not otherwise express.[5] Thus were

---

[3] Cook, *Born to Die*: 137–40; Hanns J. Prem, "Spanish Colonization and Indian Property in Colonial Mexico, 1521–1620," *Annals of the Association of American Geographers* 82, no. 3 (1992).

[4] Tutino, *Making a New World*: 36–44.

[5] Susan Schroeder has explored the loose network of Nahua historians based in Mexico City who corresponded and shared materials during the early seventeenth century. See Susan Schroeder, "Chimalpahin Rewrites the Conquest: Yet Another Epic History?," in *The Conquest All Over Again: Nahuas and Zapotecs Thinking, Writing, and Painting*

produced the great native and mestizo chronicles of New Spain, some of the most important early works of American history by non-Europeans. They remain critical to empirical studies of Nahua and Mesoamerican history today.

Yet while scholars often turn to the cacique-chroniclers for "indigenous" accounts of Mexican history, they must be understood within their own political and historiographical context. Unlike their predecessors, they were neither tlatoque-governors nor the heirs to cacicazgos. Indeed, some were mestizos. Yet they were nonetheless allied with the historic lineages of Anahuac both genealogically and personally, and their work derived from or built upon the cacique historical accounts of previous decades.[6] These affiliations helped shape the chronicles: While largely addressing pre-Hispanic history, they were nonetheless framed and structured according to the concerns and rhetorical needs of the anxious and frustrated postconquest lords who were their forebears, their relatives, their peers, and their sources. The result was a blend of hagiography and patriotic history that, not coincidentally, elevated the status of the chroniclers themselves: They were, after all, descended from the great rulers of whom they wrote. We must, therefore, acknowledge the texts' political contours; according to Rolena Adorno, the chroniclers' "re-evaluation of the past has a present-oriented objective."[7]

In this sense, the native and mestizo chroniclers echoed and elaborated upon the agenda of the ladino caciques of previous generations. Importantly, they were among the first to fully embed the iconic cacique emphases on primordiality, fealty, and orthodoxy into linear historical narratives – thereby synthesizing into the epistemologically authoritative form of *history* the ideas, themes, and symbols their grandparents had

---

Spanish Colonialism, ed. Susan Schroeder (Portland, OR: Sussex Academic Press, 2011), 106–09.

[6] José Rubén Romero Galván and Rosa Camelo, "Fray Diego Durán," in *Historiografía novohispana de tradición indígena*, ed. José Rubén Romero Galván (México: Universidad Nacional Autónoma de México, 2003); Josefina García Quintana, "Fray Bernardino de Sahagún," in *Historiografía novohispana de tradición indígena*, ed. José Rubén Romero Galván (México: Universidad Nacional Autónoma de México, 2003).

[7] Salvador Velasco similarly notes that they "imagined the past to live in the present," that their historiography was intended to "affirm or retain a political, social, and cultural position. Edmundo O'Gorman, meanwhile, views the collected works of don Fernando de Alva Ixtlilxochitl as a sort of extended *probanza de méritos y servicios*. Adorno, "'Indio ladino" as Historian," 400; Alva Ixtlilxochitl, *Obras históricas*: v. 1, 211; Salvador Velazco, *Visiones de Anáhuac: Reconstrucciones historiográficas y etnicidades emergentes en el México colonial: Fernando de Alva Ixtlilxóchitl, Diego Muñoz Camargo, y Hernando Alvarado Tezozómoc* (Guadalajara: Universidad de Guadalajara, 2003), 269.

invoked as rhetorical tactics before colonial tribunals. The narrative format enhanced the implications of such stories in subtle, yet powerful ways: It was precisely the lords' nobility and wisdom that inspired their alliance with Castile, it was their heroism that enabled its triumph, and it was their Christian zeal that sustained it and gave it meaning. By attuning Mesoamerican antiquity to the religious and political imperatives of the postconquest native nobility, the chroniclers legitimated the ideal of cacique amparo and distinction under Spanish rule.

Yet this act changed as well as preserved native history. The cacique-chroniclers were patriotic antiquarians, but they were also educated, semipublic figures working within the political, linguistic, and discursive structures of their own age. The act of translating and incorporating oral and pictorial records into Spanish-language narratives imposed the rigidity of written prose on what had been a far more fluid and polysemous Mesoamerican mode of history-keeping.[8] The result was a "hybrid historiography" that drew from both native and Spanish narrative traditions but was holistically distinct – in all cases ambiguous and innovative, characterized by shifting perspectives, strategic omissions, and the marriage of local memory with Christian universal history.[9]

Most importantly, the cacique-chroniclers helped refine and transmit some of the most prominent motifs of Novohispanic patriotism, such as the memory of Tetzcoco's golden age, the imperial destiny of the Mexica who founded Tenochtitlan, and the exceptional character of Tlaxcala. (The Otomís of Querétaro left no great chronicles from this era, and their fame would not spread until the late-seventeenth century.) They also expressed what would become a characteristic feature of Novohispanic and Mexican patriotic memory: The frustrating sense that their contemporaries had forgotten their own glorious heritage, a self-ignorance that allowed outsiders to erroneously disregard Anahuac as either savage or inconsequential. Accordingly, this chapter examines several of the most

---

[8] See, for example, Enrique Florescano, "La reconstrucción histórica elaborada por la nobleza indígena y sus descendientes mestizos," in *La memoria y el olvido: Segundo Simposio de Historia de las Mentalidades* (México, D.F.: Instituto Nacional de Antropología e Historia, 1985); Walter Mignolo, *The Darker Side of the Renaissance: Literacy, Territoriality, and Colonization* (Ann Arbor, MI: University of Michigan Press, 1995), 69–143.

[9] Pablo García Loaeza, "Estratégias para (des)aparecer: la historiografía de Fernando de Alva Ixtlilxochitl y la colonización criolla del pasado prehispánico" (Ph.D. diss., Indiana University, 2006); Leisa A. Kauffmann, "Hybrid Historiography in Colonial Mexico: Genre, Event, and Time in the 'Cuauhtitlan Annals' and the 'Historia de la nación chichimeca'" (Ph.D. diss., University of Illinois at Urbana-Champaign, 2004); Lienhard, *La voz y su huella*: 104.

important examples of native and mestizo alphabetic historiography from the era, highlights their contributions to Novohispanic patriotic legends, and considers their relationship to the Franciscan Juan de Torquemada's *Monarquía indiana* (1615), a premier foundation of the Mexican creole tradition. Torquemada's account of Anahuac was, to a large degree, a synthesis of multiple generations of cacique-Franciscan historiography, and achieved with the input of the cacique-chroniclers themselves. Thus, although they were virtually unknown in the contemporary Hispanic literary world – unlike their Peruvian contemporary and analog, "El Inca" Garcilaso de la Vega (1539–1616), who won renown during his own lifetime – the cacique-chroniclers had a substantial, if unheralded influence on all subsequent creole historiography.

Acolhua chronicles and the golden age of Tetzcoco

Perhaps nowhere in colonial central Mexico did local native elites more intricately and extensively preserve details of their origins than in Acolhuacan. Tetzcoco boasted of an unusually strong historiographical tradition well prior to the Spanish arrival, as its tlatoque famously maintained a "general archive" of painted records in the palace complex of Nezahualpilli.[10] Although Cortés's Tlaxcalteca allies burned the archive during the conquest, its existence suggests that the Acolhua elite preserved a comparatively elaborate historical consciousness.[11] This, perhaps, facilitated extensive postconquest historical record-keeping that exceeded even that of Tenochtitlan, evinced during the early colonial period not only in the detailed accounts of such leaders as don Hernando Pimentel, but also by grand pictorial histories of dynastic genealogy and resource rights produced by the sons of Nezahualpilli, the most prominent of which were the *Codex Xolotl* and the *Mapas Quinatzin* and *Tlotzin* and other accounts from lesser towns in the Acolhua realm.[12] Collectively, these

---

[10] Juan Bautista de Pomar, *Relación de Texcoco*, ed. René Acuña, Relaciones geográficas del siglo XVI (México: Universidad Nacional Autónoma de México, 1986), 46; Horcasitas, "Los descendientes de Nezahualpilli."

[11] The Tlaxcalteca burned the palace complex of Nezahualpilli in the wake of the Noche Triste, presumably to punish Coanacochtzin for joining the Tenochca. See "Tetzcoca Accounts of Conquest Episodes," in Chimalpahin Cuauhtlehuanitzin, *Codex Chimalpahin*: v. 2, 188–89.

[12] For detailed expositions of the Acolhua pictorial corpus, see Eduardo de Jesús Douglas, *In the Palace of Nezahualcoyotl: Painting Manuscripts, Writing the Pre-Hispanic Past in Early Colonial Period Tetzcoco, Mexico* (Austin, TX: University of Texas Press, 2010); Lori Boornazian Diel, *The Tira de Tepechpan: Negotiating Place under Aztec and Spanish Rule* (Austin: University of Texas Press, 2008).

accounts relayed a vision of preconquest Tetzcoco as a society of great wealth, culture, and refinement. By the late-sixteenth century, Acolhua history-keepers were writing in Spanish, but their patriotic and genealogical commitments endured, rooted in memories of Nezahualcoyotl and his golden age in Tetzcoco. It was Nezahualcoyotl who had elevated Tetzcoco to its exalted place in Anahuac; to be an Acolhua noble was to be his descendant, and vice versa.

The first alphabetic chronicler of fifteenth-century Tetzcoco was Juan Bautista de Pomar, a mestizo grandson of Nezahualpilli. Pomar's father was Antonio de Pomar, a middling Spaniard, and his mother was María Ixtlilxochitl, the daughter of one of Nezahualpilli's noninheriting wives or concubines. He was, therefore, not a nobleman, and was not afforded the honorific *don*. Nonetheless, he aligned with the legal and political efforts of the Tetzcoca nobility, as he was close with the son of don Hernando Pimentel and other descendants of Nezahualpilli, and his incomes derived from local labor. He belonged to their world, and his voice was theirs.[13]

As a bilingual and mestizo ally of the royal lineage, Pomar authored Tetzcoco's relación geográfica in 1582. Reflecting the influence of the Acolhua origins story as represented in the painted manuscripts – as well as the earlier efforts of don Hernando Pimentel – Pomar's account revolved around the accomplishments of Nezahualpilli and Nezahualcoyotl. Born in 1402, Nezahualcoyotl was the heir to the Chichimeca chieftains who had first subdued and settled in central Mexico. Before he could claim his legacy, however, the Tepaneca of Azcapotzalco killed his father and forced him into hiding. After years in exile, however, the young prince heroically defeated Azcapotzalco and regained his rightful domain.[14] Once victorious, Nezahualcoyotl founded a new empire in Acolhuacan, and appointed the tlatoque of its various provinces. In this way, Pomar portrayed Nezahualcoyotl's reign as the cornerstone and reference point for all noble lineages in the region.

---

[13] See Power of Attorney of don Francisco Pimentel in Favor of Juan de Pomar, Tlaxcala, July 29, 1593, AGN-T 1740, exp. 1, ff. 146r-48v; "Cedula a favor de los descendientes de Nezahualpilli," Mexico, May 16, 1602 in Alva Ixtlilxochitl, *Obras históricas*: v. 2, 292–93.

[14] Tezozomoc of Azcapotzalco defeated Ixtlilxochitl I of Tetzcoco in 1419; the latter's son, Nezahualcoyotl, was forced into exile. When Tezozomoc died in 1426, Nezahualcoyotl took advantage of the ensuing succession crisis to assemble a coalition against Azcapotzalco, culminating in the Tepaneca War of 1427–28. The resulting political order in Anahuac was defined by the Triple Alliance of Tenochtitlan, Tetzcoco, and Tlacopan.

In Pomar's account, Nezahualcoyotl's diplomatic triumphs and astute statecraft cultivated the flowering of civility, science, and art in Tetzcoco. His descriptions seem carefully chosen to undermine Spanish inclinations to regard preconquest society as either brutal or licentious or both. Both Nezahualcoyotl and his successor Nezahualpilli were "very virtuous men" who espoused "good habits and an honest way of life." Although absolute despots, they "always comported themselves with rectitude and justice," and the people "never stopped speaking well of [them], as they were free from afflictions and labor." Loved in peacetime and feared in war, Nezahualcoyotl and Nezahualpilli promoted moral development, encouraging virtue and bravery while harshly punishing vice and sloth. Treason – "such an abominable sin!" – was the worst offense, followed by crimes of the flesh such as adultery, homosexuality, rape, theft, and drunkenness, each of which merited immediate death.[15] Unfortunately, Tetzcoco's greatness in those days had been forgotten "due to a lack of letters," he lamented, yet "the things that are told, especially about Nezahualcoyotzin, do not deserve to remain buried."[16]

Significantly, Pomar also ascribes quasi-Christian values to his grandfather and great-grandfather. He did not ignore the Tetzcoca pantheon – he described the "idols," "devils," and religious ceremonies of the pre-Christian era in rich (and bloody) detail – yet he also portrayed them as foreign impositions; the tyrannical Mexica, Pomar explained, had forced the Tetzcoca to adopt human sacrifice and the deities that required it.[17] While the common people were given to superstition, the Tetzcoca leadership did not revere the idols in their hearts, and any veneration they displayed was theater for the masses. "Some of them understood the delusions in which they lived," he reported, and "achieved knowledge of the immortality of the soul."[18] Most significantly, Pomar echoed the Franciscans in portraying the Tetzcoca tlatoque as moral philosophers who, despite lacking revelation and the institutional Church, had arrived at a partial understanding of the Christian God through reason alone.[19] Nezahualcoyotl, unblinkered by the idols, dedicated himself to the unitary "true God and Creator of all things" whom he called (among many

---

[15] Pomar, *Relación de Texcoco*: 75–78, quote from 77.

[16] Ibid., 51–52.

[17] Ibid., 54–69.

[18] Ibid., 61–62.

[19] This was not heretical; St. Augustine argued that while the sacraments were necessary for salvation, one could arrive at some knowledge of God by way of reason alone, as reason itself was a divine gift to humans. Brading, *The First America*: 259.

other honorific epithets) *"in tloque in nahuaque,* which is to say 'the lord of heaven and earth,'" a formless and invisible omnipresence that both designed and "sustained everything He had made and created." Nezahualcoyotl's meditations also taught him that "after death the souls of the virtuous went to reside" with the Creator, while those of the evil were condemned to a "place of punishment and horrible labors."[20] According to Pomar, Nezahualcoyotl had already seeded the spiritual landscape of Tetzcoco with Christian truths; they awaited only the institutional Church to flourish and bear fruit.

Pomar's account was the most elaborate, but the *relaciones geográficas* of nearby Acolman and Tepechpan indicate that different branches of the Acolhua nobility retained similar memories. Although written by Spanish officials, their historical components so closely parallel Pomar's *Relación de Tetzcoco* that they clearly derived from the same collective memory, if not the same sources. Both echo Pomar's descriptions of Tetzcoco's golden age and his portrayal of Nezahualcoyotl as a proto-Christian founder of Acolhua unity, over a century after his death.[21]

By far the most influential non-Spanish chronicler of the era, however, was don Fernando de Alva Ixtlilxochitl (c. 1578–1650), the author of at least five major accounts of Tetzcoca and Acolhua history and the compiler of a major collection of indigenous primary sources – mostly but not exclusively of Acolhua provenance – that (as we will see in subsequent chapters) played an overarching role in the later development of Mexican creole and national consciousness.[22] As the second son of doña Ana Cortés (1561 to c. 1655), the cacica of San Juan Teotihuacan, don Fernando himself did not stand to inherit a cacicazgo, much less a tlatocayotl.[23] Yet by publicizing the ancient grandeur of his Acolhua ancestors, their friendship with Castile, and their commitment to the Church, he secured an honorable (if modest) career in viceregal

---

[20] Pomar, *Relación de Texcoco*: 69–70.
[21] In Acolman, the informants were governor don Diego Vázquez, alcalde don Guillermo de San Francisco, regidores Lucas de Molina, don Cristóbal de Santiago, and Pablo Cihua Tecpanecatl, and principales don Juan Bautista, Diego Atecpanecatl, and Antonio de Santiago. In Tepechpan, the informants were don Antonio de Estéban and don Diego de Sándoval. See the "Relación de Tequizistlan y su partido," in Acuña, *Relaciones geográficas del siglo XVI,* v. 7, 211–51.
[22] Camilla Townsend, "The Evolution of Alva Ixtlilxochitl's Scholarly Life," *Colonial Latin American Review* 23, no. 1 (2014): 1–17.
[23] The colonial history of the Teotihuacan cacicazgo is in Guido Munch Galindo, "El cacicazgo de San Juan Teotihuacán durante la colonia, 1521–1821" (Mexico: Instituto Nacional de Antropología e Historia, 1976).

government. His earliest work, the *Compendio histórico del reino de Tetzcoco* (~1608), earned the attention of the viceroy, who later appointed him *juez-gobernador* (judge-governor) in several native communities, including Tetzcoco in 1613.[24] He also preserved the papers of don Francisco Verdugo Quetzalmamalitzin-Huetzin, his great-grandfather who was cacique in Teotihuacan (r. 1533–63), which he brandished several times to defend his mother's estate against rivals.[25]

There was another subtle, yet equally urgent factor behind Alva Ixtlilxochitl's interest in Acolhua history. After three generations in which daughters had inherited the Teotihuacan cacicazgo, the last two of whom had married Spaniards, don Fernando and his siblings were neither Indians nor mestizos according to colonial classification schemes. Rather, they were "castizos" with one native and three Spanish grandparents. Indeed, their mixed heritage left the Alvas vulnerable to charges that they were, in the words of their rivals, "all of them Spaniards," and therefore in violation of the prohibition against mestizos holding cacicazgos.[26] Yet while born, raised, and educated in the nucleus of Hispanic culture in Mexico City, as heirs to a cacicazgo they inherited the social and economic agenda of the native nobility. Thus, while many native lineages felt compelled to adopt a Hispanic bearing to safeguard their privileges and ascend within colonial hierarchies – for example, by sporting Spanish dress and intermarrying with creoles – circumstances required the precise opposite of the Alvas: As castizos, they were compelled to overtly perform and represent themselves as Indian lords rather than mestizo or creole gentlemen. Accordingly, the chronicler studiously avoided acknowledging his own predominately Spanish heritage. In seeking positions in the Indian republic, he discarded his father's name (he was born Fernando de Alva Peraleda), adopted the honorific *don*, and assumed the surname Ixtlilxochitl, after his famed great-great-grandfather, the Indian

---

[24] See "Nombramieno de juez gobernador de la ciudad de Texcoco a favor de don Fernando de Alva Ixtlilxochitl," Dec 10, 1612; and "Nombramiento de juez gobernador de Tlalmanalco a favor de don Fernando de Alva Ixtlilxochitl," Dec 13, 1617 (Alva Ixtlilxochitl 1977, 336–37), in Alva Ixtlilxochitl, *Obras históricas*: v. 2, 334–37. While the viceroy frequently appointed outsiders, judge-governor was an office technically reserved for those from the local ruling class. See Connell, *After Moctezuma*: 23–25; Haskett, *Indigenous Rulers*: 5, 82–85, 100–04.

[25] Alva Ixtlilxochitl, *Obras históricas*: v. 2, 294–333; Munch Galindo, "Cacicazgo de San Juan Teotihuacán," 45–46.

[26] See "Diligencias sobre ser españoles los descendientes de Juan Grande," Teotihuacan, Sep 28, 1643, in Alva Ixtlilxochitl, *Obras históricas*: v. 2, 354–69, quote from 58; Royal Decree of Felipe II, Madrid, Mar 11, 1576, RLI-VI, 7.6.

conquistador of Tetzcoco.[27] Eager for cultural allies among the native leadership, the viceroyalty obliged, and received Alva Ixtlilxochitl as a cacique of lineage.[28]

Don Fernando collected physical documents as well as oral traditions and songs.[29] Most importantly, he synthesized diverse colonial sources, native and Spanish, into linear narratives modeled on European chronicles. He interviewed elderly relatives and acquaintances about Acolhua history and genealogy, and he acquired the *Codex Xolotl* and the other pictorial artifacts of the early colonial legal campaigns of the children of Nezahualpilli. Alva Ixtlilxochitl also compiled the most important alphabetic texts of the sixteenth-century Acolhua nobility, including Juan de Pomar's relation and the accounts of the tlatoani-governor don Hernando Pimentel Nezahualcoyotl, his son don Francisco Pimentel, and other nobles of Tetzcoco.[30] Don Fernando also benefitted from the antiquarian groundwork of his great-grandmother's half-brother, don Alonso Axayacatl Ixhuetzcatocatzin of Iztapalapa, the educated ladino whom we met in Chapter 3, and whose role in sixteenth-century cacique memory transmission is underappreciated. Don Alonso was connected to the Tetzcoca via his mother and wife; the former, doña Beatríz Papantzin, was a widow of Emperor Cuitlahua who remarried to Ixtlilxochitl of Tetzcoco in 1524, while the latter, doña Juana, was a granddaughter of Nezahualpilli and daughter of don Jorge de Alvarado Yoyontzin, tlatoani of Tetzcoco in 1532–33. As an exemplar of Indian hidalguía and Latinity, the viceroy appointed don Alonso judge-governor of Tetzcoco sometime during the crisis years after 1564. While there, he compiled painted records of the Tetzcoca lineage, and produced histories of Anahuac in alphabetic Nahuatl. After he died in 1583, don Alonso's daughters preserved his library; decades later, they showed it to Alva Ixtlilxochitl, who incorporated it into his own.[31]

---

[27] Ibid., v. 1, 17, 21.

[28] The crown regarded don Fernando as a descendant of don Fernando Cortés Ixtlilxochitl and Nezahualpilli; it never mentioned his Spanish father and grandfather. See "Real cédula a favor de don Fernando de Alva Ixtlilxochitl," Madrid, May 20, 1620, in ibid., v. 2, 343.

[29] Torales Pacheco, "Don Fernando de Alva Ixtlilxochitl, Historiador Texcocano," in *Historia general del estado de México*, ed. Rosaura Hernández Rodríguez and Raymundo César Martínez (Toluca: Colegio Mexiquense, 1998).

[30] Alva Ixtlilxochitl, *Obras históricas*: v. 2, 137.

[31] Ibid., v. 1, 286. See also Chaplaincy of don Alonso Axayacatl, Mexico, 1618, AGN-BN 185, Exp. 90; and "Relación de Mexicaltzingo y su partido," in Acuña, *Relaciones geográficas del siglo XVI*, v. 7, 38.

Collectively, the works of don Fernando de Alva Ixtlilxochitl echo the native nobility's inclination to blur or downplay any political ruptures between the old kingdoms of Anahuac and the new viceroyalty. He adopted the "long view" of Mexican history that linked contemporary native leaders to pre-Hispanic dynasties, thereby emphasizing their ongoing survival and relevance. For example, in 1621 Alva Ixtlilxochitl commissioned a Nahuatl account of his mother's lineage, *Ytlahtollo yn Teotihuacan tlahtocaiotl yn iuh ypan ca tlatocahuehueamatl* ("Account of the Kingdom of Teotihuacan According to Old Royal Documents").[32] The *Ytlahtollo* traces the cacicazgo of Teotihuacan to its first settler, a fourteenth-century Chichimeca chieftain named Tochinteuctli. Teotihuacan gained stature under Quetzalmamalitzin (r. 1431–83), an ally (and later son-in-law) of Nezahualcoyotl, who elevated Teotihuacan to a tlatocayotl and appointed Quetzalmamalitzin chief justice of the tribunal responsible for the Acolhua nobility. The account continues unbroken into the modern era, listing each descendant of Quetzalmamalitzin up to 1621 – thereby casting don Fernando's mother as the direct and uncontested heir to some of the most powerful tlatoque of the old Acolhua federation.[33]

Alva Ixtlilxochitl also sought, quite explicitly, to redeem his native ancestors from Hispanic contempt and ignorance, memorably declaring Mesoamerica's history to be "no less [important] than those of the Romans, Greeks, Medes, and other [renowned] Gentile republics."[34] To these ends, his account of pre-Columbian Mexico reads as a medieval chronicle, dubious to skeptics yet alluring to romantics and patriots, in which great monarchs governing by divine right strove always to expand their domains, enrich and beautify their realms, and edify their people.[35] In don Fernando's works, Anahuac's tlatoque were "kings" and "princes" who, in between hunting excursions and pleasure cruises, filled their "courts" with "poets," "philosophers," and "scientists." Their relatives and vassals, meanwhile, were "grandees" and "seigniors"

---

[32] "Ytlahtollo yn Teotihuacan tlahtocaiotl yn iuh ypan ca tlatocahuehueamatl," in PRT, 379–96.

[33] Teotihuacan was one of the fourteen "provinces" with independent tlatoque in Acolhuacan; of those fourteen, the tlatoani of Teotihuacan ranked among the six grandees immediately beneath the Tetzcoca tlatoani himself. See Carrasco, *Tenochca Empire*: 136–66; Alva Ixtlilxochitl, *Obras históricas*: v. 2, 89.

[34] Alva Ixtlilxochitl, *Obras históricas*: v. 1, 525.

[35] See Pablo García Loaeza, "Deeds to be Praised for All Time: Alva Ixtlilxochitl's *Historia de la nación chichimeca* and Geoffrey of Monmouth's *History of the Kings of Britain*," *Colonial Latin American Review* 23, no. 1 (2014): 54, 58–61.

in a classically feudal network of political relationships. By way of astute statecraft, which involved clever (and sometimes hilarious) intrigue as often as honest diplomacy and open conflict, they built Acolhuacan into a realm of fantastic prosperity and high culture. This insistence on equivalence with the great civilizations of the ancient Mediterranean explains the degree to which don Fernando indulged in detailed descriptions of Acolhua refinement, from the sumptuousness of its fabrics, to the pomp of its festivals, to architecture "of such admirable and marvelous craftwork [that it] seemed to surpass human industry."[36] By hailing such luster at the colonial nadir of indigenous population collapse and impoverishment, Alva Ixtlilxochitl self-consciously challenged contemporary Spaniards who scorned native peoples as weak, lazy, and backward.

In addition to their antiquity and sophistication, don Fernando was always careful to emphasize Acolhua contributions to the conquest and evangelization of Anahuac, and in particular those of his direct ancestors. His earliest and most complete account of the Spanish invasion comes from the final sections of the *Compendio histórico del reino de Texcoco*, and centers on the author's namesake (don Fernando Cortés) Ixtlilxochitl (1500–31). After the death of his father Nezahualpilli in 1515, the ambitious young Ixtlilxochitl disputed the claims of his half-brother, the Mexica-supported Cacama, from his stronghold at Otumba. When the Spaniards arrived in the midst of this rebellion, Ixtlilxochitl seized the opportunity to leverage them against Cacama and the Tenochca.[37] Although Cortés rarely credited native allies in his letters, Alva Ixtlilxochitl portrayed Ixtlilxochitl as an indispensable key to the Spaniards' success. Haplessly ignorant of the land and supercilious in their quest for gold, the Christians would certainly have failed were it not for Ixtlilxochitl's wise counsels and heroic perseverance.[38] Don Fernando also portrayed his great-great-grandfather as almost singularly responsible for the Christian conversion of Tetzcoco. After emerging triumphant from the war against Tenochtitlan, Ixtlilxochitl was struck with a fierce desire for Christian salvation. Upon the arrival of the twelve Franciscan friars in June of 1524, he promptly renounced polygamy and demanded baptism for himself and his wife Papantzin. In honor of his godfather and sponsor, he became don Fernando Cortés, and his wife

[36] Alva Ixtlilxochitl, *Obras históricas*: v. 2, 116.
[37] Alva Ixtlilxochitl, *Obras históricas*: v. 1, 462–76.
[38] See María Vittoria Calvi, "El diálogo entre españoles e indígenas en la XIII Relación de Fernando de Alva Ixtlilxóchitl," *Quaderni ibero-americana* 72 (1992); Velasco, *Visiones de Anáhuac*: 65–95.

doña Beatríz. The other sons of Nezahualpilli soon followed, including the then-tlatoani (don Pedro de Alvarado) Coanacoch. According to his chronicler and descendant, Ixtlilxochitl's zeal was such that he became a crusader in his own right, threatening to execute those, like his mother (doña María) Tlacoxhuatzin, who remained attached to the old ways.[39] It was primarily due to Ixtlilxochitl, he argued, that "the evangelical law was established and the city of Mexico was won ... with less labor and loss than it would have otherwise cost."[40]

Finally, like Pomar before him, Alva Ixtlilxochitl followed the Franciscans in weaving Christian providentialism into ancient Tetzcoco, situating the Acolhuaque within a teleological history of the American Church beginning centuries before the Spaniards' arrival. The effect was to posthumously convert his pagan ancestors into the protagonists of a long-term vision of Mexico's inevitable evangelization; like the prophets of the Old Testament, the kings of Tetzcoco prepared, knowingly or not, for the eventual arrival of the gospel into Mexico. There were precedents for this tactic in late-medieval and early modern Hispanic letters and politics. It echoed, for example, some Jewish and ex-Jewish communities in fifteenth-century Iberia, who valorized non-Christian ancestors such as King David – and therefore themselves – before a hostile Christian audience by emphasizing their role in the historical unfolding of Christ's victory.[41] The Franciscans of contemporary New Spain, moreover, were frequently inclined to interpret Anahuac as Augustine did Rome – as the political mechanism by which God prepared for the spread of the gospel.[42]

Teleology and providence are implicit themes of Alva Ixtlilxochitl's magnum opus, the unfinished epic known as the *Historia de la nación chichimeca* – which, as evidenced by its verbatim opening chapters, grew out of the *Yhtlahtollo in Teotihuacan tlatocaiotl*. Like its biblical model, it is both a chronicle of a people – in this case the Acolhuaque and their Chichimeca ancestors – as well as a teleological account of the unfolding of a divine plan eons in the making. Unlike his earlier works, which center on the immediate preconquest generations, the *Historia de la nación*

---

[39] Alva Ixtlilxochitl, *Obras históricas*. v. 1, 491–93.

[40] Ibid., v. 1, 450.

[41] See David Nirenberg, "Enmity and Assimilation: Jews, Christians, and Converts in Medieval Spain," *Common Knowledge* 9, no. 1 (2003).

[42] For explorations into this notion, see Jongsoo Lee, *The Allure of Nezahualcoyotl: Pre-Hispanic History, Religion, and Nahua Poetics* (Albuquerque: University of New Mexico Press, 2008), 96–127; García, "Estratégias para (des)aparecer," 59–69.

chichimeca opens at the beginning of time, inscribing the Mesoamerican "Legend of the Suns" – which told of the existence of four previous eras, or "suns," before the present one – into the Judeo-Christian story of the Creation and the Flood. It follows this with an account of the decline of the historic Tolteca civilization, which the author dates to the ninth century, and the arrival into Anahuac of the great Chichimeca chieftain Xolotl and the process by which he and his heirs established a great empire in Acolhuacan over the next five centuries. Yet it is more than a simple chronicle, as embedded throughout the text are omens of Mexico's spiritual destiny, some more overt than others. Don Fernando signaled this agenda in the early chapters by invoking the increasingly popular creole notion that St. Thomas the Apostle had preached in America. The *Historia* tells that, shortly after the death of Jesus in the year *Ce-Acatl* (1-Reed), a white, bearded sage appeared in central Mexico. Calling himself Quetzalcoatl and bearing a cross called "the Tree of Health and Life," he settled in Cholula and instructed the people in the ways of virtue. After a time, however, Quetzalcoatl departed to the east, but not before declaring that others would return to fully realize his moral vision.[43]

Nezahualcoyotl, however – described as "the most powerful, valiant, wise, and successful prince and captain that has ever existed in this new world" – is the primary hero of the *Historia's* teleology.[44] Like Pomar, Alva Ixtlilxochitl told that the venerated tlatoani rejected the "enemy demons" of pre-Hispanic religion in favor of a creator God called *in tloque in nahuaque*, and understood the immortality of the soul as well as the notions of eternal punishment and reward.[45] Yet Alva Ixtlilxochitl went further, depicting Nezahualcoyotl as an Old Testament prophet in his own right. According to the *Historia*, in 1467 – also Ce-Acatl – the tlatoani predicted the collapse and religious rebirth of Anahuac. While attending the inauguration of a new temple dedicated to the Mexica deity Huitzilopochtli, Nezahualcoyotl foretells that in another Ce-Acatl – it was no secret that 1519 was such a year – "the temple that is now being revealed will be destroyed." It would be a cataclysmic event, he warned: "Malice, vice, and sensuality will ripen, ensnaring men and women from

[43] Alva Ixtlilxochitl, *Obras históricas*: v. 2, 8–9.
[44] Ibid., v. 2, 136. Georges Baudot calls Nezahualcoyotl don Fernando's "providential prince." See Georges Baudot, "Nezahualcóyotl, príncipe providencial en los escritos de Fernando de Alva Ixtlilxóchitl," *Estudios de cultura nahuatl* 25 (1995); García, "Estratégias para (des)aparecer," 101, n. 54; Patrick Lesbre, "El Tetzcutzinco en la obra de Fernando de Alva Ixtlilxóchitl," *Estudios de cultura nahuatl* 32 (2001).
[45] Alva Ixtlilxochitl, *Obras históricas*. v. 2, 132–33, 36–37.

a tender age, and the people will rob each other's homes." Implicitly invoking the prophecy of Quetzalcoatl, Nezahualcoyotl also foresees that a path of righteousness would be revealed, allowing people to escape the discord: "In that time the tree of light, health, and sustenance will arrive." His prescription could have been drawn from any seventeenth-century Novohispanic sermon: "To free your children from these vices and calamities," advised the tlatoani, "ensure that from a young age they commit themselves to virtue and good works."[46]

In this way, Alva Ixtlilxochitl aligned a hagiography for pagan ancestors with the Christian imperatives of his colonial milieu. It was a careful balance between rupture and continuity in Mexican history that allowed him to cast his heritage as both ancient and prestigious as well as newly reborn within the Church. It also offered the moral grounds from which to subtly criticize his contemporary society by contrasting it with Tetzcoco's golden age.[47] According to the chronicler, preconquest Tetzcoco was a place of law, refinement, and virtue – as well as a land with a reasoned knowledge of the Christian God, lacking only biblical revelation.[48] Its destruction, therefore, while perhaps teleologically necessary, had mixed results; while it ushered in the "Tree of Light and Health" – invoking a common Christian image – it also provoked a moral crisis resulting in widespread and unrestrained greed and vice. Injecting his own voice, the chronicler noted that "all these changes, and the rise in immorality, have come perfectly true."[49] Behind this bit of righteous moralizing, meanwhile, is an undercurrent of purposeful – or, more intriguingly, presumptive – syncretism, as the Christian image of the Edenic Tree of Life paralleled the ancient Nahua belief in the Tree of Tamoanchan, the tree of origins from which sprung time and existence.[50] Yet who were the sinners of whom Nezahualcoyotl spoke: the conquered natives, or the Spanish conquerors? As the descendant of an indigenous conqueror, did he make the distinction?

[46] Ibid., v. 2, 132–33.

[47] Leisa A. Kauffmann, "Figures of Time and Tribute: The Trace of the Colonial Subaltern in Fernando de Alva Ixtlilxochitl's *Historia de la nación chichimeca*," *The Global South* 4, no. 1 (2010).

[48] Adorno, "'Indio ladino' as Historian," 389–90; Brading, *The First America*: 259.

[49] Alva Ixtlilxochitl, *Obras históricas*: v. 2, 132–33.

[50] The Nahua painters of the Florentine Codex had alluded to such a link. See Magaloni Kerpel, "History Under the Rainbow: The Conquest of Mexico in the Florentine Codex," in *Contested Visions in the Spanish Colonial World*, ed. Ilona Katzew (Los Angeles: Los Angeles County Museum of Art, 2011), 92–5.

The work of don Fernando de Alva Ixtlilxochitl expresses, as much as any other, the peculiar array of interests that characterized the caciques' historical vision. It aspired toward an elusive harmony between pro-Indian and pro-Spanish imagery. Too much pro-conquest triumphalism would implicitly challenge the caciques' historic legitimacy. Unrestrained pride in Aztec Anahuac or lamentations on its decline, on the other hand, were inherently critical of the conquest, and therefore anathema to the quest for noble privileges based on services to the crown. Don Fernando's bridge between Anahuac and New Spain was the retroactive "conversion" of his own ancestors – and in particular Nezahualcoyotl – into providential, pre-Christian heroes, a tactic that required not only narrative skill, but also a degree of strategic omission and ambiguity.

Not coincidentally, such qualities also characterized the brand of creole patriotism Alva Ixtlilxochitl helped so much to inspire. According to Edmundo O'Gorman, the *Historia de la nación chichimeca* is "of the utmost importance in the complex process of the formation of Novohispanic consciousness and, ultimately, of national consciousness [in Mexico]."[51] The elite Acolhua historical vision as related by Alva Ixtlilxochitl continues to permeate contemporary notions of the pre-Columbian past and the exalted place of Tetzcoco in Mexican memory – it was Anahuac's university, the Mexican Athens, where its loftiest and most sophisticated qualities flourished to their greatest extent. Unpublished in his lifetime, his works and his perspectives were adopted, transcribed, and circulated by subsequent generations of creoles interested in Mexican history. Due in part to these efforts, Nezahualcoyotl remains a celebrated icon of Mexico's ancient cultural heritage today; his heroic visage, along with one of his poems, even graces the contemporary 100-peso note. Nezahualcoyotl is far more famous today than the humble seventeenth-century chronicler, his great-great-great-great-grandson, who did so much to shape his memory.

Destiny and doom in imperial Tenochtitlan: don Hernando de Alvarado Tezozomoc

Among the chroniclers of the era, the voice of imperial Tenochtitlan and its ruling lineage was that of don Hernando de Alvarado Tezozomoc. While several contemporaries likewise set down the Mexica version of history – most prominently Chimalpahin, but also non-noble partners

---

51 Alva Ixtlilxochitl, *Obras históricas*: v. 2, 218.

of the Franciscans such as Cristóbal del Castillo – they did so as out-siders rather than as representatives of the dynasty and guardians of its memories.[52] Don Hernando was the son of don Diego de Alvarado Huanitzin, who had restored the dynasty in 1538 under Viceroy Men-doza, while his mother was doña Francisca de Moctezuma, the daugh-ter of the late huei tlatoani. Thus, although never himself governor, he moved within the highest ranks of postconquest Tenochtitlan, and was likely the official history-keeper of the royal family.[53] Accordingly, his Spanish-language *Crónica mexicana*, or *Mexican Chronicle* (1598), nar-rates Mexica history as preserved among their most noble descendants. In their telling, the Mexica were chosen by fate and otherworldly forces to conquer and rule over all of Anahuac. But the gods are fickle, and withdrew their favor just as quickly.

Unlike many cacique histories, the *Crónica mexicana* is relatively unin-flected by any immediate personal or political agenda. It was not a mech-anism for social or professional ambition, as in addition to being quite old when he began writing, don Hernando was already well-provisioned as an interpreter for the Royal Audiencia.[54] This distinguishes him from his much younger contemporary, the fourth-generation Mexico City cas-tizo don Fernando de Alva Ixtlilxochitl, whose links to historic Tetzcoco were more abstract and intellectual. Second, unlike the account of Juan de Pomar, the *Crónica* was not occasioned by – and therefore sensitive to – Spanish concerns such as the relaciones geográficas. The narrative reflects only its sources and the author's literary and scholarly priorities, which were, it seems, largely antiquarian and patriotic. Don Hernando's chronicle tells of the Mexica's legendary origins at Chicomoztoc (the Seven Caves) in Aztlan, their years of wandering under the guidance of

---

[52] Chimalpahin's *Crónica mexicayotl* (1609) – often misattributed to Tezozomoc, who merely contributed a brief introduction – recounts Mexica history based on Mexica sources. Chimalpahin was from Chalco-Amecameca, and represented himself as an antiquarian and compiler rather than a voice of the Tenochca dynasty. Meanwhile, Castillo – an outsider and a commoner – saw himself as a mere "translator." See Chi-malpahin Cuauhtlehuanitzin, *Codex Chimalpahin*. v. 1; Cristóbal de Castillo, *Historia de la venida de los mexicanos y de otros pueblos e historia de la conquista*, trans. Fed-erico Navarrete Linares (Mexico: Cien de México, 2001). On the authorship of the *Crónica mexicayotl*, see Schroeder, "The Truth about the *Crónica mexicayotl*."

[53] Susan Schroeder notes that in Nahua tradition his holding this position would have precluded his involvement in municipal government. Schroeder, "The Truth about the *Crónica mexicayotl*," 235–36.

[54] Romero Galván, *Los privilegios perdidos*: 85–94. Romero Galván notes that it is prob-able that don Hernando was a student at the Colegio de Santa Cruz in Tlatelolco, but this cannot be confirmed.

the prophetic priest-deity Huitzilopochtli, their immigration into central Mexico, and the foundation of the future imperial capital of Tenochtitlan on the island of Mexico. This was the historical self-representation and justification of an imperial power, detailing its rise from poverty and obscurity to glory and prosperity through providence, martial ingenuity, and the militaristic cult of a titular deity.[55] Along with his creole contemporaries Diego Durán and Juan de Tovar, who worked with the same sets of sources, Tezozomoc helped transmit the legends of imperial Tenochtitlan into the broader Novohispanic consciousness.[56]

Yet the *Crónica mexicana* is also, like its contemporaries, a creature of the colonial milieu, subject to all the rhetorical and religious imperatives implied therein. And therein lies its uniqueness: The author overlay the traditional Mexica origin story with the perspective and sensibilities of a Novohispanic cacique. Don Hernando was the grandson of Moctezuma, but he was also a Christian vassal of the Spanish king, and his history reflects this "hybrid identity."[57] In its often surprising twists and complexities – at once proud of and hostile toward Mexica culture and society – we can sense how don Fernando, as an heir to the old lords of Mexico, gathered and reassembled the fragments of a shattered cosmology. In the Mexica tradition, fate and destiny had elevated Tenochtitlan to imperial glory; in Tezozomoc's account, fate and destiny also sealed its eventual destruction.

Like its preconquest and early postconquest antecedents, the *Crónica* traces the Mexica to a primordial, barely conceivable antiquity. Although set in real places and in earthly time, the first chapters detail the emergence of Huitzilopochtli's potency and the covenants he forges with his people.[58] Entire centuries are condensed into mere sentences, the supernatural converses freely with the natural, and the line between history and myth is both shifting and permeable. Yet beginning with the reign

---

[55] Elizabeth Hill Boone, "Manuscript Painting in Service of Imperial Ideology," in *Aztec Imperial Strategies*, ed. Frances Berdan (Washington, DC: Dumbarton Oaks, 1996).

[56] These sources were the famous *Tira de la peregrinación* (~1530s) and its various alphabetic renderings, most prominently the "Crónica X," an inferred source, either an earlier text now lost or an oral tradition. María Castañeda de la Paz suggests these items once constituted a single volume viewed by Tezozomoc, Durán, Tovar, and others. See Castañeda de la Paz, "El Códice X o los anales del "Grupo de la Tira de la Peregrinación." Copias, duplicaciones, y su uso por parte de los cronistas." See also Romero Galván, "La Crónica X."; Romero Galván, *Los privilegios perdidos*, 96–105; Velazco, *Visiones de Anáhuac*: 207–15.

[57] Velazco, *Visiones de Anáhuac*: 205.

[58] Hernando de Alvarado Tezozomoc, *Crónica mexicana* (Madrid: Dastin, 2001), 53–64.

of Acamapichtli, the fourteenth-century nobleman of Culhuacan who founded the Tenochca tlatocayotl, the narrative firmly enters the realm of history, detailing the political and diplomatic challenges and triumphs of the Mexica in Anahuac. Indeed, most of the *Crónica* may be said to be hyper-historical, inasmuch as it reflects the oral histories that were its primary sources. The action is driven forward by supposedly verbatim dialogue between the notables of fifteenth-century Tenochtitlan such as Itzcoatzin, Moctezuma the Elder, and their cihuacoatl Tlacaeleltzin. The narrative pretense of directly quoting the long deceased – also ubiquitous, for example, in the chronicles of Alva Ixtlilxochitl – seemingly converts the reader into a direct witness to history in the manner of the Nahua oral tradition.[59] The contrast with the mist-enshrouded opening is stark, but the effect is to dignify the Tenochca rulers: Their destiny was glory from the beginning, but only achieved through sacrifice and conflict.

Don Hernando's primary purpose was to translate the Mexica origin story as he had received it, not to report merits and claim privileges. Nonetheless, his account of the Spaniards' arrival is notable because he refuses to acknowledge any real resistance to the conquistadors. Instead, he presents Moctezuma's role in the conquest as predicated entirely on his utter belief in Quetzalcoatl's eventual return, allowing the author to incorporate Cortés and Spanish rule into Mexica teleology, making sense of them in Mexica rather than Christian terms. That is, the Quetzalcoatl myth enabled Tezozomoc to reconcile the collapse of Tenochtitlan with the story of its divinely ordained rise: The Christian God did not unmake Tenochca sovereignty, it was written in the Mexica's own prophetic tradition. The result is an assertion of patrimony and heritage that nonetheless remains faithful to the religious and political imperatives of Spain's composite monarchy. Imperial Tenochtitlan was part of a heavenly plan; yet so, also, was viceregal New Spain.

To be specific, the *Crónica* tells that, years before the Spaniards' arrival, numerous omens reminded Moctezuma that he merely occupied a throne that in reality belonged to Ce-Acatl Quetzalcoatl, a ruler of the Toltecs, whom the Mexica viewed as the original civilizers of Anahuac. "The elders," Moctezuma explained to one of his advisers, "understood

---

[59] According to Salvador Velazco, "because Alvarado Tezozomoc adopts a European narrativity – his is a chronicle organized in chapters and episodes, following the written model that the new culture put at his disposal in the colonial situation – Nahua orality is, in reality, what sustains the diegesis, the history, the account." Velazco, *Visiones de Anáhuac*, 209–13, quote from 212–13.

clearly that their god Quetzalcoatl would return to rule in Tula and its entire realm," that he would come from the east, and that he would take back what was already his, "for this throne and majesty are his, which I have only on loan from him as his lieutenant."[60] After observing certain presages, including a giant cloud of glowing white smoke in the form of a man coming from the east at midnight, Moctezuma consulted his counterpart, Nezahualpilli. The latter responded bluntly: "If it is the will of the gods that all this should end, what can I say?"[61]

Thus, when the Spaniards arrived, Moctezuma's response was utter fatalism, submission, and capitulation – hardly eager alliance in the manner of Ixtlilxochitl of Tetzcoco, but neither was it resistance. "I truly believe [Cortés] to be the Çe Acatl," he remarked, "the walking god of the One Reed."[62] The soothsayers he commissioned agreed, telling him that upon his return Quetzalcoatl would appear in a different form than he had in the past, and that those he brought with him would be "very ferocious and valiant, in strange garb," and speaking a foreign tongue.[63] Don Hernando also recorded that Moctezuma voluntarily transferred his rule to the Spaniards. Yet the emperor's grandson goes further than even Cortés, a man notorious for his hubris; in the *Crónica mexicana*, the supposed transfer of rule is proposed immediately upon the Spanish landing on the coast. Upon learning of their arrival, Moctezuma appoints an emissary and instructs him to test whether Cortés was Quetzalcoatl. "If it indeed be him," he orders, "then pray him and beg him humbly to come and enjoy his chair and throne that I guard as his lieutenant."[64]

Finally, of all the non-Spanish chroniclers of the era, Tezozomoc exhibited perhaps the most conflicted and ambivalent relationship to the thorny issue of pre-Hispanic religion. His history is an origins account of Mexica glory, yet he does not ignore or avoid the most notorious aspects of its martial theology. Instead, he opts to portray the Mexica as a civilization under the dominion of the devil. Huitzilopochtli is not merely an "idol" in

---

[60] Alvarado Tezozomoc, *Crónica mexicana*: 470–71.

[61] Ibid., 439–41. Alva Ixtlilxochitl offers a similar version of this episode. He records that the glowing cloud appeared in 1510, and that Nezahualpilli, as a man of "science," understood that it heralded the inevitable destruction of the empire his father had helped build, and advised Moctezuma to accept the ephemerality of his power. Alva Ixtlilxochitl, *Obras históricas*: v. 2, 181–82.

[62] Alvarado Tezozomoc, *Crónica mexicana*: 474.

[63] Ibid., 476.

[64] Ibid., 471.

the *Crónica;* he is also a demon – or even Lucifer himself – surrounded by lesser devils in an unholy mirror of Jesus and the saints.[65] This trope, common among the Franciscans with whom don Hernando was acquainted, served a number of rhetorical purposes. Far from a blanket dismissal of indigenous civilization, in the context of sixteenth-century Hispanic debates over the rationality of Indians, to emphasize the role of the devil was semiapologetic.[66] If abhorrent practices were the result of infernal trickery, then they did not implicate native peoples themselves. In other words, to equate Huitzilopochtli with Christianity's devil was a subtle argument for, rather than against, the rationality and moral equality of Indians. Inserting the devil into his account also allowed Tezozomoc to preserve the essential narrative of the Mexica imperial history he had inherited, which was partially predicated on the potency and consequentiality of Huitzilopochtli. If the chronicler had represented the deity as merely an inert figure of carved stone, he would have had to restructure and reinterpret the entire story of the Mexica's rise, which was underwritten by supernatural forces. Both Huitzilopochtli and the Christian God have agency in the *Crónica mexicana.*

By blaming Mexica religious practices such as human sacrifice on the devil, don Hernando affords himself the narrative liberty to openly and ferociously condemn them. During these moments the colonial elements of the *Crónica* overwhelm its adherence to Mexica oral tradition. Don Hernando describes certain rituals and events in gruesome detail, making a clear and obvious show of his distaste. In one example, the three rulers of the Triple Alliance invite kings from distant lands to attend a celebration. A succession of Tlaxcalteca war prisoners is brought forth, and a "celebration of cruelty and great slaughter (*carnicería*)" begins. After sumptuously feeding and adorning the captured enemies, the Mexica bind them to a large round stone (*temalacatl*) and subject them to mocking combat until their legs buckle. At that point, each "poor Indian" (*miserable indio*) is forced onto his back while five priests pry open his chest, remove his still-beating heart, smear blood on the statue of Huitzilopochtli, and burn the heart in an "infernal brazier" (*cuauhxicalli*). The author notes that at this point in the ritual the hollowed corpses might leap to their feet and

---

[65] Ibid., 418.

[66] See Brading, *The First America*: 105–07. Brading indicates that Franciscan chroniclers gave the devil agency in Mexican history so as to reconcile their admiration for the grandeur of Mesoamerican civilization with their abhorrence for native religious practices.

stumble several steps before finally collapsing.[67] In thus describing such events – and using the term *miserable indio* in doing so – don Hernando temporarily shed the voice of Mexica tradition. There were no "Indians" in pre-Hispanic America, while *miserable* was the Castilian legal designation for those to whom Christian charity obliged special leniency and favor, such as orphans and widows – and, in imperial law, Indians.[68] The words *miserable indio* derived entirely from a colonial perspective, and not at all from his acquaintance with Tenochca royal memory.

The ultimate effect is ambiguous and sometimes contradictory, as don Hernando both lauds and condemns imperial Tenochtitlan. He explicitly curses some of the customs of his ancestors, yet also valorizes them by faithfully transmitting their origin story and hailing their wisdom and courage. The fragmented spiritual perspective of a Nahua nobleman steeped in both pre-Hispanic memories and colonial ideologies is revealed in one passage, Moctezuma's lament upon learning that Cortés intended to approach Tenochtitlan. "And so it is that the gods have wearied and left us to the control of strangers," he cries, "they, our gods, the era and the lord, Tloque yn Nahuaque, our lord, the night, the air, to their will."[69]

With a moral sensibility straddling two distinct intellectual, religious, and cultural traditions, the *Crónica* is far more ambiguous than the overtly hagiographical accounts from Acolhuacan. The reader is at all times aware that Tezozomoc was the grandson of Moctezuma and an heir to the imperial legacy he so richly details. Indeed, his lineage was central to his claim to authorial reliability, insisting that his was the only official account of the Tenochca royal family.[70] In doing so, however – in purporting to transmit in its entirety the historical knowledge of a fallen imperial capital – he inadvertently drew attention to a subtle, yet ubiquitous contrast permeating the entire chronicle: the state of Tenochtitlan's royal dynasty before and after the imposition of Spanish rule.[71] Yet

---

[67] Alvarado Tezozomoc, *Crónica mexicana*: 409–10. Tezozomoc was describing one of the ceremonies of imperial intimidation and theater that accompanied Tenochca expansion. See Inga Clendinnen, *Aztecs: An Interpretation* (Cambridge: Cambridge University Press, 2000), 88–104; Emily Umberger, "Art and Imperial Strategy in Tenochtitlan," in *Aztec Imperial Strategies*, ed. Frances Berdan (Washington, DC: Dumbarton Oaks, 1996), 97.

[68] RLI-II, 5.5; Borah, *Justice by Insurance*: 15–16.

[69] Alvarado Tezozomoc, *Crónica mexicana*: 481.

[70] Chimalpahin Cuauhtlehuanitzin, *Codex Chimalpahin*: v. 1, 62–63; Schroeder, "The Truth about the *Crónica mexicayotl*," 237.

[71] See Romero Galván, *Los privilegios perdidos*: 153–58.

there are no overt lamentations of decline or pleas for restoration in the *Crónica*; Tezozomoc's resignation echoed that of his grandfather.

The stoics of Tlaxcala: Diego Muñoz Camargo

While some Tlaxcalteca were involved with the Franciscan ethnographical projects of the sixteenth century, historiography in Tlaxcala developed somewhat autonomously from that of Anahuac, reflecting both its preconquest independence and its special postconquest exemptions and privileges.[72] Its greatest representative was Diego Muñoz Camargo (c. 1528–1600), the son of a Tlaxcalteca woman and a Spaniard. Although his perspective clearly reflected his bilingual and mestizo status and upbringing, as an adult he owned lands in Tlaxcala and aligned with its traditional nobility, even marrying the Tlaxcalteca noblewoman doña Leonor Vázquez. In the 1580s he became the official procurador and advocate for Tlaxcala, charged with representing its interests before the viceroyalty – a role he performed for over a decade. Most consequentially, in the 1590s Muñoz Camargo helped organize and provision the 400 Tlaxcalteca families who migrated to the northern frontiers under Viceroy Velasco II. Reflecting his status among the Tlaxcalteca elite, his bilingual son (also named Diego Muñoz Camargo) married doña Francisca Pimentel Maxixcatzin – who as a descendant of both the Maxixcatzins of Tlaxcala and the Pimentels of Tetzcoco was the highest-ranking woman in Tlaxcala.[73]

Thus, despite his mixed heritage, like Juan de Pomar of Tetzcoco Muñoz Camargo was a reliable voice for Tlaxcala's nobility and a natural choice to write its relacion geográfica. Modern scholars have questioned the extent to which the resulting *Historia de Tlaxcala* (1585) identifies with its author's native ancestry, as its narrative voice is overtly Hispanic rather than indigenous – for example, it refers often in the first-person

---

[72] An example of Franciscan-Tlaxcalteca collaboration is the *Anónimo mexicano*, a history of Anáhuac and Tlaxcala written by one or more Tlaxcalteca in the late-sixteenth or early seventeenth century. The document is related to the researches of fray Juan de Torquemada, as either a source or a rough translation. See *Anónimo mexicano*, trans. Richley H. Crapo and Bonnie Glass-Coffin (Logan, UT: Utah State University Press, 2005).

[73] Charles Gibson, "The Identity of Diego Muñoz Camargo," *Hispanic American Historical Review* 30, no. 2 (1950); Velazco, *Visiones de Anáhuac*: 132; Torquemada, *Monarquía indiana*: v. 5, 63–64. The Diego Muñoz Camargo with whom Torquemada was acquainted was the historian's son, not the historian himself.

plural to "we Spaniards."[74] The confusion can be partially resolved if we recognize Muñoz Camargo as a representative of the caciques' peculiar agenda rather than that of the Tlaxcalteca more generally; as Salvador Velazco argues, his history reflects the "coalition of interests" between the sons of conquistadors and the Tlaxcalteca aristocracy.[75] Seen holistically, the essential rhetorical thrust of the *Historia* is apology. It betrays deep affinities for the community where he was born and lived, and he even traveled to Madrid to personally deliver it to Felipe II.

The *Historia* is an admiring, yet not hyperbolic portrait of precontact Tlaxcala. It describes an organized and sophisticated confederation consisting of four autonomous kingdoms, though not without its fair share of dissension and internal conflict. Governed by a mostly wise caste of leaders vigilant against tyranny and oppression, Tlaxcala emerges as a fiercely independent society with republican tendencies. For example, the chronicler recounts an episode in which Tlacomihua, the lord of Ocotelolco (one of the four independent districts of the confederation), led a popular rebellion against Acantetehua, who had become a tyrant. While describing the coup as an "atrocity" and "treason," he nonetheless insists that Tlacomihua enjoyed the support of the people, and that among his descendants was Maxixcatzin, the venerable tlatoani who helped secure the Tlaxcalteca alliance with Castile.[76] Muñoz Camargo also emphasizes the Tlaxcalteca dedication to the rule of law. He describes the debate over the proper punishment for Xicotencatl the Younger, the acting lord of the district of Tizatlan who abandoned Cortés during the battle for Tenochtitlan (perhaps to be with a lover). Although Xicotencatl was the powerful scion of a venerable house, Maxixcatzin imprisoned him for treason and gave him to Cortés for execution. Nobody was above the law; Xicotencatl had violated Tlaxcala's "rigorous" warrior codes, explained Maxixcatzin, and merited punishment.[77]

Muñoz Camargo's contemporary Spanish readers would have sensed implicit analogies to the virtuous pagan civilizations of Western antiquity such as Sparta or Rome – a historical framework already common in the Franciscan accounts with which Muñoz Camargo was familiar.

---

[74] Muñoz Camargo's cultural affinities shift back and forth in his prose. See Marilyn Miller, "Covert Mestizaje and the Strategy of "Passing" in Diego Muñoz Camargo's *Historia de Tlaxcala*," *Colonial Latin American Review* 6, no. 1 (1997).

[75] Velazco, *Visiones de Anáhuac*: 127–95, quote from 94–95.

[76] Diego Muñoz Camargo, *Historia de Tlaxcala*, ed. Alfredo Chavero (Mexico: Oficina tip. de la Secretaría de Fomento, 1892), 73–78.

[77] Ibid., 85.

By portraying pre-Hispanic Tlaxcala as a place where duty and logic triumphed over passion and emotion, Muñoz Camargo exploited the early modern Hispanic appreciation for the stoic virtues, which Counter-Reformation thinkers understood as commensurate with the lessons of Christian revelation.[78] The narrative effect was subtle, but real: The alliance between the stoics of Tlaxcala and the Christians of Castile was natural and organic, built upon shared values rather than opportunism, coercion, or weakness.

As the archetypal community of Indian conquistadors – and after five decades of active negotiations for royal recognition and rewards – Muñoz Camargo did not lack for anecdotes symbolizing Tlaxcala's support for the Spanish crown. Indeed, the *Historia* translated the imagery of the *Lienzo de Tlaxcala* into prose, and the chronicler even attached 156 ink drawings copied from the tapestry to his history.[79] Yet the written narrative format allowed Muñoz Camargo to further elaborate upon the issue of Tlaxcalteca valor. The message was the same: Without Tlaxcala, there would be no New Spain. Like the *Lienzo*, the *Historia* omits any mention of Tlaxcala's initial resistance to the Spanish intrusion. Although Cortés had reported that the Tlaxcala-Castile alliance was only achieved after two weeks of fierce combat resulting in the deaths of one Spaniard, two horses, and many local enemies, Muñoz Camargo conspicuously attributed the violence to local Otomís unaffiliated with the Tlaxcalteca.[80] The chronicler tells instead of respectful diplomacy between Cortés and the four tlatoque of Tlaxcala, portraying the latter as cautious statesmen seeking the wisest course of action. After some debate exemplifying the ideals of pagan stoicism and natural wisdom, they decided to receive Cortés peacefully. In the meantime, "they ceased the sacrifices to their infernal gods, their rites, and superstitions, with extreme

---

[78] See Peer Schmidt, "Neoestoicismo y disciplinamiento social en Iberoamérica colonial (siglo XVII)," in *Pensamiento europeo y cultura colonial*, eds. Karl Kohut and Sonia V. Rose (Frankfurt and Madrid: Vervuert, Iberoamerica, 1997).

[79] Travis Barton Kranz, "Visual Persuasion: Sixteenth-Century Tlaxcalan Pictorials in Response to the Conquest of Mexico," in *The Conquest All Over Again: Nahuas and Zapotecs Thinking, Writing, and Painting Spanish Colonialism*, ed. Susan Schroeder (Portland, OR: Sussex Academic Press, 2011), 53.

[80] Muñoz Camargo, *Historia de Tlaxcala*: 185; Travis Barton Kranz, "Sixteenth-Century Tlaxcalan Pictorial Documents on the Conquest of Mexico," in *Sources and Methods for the Study of Postconquest Mesoamerican Ethnohistory, Provisional Version*, eds. James Lockhart, Lisa Sousa, and Stephanie Wood (University of Oregon Wired Humanities Project 2007), 16–17.

fervor and care."[81] The Spaniards' bloody escape from Tenochtitlan also provided an opportunity for the Tlaxcalteca to demonstrate their loyalty and bravery. At one point, Cortés was captured by the Mexica. Yet before they were able to subject him to the horror of the sacrificial stone, a valiant Tlaxcalteca warrior named Antonio Temazahuitzin rescued him and allowed him to escape. During the ensuing struggle, Temazahuitzin fell into a bog and was himself captured (although he was later reclaimed by his compatriots and Spaniards with horses).[82]

Like contemporary chronicles, Muñoz Camargo's treatment of Tlaxcalteca religiosity was complicated and ambivalent, yet ultimately apologetic. While overtly scornful of the pagan practices of his mother's ancestors, he defended them from charges of savagery by resisting the worst hyperbole regarding preconquest barbarity, deflecting blame for offensive practices and locating quasi-Christian sensibilities in unlikely preconquest places. For example, Muñoz Camargo acknowledged human sacrifice and anthropophagy in Tlaxcala, but insisted that the practices were only recent, and in some sense aberrant, additions to local religious practice – devilish mischief that had corrupted and deceived a once-virtuous people. The idols, he explained, originated as patriotic commemorations of local heroes. Unfortunately, the devil tricked later generations into attributing supernatural powers to the images. Human sacrifice and cannibalism were also demonically inspired detours from Tlaxcala's fundamentally admirable legacy.[83] Thus, like don Hernando Alvarado Tezozomoc, Muñoz Camargo deployed allegations of diabolic intervention to apologize for rather than impugn the reputation of a pre-Hispanic society. "They never knew – nor did they understand – the deceit under which they lived," he concluded, "until they were baptized and made into Christians."[84]

Despite its more notorious aspects, Muñoz Camargo portrayed Tlaxcalteca religion as a legitimate source of moral development, in some ways mirroring the submissive rituals of Christian piety. The Tlaxcalteca spent years cultivating and educating their children in the importance of humility. "They prayed often," and when they addressed the idols, they did so with great reverence, neither looking directly at them nor spitting

[81] Muñoz Camargo, *Historia de Tlaxcala*: 183–85.
[82] Ibid., 223–24.
[83] Ibid., 141–42.
[84] Ibid., 130.

or squirming impatiently. In departing their presence, they backed away "with much modesty," their heads lowered. Somewhat incongruously, Muñoz Camargo notes that they did this while speaking to the devil.[85]

Most significantly, however, was the chronicler's cautious foray into preconquest metaphysics, which, like Alva Ixtlilxochitl, he portrayed as containing a substantial, if subterranean, proto-Christian element. "Before we proceed," he wrote,

> it is important that I address the knowledge that they had of one sole God (Muñoz Camargo's capitalization) and one unitary cause that was the substance and origin of all things; and it was thus: as all of the gods that they adored were the gods of springs, rivers, fields, and other false gods, with each thing attributed to its own god, they concluded by saying "Oh God within whom all things are," which is to say the *Teotloquenahuaque*, or, as we would say today, "that person by whom all things are made possible, that attending cause of all things, which is of a single essence."

Cautiously, Muñoz Camargo argued that this conception of an ultimate deity was proof that the Tlaxcalteca possessed "a trace" of the idea that there was one God above all other gods. They also understood eternity and the immortality of the soul, of "another life in which they would live alongside the gods in eternal pleasure, pastimes, and rest."[86]

Muñoz Camargo wrote at a time when many Spaniards were turning skeptical of the sincerity of Christianity in Mexico.[87] He obviated such concerns *vis a vis* Tlaxcala by depicting its leadership as driven to baptism out of sincerely reasoned spiritual inspiration. After securing friendship, they ask Cortés to explain the Castilians' religion. The conquistador responds with a brief summary of Christian doctrine, worries that the devil had misled his hosts into their cruel superstitions, and invites them to receive baptism.[88] The four tlatoque then weigh the moral and political implications of what they have heard. They concede that their "idols"

---

[85] Ibid., 142–43.

[86] Ibid., 129–30. Muñoz Camargo's original Spanish definition is "aquella persona en quien asisten todas las cosas, aquella causa de todas las cosas acompañadas, que es sólo una esencia."

[87] The Third Mexican Church Council (1585), held the same year that Muñoz Camargo and the Tlaxcalteca delegation delivered their relación to Madrid, declared Indians, mestizos, and Africans as people with "natural defects" who, except in extraordinary circumstances, were ineligible for positions of authority within the Church (although Felipe II later softened this policy *vis a vis* Indians and mestizos). See RLI-I, 1.7. See also Stafford Poole, "Church Law on the Ordination of Indians and *Castas* in New Spain," *Hispanic American Historical Review* 61, no. 4 (1981).

[88] Muñoz Camargo, *Historia de Tlaxcala*: 193–97.

were merely inanimate statues, but nonetheless emphasize their important role in the life of the community. In an eloquent speech, Maxixcatzin of Ocotelolco proclaims the difficulty of simply discarding ancient and revered traditions:

How can you expect us, oh valiant Captain, to so easily allow violent and sacrilegious hands to profane the gods whom we so respect and esteem? Why would you desire such a difficult thing, altering our hearts such that we would ever . . . break such an inviolable code? . . . When [the gods] see that men on earth disrespect them, they send us famines, pestilence, and other disasters, misfortunes, and calamities, discarding us and expelling us, accursed, from their favor, and they would neither speak nor respond to us any longer; the sun, moon, and stars would become angry with us, and would no longer show us their light and clarity. Understand, lord and feared knight of the white and bearded gods, what you attempt; we love you very much, and we beg you not to do this . . . . We consider it a very small thing to put ourselves at your service [in the war against the Mexica], for this is nothing in comparison to what you have asked.[89]

Nonetheless, according to Muñoz Camargo, the lords inform the people of the new ideas, and all of Tlaxcala engages in deep religious introspection. Some argue in favor of the old traditions, while others are inspired by the notion of an omnipotent Creator that required only prayers and water baptisms rather than blood offerings and sacrifices. Still others wonder why the Castilian deity could not merely be added to Tlaxcala's pantheon alongside the others.[90] In the end, however, the Tlaxcalteca nobles stoically reason in favor of baptism and tear down the idols. Much of the population soon follows, celebrating with banquets and festivities. Although some continued to revere their idols in secret, they were soon eradicated entirely. During the pandemic of 1576, some elderly nobles demanded baptism, admitting they had never received it previously, and Tlaxcala became a place of unanimous Christian purity.[91]

Thus did Muñoz Camargo solidify the textual basis for the growing colonial legend of Tlaxcalteca exceptionalism. In his account, Tlaxcala's lords were nothing if not sincere Christian subjects of Spain. Unsurprisingly, toward the end of his chronicle Muñoz Camargo did not fail to retell Motolinia's story of Cristobalito Acxotecatl and the other child-martyrs of Tlaxcala, as these "merited eternal memory."[92] A primary difference between the *Historia de Tlaxcala* and earlier accounts such as

[89] Ibid., 197–99.
[90] Ibid., 202.
[91] Muñoz Camargo, *Historia de Tlaxcala*: 203–05.
[92] Ibid., 244–49, quote from 45.

the *Lienzo de Tlaxcala* or the testimonies of conquest-era natural lords, then, was its retroactive valorization of pre-Hispanic Tlaxcala according to colonial ideals of religious and cultural merit. In Muñoz Camargo's vision, the storied Tlaxcala-Castile alliance was built on more than political convenience. It was inspired and underwritten by the stoic honor of the Tlaxcalteca leadership, who possessed wisdom sufficient to understand the truth once it had been revealed.

The cacique-chroniclers and Torquemada's *Monarquía indiana*

As we have seen, certain Spaniards in the sixteenth century were well acquainted with Anahuac's long history. Some of them – especially those linked to the native nobility, such as the husbands of noblewomen, the friars, and secular administrative officials – were inclined to represent Anahuac as the political (if not cultural) predecessor to New Spain. Yet early creoles more generally – the immediate heirs to the conquerors – remained largely hostile to native history, as their fortunes were founded upon encomiendas, and therefore the notion that their fathers had pacified an evil and savage land. By the late-sixteenth century, however, most encomiendas had escheated, and creole literature entered a new phase. The basic narrative remained the same – the devil reigned in Anahuac, while Cortés led heaven's army on earth – but hints of an emotional identification with Mexico and its history began to complicate simplistic accounts of good and evil.[93]

Importantly, Baltasar Dorantes de Carranza's 1604 defense of the rights of conquerors and their descendants, *Sumaria relación de las cosas de la Nueva España* (*Summary Relation of the Things of New Spain*), was based not only on conquest accounts, but also on Tezozomoc's *Crónica mexicana* and the sympathetic history of fray Diego Durán. This adds a partially incongruent dimension, a half-realized creole sympathy, to what is otherwise a history of good triumphing over evil; specifically, his paean to the conquistadors is spliced with references to Nahua and Mexica history, such that they become the same story. A fragmented sense of continuity thus informs the text, a mentality that aligns, perhaps, with his overt approval of the cacica-conquistador marriages that followed the conquest. Carranza begins in the distant past, and echoes Tezozomoc's account of the Aztec pilgrimage to central Mexico – including

---

[93] Jorge Cañizares-Esguerra highlights these accounts as versions of "the Satanic epic." See Jorge Cañizares-Esguerra, *Puritan Conquistadors: Iberianizing the Atlantic, 1550–1700* (Stanford: Stanford University Press, 2006), 35–53.

the mythic and supernatural elements – as well as the story of Nezahual-pilli's prophecy regarding the ruin of the Mexica empire.[94] While he stresses the "cruelty" and "brutality" of the Aztecs, he betrays fleeting moments of admiration; for example, he hails Tlacaeleltzin, the engineer of Mexica supremacy after 1428, as "another Cid" whose heroics would never be forgotten.[95] He expounds at length upon the "ingenuity" and "skill" of the Indians who cultivated that "mouthwatering" and "precious tree," the cacao.[96] At other points he defends native culture from charges of savagery, pointing out, for example, that while many considered earrings to be ugly and barbaric, some women in Spain also wore them.[97]

Other contemporary accounts not based on indigenous sources likewise betray some measure of affinity for and knowledge of Mexico's ancient heritage, even as they presumed its validity to be a direct result of its conquest by Christian Spaniards. Antonio de Saavedra y Guzmán's *Peregrino indiano* (*American Pilgrim*, 1599) is a poetic paean to Cortés as God's champion against the devil and his Mexica army. Yet the poet allows himself a timid moment of sympathy for the conquered; citing his Mexican origins and apologizing for his insolence, he explicitly declines to dwell, as others had, on the savagery of native religion, offering instead praise for Mexica martial prowess and discipline.[98] Similarly, in his homage to Mexico City, *La grandeza mexicana* (*Mexican Greatness*, 1603), the Spanish transplant Bernardo de Balbuena briefly hails its "fierce" and "barbarous" origins, the eagle atop the cactus, and its impressive rise to become the capital of an empire that "united a thousand crowns into one."[99] In his own historical poem, *Canto intitulado Mercurio* (*A Song Titled Mercury*, 1603), the relocated Spaniard Arias de Villalobos describes an ancient city to the viceroy, beginning not with the arrival of the Spaniards in 1519, but with the foundation of Tenochtitlan in 1325. Indeed, the entire first half of the poem recounts the achievements of the Mexica emperors, and the Spaniards do not appear until the second act.[100]

[94] Dorantes de Carranza, *Sumaria relación*: 18–21.
[95] Ibid., 166.
[96] Ibid., 108–09.
[97] Ibid., 167–68.
[98] Antonio de Saavedra y Guzmán, *El peregrino indiano* (Madrid: Iberoamericana, 2008), 216. I am grateful to David A. Boruchoff for assistance in interpreting this stanza.
[99] Bernardo de Balbuena, *La grandeza mexicana* (Mexico: Editorial Porrúa, 1980), 69–70.
[100] Arias de Villalobos, "Canto intitulado Mercurio," in *México en 1623, por el Bachiller Arias de Villalobos, Documentos inéditos o muy raros para la historia de México*, ed. Genaro García (Mexico: Librería de la Viuda de Ch. Bouret, 1907), 185–280.

Early creole poetry, however, was more allegorical than historical. It was left to a diligent Franciscan friar, Juan de Torquemada (d. 1624), to synthesize the vast store of knowledge produced by the cacique-Franciscan collaborations of earlier generations. Born in Spain but raised in Mexico, Torquemada was the official chronicler of the local Franciscans. While stationed at Tlatelolo, he had privileged access to the many artifacts preserved there. In this sense Torquemada's magisterial *Monarquía indiana* was the culmination of the early cacique-mendicant project, as it narrated Mexican history "according to the accounts of the Indians."[101] In twenty-one dense and detailed volumes, the author recounted the creation of the earth, the earliest human settlements in Mesoamerica, the pilgrimage from Aztlan, the rise of Tenochtitlan, the Spanish conquest, and the establishment of the Church and viceroyalty. In doing so, it was the first work by a non-native author to acknowledge multiple cycles of civilization in central Mexico prior to the fourteenth century.[102] *Monarquía indiana* would remain a primary reference on Mesoamerican history well into the nineteenth century, and it is difficult to overstate its influence on the shape and content of the creoles' emerging patria.

Yet along with an exhaustive list of biblical, classical, and canonical authorities, *Monarquia indiana* relies on the reports of the Nahua and Otomí leadership. Torquemada's work was collaborative from the very beginning. Not only was he deeply familiar with the Franciscans' vast collection of ethnographic materials, but he also maintained personal and intellectual contacts among the contemporary native nobility as a Franciscan, as a speaker of Nahuatl and Otomí, and as an historian of Anahuac. Such contacts, along with others he met while evangelizing in Otomí regions to the north and along the gulf coast, place Torquemada squarely within the elite native realm of the era.[103] Torquemada did not hide his reliance on the information and assistance they provided, especially in the compilation and translation of oral histories and pictorial sources, and elite indigenous historical perspectives are amply represented in his tome. By their inclusion into the colonial-era's most widely cited text on Mesoamerican history, the historical interpretations and emphases of Diego Muñoz Camargo, don Hernando Alvarado

---

[101] See, for example, Torquemada, *Monarquía indiana*: v. 1, 49.
[102] Brading, *The First America*: 273, 79.
[103] Miguel León-Portilla, "Fuentes de la monarquía indiana," in Torquemada, *Monarquía indiana*: v. 7, 97–98.

Tezozomoc, don Fernando de Alva Ixtlilxochitl, and the elite native social caste they represented were transmitted to a broader Hispanic audience. Thus did generations of creoles absorb images of Tlaxcalteca republicanism, Mexica glory, and Tetzcoca refinement.

Torquemada's many contacts among the central Mexican indigenous elite can be documented. He was close to the Tlaxcalteca nobility, including Diego Muñoz Camargo and his son, who married into the Maxixcatzin lineage of Ocotelolco. (It was the latter, declared Torquemada, who convinced him of the previous existence of a race of giants in prehistoric Mexico by describing a skull he had seen in Tlaxcala.)[104] He also claimed to have known, prior to his death, the venerable Tlaxcalteca cacique don Antonio Calmecahua Acxotecatl, renowned for his heroism during the sack of Tenochtitlan, and a relative of the child-martyr Cristobalito Acxotecatl.[105] In echoing the famous tale of the three murdered boys, Torquemada named Tlaxcala the "Bethlehem" of the New World: It was in Tlaxcala where Christianity was first born in America, and it was there where an American Herod had first slaughtered innocents in defense of the old order.[106] Although it is interspersed with lengthy digressions on classical and Christian moral and political philosophy, Torquemada's account tracks Muñoz Camargo's story of the emergence of the Tlaxcalteca confederation through the same series of internal and external conflicts, including the overthrow of Acantetehua.[107] Tlaxcala emerges in Torquemada's account as a freedom-loving republic that stood strong and independent against hostile neighbors who considered them of inferior stock. As for its government, he labeled it "aristocratic" in the Aristotelian sense, a confederation governed by four kings who consulted with the provincial nobility in matters of both peace and war.[108]

Torquemada maintained many links to the guardians of the Mexica legacy as well. Indeed, Torquemada learned Nahuatl from none other than don Antonio Valeriano himself, the esteemed prodigy of Azcapotzalco who had become governor of Tenochtitlan. Torquemada praised don Antonio in the highest terms as a student would a beloved teacher, and remembered keeping him company on his deathbed in 1605.

---

[104] Ibid., v. 1, 54.
[105] See Muñoz Camargo, *Historia de Tlaxcala*: 224; Robert Haskett, "Dying for Conversion: Faith, Obedience, and the Tlaxcalan Boy Martyrs in New Spain," *Colonial Latin American Review* 17, no. 2 (2008), 186–87.
[106] Torquemada, *Monarquía indiana*: v. 5, 156–57.
[107] Ibid., v. 1, 371–75.
[108] Ibid., v. 4, 61.

The dying don Antonio also gave Torquemada several incomplete texts he had been working on in both Latin and Nahuatl.[109] He associated formally, meanwhile, with the cabildo members of Tenochtitlan and Tlatelolco, some of whom were the children and grandchildren of the erudite caciques of the sixteenth century, such as don Antonio Valeriano the Younger, the elder's grandson and likewise governor of Tenochtitlan, as well as don Melchior de Mendoza, the son of don Diego de Mendoza Imauhyantzin and likewise governor of Tlatelolco.[110]

In the 1590s, Torquemada lived with the Franciscan community in Mexico City, which was attached to the Indians' church of San José, where he assisted with religious rites and festivals.[111] After 1604, when he took up residence in Tlatelolco, Torquemada had access to the same historical sources as don Hernando Alvarado Tezozomoc, including the *Tira de la peregrinación* and its alphabetic derivations. He was doubtless familiar with the old cacique himself, as they were both highly prominent and moved in the same circles. His account of the rise of the Mexica, therefore, tracks the traditional origins story closely – although he expresses caution and skepticism with regard to its mythic elements.[112] Elsewhere, Torquemada wrote that "according to the paintings that the most curious of these native Indians possess, and that I at present have in my own possession," the Mexica were inspired to leave Aztlan at the behest of a bird, whose trills were interpreted by priests as a sign. Upon leaving their homes, the devil appeared to them in the form of the idol Huitzilopochtli, and indicated that they were to be his chosen people, and to henceforth call themselves "Mexicans."[113] After long years of wandering – which Torquemada compares to the Israelites in Egypt – the starving and homeless Mexicans arrived into central Mexico, where they were both scorned and feared. Dressed only in leaves and reeds and surviving on a meager diet of aquatic creatures, they witnessed a prodigious sign on an island in the midst of Lake Texcoco: A magnificent eagle, resting atop a nopal cactus growing out of a rocky crag (Figure 5).[114] While Torquemada's tone

---

[109] Ibid., v. 5, 176–77.

[110] Miguel León-Portilla, "Fuentes de la *Monarquía indiana*," in ibid., v. 7, 98; Chimalpahin Cuauhtlehuanitzin, *Codex Chimalpahin*: v. 1, 175.

[111] Chimalpahin records Torquemada's presence at several indigenous religious functions. See Chimalpahin Cuauhtlehuanitzin, *Annals* 69, 73.

[112] Torquemada, *Monarquía indiana*: v. 1, 49.

[113] Ibid., v. 1, 114–15.

[114] Ibid., v. 1, 132.

FIGURE 5 The foundation of Tenochtitlan, from *Codex Tovar*. Courtesy of the John Carter Brown Library at Brown University.

is generally measured and disinterested, he loses composure somewhat in his account of the rise of Tenochtitlan, remarking

I do not think it irrelevant to recall at this point the bustling and very illustrious city of Rome, capital during the time of the Gentile kingdoms and empires and today of all Christendom; and the reason I am moved [to say] this is that it seems to me to resemble the Mexican case in the majority of its aspects. And we can conclude by this similarity that [God] chose this city to be the head of the Church in the New World, just as [He] chose that of Rome for the same purpose in that [world] we call the Old. [God's] victory in this [world] was no less than it was in the other, stealing from [the devil] a city that came to be called the capital of all the realms of these Indies.[115]

However, Torquemada's most detailed accounts pertain to Acolhuacan. Indeed, despite his fondness for the Mexica origins story, Torquemada seems to have regarded his Acolhua sources as more reliable and historical, and less inflected by legend. While he frequently expresses reservations about the semimythic character of the Mexica histories, he addresses the Acolhua sources more or less directly, and comments on their details in much greater length. His chronicle of Anahuac, for example, carries a distinctly Acolhua perspective: The Chichimeca ancestors of the Acolhuaque were the first to populate the area after the fall of the Toltecs, and the early political history of the region is indistinct from the elite Acolhua version of events.[116]

This warmth toward Acolhua history reflects his close relationship with don Fernando de Alva Ixtlilxochitl, the premier Acolhua historian of the era, who assisted him in the compilation and translation of pictorial records.[117] Indeed, both Alva Ixtlilxochitl's *Historia de la nación chichimeca* and Torquemada's *Monarquía indiana* date the beginning of Anahuac's contemporary era to the migration of the Chichimeca chieftain Xolotl and his Acolhua descendants. Most tellingly, Torquemada emphasizes Nezahualcoyotl's place in central Mexican history, devoting many words to his achievements and exploits. Besides representing him as one of the main protagonists and victors of the Tepaneca War, Torquemada echoes the elite Acolhua memory of Tetzcoco's golden age under Nezahualcoyotl, whom he portrays as a leader of great justice and wisdom. Citing "books" that had belonged to the postconquest tlatoani don Antonio Pimentel [Tlahuitoltzin], the son of Nezahualpilli and uncle of

---

[115] Ibid., v. 1, 396.
[116] See ibid., v. 1, 103–05.
[117] Brading, *The First America*: 279–81.

don Hernando Pimentel Nezahualcoyotl, he marvels at Nezahualcoyotl's genius, wealth, and princely virtues.[118] He was such an effective ruler that, through astute policies and governing tactics not a single uprising or riot occurred during his reign – an accomplishment that would have struck someone in the raucous milieu of colonial Mexico City as quite marvelous. "I say," he remarked, "that I have never read, in any of the many histories I have encountered, of any king in the world" who accomplished such a feat.[119] Although he judged the guilty rigorously – punishing sodomy and treason with death – he was dedicated to fairness and justice, and was much given to clemency and forgiveness for those who deserved it. "He was generous toward the poor, the sick, widows, and the elderly," gushed Torquemada, "and many of his rents he distributed to feed and clothe the needy." "There was no father more loving toward his children," he concluded.[120]

The Alva Ixtlilxochitl family was linked by blood to the royal lineages of Acolhuacan, but they were also fully connected to and invested in the erudite Hispanic world.[121] The relationship between Alva Ixtlilxochitl and Torquemada in particular seems to have been one of mutual respect and tutelage, inasmuch as each learned from the other. The former's efforts to compile and narrate the Acolhua historiographical tradition was largely completed by 1608, when he presented the *Compendio histórico* to the native cabildos of Acolhuacan, and Torquemada clearly read and utilized it in his own *Monarquía indiana* of 1615. In turn, Alva Ixtlilxochitl in his later work overtly cited the *Monarquía indiana* and expressed admiration for Torquemada, hailing him as the man who first revealed the secrets of the ancient paintings and songs.[122] It was likely through Torquemada that Alva Ixtlilxochitl acquired, among other Franciscan treasures, the *Codex Chimalpopoca*, which contains the important *Annals of Cuauhtitlan* and the *Legend of the Suns*: The account of the destruction of several prehistoric civilizations in Mexico that both the friar and the cacique reinterpreted according to Noah's Flood. Finally,

---

[118] Torquemada, *Monarquía indiana*: v. 1, 231.

[119] Ibid., v. 1, 234.

[120] Ibid., v. 1, 229–31., quote from 231.

[121] Amber Brian situates both the work of don Fernando as well as his brother, Bartolomé de Alva, in the broader intellectual world of early seventeenth-century Mexico. See Amber Brian, "The Alva Ixtlilxochitl Brothers and the Nahua Intellectual Community," in *Texcoco: Prehispanic and Colonial Perspectives*, eds. Jongsoo Lee and Galen Brokaw (Boulder: University Press of Colorado, 2014).

[122] Alva Ixtlilxochitl, *Obras históricas*: v. 2, 137.

Torquemada and Alva Ixtlilxochitl offer similar accounts of the Tolteca deity Quetzalcoatl as a bearded white man who implemented good customs in Cholula before departing and promising to return.[123]

Conclusion

The *Monarquía indiana* was a cornerstone of historical awareness among Mexico's Spanish-speaking population, the means by which subsequent generations of creoles would learn of the distant history of their adopted land. Yet as the friar himself was the first to admit, his work synthesized over six decades of collaboration and communication between the Franciscans and the natural lords. The cacique-chroniclers who shared their materials and knowledge with Torquemada and his predecessors are far less famous today than he, yet their presence haunts the *Monarquía indiana*, evident not only in the story of its production, but also its content and thematic emphases, especially the Tetzcoca Athens, the imperial destiny of the Mexica, and Tlaxcalteca exceptionalism. Such legends were fundamental to elite native self-representation, sources of pride in an otherwise dark time of disease and dispossession. They permeate Torquemada's synthesis, and would influence the creole perception of Anahuac – and therefore their own patria – for generations to come.

[123] Torquemada, *Monarquía indiana*: v. 1, 351–52.

5

Cacique-hidalgos

Envisioning ancient roots in the mature colony

My party has been and is currently in possession of [the title of] cacique, just as his parents and ancestors manifestly were as descendants of the kings of this realm.... May it serve Your Highness to [receive] information from my party [about their origins and descent, and command] that they be protected and maintained in the ... quasi-possession [of] all the privileges, exemptions, and prerogatives [justly pertaining] to them as caciques.
Probanza of don Alexandro de la Mota, 1744[1]

[Supposedly] there is no immediate application to investigating with curiosity our domestic histories, nor is there to be any reward. [Nonetheless] it seemed desirable to me to serve my affections with news of the kings, emperors, governors, presidents, and viceroys who have governed this Very Noble and Imperial City of Mexico from its foundation to the present time, without relying upon certain [Spanish] authors who merely listed them in order, with perhaps some errors ... To these ends, I consulted some ancient annals of the Mexicans beginning with the year 1402, along with others of their paintings.
Don Carlos de Sigüenza y Góngora, 1680[2]

On July 27, 1621, the people of Mexico City assembled to commemorate the ascension of the new king, Felipe IV. The ceremonies were rich with baroque color and pomp, and the poet-cleric Arias de Villalobos – born in Spain yet a longtime resident of Mexico – was commissioned to

---

[1] Petition and Probanza of don Alexandro de la Mota, Mexico, Feb 6, 1744, AGI-I 239, N.6, ff. 78r-78v.
[2] Carlos de Sigüenza y Góngora, *Noticia chronológica de los gobernantes mexicanos*, Mexico, 1680, LL, n.p.

document the spectacle as well as honor it with verse. As was customary, the participants were organized according to their social rank and political associations. The viceroy and the audiencia led the proceedings, followed by the members of elite institutions such as the Royal University, the Metropolitan Cathedral, and the Mexico City cabildo. Gathering in front of the viceregal palace, they were approached by representatives of the city's many civic, religious, and professional corporations. Amidst the continuous throbbing of trumpets, flutes, and ceremonial firecrackers, each in succession publically declared their allegiance to the new king.[3]

Among their number were seventeen emissaries of the Indian republics of Tenochtitlan and Tlatelolco, led by governors don Antonio Valeriano the Younger and don Melchor de San Martín, who approached the dais and offered gifts of native craftwork and flowered wreaths. Through an interpreter, the two governors proclaimed themselves part of the royal body "as native vassals of these its realms and domains, saying in their mother tongue that... they are and would be in favor of His Majesty, just as their glorious fathers and grandfathers had been."[4] Upon the conclusion of these formalities, fireworks were launched from several canoes on Lake Texcoco. According to Villalobos, "these were a spectacle, as within them [could be seen] the image of King Moctezuma and others of his native caciques, kneeling before a royal lion bearing the arms of the State, in allusion to his new king and lord, the Lion of Spain."[5]

Rich with political and religious symbolism, such theatrics were an important means by which colonial rulers publically asserted and legitimated their own authority. The ritual participation of the native nobility in such spectacles was crucial, as it symbolized the just and benevolent foundations of Spanish rule in Mexico – in this case, by invoking the old story of Moctezuma's donation as well as the imperialist fiction of indigenous "gratitude" for conquest.[6] For caciques, meanwhile, such ceremonies reaffirmed their semiprivileged status as colonial intermediaries and lords of lineage. Yet as we have seen, the notion of voluntary alliance between the crown and the natural lords implicitly presumed and asserted a certain political continuity between Anahuac and New Spain. If Moctezuma had knelt, his realm was integrated intact into Spain's

---

[3] Arias de Villalobos, "Obediencia que México, cabeza de la Nueva España, dio a la majestad del rey don Felipe de Austria....," in García, *México en 1623*, 141–72.

[4] Ibid., 173–74.

[5] Ibid., 174–75.

[6] See Linda A. Curcio-Nagy, *The Great Festivals of Colonial Mexico City: Performing Power and Identity* (Albuquerque, NM: University of New Mexico Press, 2004), 41–58.

composite monarchy, donated and inherited rather than displaced or destroyed. It was a fanciful version of history, but it was essential to the public agendas of Indian and Spanish governors alike. In this sense, both groups conspired to append an Aztec heritage to the Hispanic colony.

This chapter enters the baroque era of genealogical and patriotic myth-making in New Spain. Specifically, it examines how and why native elites and some creoles in the seventeenth and early eighteenth centuries retrofitted New Spain with an indigenous heritage via stories of caciques who allied with the Spanish king. For different reasons, both native lords and their creole contemporaries found it useful to emphasize Indo-Hispanic comity while downplaying memories of bloodshed and exploitation. As the caciques portrayed themselves as loyal participants in Spanish colonialism, creoles felt increasingly comfortable with and attracted to the idea of an Aztec heritage. By 1700, elite urban creoles had constructed a discrete Novohispanic patria atop an indigenous history as they knew it from the caciques. And while they typically embraced an abstract, hermetic, and disindigenized version of Anahuac, some creoles extended their sympathies to the intimate realm of genealogy. In late-colonial Mexico, native and creole elites alike boasted of noble Aztec ancestors.

Cacique blood and the construction of native hidalguía

New Spain reached its demographic nadir in the early seventeenth century, and with it the social and economic condition of the indigenous nobility continued to erode. The era of dynastic cacique-governors was past, many cacicazgos had been carved up and alienated, macehualtin and mestizos had entered the Indian republics, and a substantial portion of the central Mexican elite had married Spaniards, their children belonging to that world. To some outsiders, it seemed that the Indian nobility had disappeared, a perception captured in a 1754 report by the Archbishop of Mexico. Most of the old lineages, he wrote, had intermarried with Spaniards and were "no longer Indians"; the rest, he sniffed, were indistinguishable from commoners, although they were perhaps less likely to go barefoot.[7]

Yet such observations were overwrought, as a hereditary indigenous elite persisted in many regions, and continued to influence the social,

---

[7] Archbishop Manuel José de Rubio y Salinas to Fernando VI, AGI-M 1937, ff. 88–90.

economic, and political life of the colony.[8] Indeed, their social diminishment compelled further rounds of historical self-fashioning, and therefore a renewed emphasis on histories of ancient grandeur and Indo-Hispanic alliance. While few enjoyed the lands, rents, and political authority of their ancestors, they still asserted cacique legal status, and not merely for its psychic income and residual prestige: Among other privileges, caciques remained exempt from royal tributes, a powerful motivator that encouraged otherwise penniless and unpropertied descendants to seek viceregal confirmation and amparo. As both crown tax collectors and the Indian republics derived income from such levies, they often challenged those would-be caciques claiming noble exemptions, leading to a bulky caseload.

Thus cacique genealogy remained relevant into the seventeenth and eighteenth centuries, with preconquest ancestry still the clearest indicator of merit. Savvy petitioners seldom arrived before colonial officials without graphic or textual proofs of pedigree, including notarized concessions of privileges won in earlier generations.[9] Others commissioned official inquiries into local oral traditions, while still others invented noble traditions outright with forgeries and falsifications. Some were successful, though many were not – and still more became mired in the endless process of colonial justice. Indeed, the volume of amparo petitions reveals the disjuncture between what imperial law promised and what noble Indians experienced.[10] Nonetheless, for all its inefficiencies, there was a real expectation of rule of law in New Spain, and subjects continued to pursue legal protections with tales of ancestral greatness.[11]

In some ways, cacique testimonies in the mature colony remained essentially unchanged from their sixteenth-century antecedents, although after generations of postconquest intermarriage their ancestral identities

---

[8] Chance, "Indian Elites in Late Colonial Mesoamerica."

[9] Scholars have documented how indigenous leaders preserved sixteenth-century historical records into the late-colonial era. See, for example, Michel R. Oudijk and María Castañeda de la Paz, "El uso de fuentes históricas en pleitos de tierras: la *Crónica X* y la *Ordenanza de Cuauhtémoc*," *Tlalocan* 16 (2009).

[10] There is a bias in this chapter toward favorable rulings, reflecting the contents of the Tributes catalog at the Archivo General de la Nación in Mexico City. In favorable rulings, several copies were made, with one for the successful petitioner and another dispatched to the relevant provincial magistrate. As a result, many archived items that include the full petition, probaza, and witnesses' testimonies come from favorable rulings. In unfavorable cases, the testimonials (if they exist) remain buried in the scribes' books.

[11] Owensby, *Empire of Law*: 304–07.

grew more elaborate. Such was the case with the important Guzmán Izt-lolinqui lineage of Coyoacan, which for over 200 years fought to main-tain the noble benefices of don Juan de Guzmán (d. 1569), addressed in Chapter 3. Don Juan's various concessions – along with the 1573 tes-tament of his son and heir – were treasured heirlooms. The 1670s and 1680s saw a flurry of genealogical disputation as separate branches of the family jockeyed for the cacicazgo by slurring the others as "usurpers" and "intruders." A memorial of 1678, linked to the great-great-grandson of don Juan, detailed the maternal ancestry of Quauhpopocatzin of Coyoa-can, the Spanish-aligned tlatoani who perished during the conquest. It reported that Quauhpopocatzin descended from both Mexica nobility as well as Tezozomoc (d. 1426), the great leader of imperial Azcapotzalco. They also appropriated Nezahualcoyotl's considerable prestige via doña Mencía de la Cruz, the Tetzcoca wife of don Juan de Guzmán.[12] Thus did the dynastic traditions of Anahuac continue to inflect disputes well into the late-colonial period.

Yet in other ways the rhetoric of pedigree evolved considerably after 1600. This was in part a result of legal ambiguity *vis a vis* the succession rules of cacicazgos: While officially subject to Iberian rules of primogen-iture, other noninheriting descendants who credibly linked themselves to a prominent preconquest or conquest-era lord might claim the "quasi-possession" of tribute exemptions: A privileged tax status that theoret-ically passed, like property, from parents to children. Thus did some native elites adopt a social identity and posture more analogous to the multitudinous hidalgos of Iberia than the old teteuctin of Anahuac. In early modern Spain, wealth and landownership were frequent, but not necessary markers of noble status, and impecunious hidalgos in rural areas could often be seen plowing fields alongside their more vulgar con-temporaries. More important than landed wealth in determining Spanish hidalguía were tax privileges and heraldry, to which even the most hum-ble hidalgos clung tenaciously. Both were also easier to invent than land titles; indeed, Teofilo Ruiz traces families of humble origins who ennobled their lineages simply by assuming aristocratic lifestyles and producing

---

[12] See Succession of the Cacicazgo of Coyoacan, AGN-VM 241, Exp. 5, ff. 1–70. The expediente is marked as number five, but it is actually sixth in the volume. Chimal-pahin confirms this genealogy: Maxtla, one of the sons of Tezozomoc of Azcapotzalco, was installed as ruler of Coyoacan. The 1678 document lists Maxtla as "Meztlazin" and Quauhpopocatzin as "Acapopocatzin." See Chimalpahin Cuauhtlehuanitzin, *Codex Chimalpahin*: v. 1, 128–29; Gibson, "Aztec Aristocracy," 186–88; Horn, *Postconquest Coyoacan: Nahua–Spanish Relations in Central Mexico, 1519–1650*: 48–55.

documents attesting to tax privileges.[13] This characteristically Spanish mode of upward mobility took root in America as well, including among non-Spanish lineages that retrofitted it to their own ancestral and religious particulars in a practice that María Elena Martínez aptly named "genealogical fictions."[14]

Thus, in a departure from Nahua tradition, by the mid seventeenth century many savvy caciques, particularly in the urban milieu of Mexico City, insisted that their noble quality derived from blood alone so as to secure favored tax status.[15] This phenomenon contributed to the emergence of a new social subgroup we might call "cacique-hidalgos": Those who boasted of elite blood and modest privileges, yet who enjoyed few if any patrimonial lands and rents. Such individuals, often the second sons and daughters of caciques, were perhaps indistinguishable from commoners but for their legal exemptions and coats of arms, which they guarded jealously. The proliferation of cacique-hidalgos continued until the 1720s and 1730s, when the centralizing Bourbon monarch reversed the Hapsburgs' general reluctance to meddle in Indian successions and restricted cacique-specific privileges to eldest sons.[16]

This process played out before Spanish officials whenever the children of caciques protested their inclusion on the tribute rolls. For example, in the early seventeenth century don Diego Alonso of Coyoacan – a great-grandson of don Juan de Guzmán Iztlolinqui – relocated to Mexico City. In 1635, he was indignant at finding himself listed as a common tribute-payer and repartimiento (draft) laborer in San Juan Tenochtitlan. He could not be subject to such common obligations, he argued, as the noble rights of caciques were inherent to his person as a descendant of don

---

[13] Teofilo F. Ruiz, "Discourses of Blood and Kinship in Late Medieval and Early Modern Castile," in *Blood and Kinship: Matter for Metaphor from Ancient Rome to the Present*, eds. Christopher H. Johnson, Bernhard Jussen, David Warren Sabean, and Simon Teuscher (New York: Berghahn, 2013), 121. See also Teofilo Ruiz, *Spanish Society, 1400–1600* (Harlow, England: Pearson Education Ltd., 2001), 75–79, 103–05; Elliott, *Imperial Spain, 1469–1716*: 220–24.

[14] María Elena Martínez, *Genealogical Fictions: Limpieza de Sangre, Religion, and Gender in Colonial Mexico* (Stanford: Stanford University Press, 2008), 91–141. See also Nikolaus Böttcher, Bernd Hausberger, and Max S. Hering Torres, eds. *El peso de la sangre: Limpios, mestizos, y nobles en el mundo hispánico* (México: El Colegio de México, 2011).

[15] John Chance argues that nobility was more attached to the noble estate (*teccalli*) than to blood. See John K. Chance, "The Noble House in Colonial Puebla, Mexico: Descent, Inheritance, and the Nahua Tradition," *American Anthropologist* 102, no. 3 (2000).

[16] Gibson, "Aztec Aristocracy," 185–86.

Juan de Guzmán, Quauhpopocatzin, and the ancient rulers of Coyoa-can, even though he maintained few links to its land and tribute base.[17] Don Diego even acquired a statement of support from the cabildo of San Juan Tenochtitlan and its governor, don Pascual Cristóbal, who made the dubious assertion that, while the petitioner had indeed paid tributes in the past, they were voluntary contributions for the common good rather than his due as a commoner. The governor's support is unsur-prising, as it involved not a dispute over land, but an expansive inter-pretation of the rights of indigenous nobles. Significantly, don Pascual termed don Diego a *caballero de privilegio* (a nobleman with privileges); more so than "cacique," this label emphasized rights derived from noble ancestors rather than from an estate or service in the Indian republic. It also implied a presumptive or willful denial of any qualitative difference between Spanish and Mexican noble bloodlines.

Don Diego's efforts succeeded, and his name was stricken from the tribute rolls. But the family was not finished, and sought to confirm that the exemption was truly hereditary. Three years later his son (also named Diego Alonso) resubmitted his father's information in a bid for preemptive amparo, likewise styling himself a caballero de privilegios; he, too, was successful.[18] In this way, father and son leveraged their remote links to a Mesoamerican lineage to reinvent themselves as hidalgos, with privileges derived from blood alone.

The possibility of de-linking cacicazgos from the tax status of caciques held deep implications for native noblewomen, who otherwise stood to inherit little.[19] This is shown by the case of doña Catalina de Alvarado, of one of the most prestigious families in Tetzcoco. The Alvarados descended from the tlatoani don Jorge de Alvarado Yoyontzin (r. 1532–33), whose daughter, doña Juana, married don Alonso Axayacatl Ixhuetzcatocatzin of Iztapalapa.[20] In 1638 doña Catalina, who inherited no lands, requested and received tribute exemptions by reason of lineage alone. Through an interpreter, she requested confirmation of all the legal privileges that "the other caciques of New Spain are accustomed" on account of her "con-siderable quality, merit, and legitimate rights." She supplemented her petition with the familiar declaration of natural lordship: "My parents and grandparents were always afforded the recognition and services of

---

[17] Petition of don Diego Alonso of Coyoacan, Mexico, Mar 30, 1635, AGN-TR 45, Exp. 4, f. 42–43.

[18] Genealogy of Diego Alonso, Mexico, Feb 12, 1638, AGN-TR 45, Exp. 4, 48.

[19] Gibson, "Aztec Aristocracy," 192.

[20] See Figure 4. Chimalpahin Cuauhtlehuanitzin, *Codex Chimalpahin*: v. 1, 166–67.

caciques as descendants and legitimate successors to the kings and natural lords [of Tetzcoco] and its provinces during pagan times."[21] As we will see, the extension of tribute exemptions to cacica women was also important because it incentivized the assumption, though never without controversy, of cacique identities by their mestizo and castizo children and grandchildren, often culturally Hispanic (the Alvas of Teotihuacan being a premier early example of this phenomenon).

Similarly in 1661, don Juan García Bravo de Lagunas, an Andean nobleman resident in Mexico City (labeled *Inga,* or Inca), claimed exemptions on behalf of his wife, doña Agustina Mendoza de los Reyes Moctezuma, the great-granddaughter of don Diego de Mendoza Imauhyantzin, tlatoani of Tlatelolco and ally to Viceroy Mendoza. His wife's family claimed, dubiously, to have descended from both Moctezuma II and Cuauhtemoc, and adorned itself with the gaudy surname of Mendoza Austria y Moctezuma.[22] Don Juan García argued that his wife was entitled to all the noble privileges and exemptions conceded to the Mendozas of Tlatelolco over a century earlier in recognition of don Diego's heroics during the Mixton War. Yet doña Agustina was being denied her rightful privileges because her cousin possessed and was refusing to share the concession of arms and other documents attesting to the family's quality, which included a portrait of don Diego Imauhyantzin himself kneeling before Carlos V. The case involved no land, but merely the quasi-possession of tax exemptions.[23]

The almost talismanic name "Moctezuma" – which Spaniards held in high esteem – continued to pay dividends to those who could claim it. A prominent Nahua family by that name lived in Actopan, northwest of Pachuca. In 1726, a recently widowed cacica named doña María Rosas Moctezuma claimed to be "one of the noblest (*principalísimas*) cacicas of

21　Merits of doña Catalina de Alvarado, Mexico, Dec 7, 1538, AGN-I 11, Exp. 72, f. 56.

22　As María Castañeda de la Paz and others have demonstrated, the Mendoza Austria Moctezuma lineage is shrouded in misinformation, largely due to a series of forgeries, and its true origins are difficult to assess. See Chimalpahin Cuauhtlehuanitzin, *Codex Chimalpahin*: v. 1, 99, 173; María Castañeda de la Paz, "Apropiación de elementos y símbolos de legitimidad entre la nobleza indígena: el caso del cacicazgo tlatelolca," *Anuario de Estudios Americanos* 65, no. 1 (2008), 25–28; Rebeca López Mora, "El cacicazgo de Diego de Mendoza Austria y Moctezuma: Un linaje bajo sospecha," in *El cacicazgo en Nueva España y Filipinas*, eds. Margarita Menegus Bornemann and Rodolfo Aguirre Salvador (México: Universidad Nacional Autónoma de México, Plaza y Valdés, 2005), 219–21. See also PRT, 80, 194, 196, 200; and "Concession of Arms to don Diego de Mendoza Austria Moctezuma, Madrid, Aug 16, 1563, in Fernández de Recas, *Cacicazgos*, 14–15.

23　Petition of don Juan García Bravo de Lagunas Inga, Mexico, Nov 23, 1661, AGN-I 19, Exp. 471, ff. 263v-264v.

this jurisdiction," and took active measures to confirm the privileges of her sons. Producing baptismal certificates and a genealogy, she emphasized her descent from past governors of Actopan's Indian republic and her residence in the local tecpan. The Spanish *fiscal* (legal aide) who examined her case, however, focused almost entirely on her name. "The surname Moctetzuma," he noted, indicated that she and her children belonged among the "first [families] of this jurisdiction," and recommended the confirmation of their exemptions.[24] Tellingly, a Spanish witness and resident of Tula expressed respect for the family by describing them as hidalgos: "They are very gentle (*caballerosos*) and of superior uprightness (*obligación*), as they are descended directly from Emperor Moctezuma" and exuded the same grace as their famous forebear. Such was their noble quality, he continued, that they bore themselves "as if they were white," and their lifestyle and manners were those of "the most hidalgo Spaniard." Believing such things hereditary, he concluded that this was proof of the "royal blood that enlightens them."[25]

In addition to official declarations of royal favors dating to the first postconquest decades, native petitioners also continued to submit – and Spanish officials continued to accept – pictorial and nontextual proofs of merit. This was especially true in cases where litigants sought to establish immemorial or primordial rights. As Elizabeth Hill Boone notes, Spaniards perceived pictorial documents to be "ancient" and therefore somewhat more authoritative, an epistemological approach to Indian justice that encouraged native litigants to continue producing painted manuscripts – many of which they manipulated for the appearance of deterioration and a more archaic aesthetic feel.[26] The histories that derived from such pictorial records differed from those linked to early colonial testimonies pertaining to noble recognition. They were far more likely to include the quasi-mythical flourishes more characteristic of collective memories and oral traditions, and to emerge in the documentary record as misty narratives freely blending realism with supernatural episodes and legendary events.[27]

---

[24] Probanza of doña María Moctezuma, Cacica of San Nicolás de Actopan, Actopan, Jan 11–12, 1726, AGN-TR 33, Exp. 8, ff. 68r–72r.

[25] Testimony of Miguel de Zetina of Tula, Actopan, Jan 5, 1726, AGN-TR 33, Exp. 9, f. 82r.

[26] Elizabeth Hill Boone, *Stories in Red and Black: Pictorial Histories of the Aztecs and Mixtecs* (Austin: University of Texas Press, 2000), 245–49.

[27] Some scholars have employed the neologism "mythistory" to describe colonial accounts, both native and Spanish, that blended historical and mythic elements – for example, by assigning natural locations and dates to supernatural events. See Matthew Restall,

For example, in 1647 no fewer than twelve noblemen from Tenochtitlan and Tetzcoco augmented their demands for tribute exemptions with an elaborate history they described as a Spanish "transcription" of "paintings and characters" commissioned by don Gabriel García of Tetzcoco and attesting to the heroics and nobility of their ancestors. Projecting colonial concepts into the precolonial past, don Gabriel insisted that the purpose of the transcription was to document the "cacicazgos" that his ancestors "and other ancients won in pagan times."[28] Reflecting its oral and pictorial origins, the document's narrative is nonlinear, and portrayed their forebears as victorious rulers who built an empire through bravery and sacrifice. The account is striking inasmuch as it converts fragmented memories of the Tepaneca War and the rise of the Triple Alliance into a humble plea for the favor of the Spanish king. It also betrays no sense of distinction between the pre-Hispanic and colonial eras; the cacique lineages of Tenochtitlan and Tetzcoco stretched, unbroken, into the distant past.

When the nobles [*principales*] of the City of Mexico and the Realm of Texcoco went out to battle and conquer [they went as one] with the primary motive of conquest, and they conquered the majority of the lands of Chichimeca Indians, as is clear and apparent by antiquity and the true traditional paintings from pagan times, the truth of which is evident from the nobility, valor, and quality of the *caballeros* [gentlemen, yet connoting knighthood and horseriding], principales, caciques, and lords who went to occupy [those lands], whose valor is very clear from the native [*natural*] blood of their noble births; some of these warriors came to reign by direct line of inheritance, possessing as they did the rights to the realm of the City of Texcoco and the City of Mexico that later came to be ruled by Moctezuma, the fifth king of Mexico, and Nezahualcoyotl, who was [king] in Texcoco, and Moctezuma was [king] in the year 1086 (sic).

According to the transcription, both the elders and "well-informed youths [*mozos muy entendidos*]" of Tenochtitlan and Tetzcoco remembered that the heirs to Moctezuma and Nezahualcoyotl continued to enjoy the "privileges, lands, cacicazgos, grants, and estates" their ancestors had won as "noble and lofty caballeros and warriors of known property and descent [and] very ancient reputation." An account of several battles followed. Ten captains of Tenochtitlan and Tetzcoco convened a war council and

"Spanish Creation of the Conquest of Mexico," in *Invasion and Transformation: Interdisciplinary Perspectives on the Conquest of Mexico*, eds. Rebecca P. Brienen and Margaret A. Jackson (Boulder, CO: University Press of Colorado, 2008), 94.

[28] Transcription of the Genealogy of Necoametl and Other Ancients, Mexico, Jan 24, 1647, in Fernández de Recas, *Cacicazgos*, 44.

mustered forces to march against an unnamed "enemy" at Culhuacan. They then pursued their foes throughout "New Spain" for four years, reaching as far as the north coast, gaining land and "cacicazgos" along the way. Their victories were not easy, however, as they were fraught with "infinite labors," and they "spent their wealth and their lives in many dangers and risks."[29] In separate testimony from the same proceedings, the nobles of Tenochtitlan supported don Gabriel's transcription and re-clarified their objectives: As the "children and descendants by direct line of the true principales and nobles that King Moctezuma kept in his house and palace," and as the heirs to the war captains of imperial Tenochtitlan, they had always enjoyed "continued and ample concessions [and] liberties." It was only just, they concluded, that these ancient privileges, so nobly won through sacrifice and heroism, be protected and preserved by the Spanish king and his viceroy.[30] Such demands indicate an historical sensibility neither inclined to distinguish between the preconquest and postconquest eras, nor the political regimes governing both.

Services: mythologizing Indian conquistadors

During the expansionist phase of Spanish Mexico, the invaders relied heavily upon native auxiliaries drawn from the central areas. In Guatemala, the Yucatán, and throughout the north and west, the blood and sweat of warriors, porters, cooks, and guides from Tenochtitlan, Tetzcoco, Tlaxcala, and other communities enabled the Spaniards' endeavors. Significantly, many of these native allies remained in the areas they helped to "pacify" and "reduce" to Spanish rule. Enticed by promises of favors such as tribute exemptions and access to land, they agreed to settle among the newly conquered peoples as provincial deputies of colonial administration. Logically, such settlers (and their descendants) distinguished themselves from those they had conquered.[31]

---

[29] Ibid., 44–45.

[30] Testimony of don Fernando de Alvarado, don Alonso de San Francisco, don Andrés de Santa María, and the Principales and Vecinos of Tenochtitlan, Mexico, Jan 24, 1647, in Fernández de Recas, *Cacicazgos*, 45–46.

[31] See Florine Asselbergs, *Conquered Conquistadors: The Lienzo de Quauhquechollan: a Nahua Vision of the Conquest of Guatemala* (University Press of Colorado, 2008); Laura E. Matthew, *Memories of Conquest: Becoming Mexicano in Colonial Guatemala* (Chapel Hill: University of North Carolina Press, 2012); Yanna Yannakakis, "The Indios Conquistadores of Oaxaca's Sierra Norte: From Indian Conquistadors to Local Indians," in *Indian Conquistadors: Indigenous Allies in the Conquest of Mesoamerica,*

Yet due to shifting political winds and the ephemerality of Spanish guarantees, within a few generations the descendants of Indian conquistadors found themselves treated as "Indians" within the colonial caste system. Fearing the dilution and loss of hard-won privileges, they produced new histories, graphic and textual, commemorating their services to the king, with the *Lienzo de Tlaxcala* being the premier early example of the genre. Such accounts stressed the relative merit of Indian conquistadors above other native communities. Indeed, in some cases their authors and artists did not differentiate between themselves and Spaniards; rather, they distinguished themselves and the Spaniards – collectively, the "Christians" – from their common enemies. With more distance from conquest era, however, stories of Indian conquistadors began to accumulate narrative flourishes more characteristic of legends. Rather than detail specific services in the manner of the *Lienzo de Tlaxcala*, memories of services in the mature colony grew increasingly grandiose, idiosyncratic, and laced with mythic elements – compressing centuries, conflating multiple people, and rearticulating history according to highly local and orally transmitted memories.

As we have seen, the Tlaxcalteca and the Otomís of Querétaro were among the most successful at eliciting privileges for conquest-era services, but we encounter similar efforts across New Spain. A particularly rich example comes from the Acolhua region, where local leaders sought to invent cacicazgo rights with a self-aggrandizing account of the conquest. Appearing before Spanish officials in 1617, the governors and cabildos of Axapusco and Tepeyahualco commissioned transcriptions of several documents that they claimed to have inherited, and which seemingly certified their possession of a number of local lands. The first was a 1537 order of Carlos V declaring the caciques of Axapusco and Tepeyahualco exempt from all forms of tributes and taxation in recognition of unspecified services toward the "wellbeing, spread, and utility of the Holy Catholic Faith . . . and the royal crown."[32] The second document, however, which the procurador described as "ancient" and in a state of deterioration, purported to be a grant of Hernando Cortés himself dated 1526, five years after the fall of Tenochtitlan and one year after the death of Coanacoch of

---

eds. Laura E. and Michel R. Oudijk Matthew (Norman, OK: University of Oklahoma Press, 2007).

[32] Royal Order of Carlos V, Zaragoza, Nov 2, 1537, "Real Ejecutoria de los caciques de Axapusco," in García Icazbalceta, *Colección de documentos para la historia de México*, 21–22, quote from 21.

Tetzcoco. In it, Cortés rewarded two caciques, don Estéban López Tlama-panatzin and don Francisco Montezuma Atonaletzin, for their ample ser-vices during the conquest, which he described in sublime detail.[33] The account is a forgery, but it exemplifies the themes and tropes of ideal-ized loyalty that colonial administrators expected from allied caciques.[34] Specifically, such petitioners hoped to derive seventeenth-century favors by crediting their ancestors for the success of the conquistadors. They also, in the manner of the cacique-chroniclers of the era, located prophetic knowledge of Christianity and the Spanish invasion in the pre-Hispanic era.

Purporting to be a first-person relation of Cortés, the document tells that Tlamapanatzin and Atonaletzin arrived to greet the Spaniards only three days after they had landed at Veracruz, as part of the diplomatic con-tingent sent by Moctezuma. Yet the two emissaries had a secret agenda. Despite their own Mexica heritage, they complained, Moctezuma had stolen their wealth, demanded excessive tributes, and eaten many of their children. Besides, they much desired to know and serve the one true God. Pledging themselves to Carlos V, they promised essential assistance against the Mexica; in return, Cortés pledged to support their inherited rights to land and governance.[35]

Over the following months, Tlamapanatzin and Atonaletzin repeatedly demonstrated their value. First, they revealed several painted histories of Tenochtitlan, explaining that in the year 1384 during the reign of Emperor Acamapichtli – somehow citing the Christian calendar – a white, bearded sage dressed like a Catholic priest and carrying a book appeared in central Mexico. In a strange tongue, he exhorted the people to live virtuously and work for peace, and to end human sacrifice and cannibalism. They were also to reject their idols, as the legitimate rulers of Mexico – the "children of the sun" – were drawing near, to govern for the benefit of all.[36] The

---

[33] Grant of Cortés to Tlamapanatzin and Atonaletzin (forgery), Mexico, Dec 16, 1526, in ibid., 4–21.

[34] The nineteenth-century Mexican collectors who first examined the account, Joaquín García Icazbalceta and José Fernando Ramírez, accepted the legitimacy of the document and rationalized its many inconsistencies and anachronisms as both a historical account and as an example of an early colonial land grant. Occam's Razor, however, merely sug-gests a forgery, as Charles Gibson argued. See García Icazbalceta, Introduction to "Real Ejecutoria de los caciques de Axapusco," x-xxiii, and Gibson, "Aztec Aristocracy," 192–93.

[35] Grant of Cortés to Tlamapanatzin and Atonaletzin, 5–7, 18.

[36] Ibid., 11–12.

Spaniards immediately rewarded Tlamapanatzin and Atonaletzin with baptism.

From then on, the pair acted as double agents, supplying Cortés with the crucial inside information that ultimately enabled his victories. While in Tenochtitlan, the two informed Cortés of the attack on the garrison at Veracruz, and assisted with the seizure of Moctezuma. In disarray following their escape from the city, they found critical succor and medicine in Axapusco, where they were allowed to place crosses and saints' images. And finally, the loyal teteuctin provided critical tactical advice: "[Tlamapanatzin and Atonaletzin] advised us not to accept war in the mountains," Cortés supposedly remembered, "but to meet them directly in the plains, so that we could ride the horses."[37] Finally, three days after the surrender of Cuauhtemoc, full of joy, the two lords arrived into Tenochtitlan to congratulate their allies and claim their rewards.[38] Grateful to his two friends, Cortés declared them "legitimate natural lords... and descendants of kings" in perpetuity, and their lands forever exempt from encomiendas, royal tributes, and other forms of taxation.[39]

The account was first transcribed and notarized on March 29, 1617, and descendants of the two caciques resubmitted it in 1694, 1755, and again in 1764. They were unsuccessful; challenged in the mid eighteenth century by local rivals who resisted the audacious invention of a new cacicazgo in community lands, they were sent to prison for the forgery.[40] The entire episode – and the willingness to commit fraud – reveals how valuable a perceived record of services might be.

The mid seventeenth century was also a time of myth-making among the Otomí conquerors of the Bajío, the descendants of the early colonial migrations of Spanish-aligned groups from Xilotepec and Tula (Hidalgo). Among these Otomí auxiliaries were don Fernando de Tapia Connin, his wife's nephew don Nicolás de San Luis Montañez, and don Pedro Martín del Toro; after establishing themselves as local landowners and governors, their children intermarried, helping to preserve their sense of distinction into subsequent generations. Despite Spanish settlement and

---

[37] Ibid., 16.
[38] Ibid., 18.
[39] Ibid., 18–21.
[40] Gibson, "Aztec Aristocracy," 193. Gibson does not clarify whether he believes the forgery dates to the early seventeenth century, as I believe based on the notarized date of the account's first "transcription," or to the eighteenth century, when the fraud was revealed.

the stabilization of the frontier toward 1600, descendants of the original migrants continued to represent themselves as a distinct conqueror elite, invoking ancestral services to emphasize their superiority over other locals. Indeed, because the Otomí caciques were not native to the area – and because their privileges derived entirely from conquest rather than a pre-Hispanic lineage – unlike their central Mexican contemporaries, the Otomí histories say little about the preconquest era. Rather than ancient bloodlines, they emphasized conquest-era victories and their critical role therein. Querétaro had little history, they implied; its prosperity derived from the heroics of its noble Otomí founders.

Francisco Martín de la Puente was the nephew and godson of don Pedro Martín del Toro. He was also related, through marriage, to the heirs of don Fernando de Tapia Connin. Sometime after 1649, he produced a historical text – a mixture of poor Castilian, Otomí and graphic images – that was partially a genealogy and partially a heroic account of his uncle during the "Christian" conquest and pacification of the "barbarous" Chichimecas. Blending history, oral tradition, legend, and wishful thinking, the account followed don Pedro as he migrated into the area and subjugated region after region for the Spanish crown.[41]

In 1520, the account began; a king named "García" reigned in Chapa de Mota, in the province of Xilotepec. García came from an independent dynasty, but his sovereignty came to an end under his son, Águila Real Chica (Spanish: "Royal Eagle the Younger"), who suffered defeat at the hands of "the Great Monarch Moctezuma." Unable to resist, Aguila Real Chica submitted and, at Moctezuma's command, planted an ahuehuete tree to symbolize the new peace. For five generations henceforth, the descendants and relatives of Águila Real Chica – whom the narrator calls "our very ancient grandparents, great-grandparents, governors and lords, fathers, uncles, cousins, and other ancestors" – governed the Otomí of Xilotepec and settled numerous towns in the area. When the Spaniards arrived, the Otomí were already engaged in a series of wars with the Tarascans of Michoacan, yet "these caciques helped the Spaniards in everything [they did], guiding them (*acaudillandolos*)" and assisting in the propagation of the Holy Gospel, assigning saintly patrons to each pueblo. Once victorious, they settled Querétaro, San Miguel el Grande,

---

[41] Wright, *Conquistadores otomíes*, 37. A 1703 court translation and description of the document – which Wright describes as bad – is in Fernández de Recas, *Cacicazgos*, 239–45. The volume also includes six facsimile images of the graphic portions of the original document (unnumbered).

Celaya, Acámbaro, and the other major pueblos of the region, and then "the native inhabitants lived in peace and tranquility, each one enjoying what pertained to him."[42]

Don Pedro Martín del Toro – whom his nephew describes as "brave, [and] who spoke neither Mexican (Nahuatl) nor Castilian well, because he was of the Otomí nation" – was among the migrants from Xilotepec who had "endured infinite labors because of the ruggedness of the land and the hungers that afflicted them."[43] The account tells that after settling in the region alongside his brother and three sisters, don Pedro guided the Spaniards in the "discovery and pacification" of the lands to the northwest, mentioning no fewer than twenty-one "outposts" and pueblos that the cacique and his "army" (*ejército*) helped bring under Spanish control, from San Juan del Río all the way to Zacatecas. The narrator even credited his uncle with the settlement of Guanajuato and the discovery of its rich veins of silver. Once the region had been pacified, don Pedro became a frontier captain for the viceroy, his "valor and effort" "striking fear into the [infidel] Chichimecas" that refused to join the settlements.[44] Soon thereafter, in 1534, don Pedro Martín, don Francisco (sic) de Tapia, and other Otomí leaders founded Querétaro and assisted in the evangelization of the reluctant Chichimecas. They remained indispensable for decades, participating in the later pacifications of Nueva Vizcaya (Durango and Chihuahua) and the northeastern coast.[45]

Similar to those of native conquistadors elsewhere, the graphic component of Francisco Martín de la Puente's account erases the social and ethnic distance between his ancestors and Spaniards.[46] The first folios depict don Pedro Martín del Toro and his forces armed with bows and arrows, fighting alongside the Spaniards armed with arquebuses and swords. Subsequent images indicate victory by depicting don Pedro triumphant over the body of his defeated enemy, and express a sort of honorary Hispanization as he wears Spanish clothing and wields a sword. The glossator explains that "as a sign of gratitude and for the good that he had done the Spaniards gave him some of the weapons they carried and dressed him

---

[42] Transcription of an Account of Francisco Martín de la Puente, Mexico, June 28, 1703, in Fernández de Recas, *Cacicazgos*, 239–40.

[43] Ibid., 245.

[44] Ibid., 241–42.

[45] Ibid., 244–45.

[46] See, for example, Asselbergs, *Conquered Conquistadors*: 208.

in the Spanish fashion, naming him Captain of the Huachichiles (sic), conqueror of the inner lands."[47]

The conquistador identity remained prominent among regional Otomís for generations, long after the ebbing of the old Chichimeca frontier, and continued to play a role in their social and legal agendas. In 1697, don Juan Sánchez, a cacique of Tecozautla east of Querétaro, petitioned for tax exemptions by invoking the memory of the famed Otomí conquerors. His grandfather had been don Cristóbal de la Barcena, mentioned in the Otomí accounts as a companion of don Pedro Martín del Toro and don Nicolás de San Luis Montañez.[48] Referring to him as yet another "captain of the Chichimeca Frontier" and citing "instruments in the Otomí language," his petition detailed the hardships don Cristóbal had endured in service to the viceroys. "In ancient times," recalled one old cacique through an interpreter, "the Chichimeca Indians of the Sierra Gorda were rebelling, and every day they rose up and killed the Indians of this pueblo and burned their houses, and the ancestors of don Juan Sánchez favored the Indians of this pueblo."[49] Another witness told that "the grandfather of don Juan Sánchez, having obtained the position of Captain of the Frontiers of this pueblo and the Sierra Gorda in ancient times, protected this pueblo of Tecosautla [from the Chichimecas] at his personal cost."[50]

In another dispute, from Aculco (south of San Juan del Río) in the 1720s, two brothers, don Juan and don Bacilio García de la Cruz, had successfully removed their names from the tribute rolls by claiming to be the descendants of don Nicolás de San Luis. However, a local cabildo officer protested the ruling and demanded back taxes; the legendary don Nicolás had left no heirs, he argued, and therefore none could claim his legacy. In response, the Garcías produced a treasured family heirloom: an old copy of don Nicolás's 1557 viceregal confirmation as Captain of the Chichimeca Frontier. With the support of several local Spaniards, they

[47] Transcription of an Account of Francisco Martín de la Puente, Mexico, June 28, 1703, in Fernández de Recas, *Cacicazgos*, 243.

[48] In 1554 don Nicolás named his wife as doña Juana Mendosa de Barsena. See Merits and Services of don Nicolás de San Luis Montañez, Xilotepec, Feb 6, 1554, in Valentín Frías, ed. *La conquista de Querétaro* (Querétaro: Escuela de Artes del Señor San José, 1906), 79. See also Transcription of the Account of Francisco Martin del Toro, in Fernández de Recas, *Cacicazgos*, 245.

[49] Testimony of don Vicente Mexcohual y Luna, Xilotepec, Aug 3, 1697, AGN-TR 50, Exp. 2, f. 13.

[50] Testimony of don Nicolás de la Barcena, Xilotepec, Aug 3, 1697, AGN-TR 50, Exp. 2, f. 11.

argued that don Lucas was only disputing their claims because he was personally ill-disposed toward them. They were successful, suggesting that the services of the original Otomí conquerors continued to pay dividends for two centuries.[51] In Chapter 6, we will examine how Querétaro's Franciscans adapted and glorified Otomí memories to promote civic patriotism and their own institutions.

Ancestral appropriation: mestizo and creole "caciques"

In the sixteenth century, many marriages occurred between Spanish men and the daughters of caciques. In some cases, the mestizo and castizo offspring of such unions, often culturally Hispanic, continued to represent themselves as heirs to the noble lineages of Anahuac, the Cano-Moctezumas of Mexico City being a prominent example. By law, mestizos were forbidden to inherit cacicazgos, but the prestige of pedigree derived informally from culture as much as from the law, and could facilitate upward mobility within the increasingly byzantine colonial caste system and its hierarchies. In Mexico, mestizos of noble lineage sometimes cited their Spanish heritage – and "Spanish lifestyles" – in their own favor, as evidence of their superiority over native commoners. Conversely, Hispanic mestizos and castizos with some ancestral link to the Mesoamerican nobility might also cite it as evidence of noble quality, especially after 1697, when (as we will see in Chapter 7) the crown declared caciques equal to hidalgos. In this way, some mestizos, castizos, and even creoles identified, in the most intimate of ways, as the heirs to Anahuac and its noble bloodlines. The creole appropriation of Mexico's antiquity, it seems, was not solely a romantic or intellectual phenomenon; it also occurred genealogically, through blood.[52] That is, some in the late-colonial world belonged fully to the creole realm, yet derived, by way of a distant cacique or cacica ancestor, prestige and identity as descendants of tlatoque and teteuctin. Nonetheless, those whom we might call

---

[51] Don Lucas Magos Barsena y Cornejo v. don Basilio and don Juan García de la Cruz, Xilotepec, Mar 31, 1721, AGN-TR 11, Exp. 8, ff. 72–110.

[52] This pattern existed also in the Andean highlands, where despite a general preference for endogamy and an ideal of "Incaness," over generations noble indigenous families accumulated many social, economic, and genealogical ties to the provincial creole elite. See Garrett, *Shadows of Empire: The Indian Nobility of Cusco, 1750–1825*: 76–86, 100–02; Cahill, "A Liminal Nobility: The Incas in the Middle Ground of Late Colonial Peru."

"castizo-creoles" studiously avoided identifying with Indians in any cultural or ethnic sense. Noble Aztec ancestors might have been prestigious, but indigeneity was not. The distinction was possible only by way of an arcane blend of both genealogical assertion and omission, both remembering and forgetting.

That genealogy sometimes mattered more than culture with respect to cacique privileges is evident from the case of don Hipólito de Alvarado of Mexico City, described by legal aides as a Spanish-speaking tradesman in Spanish attire. In 1660 don Hipólito suffered the indignity of finding his name listed on the tribute rolls. He protested to the audiencia, offering a detailed ancestral account as the basis for his claimed exemptions. Despite his mestizo appearance and Hispanic bearing, he was, he insisted, of noble blood, a direct descendant of "Hatlacaguapan, king of Texcoco during pagan times," and thus "a noble person" who could not be subject to tributes. The audiencia accepted don Hipólito's request, affirmed his status as a noble "cacique Indian," and granted his exemptions.[53]

In some cases, not only were Hispanic ancestors and cultural expressions overlooked, they could count in one's favor. In 1726, a cacique in Actopan – the stepson of doña María Moctezuma mentioned above – sought to have his noble exemptions confirmed and protected. While he could not boast of the same royal blood as his mother and stepsiblings who bore the Moctezuma name, the petitioner cited his maternal grandmother as doña Bernardina de Belasco, who traced her ancestry to none other than Viceroy Luis de Velasco. As such, the petitioner and his family were highly "venerated by everyone in this place."[54] Ironically, his Spanish witnesses cited his Hispanized bearing and lifestyle as proof of his elite ancestry, describing him as one who went about with a sword and dagger "as a symbol of his nobility."[55]

Similarly, in 1740, a group of fourteen brothers and sisters from Chiautla, near Tetzcoco, complained to the audiencia upon finding themselves listed on the tribute rolls. Some of them had even been thrown in

---

[53] Probanza of Hipólito de Alvarado, Mexico, June 16, 1660, in Fernández de Recas, *Cacicazgos*, 41–43. The ancestor cited by both don Hipólito and his witnesses is given, variously, as Hacahuapan, Hatlacaguapan, Hatlacahuapan, Hacaguapan, and Atlacahuapan.

[54] It is unclear whether this refers to the elder Velasco (r. 1550–64) or the younger (r. 1590–95, 1607–11). Probanza of don Juan Daniel de Medina, Actopan, Jan 5, 1726, AGN-TR 33, Exp. 9, ff. 80v, 86.

[55] Testimony of Juan Alfonso de la Cruz, Actopan, Jan 5, 1726, AGN-TR 33, exp. 9, f. 86.

prison for refusing to pay the required back taxes. They should be exempt, they argued, because not only were they descended from noble Indians on their mother's side – she was the daughter of a former governor of Chiautla – but their father was Spanish. This made them doubly exempt, released from common tribute obligations by way of both their maternal and paternal ancestries. The fiscal and the audiencia conceded, striking their names from the lists and ruling that as the "legitimate children of a Spaniard and an Indian held and reputed as caciques" they should enjoy all the rights and privileges pertaining to caciques in general.[56] Later generations, Spanish-speaking mestizos all, continued to reference the 1740 ruling to protect their exemptions as "caciques" as late as 1780.[57]

Of course, those who were sufficiently Hispanized in their appearance, customs, and family connections would never be mistaken for native tribute-payers, and were not required to defend their noble character. Yet some still capitalized on the cachet and prestige of an elite native lineage, particularly in the eighteenth century when caciques and hidalgos were legally equivalent. In 1728, Marcos de Mendoza Valdés Guzmán y Cárcamo, a *vecino* (respected resident) of Mexico City, arrived before the audiencia "in defense of his rights."[58] Mendoza clearly belonged to the Hispanic realm. His *probanza* (legal proof of merits) boasted of noble Iberian roots, and began by delineating and hailing the grand heritage of his many surnames. "The House of Cárcamo" he reported, "is very ancient and of great and renowned quality," and many of its members in Spain were "brave heroes greatly esteemed for their quality, scholarship, virtue, and memorable deeds."[59] Similarly, the Valdés family counted among its own many esteemed royal officials, while the Silvas were honored by their descent from a Portuguese countship. As for the Guzmáns, they were ennobled by "the illustrious blood of the Catholic Kings," and counted as kin not only the infamous conquistador Nuño de Guzmán, but also St. Dominic himself.[60]

Such Iberian origins notwithstanding, don Marcos insisted on styling himself a "cacique principal" before the audiencia, and submitted a second series of documents as proof, including a probanza that his uncle,

[56] Petition and Probanza of don Pedro Ponce de Leon and Consort, Chiautla, Mar 1740, AGN-TR 35, Exp. 10, ff. 307–42.

[57] Ibid., ff. 346–53.

[58] Information of don Marcos de Mendoza Valdés Guzmán y Cárcamo, Mexico, Jan 15, 1728, in Fernández de Recas, *Cacicazgos*, 68–81, quote from 69.

[59] Ibid., 70.

[60] Ibid., 70–72, quote from 72.

Nicolás de Silva López Moya Carreño y Valdés, had produced thirteen years earlier, in 1715. Silva had been a creole tailor of Mexico City who claimed to have descended from the first Spanish conquistadors on his father's side. His mother's background, however, was more complex, and involved several non-Spanish ancestors. To certify her quality, Silva submitted a proof from 1648 in which her brother, Alonso Carreño y Valdéz, received official recognition as "Spanish" despite having a dark complexion (*no obstante ser moreno de rostro*). Meanwhile, Silva's grandmother was Beatríz González de Saravia, described in the 1648 case as a respected Spanish resident (*vecina*) of Mexico City.[61] In his own testimony, Silva referred to this woman as Beatríz Cano González de Saravia y Moya.[62]

The mixed ancestry of the woman Beatríz Cano played an important role in the 1715 probanza, which came attached to what the magistrate described as

a genealogy of cacique Indians, copied from those paintings which, in pagan times, served as instruments for the perpetual remembrance of their deeds, rights, and actions, which their ancestors conserved with verbal explication... [made credible with] song, the accompaniment of *mitotes* (drums)... which was how they commemorated their histories on the days of public festivals. Even today these rituals take place, both because they are accustomed to that ancient style, as well as because of the imprecision from which their language and reasoning suffered in those times due to the lack of writing.[63]

The painted genealogy that the magistrate described traces Beatríz Cano and her family through eleven prominent ancestors to the pre-Hispanic tlatoque of Tenochtitlan. Purporting to be itself the copy of an "original map" dated to "one hundred and forty-five years since the foundation of Mexico," it begins with Chimalpopoca, huei tlatoani in the early fifteenth century, and continues through Emperor Moctezuma and into the colonial period. The genealogy ends with the heirs of a Francisco Cano Yecateuh, depicted as a native conquistador carrying a *macahuitl* (a wooden club with obsidian blades) who had received a coat of arms. His descendant, Beatríz Cano, stands in the bottom-right corner, a white-skinned woman in elegant European dress (Figure 6).[64]

Like the litigants themselves, the map both embraces and distances itself from its own native heritage. It is self-consciously "Aztec" in style,

[61] Information of Alonso Carreño y Valdés, Mexico, Oct 5, 1648, in ibid., 76.
[62] Probanza of Nicolás de Silva Moya Carreño y Valdés, Mexico, Jan 28, 1715, in ibid., 73, 74.
[63] Description of the Painted Map of Nicolás de Silva, Mexico, Mar 15, 1715, in ibid., 77.
[64] Ibid., 78–80.

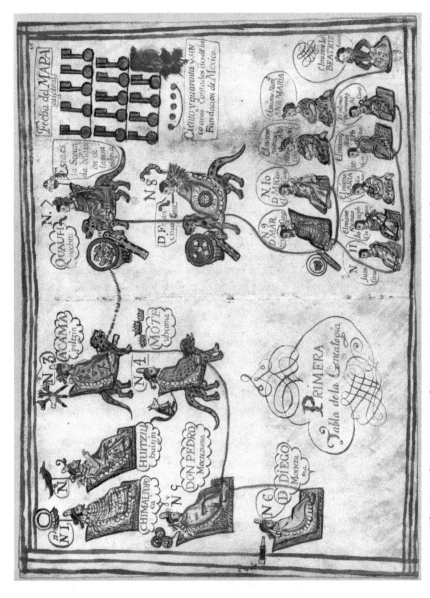

FIGURE 6 The Tenochca ancestry of Beatríz Cano de Saravia, early 18th century. Bibliothèque Nationale de France.

170

as it adorns the indigenous ancestors of the creole tailor with feathered headdresses and identifies them with name glyphs – artistic signals of indigeneity that seem to have convinced the magistrate of the map's authenticity. The various Mexica luminaries sit atop ferocious jaguars, while their Indian and mestizo descendants rest on reed mats. It also dates itself from the year of the foundation of Tenochtitlan, following Mexica tradition. Yet the genealogy was also a fanciful and romanticized representation of history, if not an outright forgery. The chronology of the Mexica tlatoque is confused; Acamapichtli (d. 1395) is listed as the third in the lineage, after both his son and grandson, Huitzilihuitl and Chimalpopoca. While some of the name glyphs are accurate, others bear no clear connection to the historical figures they purport to represent. And although the Spanish gloss records the date of the original document as "one hundred forty-five years since the foundation of Mexico," in the traditional native notation the number actually reads 285 (with each flag representing twenty years, not ten).

Thus, it seems the artist was familiar with Nahua artistic and historical conventions yet not truly of that world, in a sense paralleling the vaguely "indigenous" ancestry of the eighteenth-century castizo-creole Nicolas de Silva.[65] Most strikingly, the map visually denies any cultural or blood links between the petitioners and their supposed native forebears, even as the map revels in a grand Aztec heritage. The genealogy casts each generation with a lighter complexion than the last; while Chimalpopoca and the ancient kings are painted a mild bronze, the Canos are significantly lighter, with a ruddy splotch on each cheek. Beatríz Cano, meanwhile, is completely white, with no hint of color, leaving it ambiguous at what point in time the family ceased to be "Indian" and began to be "Spanish." Her descendants who commissioned the genealogy claimed the noble prestige of a cacique lineage, yet they in no way conceded their social privilege as white creoles descended from Spaniards.

The Cano genealogy was not unique; it belonged to a genre. It and other contemporary examples visually depict the complex ways that some creole elites in late-colonial Mexico strategically understood and represented their own ancestral connections to Anahuac. According to Eduardo Douglas, "from pre-Hispanic Nahua to colonial Indian, from Indian to

[65] Justyna Olko, "Remembering the Ancestors: Native Pictorial Genealogies of Central Mexico and Their Pre-Hispanic Roots," in *Mesoamerican Memory: Enduring Systems of Remembrance*, eds. Amos Megged and Stephanie Wood (Norman, OK: University of Oklahoma Press, 2012), 62–63.

mestizo, and from mestizo to Spaniard," such ancestral reckonings chart "one of many possible narratives of indigenous experience" in New Spain.[66] Despite existing squarely within the Spanish cultural realm, Silva and his nephew called themselves "caciques" and claimed a cacique's heritage to showcase their genealogical quality. In contrast to Alonso Carreño, who in 1648 required legal protections due to his dark skin, just decades later his nephew emphasized a native heritage to demand favor from the viceroyalty.

Spanish blood, Mexican memories: Sigüenza y Góngora and the cacique archive

As scholars of the colonial era are well aware, those with cacica great-grandmothers were not the only creoles in baroque New Spain to adopt Anahuac as their own heritage. For antiquarian and patriotic reasons, an influential handful of creole intellectuals in the late-seventeenth century, with no known native ancestors, labored to collect and disseminate knowledge of Mesoamerican history with an epistemological emphasis on native-authored sources such as painted manuscripts, alphabetic texts, and the oral memories of highborn and elderly Indians. By gathering and investigating such materials, they compiled what Anna More has termed the "creole archive" of New Spain: A collection of physical artifacts its owners understood as the embodiment of Mexico's ancient legacy and proof of its greatness. As masters of the archive, the creoles postured as the authoritative guardians of Mexican history and its secrets.[67]

At the center of this increasingly assertive creole identity was don Carlos de Sigüenza y Góngora (1645–1700), the mathematician, scientist, and poet renowned even today as one of the greatest intellectual figures in Mexican history. As we know, Sigüenza was not the first non-Indian in New Spain to claim Anahuac as his own heritage, nor even to stress the authority of cacique historiography; such notions were ubiquitous in the Franciscan works of the previous century, including Torquemada's *Monarquía indiana*. Yet it was Sigüenza who did the most to popularize

---

[66] Douglas addresses a similarly blended genealogy from 1750s Tetzcoco, and contextualizes it within colonial indigenous art history in general. See Eduardo de Jesús Douglas, "Our Fathers, Our Mothers: Painting an Indian Genealogy in New Spain," in *Contested Visions in the Spanish Colonial World*, ed. Ilona Katzew (Los Angeles: Los Angeles County Museum of Art, 2011), 131.

[67] More, *Baroque Sovereignty*.

the notion that native history – as known through cacique texts – was the forerunner to his and his compatriots' incipient patria. Temperamentally and ideologically, Sigüenza y Góngora aligned with the Jesuits, with whom he trained while young, and among whom he found his most likeminded cohort. The Jesuits were the most consistent advocates of indigenous education, and along with the Franciscans tended to view Anahuac as America's Rome, a worthy and admirable foundation upon which to construct a new Christian society. It is no coincidence that upon his death Sigüenza willed the bulk of his Mesoamerican collection to the Jesuits, nor that later Jesuits embraced him as one of their own, despite his early departure from their company.[68]

Like Torquemada, the Franciscans, and the Jesuits before him, Sigüenza's process of patriotic self-discovery relied heavily upon elite native historical accounts, in this case, those of the Alva (Cortés Ixtlilxochitl) family, the castizo caciques of San Juan Teotihuacan. Sigüenza was a friend and partner of don Diego, don Felipe, and don Juan de Alva, sons of the great Acolhua chronicler and collector don Fernando de Alva Ixtlilxochitl. Don Juan was, like his father and grandfather before him, an interpreter with the Mexico City Audiencia, while Sigüenza owned lands and properties in and around Teotihuacan. In this way he befriended the Alva brothers, and occasionally lent his legal expertise (and political connections) to the maintenance and preservation of their cacicazgo.[69] The relationship was close, such that the Alvas even named Sigüenza executor to their estates.[70] In what is certainly one of the most important and consequential episodes in Mexican intellectual history, don Juan gifted to Sigüenza his late father's entire library, the greatest compilation of native Mexican historical and ethnographical sources then in existence.[71] More than any other event in colonial history, Sigüenza's acquisition of

---

[68] See Francisco Javier Alegre, *Memorias para la historia de la Provincia que tuvo la Compañia de Jesús en Nueva España*, 2 vols. (México: Talleres Tipográficos Modelo, 1940), v. 2, 18–19.

[69] Cacicazgo of Teotihuacan, Apr 27, 1682, AGN-VM 232, Exp. 1, ff. 71–77.

[70] Petition of don Diego de Alva, Teotihuacan, Apr 22, 1682, AGN-VM 232, Exp. 1, f. 4. See also Munch Galindo, "Cacicazgo de San Juan Teotihuacán"; Brading, *The First America*: 366.

[71] Brading, *The First America*: 366; Cañizares-Esguerra, *How to Write*: 221–25; Georges Baudot, "Sentido de la literatura histórica para la transculturación en el México del siglo XVII: Fernando de Alva Ixtlilxóchitl," in *Reflexiones lingüisticas y literarias, vol. II – Literatura*, eds. Rafael Olea Franca and James Valender (México, D.F.: El Colegio de México, 1992); Amber Brian, "The Original Alva Ixtlilxochitl Manuscripts at Cambridge University," *Colonial Latin American Review* 23, no. 1 (2014).

Alva Ixtlilxochitl's materials symbolizes the creole adoption of indigenous Mesoamerica as their own heritage.

As the library was never fully catalogued before it was scattered upon Sigüenza's death in 1700, it is difficult to reconstruct in its entirety.[72] However, it is clear that the collection contained some of the most important artifacts of the sixteenth-century Franciscans, along with others produced by the sons of Nezahualpilli – including the great pictorials of Acolhuacan – and the series of Nahua accounts known today as *Codex Ixtlilxochitl*, not to mention Alva Ixtlilxochil's own unpublished writings.[73] In short, the library embodied the accumulated historiographical efforts of the postconquest natural lords and their immediate descendants, reflecting not only Alva Ixtlilxochitl's own activities as a writer and collector, but also his contemporaries Tezozomoc and Chimalpahin, as well as such sixteenth-century nobles as don Alonso Axayacatl Ixhuetzcatocatzin and the Acolhua nobility. In the 1670s, then, what had theretofore been a rapidly decaying monument to postconquest cacique self-advocacy and historical preservation achieved new life as the core of the creoles' own archive, and a major basis for all subsequent patriotic historiography.[74] Unsurprisingly, the Alva Ixtlilxochitl library looms behind most of Sigüenza's historical musings – and therefore, given his prominence in the erudite colonial world, Mexican creolism itself. While Sigüenza explicitly cautioned against accepting Alva Ixtlilxochitl's exaggerated representation of Anahuac's grandeur uncritically, he seems to have done so primarily to burnish his own authority by signaling a commitment to skepticism and reason.[75] Nonetheless, a defining feature of Sigüenza's many writings is his inclination to perceive cacique sources as epistemologically superior. As Sigüenza wrote in 1684, his renowned insights into ancient Mexico derived "from much communication I have had with the Indians, to find out their [history]."[76]

---

[72] Irving Leonard, *Don Carlos Sigüenza y Góngora, a Mexican Savant of the Seventeenth Century* (Berkeley: University of California Press, 1929), 93–95.

[73] Elías Trabulse, *Los manuscritos perdidos de Sigüenza y Góngora* (México, D.F.: El Colegio de México, 1988).

[74] Josefina Muriel, "La mexicanidad de don Carlos de Sigüenza y Góngora manifiesta en su *Paraíso occidental*," in *Carlos de Sigüenza y Góngora: Homenaje 1700–2000*, ed. Alicia Mayer (Mexico: Universidad Nacional Autónoma de México, 2000), 71.

[75] See Alva Ixtlilxochitl, *Obras históricas:*, v. 1, 168.

[76] Carlos de Sigüenza y Góngora, *Parayso occidental, plantado, y cultivado por la liberal benefica mano de los muy católicos, y poderosos Reyes de España Nuestros Señores en su magnifico Real Convento de Jesús María de México* (Mexico: Juan de Ribero, 1684), f. ixr.

Accordingly, Sigüenza absorbed one of the implicit presumptions of Alva Ixtlilxochitl's cacique archive: That New Spain was the direct successor to Anahuac. He made this perceived link explicit in the famous triumphal arch he designed for the arriving viceroy in 1680, which featured the eleven tlatoque of imperial Tenochtitlan in a "theater of virtues," in which each Mexica emperor exemplified a different aspect of the ideal prince. Itzcoatzin, for example, embodied Prudence, while his successors Moctezuma I and Axayacatzin were models, respectively, of Piety and Fortitude.[77] Sigüenza was explicit regarding his intentions: First, modern Spanish viceroys could and should learn from the pagan rulers of old Tenochtitlan – who, he explained, erred not in the type but only in the object of their religious devotion.[78] Second, and most importantly, the modern viceroys were the direct successors to the old tlatoque. The Spanish conquest was not a complete break with Mexican history, and the colonial entity of New Spain had an indigenous past. With his arch, Sigüenza transformed New Spain from a colonial outpost of the Western world into a discrete American kingdom with a long and storied past, and the viceroy from a Spanish administrator into the latest heir of an ancient American tradition.

Echoing the cacique-Franciscan literature, Sigüenza also drew analogies between imperial Tenochtitlan and the great cities of Greco-Roman antiquity.[79] In a 1684 paean to a crown-sponsored convent in Mexico City, *Western Paradise (Paraíso occidental)*, he insisted that, like Spain, Mexico boasted of an imperial legacy "of no lesser esteem." Citing Alva Ixtlilxochitl, he described the *cihuatlamacazque* ("women-priests"), the priestesses of imperial Tenochtitlan. Glossing over their many important roles within the religious life of the altepetl, including their participation in the rituals of human sacrifice, Sigüenza emphasized their unmarried and secluded status.[80] While their religion was demonic, he wrote, the priestesses nonetheless modeled an exquisite chastity and piety, demonstrating that the ancient Mexicans understood the true nature of feminine virtue, despite their idolatry. Indeed, like their Roman counterparts, the cihuatlamacazque anticipated – and held lessons for – the holy sisters of contemporary Christendom. "The barbarian Mexicans agreed with the ancient Romans," wrote Sigüenza, "that pure virgins were necessary

---

[77] Carlos de Sigüenza y Góngora, *Theatro de virtudes políticas que constituyen a un príncipe* (Mexico: Viuda de Bernardo Calderón, 1680), 66.

[78] Ibid., 62.

[79] See, for example, ibid., 45–48.

[80] On the priestesses, see Kellogg, *Law and the Transformation of Aztec Culture*, 101.

to tend to the eternal flames [in the temples], and because both were inspired by the same impulse... the ceremonies were the same." Quoting Alva Ixtlilxochitl, whom he called "the Cicero of the Mexican language," he recounted some of the prayers offered by the cihuatla-macazque as they tended to the temples; unsurprisingly, the prayers convey the proto-Christian sensibility that Alva Ixtlilxochitl attributed to Anahuac's highborn, as well as invocations of the supreme deity Tloque Nahuaque; "Lord, and invisible God..." began the prayers, "cause of all things...."[81] Sigüenza continued, lamenting the creoles' ignorance of this and other aspects of their own heritage:

If today the repeated example of the Roman vestals inspires the pious souls of our Christian maidens, I do not know why what I have proposed here would not be more effective and profitable; but unfortunately we no longer give it the credit it deserves, as our fame has been losing, as "Mexican" and domestic, that which it deserves everywhere as "European" and "Roman" – as if God had not indiscriminately distributed his kindness to all places within His reach.[82]

Sigüenza's interpretation of how Mexico joined the Hispano-Catholic world also betrays his patriotic reading of cacique sources, and the cacique-creole inclination to blur or ignore the reality of violent conquest. Mexico's pacification and evangelization, he wrote in 1683, was less the result of the sword and more of a "spontaneous" enlightenment, in which "America recognized the perdition of its errors." That they should have done so only confirmed that preconquest Mexico was a place of great civility, with admirable traditions of erudition, scholarship, and the political life. That so many of his Spanish-speaking peers and contemporaries discounted or scorned this "venerable antiquity," Sigüenza lamented, was simply due to their ignorance of indigenous historical sources.[83]

Importantly, Sigüenza also played a role in the proliferation of patriotic memories of the foundation of Querétaro and its Otomí conquerors. In 1680 he traveled to Querétaro to report on the inauguration of a new temple dedicated to the Virgin of Guadalupe. In his account of the festivities, *Glorias de Querétaro* (*Glories of Querétaro*, 1680), he pays homage to don Fernando de Tapia Connin, his conversion, and his selfless heroics on behalf of his Spanish allies. Going further, Sigüenza honors the contemporary descendants of don Fernando and the other Otomí

[81] Sigüenza y Góngora, *Parayso occidental*: ff. 2v–3r.
[82] Ibid., ff. 4v–5r.
[83] Carlos de Sigüenza y Góngora, *Triumpho parthénico que en glorias de María Santíssima immaculadamente concebida, celebró la Pontificia, imperial, y regia Academia Mexicana...* (Mexico: Juan de Ribera, 1683), 4r.

settlers – some of whom were present as participants in the proceedings – as extraordinarily dignified and noble, reflecting their grand heritage. Yet he simultaneously exoticizes their "barbarous grandeur," portraying them as the timeless and unchanging embodiments of a distant antiquity, the stoic specters of another age. Anticipating those who would look askance at this perhaps shocking display of (noble) indigeneity, Sigüenza responded preemptively that it would be absurd for the Otomí lords to dress any other way, as their own noble traditions were sufficiently splendid.[84]

Sigüenza's works are marked by a frustration that his peers were ignoring their own heritage, to the detriment of creole society as a whole. It was the task of every intellectual to hail and transmit the proud achievements of his or her patria, yet in their ignorance Mexico's creoles preferred instead to borrow from others. His own labors were motivated by "the great love" that he had for his patria, and lamented that the full story of "the Mexicans" had yet to be told.[85] Although many considered ancient Mexico a place of barbarism, in reality it boasted of a strong tradition of scholarship, even during the late-imperial decadence of its "venerable antiquity": A native erudition unacknowledged by those "who have not read carefully the Mexican histories."[86] Thus, the feats and the accomplishments of the ancient Mexicans, which could have served to elevate the status of the American Spaniards within the crown, languished in an undeserved obscurity, "marooned on the sea of forgetfulness." How could distant nations learn of Mexico's "heroic greatness" if the "Mexicans" themselves – by which Sigüenza meant contemporary creoles – neglected it? "Enough of this silence!" he demanded.[87] As we will see, his call would be answered, first by his own companions, and then by subsequent generations who came to know the cacique archive by way of his efforts.

Don Carlos de Sigüenza y Góngora was the most famous and influential creole intellectual of his era, but he was not alone in his adoption of the caciques' vision that portrayed New Spain as the direct political successor to Anahuac. His patriotic identification with preconquest Mexico was an integral theme within a more general baroque cultural and literary movement among educated, urban, wealthy creoles. Sigüenza inherited this sentiment from others, but partially by his efforts it reached its fullest

---

[84] Carlos de Sigüenza y Góngora, *Glorias de Querétaro* (Querétaro: Ediciones Cimatario, 1945), 51.
[85] Sigüenza y Góngora, *Parayso occidental*: ixr.
[86] Sigüenza y Góngora, *Triumpho parthénico*: 4r.
[87] Ibid., 5r.

expression in the final decades of the seventeenth century and the first decades of the eighteenth. He shared his cacique treasures with contemporary Jesuits, Franciscans, secular clergy, viceregal officials, and other minds such as the nun of letters sor Juana Inés de la Cruz, in such locales as Mexico, Puebla, and Querétaro. By the 1680s, Sigüenza's associates throughout New Spain were invoking, elaborating upon, and disseminating many of the most spectacular and romantic motifs of the emerging creole vision: The notion that America had a Christian or proto-Christian history prior to 1519, that Tenochtitlan was America's Rome, and that New Spain was less the product of conquest than of a triumphant alliance between Castile and the natural lords, a partnership inspired by a shared love for king and Church. With baroque bombast and exuberance, the creole intelligentsia at the turn of the eighteenth century answered Sigüenza's call and began to construct a prestigious antiquity for their patria with the building blocks of the cacique-creole archive, one that equaled Spain's own heritage while also ennobling the creoles as its guardians and heirs.

A creolized cacique: don Manuel de los Santos y Salazar of Tlaxcala

Don Manuel de los Santos y Salazar (d. 1715) was the son of don Bernabé de Salazar of Quiahuiztlan, one of the four primary districts of the complex altepetl of Tlaxcala. Don Bernabé – by family tradition a descendant of don Bartolomé Citlalpopoca, one of the four ruling tlatoque who had first accepted baptism and allied with Cortés during the conquest – had been the governor of Tlaxcala from 1660 to 1661, and belonged to a cohort of Tlaxcalteca leaders, centered around the cabildo, who recorded Tlaxcalteca history as a means of promoting its civic tradition and integrity. Yet don Manuel's life and career went beyond the patrician culture of his father's generation, as in 1675 he entered the Franciscan community in nearby Puebla. Although health problems forced the early termination of his novitiate, the aspiring cacique-cleric eventually came to the attention of the energetic Bishop of Puebla, Manuel Fernández de Santa Cruz (r. 1677–99), who favored the education and preparation of caciques as exemplary Indians. With the bishop's guidance and patronage, in 1685 don Manuel received ordination, and spent the next three decades administering the sacraments in a number of Tlaxcalteca parishes.[88]

---

[88] For the story of don Manuel's formation and his relationship with Bishop Fernández, see Peter B. Villella, "Indian Lords, Hispanic Gentlemen: The Salazars of Colonial Tlaxcala," *The Americas* 69, no. 1 (2012).

During his years of study, don Manuel traveled throughout central Mexico, establishing ties in Puebla, Mexico City, and Xilotepec (where he had gone to learn Otomí, the most common indigenous language in Tlaxcala after Nahuatl). Circumstantial – yet ample – evidence places the cacique-priest among the influential creole intellectual circles centered around don Carlos de Sigüenza y Góngora in the early 1680s. His patron, Bishop Fernández, associated with both Sigüenza and (notoriously) sor Juana Inéz de la Cruz.[89] He was at the Royal University in Mexico City in 1680, where he would have witnessed, or at least known about, Sigüenza's triumphal arch honoring the virtues of imperial Tenochtitlan. He studied Otomí under the eminent linguist, Lic. Francisco de Aédo y Peña (1638–1731), one of the highest-ranking men of letters in contemporary Mexico City.[90] He was well-read in creole historiography, up to and including his own contemporaries, and lent his voice to characteristically creole concerns, such as the perennial debate over the "origins" of America's native peoples. For example, he admired the "very wise" Franciscan fray Agustín de Vetancurt (1620–1700), Sigüenza's collaborator, whose 1698 *Teatro mexicano* (*Mexican Theater*) was a grand expression of the creoles' longing to be recognized as a distinct patria with its own heroes and traditions.[91]

Don Manuel, therefore, was simultaneously a Tlaxcalteca patriot, a cacique of lineage, and an erudite priest with ties to the leading creole intellectuals of his time. He was a noble Indian educated and active in the elite creole realm at the very moment it was becoming self-aware and beginning to assert its distinctiveness and worth. Holistically, don Manuel's writings illustrate the thematic parallels and emotional resonances between the cacique and creole brands of patriotism. Despite working and interacting within the Hispanic professional realm, he continued to articulate, in various formats, the traditional cacique

---

[89] Sigüenza praises Bishop Fernández in *Glorias de Querétaro*, 26. The bishop, meanwhile, is most famous today for his public criticism of sor Juana under the pseudonym "Sor Filotea." See Juana Inés de la Cruz, *The Answer / La Respuesta*, trans. Electa Arenal and Amanda Powell (New York: The Feminist Press, 1994).

[90] Aédo y Peña was a secular priest and chaplain to the Hieronymites of San Lorenzo in Mexico City; he spoke Hebrew, Greek, Arabic, Nahuatl, and Otomí. From 1710 to his death in 1731, he held the chair in Otomí at the Royal University, and trained aspiring priests for service in Otomí-speaking parishes. See Bachiller of Manuel de los Santos y Salazar, Mexico City, May 7, 1684, Salazar Family Papers, f. 3; and *Gazeta de México* 44, in Nicolás de León, ed. *Bibliografía mexicana del siglo XVIII* (México: J.I. Guerrero, 1902–08), pt. 2, sec. 1, 261.

[91] Santos y Salazar, *Computo cronológico*, 228. See also Brading, *The First America*: 373–75.

legitimating narrative, synthesizing primordial rights, loyalty, and ortho-doxy into a seamless historical self-representation. In his person, the patri-otic Tlaxcalteca republicanism of his father's generation aligned neatly with the creole project to identify and glorify the native and American roots of colonial culture. Indeed, the only substantial difference between don Manuel's work and that of the creoles with whom he associated was where they directed their patriotic sentiment. Whereas the creole patriots pointed to the glories of Mexican antiquity in the broadest sense, don Manuel (like his father) focused on Tlaxcala's unique merit within the crown.

Although don Manuel suffered from chronic ailments and creeping blindness, he was dedicated to preserving and proclaiming Tlaxcala's proud republican history, and his own family's illustrious lineage. He and his father were friends and associates with the former Tlaxcalteca governor don Juan Buenaventura Zapata y Mendoza, author of the most important and comprehensive seventeenth-century account of Tlaxcalteca history, the Nahuatl *Historia cronológica de la muy noble y leal ciudad de Tlaxcala* (*Chronological History of the Very Noble and Loyal City of Tlaxcala*). After Zapata's death in 1689, his son turned the manuscript over to don Manuel, who continued to elaborate upon it for at least another fourteen years, illustrating it with glyphs and adding information and glosses that betray a bias in favor of his own lineage in Tlaxcalteca history. He was moderately cosmopolitan, as evidenced by his role in the production of contemporaneous Nahuatl annals from both Tlaxcala as well as the Tlaxcalteca community in nearby Puebla (Tlaxcalapan).[92] Finally, he investigated his own noble roots, tracing them back through multiple generations of caciques from Quiahuiztlan to don Hernando de Salazar (Tececepotzin), a governor of Tlaxcala in 1563–64, as well as tlatoani Citlalpopoca himself.[93]

Don Manuel de los Santos also mirrored the antiquarian spirit of don Carlos de Sigüenza, and spent many hours collecting and compil-ing ancient Tlaxcalteca history – an endeavor, he wrote, animated by

[92] Camilla Townsend, "Don Juan Buenaventura Zapata y Mendoza and the Notion of a Nahua Identity," in *The Conquest All Over Again: Nahuas and Zapotecs Thinking, Writing, and Painting Spanish Colonialism*, ed. Susan Schroeder (Portland, OR: Sussex Academic Press, 2011), 21–26.

[93] Salazar Genealogy, Mexico City, 1735, Salazar Family Papers, LC, f. 74r; Juan Bue-naventura Zapata y Mendoza, *Historia cronológica de la noble ciudad de Tlaxcala*, trans. Luis Reyes García and Andrea Martínez Baracs (Tlaxcala: Universidad Autónoma de Tlaxcala, 1995), 128.

his "great fondness for [his native soil]."[94] He collected, updated, and corrected a Tlaxcalteca calendar wheel originally produced in 1554 by the Franciscan Francisco de las Navas and the native governor don Antonio de Guevara.[95] Finally, sometime after 1711 he authored a history of central Mexico titled *Computo chronológico de los indios mexicanos* (*Chronological Account of the Mexican Indians*), which largely recreates and expands upon a similar account by Sigüenza, now lost, titled *Ciclografía mexicana*. In it, don Manuel reviewed, somewhat critically, twelve distinct opinions that European and creole authors had offered regarding the origins of the Indians, and tenuously endorsed the theory that they were, in fact, the descendants of refugees from biblical Ophir – which he imagined to be in Asia – who had, in different waves, fled the tyrannies of Alexander the Great and other notorious conquerors of the ancient world.[96] This he follows with accounts of the major ethnic-ancestral groups of Anahuac based largely on Torquemada's readings of Alva Ixtlilxochitl, the Acolhua painted histories, and the *Tira de la peregrinación*.[97] Thus, the *Computo cronológico* represents the intellectual labor of a Nahua cacique who received, adapted, and re-transmitted a quintessential creole project: illuminating the origins of the Indians and the ancient indigenous prehistory of New Spain by way of the texts, paintings, and "hieroglyphs" of earlier generations of caciques.[98] Yet despite his foray into creole history – which revolved around New Spain as a whole – he remained primarily dedicated to Tlaxcala, as indicated by glosses highlighting Tlaxcalteca history and genealogy.[99]

Importantly, don Manuel did not perceive, or chose not to acknowledge, any distinction between his Tlaxcalteca background and his participation in the colonial regime and its Church. Like many Nahua annals, the *Computo* makes no overt reference to the conquest, thereby representing local history as an unbroken story stretching from the year 1186 to his own time.[100] Most symbolically, in 1707 don Manuel cited his descent

---

94 Santos y Salazar, *Computo cronológico*, 226.
95 Masae Sugawara, "Boturini y los manuscritos históricos sobre Tlaxcala," in *La escritura pictográfica en Tlaxcala*, ed. Luís Reyes García (Tlaxcala: Universidad Nacional Autónoma de Tlaxcala, 1993), 219–21, 28. Georges Baudot discusses this calendar and transcribes its description by Las Navas; see Baudot, *Utopia and History in Mexico*, 476, 86–90.
96 Santos y Salazar, *Computo cronológico*, 227–29
97 Ibid., 230–35.
98 Ibid., 229.
99 Ibid., 237–38, 243.
100 Ibid., 236–43.

from the leaders of preconquest Tlaxcala in support of his request for promotion into a better parish.[101]

> I am the legitimate son of don Bernabé Antonio de Salazar and doña Phelipa Ysavel de Flores his legitimate wife, well-known nobles (*cavalleros*) of the distinguished, noble, and loyal city of Tlaxcala in the *cabecera* and district of Quiahuiztlan, proceeding by paternal line from don Bartholomé Citlalpopocatzin, one of the four kings and lords of said city, and by maternal line of Quapiotzin, also king and lord of said cabecera long before receiving the Holy Catholic Faith, grandfather of the valiant Tlahuicole, captain of the Tlaxcalan armies, whose descendants, after having voluntarily received and given obedience to the Crown of Castile, were [all of them] always honored with honorific offices in the cabildo and Republic, exercising them with all fidelity, all of them Old Christians and clean of every bad race, generation, and mix, and therefore always reputed and held [as such].[102]

This erased, in a rather spectacular way, any sense of historical rupture by conquest. The descendants of Tlaxcala's pre-Hispanic leaders were uniquely qualified, by blood, to serve in exclusive positions in the Hispanic Church. It was assertion by omission: There simply was no division of consequence between Tlaxcala and Spain, such that Tlaxcala's ancient heroes could be counted among the worthies of the Hispano-Catholic world. Don Manuel expressed this synthetic genealogical identity graphically, in a family tree later copied and elaborated upon by his nephew (addressed in Chapter 7). In tracing his roots directly to don Bartolomé Citlalpopoca, don Manuel allowed only a single distinction between his pre-Hispanic and postconquest ancestors: The former wore feathers in their hair (Figure 7).

Don Manuel de los Santos interacted with the influential generation of creole intellectuals active in Mexico City at the end of the seventeenth century. He studied with them, read their works, and incorporated them into his own. In doing so, however, he influenced the content of creole patriotism in later generations. In the late 1730s, while serving as lieutenant to the Spanish magistrate in Tlaxcala, the Italian aristocrat and devotee of the Virgin of Guadalupe, Lorenzo Boturini Benaduci (1702–53) learned of the late don Manuel by name, and collected the cacique-priest's most important works of Tlaxcalteca history – the *Historia cronológica* of don

---

[101] Diego Muñoz Camargo tells the story of Tlahuicole (1497–1518), a fierce young war captain captured and sacrificed in Tlaxcala's wars against Tenochtitlan. See Muñoz Camargo, *Historia de Tlaxcala*: 125–28.

[102] Merits of Manuel de los Santos y Salazar, Cuapiaxtla, 1707, Salazar Family Papers, f. 47r.

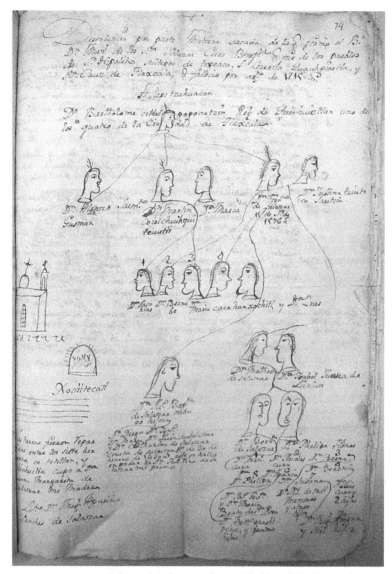

FIGURE 7 Salazar family genealogy, Library of Congress

Juan Zapata y Mendoza, the other Tlaxcala-Puebla annals, the *Computo cronológico*, and the Las Navas-Guevara calendar wheel.[103] Over

[103] Lorenzo Boturini Benaduci, *Catálogo del museo histórico indiano* (Madrid: Juan de Zúñiga, 1746), 31–32, 59, 62, 78.

the following decade, Boturini incorporated these items into his famous "Indian Museum," the most important single collection of items relating to Mesoamerican and indigenous Novohispanic history ever before assembled. The Tlaxcalteca materials of don Manuel – along with the work of Diego Muñoz Camargo – made a special impression on Boturini; "the exploits [of Tlaxcala] in the time of its gentility," he later wrote, "and even more in the conuest, deserve to be written in letters of gold."[104]

Boturini was more responsible than even Sigüenza in disseminating knowledge of Tlaxcala's unique historical identity. Boturini's disciple and collaborator, the well-connected creole gentleman Mariano Fernández Echeverría y Veytia, utilized the Tlaxcalteca collection of don Manuel de los Santos, and reproduced don Manuel's calendar wheel in his own study of Mesoamerican calendrics.[105] In 1770, the Archbishop of Mexico, Francisco de Lorenzana, utilized the remnants of the Boturini collection to write a new history of New Spain and its conquest; the volume opened with an altered version of the calendar wheel by the Tlaxcalteca cacique and priest.[106] In 1778, the Spanish priest and creole sympathizer José Joaquín de Granados y Gálvez referred to the Tlaxcalteca materials and echoed don Manuel in describing the altepetl as "so valiant, courageous, spirited, proud, and bold, that no empire was ever able to defeat them."[107] The Spanish military engineer and antiquarian Diego García Panes (1730–1811) – who spent decades surveying the land of New Spain – cited don Manuel by name as one of his primary sources on Mexican history.[108] Unsurprisingly, he lavished praise on Tlaxcala in particular, and closely echoed don Manuel's account of Tlaxcalteca exceptionalism: republican virtues, conquest-era heroics, Christian purity. Tlaxcala, explained Panes in 1789, was as renowned for its "glorious actions during the conquest" as it was "for the valor and constancy of its [ancient] inhabitants, who never fell subject to any other pagan realm." And although the contemporary

---

[104] Lorenzo Boturini Benaduci, *Idea de una nueva historia de la América Septentrional* (Madrid: Juan de Zúñiga, 1746), 150. See also Cuadriello, *Glories*: 236–43.

[105] Mariano Fernández Echeverría y Veytia, *Los calendarios mexicanos* (Mexico: Museo Nacional, 1907), plate 5.

[106] Francisco Antonio Lorenzana, *Historia de Nueva-España, escrito por su esclarecido conquistador Hernán Cortés* (México: Joseph Antonio de Hogal, 1770), 2.

[107] José Joaquín Granados y Gálvez, *Tardes americanas: Gobierno gentil y católico: Breve y particular noticia de toda la historia indiana: Sucesos, casos notables, y cosas ignoradas, desde la entrada de la Gran Nación Tolteca a esta tierra de Anáhuac, hasta los presentes tiempos, trabajadas por un indio y un español* (México, D.F.: Porrúa, 1987), 229, 37.

[108] Diego García Panes, *La conquista: selección de láminas y textos de los tomos V y VI del Teatro de Nueva España* (Mexico: San Ángel Ediciones, 1976), 22.

pueblo was but a shade of its former splendor, he admired how "its loyal residents carefully preserve[d] the royal and exceptional privileges" symbolizing the undying gratitude of the Spanish monarchs.[109]

Don Manuel, his family, and his creole fellow travelers fused neo-Aztec and Hispano-Catholic imagery into one patriotic Indo-Christian vision, perceiving or admitting no significant distinction between Tlaxcala's native lineages and Spanish colonialism.[110] This gave Tlaxcalteca history significance within – rather than in addition to – the history of New Spain. Both don Manuel and the creoles attributed an imperial (rather than local) significance to the traditional symbols of Tlaxcalteca patriotism, insinuating Tlaxcalteca icons into the broader Hispanic pantheon. Tlahuicole, Maxixcatzin, and the other heroes of ancient Tlaxcala, they implied, ennobled the Hispanic tradition alongside Hadrian, El Cid, and St. Dominic. Along with creoles such as Sigüenza, don Manuel worked to erase the distinction between the elite indigenous and creole worlds, aligning not only their contemporary identities, but also their pasts.

Conclusion

The diverse cacique petitions explored in this chapter bespeak the survival and continued influence of neo-Aztec identities into the mature colonial era, among native lineages as well as among their mestizo and creole descendants. As the Indian elite Hispanized – whether by adopting Spanish language and customs or through intermarriage and mestizaje – their memories of preconquest grandeur and conquest-era services percolated into a new realm, one dominated by the American Spaniards. This process took place historiographically – particularly with regard to the Alva Ixtlilxochitl-Sigüenza library – but it also reflected genealogical trends that had resulted in a castizo-creole gentry that was culturally Hispanic but that would, if framed properly, acknowledge and even celebrate ancestral links to Aztec Mexico. Fragmented memories and social decline propelled the sense that a great forgetting had occurred; those who most closely identified with Mexican history in a proprietary sense stepped into the vacuum, and filled it with triumphant tales of Indian–Spanish

---

[109] "Solicitud del teniente coronel D. Diego Panes, sobre que el Consulado le ayude con la cantidad que guste para el fenicimiento de la útil obra que ha escrito ... año de 1789," in Manuel Carrera Stampa, "El *Teatro de Nueva España en su gentilismo y conquista*, Diego Panes," *Boletín del Archivo General de la Nación* XVI, no. 3 (1945).

[110] Cuadriello, *Glories*: 86–93.

cooperation and mutuality. Sigüenza y Góngora did not invent Mexican creolism; he captured an already widespread sentiment in words.

Yet while the emerging creole imaginary hailed elite indigenous ancestors, it did not embrace indigeneity itself. Creoles envisioned a continuity between Anahuac and New Spain – between the old native nobility and the new creole elite – that was political, genealogical, and even religious, but somehow not also cultural, social, ethnic, or racial. In 1700 Juan Ignacio Castoreña y Ursúa (1668–1733), an acquaintance of Sigüenza who shared his patriotic vision, argued that the great creole houses were forever "ennobled" by having descended from the unions of conquistadors and native noblewomen in the aftermath of the conquest; he extended no such admiration to his mestizo contemporaries. Sigüenza himself modeled the creoles' tendency to encapsulate their admiration for Mesoamerican civilization, and disallow it to bridge the misty abyss of centuries to touch the present day. Anahuac held many edifying lessons for contemporary Christians – the solemn piety of Moctezuma Ilhuicamina and the dutiful chastity of the cihuatlamacazque – but contemporary Indians, he wrote, were "the most troublesome lot that God ever greated," a drunken rabble "without sense or reason."[111] It was left to future generations, both native and non-native, to debate precisely what had gone wrong in the intervening centuries.

[111] Carlos de Sigüenza y Góngora, *Alboroto y motín de México del 8 de Junio de 1692*, ed. Irving A. Leonard (Mexico: Museo Nacional de Arqueología, Historia, y Etnografía, 1932), 54.

6

Cacique-patrons

Mexicanizing the church

[My party] is a cacique and principal, son, grandson, and descendant by both lines of caciques and principales [and] of a known house and estate of which his ancestors have been since pagan times in immemorial possession; and all of them after this realm received the Holy Doctrine have professed and profess our Catholic religion as Old Christians without race or stain of idolatry, superstition, Judaism, sophism, or heresy.... [And] they and my party have assisted Your Majesty with special services, in the collection of royal tributes, governance, and education of the Indians, and [have contributed] to the divine cult many significant services; and [having thereby] qualified himself, [may it please Your Majesty] to qualify his legitimate children....

Probanza of don Pedro Ramírez Vázquez of Tequixquiac, 1699[1]

[Heaven], in distributing its favors, takes no notice of one's lowly and scorned condition, but of the virtues that amount to the nobility of the soul.... Because to reveal your arcane secrets, [Lord], you do not honor the great, but rather the humble..... especially in this realm, wherein the most famous and glorious apparitions of your Blessed Mother... occurred to three Indians, who among the many nations of this realm are considered to be of the lowest condition.

Francisco de Florencia, 1692[2]

If one strain of baroque-era myth-making involved asserting political and genealogical continuities between New Spain and the native

---

[1] Probanza of don Pedro Ramírez Vázquez of Tequixquiac, Mexico, Oct 31, 1699, AGN-I 34, Exp. 126, f. 129v.

[2] Francisco de Florencia, *Narración de la maravillosa aparición que hizo el arcángel San Miguel a Diego Lázaro de San Francisco*, 2 vols. (Sevilla: Tomás López de Haro, 1692). v. 2, 80.

civilizations that preceded it, another concerned religion, namely, the desire to attribute Mexican roots to the colonial Church. This was an even more complicated endeavor, as native religious practices had long been scorned as demonic in Spanish and creole accounts. Those who desired to root Novohispanic Catholicism in the Mexican tradition, then, emphasized stories of rebirth and transformation, in which the stain of idolatry and devil-worship was utterly erased. Accounts of Indian conquistadors and eager baptism helped, but early modern Hispanic theology considered religious error to be an innate, inherited quality – expressed, most famously, in the Iberian doctrine of "blood purity" (*limpieza de sangre*). "New Christians" remained tarnished by their ancestors' infidelity; only direct divine intervention could erase such profound stains, cleanse Indians of the residue of idolatry, and thereby redeem the Mexican legacy. This was simultaneously continuity and rupture: Anahuac could be an acceptable heritage for New Spain, but only after it had been retroactively purified with stories of heavenly endorsement.

This chapter explores prominent episodes in which both native leaders and creole patriots in the seventeenth- and early eighteenth centuries remembered native believers as active patrons and founders of Mexican Christianity. The religious politics of cacique self-fashioning intersected frequently with Mexican creolism in the baroque era; for distinct but related reasons, both groups confronted contemporary anti-indigenous conceits and responded with detailed, and sometimes fantastic, accounts of native religious devotion. Preempting suspicions of religious insincerity, caciques invariably included evidence of their own and their ancestors' piety in their probanzas and petitions. Their accounts included memories of baptism and the construction of churches, but also more spectacular tales of Indian evangelizers, holy warriors, and miraculous conversions. Creoles, meanwhile, disseminated stories of Indo-Christian heroes, and authenticated them via references to native testimonies and texts – in essence, attributing native roots to the Mexican Church. In some cases, native leaders assisted creole clergy in the promotion of local cults. At the deepest level, such endeavors imagined the Church as an organic and providential outgrowth of ancient Mexican history rather than the fruit of conquest and coercive indoctrination. Echoing the ladino caciques of previous generations, Mexican Christianity, they implied, derived less from conquest than from grace and enlightenment.

Church patronage as a cacique social strategy

As we have seen, explicit assertions of piety were central to cacique strategies in the sixteenth century, and they remained so into the mature colonial period. One important mode of cacique signaling was church patronage – donations of money and gifts to local parishes, religious communities, and lay brotherhoods. In the early modern Hispanic world, church patronage was as much a social practice as a religious one. It was a direct assertion of honor, as prominent and respected families were expected to distinguish themselves through gifts and services to the parish. The resulting prestige was expressed in such visible ways as conspicuous family burials beneath important locations in the church.[3] Such concerns were adopted in America by native leaders who felt likewise obligated to nurture local religious life. Prominent caciques adopted the practice early, most visibly in wills and testaments, as they leveraged their worldly wealth to provide for their souls in the afterlife as well as assert their dedication to the Church.[4] And as Caterina Pizzigoni's research into Nahuatl testaments has demonstrated, pious donations – often expressed as a *noblesse oblige* for the welfare of local commoners – remained an important way for dying caciques to signal their elite status into the mature colonial era. While the clergymen responsible for preparing believers for death always encouraged – and probably required – donations, the excessive amounts that distinguish the testaments of dying caciques are significant, as are their paternalistic attitudes toward commoners, whom they frequently referred to as their "children."[5] Cacicas were no more or less likely than men to patronize the Church, both in life and in their wills.[6]

---

[3] Teofilo Ruiz, *From Heaven to Earth: The Reordering of Castillian Society, 1150–1350* (Princeton: Princeton University Press, 2004), 44–47.

[4] The cacique-governors of the sixteenth century were quite generous in their testaments, establishing chantries and lavishing local churches with gifts. See, for example, the Testament and Chantry of don Alonso Axayacatl of Coyoacan, Coyoacan, 1581, AGN-BN 185, Exp. 90; Testament of don Antonio Cortés Totoquihuaztli of Tlacopan, Tlacopan, Apr 29, 1574, in PRT, 373–78; and the Testament of don Francisco Verdugo Quetzalmamalitzin-Huetzin of Teotihuacan, Teotihuacan, Apr 11, 1563, in Alva Ixtlilxochitl, *Obras históricas*: v. 2, 281–86.

[5] Caterina Pizzigoni, ed. *Testaments of Toluca* (Stanford: Stanford University Press, 2007), 14–18.

[6] Richard Conway, for example, details the many pious donations of women in the Cerón y Alvarado family of Xochimilco, which included the sponsorship of chantries, chapels, and confraternities. Richard Conway, "Nahuas and Spaniards in the Socioeconomic History of Xochimilco, New Spain, 1550–1725" (Ph.D. diss., Tulane University, 2009), 55–56.

The colonial Church encouraged the establishment of chantries (*capellanías de misas*) – endowments providing for regular masses to be sung on behalf of the soul of the founder – as they were a major source of revenue for the clergy.[7] For moneyed Indians no less than Spaniards, chantries were a popular mode of church patronage; they promised to reduce time in purgatory, they were a highly visible and prestigious means of expressing *noblesse oblige*, and crucially, they afforded donors a religiously meritorious means to preserve resources within the family and community. A prominent early example was the chantry of don Alonso Axayacatl Ixhuetzcatocatzin, the educated son of Cuitlahua and sometime governor of Iztapalapa and Tetzcoco who died in 1583. Don Alonso bound parts of his cacicazgo to a chantry in his home parish of San Lucas Iztapalapa, naming Francisco de Loya, his Nahuatl-speaking Spanish friend and confessor, as the first chaplain.[8] By the seventeenth century, it was increasingly common for caciques, both women and men, to establish chantries, as unlike other forms of patronage they did not require vast amounts of liquid capital. They typically ranged from modest to very modest, between 1,000 and 3,000 pesos of principal, yielding approximately 50–150 pesos (5 percent) annually in chaplain fees.[9] The Mexican Church was indeed built, to a large degree, upon native wealth.

In some cases, church patronage become part of a more overt agenda of upward mobility, something local elites might cite in support of claims to immediate privileges. A rich example comes from Tequixquiac, north of Mexico City. In 1699, the Otomí cacique don Pedro Ramírez Vázquez submitted a probanza to support his petition for noble exemptions, constructing much of his case upon his family's long tradition of pious generosity in a sort of transgenerational religious scorecard. His paternal grandfather, for example, had repaired the roof of the parish church at his own cost, "purchasing *vigas* (roof beams) and panels from Papotla

---

[7] On the spiritual and financial objectives of chantires, see Asunción Lavrín, "The Role of Nunneries in the Economy of New Spain in the Eighteenth Century," *Hispanic American Historical Review* 46, no. 4 (1966), 376–77; Ruiz, *Heaven to Earth*: 44–57; Gisela Von Wobeser, *Vida eterna y preocupaciones terrenales: las capellanías de misas en la Nueva España, 1700–1821* (Mexico: Universidad Nacional Autónoma de México, 1999).

[8] Chantry of don Alonso Axayaca in San Lucas Iztapalapa, Mexico, Mar 4, 1583, AGN-BN 185, Exp. 90bis.

[9] See, for example, Chantry of don Diego de San Francisco of Tlacopan, Mexico, 1633, AGN-BN 934, exp. 5; Chantry of 3,000 Pesos of doña Catarina de Guzmán y Moctezuma of Piastla, Mexico, 1649, AGN-BN 1819, Exp. 4; Chantry of 2,000 Pesos of doña Ana Rodríguez of Tlaxcala, Mexico, 1634, AGN-BN 1826, Exp. 5; and Chantry of 1,000 Pesos of doña Juana Petronila of Tlayacapa, Mexico, 1650, AGN-BN 1300, Exp. 3.

(DF) because there was none nearby." He had also founded a confraternity dedicated to the Immaculate Conception, donating, upon his death, no fewer than forty sheep and seven rams to support the distribution of alms. Don Pedro then listed his own donations and labors. He had "perfected the work that his grandfather began," finishing the roof of the church and baptistery, and hiring a craftsman to lift the organ to the choir. He also donated a large silver cross (214 silver pesos) to replace a wooden one that had deteriorated. He raised money to beautify an altar to the Virgin of Guadalupe, and purchased candles for festival days. Don Pedro patronized the Confraternity of the Holy Sacrament, and helped fund the entire Corpus Christi celebration of his grandfather's Confraternity of the Immaculate Conception. Finally, the civic-minded cacique contributed 106 pesos toward an urn of gilded wood and glass for the church crypt. In all, he estimated that he had given 475 pesos and 220 sheep, "all out of his own fortune, without burdening the commoners with inconveniences, taxes, or other interventions." This did not include the many funds that his personal efforts helped raise from the community.[10] Importantly, in its favorable ruling, the audiencia cited the services of both don Pedro and his grandfather as proof of the family's substantial quality.[11]

Another way that native elites insisted on religious merit was historical – by remembering ancestors who had actively contributed to the founding of the Church. In the second half of the seventeenth century, the colonial population began growing after over a century of decline, leading to increased conflicts over lands and resources. To resolve this issue as well as profit from it, the crown instituted a new round of land titling, the *composiciones de tierra*, which compelled localities to pay retitling fees to document ownership over their own lands. In many cases, native communities sought to reassert control over ancestral lands that had gone uncultivated, and attached historical accounts to their titles, falsely archaized, describing the original boundaries of community lands. These documents, commonly called "primordial titles" *(títulos primordiales)*, proliferated at the turn of the eighteenth century, and reflect both oral memories as well as contemporary concerns. As the titles' primary purpose was to secure communal lands before colonial officials, they invoke familiar themes – in particular, the notion that conquest-era caciques had eagerly embraced the gospel and facilitated its spread.

---

[10] Probanza of don Pedro Ramírez Vázquez of Tequixquiac, Mexico, Oct 31, 1699, AGN-I 34, Exp. 126, ff. 131–22.
[11] Ibid., 168.

Robert Haskett and Stephanie Wood, among others, have researched the primordial titles extensively.[12] They are diverse and eclectic, but Haskett notes that a recurring theme is eager Christianization, as their authors commemorate local church construction and evangelization; "veneration," he writes, "[is depicted as] their own idea, proof of their primordial piety and, by extension, their legitimacy."[13] (Other titles, it should be mentioned, are indifferent or even hostile toward the new faith.)[14] Thus did the titles retroactively validate their authors according to Hispanic criteria of religious merit in service to a contemporary agenda. The narrators of a title from Santa Marta Xocotepetlalpan (Distrito Federal), for example, remembered that when the friars arrived into their pueblo, the caciques gathered together and "said, 'let us thank God that He has arrived now to make us Christians,' and they fell to their knees and with longing and tears in their eyes promised before God to live quietly and pacifically in these parts; this happened in the year 1555."[15] Similarly, an eighteenth-century Spanish translation of a Nahuatl title from Los Reyes Acaquilpan (Mexico) records that, according to "the elders, our fathers, our grandfathers, our women," there had been much violence among the pueblos, but the people finally "went before God and they wept and desiring and crying out before God they stopped [fighting?] and settled down and became Christians; [it was] the year 1555."[16] The similarities between these examples, from communities only several miles apart, suggest that they shared the same author or authors.

Once again, the Otomís of Querétaro offer compelling examples of native leaders adept at navigating the imperatives of colonial rule, in this case religious self-advocacy. In the mid seventeenth century, the

---

[12] New research into the primordial titles is expanding. See Stephanie Wood, "The Social vs. Legal Context of Nahuatl *Títulos*," in *Native Traditions in the Postconquest World*, eds. Elizabeth Hill Boone and Tom Cummins (Washington DC: Dumbarton Oaks, 1998); Wood, *Transcending Conquest*; Haskett, *Visions of Paradise*: 250–96; Florescano, *Historia de las historias*: 207–66; Megged, *Social Memory in Ancient and Colonial Mesoamerica*: 76–80. See also Lockhart, *The Nahuas*, 410–18.

[13] Haskett, *Visions of Paradise*: 262.

[14] See, for example, "Título primordial de San Lorenzo Chiamilpa, Morelos," in Paula López Caballero, *Los títulos primordiales del centro de México* (México, D.F.: Consejo Nacional para la Cultura y Las Artes, 2003), 145–47. See also the Title of Santo Tomás Ajusco, which stands out for its negative portrayal of the events of the conquest; "Título primordial de Santo Tomás Ajusco," in ibid., 192–95. Stephanie Wood discusses the Ajusco title in Wood, *Transcending Conquest*: 60–76.

[15] "Título primordial de Santa Marta Xocotepetlalpan," in López Caballero, *Títulos primordiales*: 241–42.

[16] "Título primordial de Los Reyes," in ibid., 311.

descendants of the original conquerors established numerous chantries, including don Baltasar Martín, an Otomí governor and relative of Pedro Martín del Toro and Francisco Martín de la Fuente, whom we met in chapter 5. The chantries were modest, but they bespeak an ongoing relationship between the Otomí nobles and local Franciscans, who remained the primary stewards of local spirituality.[17] The Otomí caciques thus actively supported the Franciscans with their donations and gifts at a critical moment in Querétaro's development, in the years immediately prior to its 1655 elevation to the status of city. As part of the legal proceedings establishing the chantries, the caciques were required to state the precise nature and origins of their nobility, which included references to their ancestral successes over the "barbarous" peoples who originally inhabited the area. Thus, even as Querétaro acquired a Spanish-speaking majority, its religious leaders absorbed the memories of its Otomí conquistadors.[18] This relationship, as we will see, contributed greatly to one of the most enduring patriotic legends of subsequent generations: that of the miraculous stone cross of Querétaro.

No other Otomí lineage outdid the Tapias, however, with regard to church patronage. As we saw in Chapter 3, Querétaro's geographic relation of 1580 hailed don Fernando de Tapia Connin as a generous church benefactor whose efforts secured the local success of the gospel. After his death, his five children inherited his empire as well as the presumed noble obligation to nurture the moral and religious life of their pueblo. In this way they established an intimate relationship with the local Franciscans, thus helping to anchor their evangelical activities in the Bajío. This pattern was repeated elsewhere; in the Tapias' case, however, it also resulted in a unique episode in Novohispanic history: An elite cloistered community – and emblem of creole pride – founded directly upon an indigenous patrimony.

As the frontier lawlessness that so profited don Fernando de Tapia gradually subsided toward 1590, don Fernando's children could not rely on the same cycle of conquests-and-rewards that had built the family fortune. The overall distribution of new land grants in the region peaked in 1591, when peace was secured with numerous unconquered groups

---

[17] See Chantry of don Baltasar Martín and doña Magdalena of Querétaro, Mexico, 1638, AGN-BN 1452, Exp. 13; and Chantry of don Domingo Martín and doña María García of Querétaro, Mexico, 1641, AGN-BN 1454, Exp. 19.

[18] See Memorias de México, "Colegio de San Fernando agregado a la Provincia del Santo Evangelio," UCB M-M 240, ff. 114–16.

and the Tlaxcalteca settlers ventured forth to populate the north.[19] Without a frontier, allied cacique-warriors like don Fernando were less indispensable; indeed, after receiving two parcels of land in 1577, the Tapias acquired no further substantial grants.[20] Political stability also challenged the Tapias' dominance in other, more subtle ways. As the fighting subsided and commerce increased, Spaniards, Africans, and mestizos began to arrive in Querétaro in greater numbers, bringing with them Hispanic culture and institutions, and in 1578 Querétaro – previously subject to the sprawling jurisdiction of Xilotepec – acquired its own crown magistrate.[21]

Yet the Tapias endured through shrewd politics, marriage alliances, and business savvy.[22] Don Fernando's fortune was divided between five children, Catalina, Magdalena, Beatríz, María, and Diego – all of whom secured favorable marriages with caciques from across the Bajío and beyond, indicating the breadth and extent of elite Indian networks even as late as 1600. Doña Beatríz married don Francisco de León, the son of another Otomí conquistador in Acámbaro; as his widow, she acquired extensive lands to the south and west of Querétaro (more on these lands later).[23] Doña Catalina married a cacique from Taximaroa, to the south, named don Gaspar de Salazar.[24] Uniquely, doña Magdalena married a non-Otomí, don Pedro Huitzméngari, of the royal Tarascan line of Michoacan.[25] Finally, doña María's husband, don Miguel Davalos, from the Tapias' ancestral home in Xilotepec, was a sometime governor of Querétaro.[26] Don Diego, the only son, became the native governor of

---

[19] Prem, "Spanish Colonization and Indian Property in Colonial Mexico, 1521–1620," 448–49.

[20] Inventory of the Papers of don Diego de Tapia, Querétaro, Jan 12, 1615, AGI-ECJ 199A, f. 250.

[21] María Eugenia García Ugarte, *Breve historia de Querétaro* (Mexico: Fondo de Cultura Económica, 1999), 76–77; Cruz Rangel, *Chichimecas*, 79; Gerhard, *Guide to Historical Geography*, 224.

[22] Super, *La vida en Querétaro*: 179.

[23] Titles and Acts of Possession of don Cristóbal de León of Acámbaro, Apaseo, Nov 15, 1562, AGI-ECJ 200B, Pza. 36, ff. 1017–52.

[24] Cacicazgo and Estate of don Diego de Tapia, Querétaro, Dec 15, 1603, in Wright, *Querétaro en el siglo XVI*, 322–23.

[25] López Sarrelangue, *Pátzcuaro*: 169–228.

[26] Testament of doña María de Tapia, Querétaro, Aug 3, 1601, in *Documentos inéditos para la historia de Querétaro*, vol. 3 (Querétaro: Gobierno del Estado de Querétaro, 1984), 145. The Tapias maintained relations with the Otomís of Xilotepec. Indeed, José Antonio Cruz Rangel has traced the conquest activities of don Fernando de Tapia Connin as far south as his old home (much to his compatriots' frustration); see Cruz Rangel, *Chichimecas*: 76–92. Even as late as 1663, local officials mentioned "doña Clara de Tapia, a cacica Indian from the province of Jilotepeque," as the closest living heir of

Querétaro in 1581, and married twice to local Otomí noblewomen (both named doña María). Once widowed, the sisters doña Beatríz and doña María in particular continued to build wealth through astute land deals, and the former willed most of her estate to her brother upon her death in 1602.[27] When don Diego died in 1614, he was the wealthiest person in Querétaro.

The detailed 1602 testament of doña Beatríz de Tapia provides a rich and intimate window into the religious and social sympathies of this elite Otomí family. She made forty-six separate pious donations, ranging from very small (such as candle wax and cloth) to very large. Most prominently, besides routine gifts to the local Franciscans, the civic-minded doña Beatríz left assets and explicit instructions for the establishment of several local charitable institutions, including a new hospital "where they care for Indians and Spaniards" in the hills west of Querétaro.[28] "For the discharge of her conscience . . . and for the souls of the native Indians [of Querétaro], alive and deceased, for whom she was in charge," she also funded a chantry dedicated to an indigenous confraternity based in the chapel of San José de los Naturales, in the local Franciscan church. The inhabitants of the land supporting the chantry, meanwhile, were to "live as they have lived, cultivating the lands for their livelihood, and none of it shall be taken away for any reason, nor shall they pay *terrasgos* [rents]." The land was not to be sold, and the inhabitants were to be exempt from all forms of personal service to Spaniards (but not to the Otomí nobility). Acting preemptively to prevent Spanish intervention in the confraternity, she stipulated that its patrons were to be exclusively Indians.[29] Don Diego

[27] Testament of doña Beatríz de Tapia, Querétaro, May 14, 1602, AGI-ECJ 199B, R. 15, ff. 1–15.

[28] Testament of doña Beatríz de Tapia, f. 7. The farm was called "Petehé," which also means "hot water" or "aguacaliente" in Otomí, referring to the village of San Bartolomé Aguacaliente, west of Querétaro and beside the lands doña Beatríz inherited from her late husband. The hospital was never built, as don Diego de Tapia never followed through with his sister's wishes, and the lands intended to support the hospital were simply packaged into the estate of the convent of Santa Clara de Querétaro. This eventually occasioned a dispute over a century later, when the Charitable Order of Saint Hipolytus Martyr challenged the convent's right to the land based on doña Beatríz's will. See Order of St. Hipolytus, *Por la sagrada provincia de la Caridad de San Hipolyto Martyr de esta Nueva España* . . . (México: Joseph Bernardo de Hogal, 1724); and Phelipe Fuertes, *Por el Real Convento de Religiosas de Santa Clara de Jesús de la Ciudad de Querétaro en el pleito con la Provincia de San Hypólito* . . . (México: Herederos de la Viuda de Miguel de Rivera, 1725).

[29] Testament of doña Beatríz de Tapia, ff. 10–12.

and doña María de Tapia, her surviving brother and sister, were named executors.

The Tapias' most spectacular act of piety, however, occurred four years later, when don Diego bundled valuable lands he inherited from his deceased sisters doña Beatríz and doña Magdalena – with an estimated value of 50,000 pesos – to establish a Franciscan convent in Querétaro dedicated to Santa Clara; his sister doña María, meanwhile, donated its first buildings.[30] Don Diego's daughter with his second wife, the Otomí noblewoman doña María García, was doña Luisa del Espíritu Santo. Already a novice at the convent of San Juan de la Penitencia in Mexico City, doña Luisa became a founding member of the new cloister, and along with two other novices and nine black-veiled nuns arrived in April 1607 to populate the new community.[31] She later served as abbess between 1649 and 1652.[32]

With the vast Tapia fortune supporting it, the convent eventually became one of the wealthiest and most prestigious cloisters in Querétaro; as a creole visitor reported in 1734, the convent was "enriched by the plentiful rents of its territories and ample community."[33] Ironically, although its founders were local Otomís, viceregal authorities imposed antinative strictures from the very beginning, and after doña Luisa no other indigenous woman would ever join the community. While don Diego and doña Luisa, as founders, initially reserved the right to choose who would succeed them as the institution's patrons, the Viceroy Marqués de Montesclaros preferred that "for the better conservation and authority of the convent," following the deaths of don Diego and doña Luisa "it was

[30] License for the Convent of Santa Clara de Querétaro, Mexico, Mar 11, 1604, AGI-ECJ 200B, R. 37, f. 3; Donation of doña María de Tapia to the Convent of Santa Clara de Querétaro, Querétaro, Jan 15, 1605, AGI-ECJ 199B, R.8, ff. 145–48. An overview of the convent's early years is in Guillerma Ramírez Montes, *Niñas, doncellas, vírgenes eternas: Santa Clara de Querétaro (1607–1864)* (México: Universidad Nacional Autónoma de México, 2005), 49–87.

[31] Joseph Gómez, *Vida de la venerable madre Antonia de San Jacinta, monja profesa de velo negro, y hija de el Real y Religiosíssima Convento de Santa Clara de Jesús en la Ciudad de Querétaro* (México: Imprenta de Antuerpia de los Herederos de la Viuda de Bernardo Calderón, 1689), n.p.

[32] Ramírez Montes, *Niñas, doncellas, vírgenes eternas*: 79.

[33] Francisco Antonio Navarrete, *Relación peregrina de la agua corriente que para beber y vivir goza la muy noble, leal, y florida ciudad de Santiago de Querétaro* (Mexico: José Bernardo de Hogal, 1739), 14. See also Asunción Lavrín, "El convento de Santa Clara de Querétaro: La administración de sus propiedades en el siglo XVII," *Historia mexicana* 25, no. 1 (1975); Ellen Gunnarsdóttir, "The Convent of Santa Clara, The Elite and Social Change in Eighteenth-Century Querétaro," *Journal of Latin American Studies* 33, no. 2 (2001); Ramírez Montes, *Niñas, doncellas, vírgenes eternas*.

just that Indians not be called to be patrons, but rather lay Spaniards of the requisite quality." He thus "advised" don Diego and doña Luisa to concede responsibility for the convent to the king upon their deaths.[34] The Tapias acquiesced, reserving for themselves only the right to name and maintain one of two novices in the convent; however, these women were, by explicit stipulation, to be "chaste" and "virtuous" – and Spanish.[35]

Don Diego de Tapia died in 1614.[36] Doña Luisa del Espíritu Santo, who had gone deaf in her old age, died in 1663. She was buried in the church sanctuary, beneath a portrait of her father, the still-revered cacique who founded the community.[37] She was also the only documented native woman to enter the conventual life in New Spain before the eighteenth century.[38] This fact upset contemporary indigenous elites, who saw it as evidence of the unjust denial of their merit as lords and nobles. Later generations resented the Spanish usurpation of an institution built upon the pious generosity of a native lineage. According to two eighteenth-century caciques from Mexico City, the injustice was notorious, and had caused "considerable sadness for the Indian nation."[39]

Ironically, by rerouting native wealth to colonial and Church authorities – such as the viceroy, who ensured the purely Hispanic character of Santa Clara de Querétaro – cacique piety may have obstructed the development within Mexican Catholicism of a more overtly indigenous element, as it reinforced the perceived distance between the formally approved Church of the Hispanic upper classes and the tapestry of local folk practices often scorned as "superstitions" or reviled as "idolatry."[40] Nonetheless, the pious activities of the Tapias and other native elites in the mature colony illustrate that Spaniards did not monopolize Christian piety in New Spain, and that native leaders aspiring to hidalguía

---

34 Donation of don Diego and doña Luisa de Tapia, Querétaro, Dec 29, 1605, AGI-EJC 199B, R. 8, ff. 158–62.

35 Don Diego de Tapia, Proposal for the Convent of Santa Clara de Querétaro, Querétaro, Dec 29, 1604, AGI-ECJ 199B, R. 8, ff. 123–24.

36 Estate of don Diego and doña Beatríz de Tapia of Querétaro, Mexico, 1614, AGN-BN 299, Exp. 7.

37 Burial of doña Luisa del Espíritu Santo, Querétaro, Sep 23, 1663, AGI-ECJ 199B, R. 8, ff. 97–98.

38 Díaz, *Indigenous Writings from the Convent*: 34–35.

39 Representation of don Diego de Torres Vázquez Quapoltoche and don Simón de Palma to the Mexico City Audiencia, Mexico City, Feb 19, 1744, AGI-M 685, f. 14.

40 For recent studies of popular religion in colonial Mexico, see William Taylor, *Shrines and Miraculous Images: Religious Life in Mexico Before the Reforma* (Albuquerque: University of New Mexico Press, 2010); and *Local Religion in Colonial Mexico*, ed. Martin Austin Nesvig (Albuquerque: University of New Mexico Press, 2006).

were also responsible for the immense wealth and strength of the colonial Mexican Church. The practice also allowed caciques to cast themselves as co-architects of the orthodox spiritual world of New Spain. Like their Spanish counterparts, caciques cited church patronage as both an expression and an assertion of their noble status, something families emphasized as evidence of their social merit.

Jesuit education and native Christians

For different reasons, others in colonial society similarly represented native believers – and especially their leaders – as core members of the Church. As part of their overall defense of colonial culture, an influential handful of creole educators, authors, and religious historians challenged widespread suspicions regarding the persistence of native idolatry by hailing Indians who had made substantial contributions to Mexican Christianity, whether by actively sponsoring its spread or by embodying its highest ideals. The genre mostly consisted of exemplary anecdotes, based on the premise that if one Indian had achieved superior Christian virtue, then all Indians were likewise capable. The motif of the exemplary Christian Indian was a characteristic of creole literature for the entire colonial era. The early Franciscans, for example, peppered their accounts with copious references to the singular piety of Christian caciques with whom they were personally acquainted. According to Motolinia, the sincere zeal of these leaders was critical to the success of the evangelical project, as their example encouraged their compatriots to forego their reticence and request baptism. A son-in-law of Moctezuma named don Juan, for example, was so transformed by the gospel that he animated the souls of all who knew him. "As in that time few [Indians] had yet awakened from their delusions and errors," reported Motolinia, "both the natives and the Spaniards who saw [don Juan] were very edified, and marveled at him, saying that he gave them a great example."[41]

This heady triumphant spirit would not last, however, and by the late-sixteenth century a deep skepticism had set in regarding native Christianity, normally expressed in fears of persistent idolatry and insincere piety.[42] The pessimism even penetrated the Franciscans, many of whom abandoned the spirit behind the Colegio de Santa Cruz and adopted a more paternalistic vision of native Christians. Characterizing this attitude

[41] Motolinia, *Memoriales*, 56.
[42] Brading, *The First America*: 116.

at the end of the sixteenth century, fray Gerónimo de Mendieta argued – even from his post at Santiago Tlatelolco – that Indians, like innocent children, were harmed by excessive freedom and autonomy. "They are not suited to giving orders or ruling," he explained, "but to be given orders and ruled, because the degree to which they are humble and submissive when governed is the degree to which they become proud and vain when they find themselves in a high position."[43]

Others, then, assumed the mantle of native education. As in so many other ways, Mexico's religious identity and intellectual climate shifted substantially with the arrival of the Society of Jesus in 1572. Until their expulsion from the Spanish world in 1767, the Jesuits would join the Franciscans as the most important advocates of creolized visions of Mexico and its history. They did so primarily through native education; if the sixteenth-century Franciscans heralded a portentous and providential Mesoamerican antiquity, the Jesuits sought to remake the caciques as genteel and obedient Christian scholars and leaders in their own image. While both Jesuits and Franciscans praised the exceptional piety of their acquaintances among the native elite, the former were also likely to stress their aptitude for letters and advanced scholarship. As a result, a distinct Jesuit influence, whether direct or otherwise, looms behind certain colonial legends and tropes casting Indians as founders, patrons, and even leaders of Mexican Christianity.

The Jesuits began establishing Indian colleges, or residential secondary schools, in New Spain's urban centers almost immediately: Institutions dedicated to educating cacique boys in letters and the arts.[44] Thus did the Jesuits adapt and assume the spirit originally pioneered at the Franciscans' Colegio de Santa Cruz: the ideal of forming an indigenous Christian vanguard in America by educating the children of the native nobility. And like Santa Cruz de Tlatelolco, caciques often embraced the Jesuits' schools, as they promised to preserve hierarchies within the Indian republics. They were places where native lords might signal their noble distinction as well as prepare their children for the leadership roles they considered theirs by right of blood. Although administered by the Jesuits, caciques

---

[43] Jerónimo de Mendieta, *Historia eclesiástica indiana* (México: Antiguo Librería, 1870), www.cervantesvirtual.com/obra-visor/historia-eclesiastica-indiana-o/html, l. 4, c. 23; Guillermo Figuera, *La formación del clero indígena en la historia eclesiástica de América, 1500–1810* (Caracas: Archivo General de la Nación, 1965), 335.

[44] For an account of Jesuit pedagogy in native communities, see Pilar Gonzalbo Aizpurú, *Historia de la educación en la época colonial: el mundo indígena* (México: El Colegio de México, 1990).

numbered among the colleges' most important patrons, seeing them as Indian corporations, financing them, and resenting any moves to dilute their indigenous identity and character.[45]

The colleges focused largely on music, grammar, and doctrine – aspirants to the priesthood required further education elsewhere – yet for two centuries they produced a steady number of two colonial types, both of whom inclined toward the synthesis of neo-Aztec and Hispano-Catholic sympathies that characterized the cacique-creole historical vision. The first were ladino caciques, learned Christian men who understood themselves as heirs to both Mexican antiquity as well the leadership of New Spain's native population. By way of lineage and education, ladino caciques were exemplars of what Ileana Schmidt Díaz de León has termed "enlightened Indianism" (*indianismo ilustrado*), and were thus disproportionately influential in debates over the significance of indigencity and native history.[46] Next were the Jesuit teachers of cacique children, Spanish and creole pedagogues who, unlike many of their compatriots, had direct experience with native communities, spoke native languages, and sympathized with the cacique realm, its memories, and its noble Indo-Christian identity.

That the scholastically minded Jesuits would emphasize the virtues of education is unsurprising, but in central Mexico their optimism also derived from close relationships with the native nobility, some of whom stood among the Society's earliest and most generous patrons. In an episode aptly symbolizing the parallels and continuity-of-purpose between the faded Santa Cruz and the emerging Jesuit network, a year after their arrival into Mexico City with only a humble dwelling of their own, they received a major donation of labor, materials, and finances from none other than don Antonio Cortés Totoquihuaztli, the venerated Tlacopaneca tlatoani and alumnus of Santa Cruz who exemplified early colonial cacique erudition.[47] In just three months, the Indians of Tlacopan erected and beautified several buildings that would serve as the Jesuits' base in Mexico City, including a chapel in the *xacal* (thatched-roof) style. The following decade, in 1586, the Jesuits dedicated some of those properties, including the chapel, to a new college for cacique

[45] Ileana Schmidt Díaz de León, *El Colegio Seminario de Indios de San Gregorio y el desarrollo de la indianidad en el centro de México, 1586–1856* (México: Plaza y Valdés, 2012), 50–108.

[46] Ibid., 204–05.

[47] "Memorias de México," M-M 240, Bancroft Library, University of California, Berkeley, f. 190.

children, the Colegio Seminario de San Gregorio. Francisco Javier Alegre, an eighteenth-century creole Jesuit, portrayed San Gregorio as an emblem of the Society's deep gratitude for don Antonio's patronage.[48] While residents came from all over New Spain, the Jesuits maintained an explicit preference for people from Tlacopan, in recognition of its "patrons and founders."[49] Each year, the community at San Gregorio, noble Indians and their Jesuit allies, regaled the sitting governor of Tlacopan with a banquet, all to honor the memory and commemorate the generosity of don Antonio Totoquihuaztli.[50]

During most of the seventeenth century there were about fifty students residing at San Gregorio. According to a contemporary chronicler, at San Gregorio the children of Nahua and Otomí caciques were instructed in "virtue, reading, writing, and music, so that they may later govern their pueblos in a more effective and Christian manner," adding proudly that the institution and its alumni had quickly become indispensable to the civic, religious, and physical welfare of Mexico City's native sector.[51] Before returning to their home communities to serve as cabildo officers or in parishes as cantors and church assistants (*fiscales*), the residents of San Gregorio maintained busy schedules, organizing processions, administering charities, and caring for sick and needy Indians. Accordingly, it continued to draw pious donations and patronage from central Mexican caciques and sympathetic creoles throughout the seventeenth century.[52] In 1698, the creole Franciscan Agustín de Vetancurt – generally less given to hyperbole than many of his contemporaries – noted admiringly that the cacique alumni of San Gregorio were widely respected for their skill as teachers, musicians, and craftsmen.[53]

Significantly, San Gregorio was located next to its creole counterpart, the Colegio de San Pedro y San Pablo, which after 1700 was the

---

48 Alegre, *Memorias*: v. 1, 74–75.
49 Ibid., v. 2, 61.
50 Schmidt Díaz de León, *Colegio Seminario*: 102.
51 "Relación breve de la venida de los de la Compañia y su fundación en la Provincia de México, año de 1602" in Francisco González de Cossío, "Tres colegios mexicanos: Tepotzotlán, San Gregorio, y San Ildefonso," *Boletín del Archivo General de la Nación* XX, no. 2 (1949), 232–35, quote from 32.
52 Schmidt Díaz de León, *Colegio Seminario*: 50–57; Susan Schroeder, "Jesuits, Nahuas, and the Good Death Society in Mexico City, 1710–1767," *Hispanic American Historical Review* 80, no. 1 (2000), 51–55.
53 Fr. Agustín de Vetancurt, *Teatro mexicano: descripción breve de los sucesos exemplares, históricos, políticos, militares, y religiosos del nuevo mundo occidental de las Indias*, vol. 1 (Mexico: Doña María de Benavides, 1698), 35.

repository of Sigüenza's grand collection of Mesoamerican antiquities. Together, the two institutions formed a locus of the Jesuits' brand of creolism, a place where educated caciques and creoles alike contemplated Mesoamerican history within a neo-scholastic pedagogical framework. San Gregorio was one of the home institutions of the creole Nahuatl-speaker Juan de Tovar who, as with his cousin fray Diego Durán and the Tenochca nobleman don Hernando Alvarado Tezozomoc, authored a history of Mexica origins – known today as *Codex Ramírez* – based on the *Tira de la peregrinación* and its affiliated materials.[54] Under Tovar and his confreres, the Jesuits emphasized native-language studies – a fact that placed them in opposition to contemporaries demanding cultural and linguistic Hispanization – and were eager to attract those with the best command of Nahuatl, Otomí, and other languages. Indeed, the Jesuits quickly succeeded the Franciscans as the most capable students and teachers of Nahuatl. As early as 1595, one of Tovar's collegues, Antonio del Rincón (1556–1601), produced a Nahuatl grammar with Tovar's approval, that for fifty years remained the most widely used of the genre.[55] This agenda further substantiated the common ground between the Jesuits and the native leadership; indeed, in establishing the Colegio de San Gregorio, Tovar negotiated for the support of none other than don Antonio Valeriano himself, the learned governor of San Juan Tenochtitlan and brother-in-law of don Hernando Alvarado Tezozomoc.[56]

San Gregorio was not the only, or even the first, Jesuit college for cacique children. That distinction went to the Colegio de San Martín in Tepotzotlan, north of Mexico City. Like San Gregorio, San Martín was built upon a cacique's generosity. In 1581, the Otomí governor of Tepotzotlan, don Martín Maldonado, negotiated a settlement with Juan de Tovar and others: The local Otomís would assist the Jesuits in establishing their presence in the area in return for an Indian college, where

---

[54] The *Codex* has been republished recently. Juan de Tovar, *Historia y creencias de los indios de México* (Madrid: Miraguano Ediciones, 2001).

[55] Rincón is sometimes remembered as a cacique of Tetzcoco himself, but this seems to be a late-colonial distortion, one of several of its type (as we will see in Chapter 7). See Antonio del Rincón, *Arte mexicana* (Mexico: Oficina Típ. de la Secretaría del Fomento, 1885); Andrés Pérez de Ribas, *History of the Triumphs of our Holy Faith*, trans. Daniel T. Reff, Maureen Ahern, and Richard K. Danford (Tucson: University of Arizona Press, 1999), 712. See also "Relación breve," in González de Cossío, "Tres colegios mexicanos," 240–42.

[56] Schroeder, "Jesuits, Nahuas, and the Good Death Society in Mexico City, 1710–1767," 53.

noble children of seven years and older would acquire doctrine, literacy, and musical training. Don Martín also donated lands, orchards, and several mills to support the project.[57] Tepotzotlan was the home institution of Andrés Pérez de Ribas (1575–1665), a Spanish Jesuit who arrived in Mexico as a young man and spent many years chronicling the Society's early missionary efforts. Pérez was a fervent defender of native Christianity. In his enormous 1645 chronicle, *Historia de los triumphos de nuestra santa fé (History of the Triumphs of Our Holy Faith)*, Pérez de Ribas proudly highlights the successes of Jesuit colleges such as San Martín and San Gregorio in educating the native leadership. Although comparatively moderate and careful in both tone and temperament, his account stands out inasmuch as it was written during a time of deep and widespread pessimism regarding native Christianity.[58]

Like Motolinia, Pérez's defense of the Mexican Church focused heavily on anecdotes detailing the virtues of individual Indians whom he or his religious brothers knew as paragons of Christian virtue. Given his association with San Martín de Tepotzotlan, such exemplars were invariably caciques – those who had the means, the inclination and, most importantly, the requisite prestige to send their sons to reside in an elite religious community.[59] According to Pérez, the Jesuits' cacique alumni were so accomplished that news of them had reached the summit of colonial society. The archbishop himself had even ordained one outstanding student of Tepotzotlan, don Gerónimo, an almost-unheard-of honor for an Indian, and his first mass was attended by the highest-ranking clergy in the colony.[60] Another cacique seminarian and teacher, don Lorenzo, was a man of such compelling Christian devotion that he had chosen to adhere to Jesuit precepts – eschewing marriage and private wealth – even though as an Indian he was ineligible to join the Society. In recognition of his inner vocation, however, the Jesuits made him an honorary member of

---

[57] "Fundación del Colegio de Tepotzotlan," in González de Cossío, "Tres colegios mexicanos," 204, 19–22; Alegre, *Memorias*: v. 1, 138–39. Alegre names the cacique "don Francisco de Tapia Maldonado," but contemporary documents give his name as don Martín.

[58] For example, the secular priest Hernando Ruiz de Alarcón wrote his alarmist account of the occult survival of native religious practices in 1629, at precisely the same time that Pérez produced his own chronicle. See Hernando Ruiz de Alarcón, *Treatise on the heathen superstitions that today live among the Indians native to this New Spain, 1629*, trans. J. Richard Andrews and Ross Hassig (Norman, OK: University of Oklahoma Press, 1984).

[59] Pérez de Ribas, *Triumphs*: 712.

[60] Ibid., 708–09.

their community as he lay on his deathbed. "A great number of Mexican Indians attended the ceremony," Pérez recalled, "and they were happy to see this person from their nation [so] honored, [as it was] something rarely seen in that kingdom, even though he was very deserving of it."[61] He cautioned his readers not to overgeneralize such triumphs, however, as they had only come about "due to very special circumstances"; in addition to their extensive education, the native seminarians were "the sons of very great caciques."[62]

Pérez also admired the ways that native leaders had creatively appropriated Christianity by adorning it with Mexican aesthetic and ritual traditions. He described, for example, a popular ceremony that the collegians at San Gregorio in Mexico City performed during Lent, a preconquest dance called the *mitote of Moctezuma*, reimagined and reinterpreted so as to commemorate their ancestors' own integration into Christendom. During the event, a dancer representing Emperor Moctezuma was symbolically "converted"; he then began a second dance in honor of his spiritual rebirth. Lest his readers be scandalized by such pagan holdovers, Pérez assured them that the participants were not commoners given to superstitions, but rather educated caciques who, by way of their subtle command of Christian doctrine, had transformed the practice into a beautiful homage to the Church itself. It was such a moving spectacle, he insisted, that it had impressed the archbishop himself, and had even been adopted and imitated by some creole associates from the Colegio de San Pedro y San Pablo who had witnessed it.[63]

Mexicanizing the Church: apparition stories

Representations of exemplary Christian Indians appeared frequently in creole apologetic literature because they challenged outsiders who doubted the sincerity – and feared the syncretism – of Mexican Christianity. By telling of outstanding native believers, they were both envisioning and honoring a Christian Mexico distinct from, but equal to, its Spanish cousin. Yet the most spectacular way that creole authors imagined and appropriated their own Church was by relocating its roots to the land, history, and native people of Mexico. The most famous expression of this phenomenon, of course, was the growing fame of the Virgin of Guadalupe, held to have appeared some years after the conquest to a

[61] Ibid., 716–18, quote from 718.
[62] Ibid., 709.
[63] Ibid., 714–15.

Nahua commoner named Juan Diego at Tepeyac north of Mexico City, a hill previously dedicated to a mother goddess. Her image, miraculously emblazoned on Juan Diego's tilma, was preserved in a temple constructed for that purpose on the spot. The power of the Guadalupe story lay in its implicit sublimation of the history of Mexico's evangelization. In 1600 the image's fame was largely limited to a small hermitage outside of Mexico City, yet by 1700 it had become, through the efforts of a series of creole authors, the most venerated religious icon in New Spain, heralded in sermons, books, chapels, and lavish artistic homages throughout the colony.

Modern scholars have thoroughly addressed the emergence and development of guadalupanismo in both local practice and creole literature. While they disagree on the precise nature and extent of the cult in the sixteenth century, they all demonstrate that the creoles who disseminated and promoted the legends in the second half of the seventeenth century were eager to root them in native rather than Spanish memories.[64] The story of Juan Diego was first published in Spanish in 1648; six months later, a more elegant and elaborate Nahuatl account by Luis Laso de la Vega and his Nahua assistants at Tepeyac appeared. In the 1660s the Church launched an official investigation into the apparition, and another Spanish chronicle, by Luis Becerra Tanco, appeared. To prove the authenticity and antiquity of the cult, all of the Guadalupan promoters gathered testimonials and eyewitness accounts of miracles from native witnesses – the older and nobler, the better. Indigenous origins were central to the creole interpretation of the image, as they gave it an American dimension, evidence of a link between heaven and the New World that did not go through Spain.[65]

During the inquiry of 1666, for example, the first witnesses to be questioned were seven elderly Indians and a mestizo from Cuauhtitlan, most of them nobles and cabildo officers. Among the non-native testators, meanwhile, was don Diego Cano Moctezuma, a castizo-creole member of the Mexico City cabildo who claimed, falsely, to be a grandson of the huei

[64] See David A. Brading, *Mexican Phoenix: Our Lady of Guadalupe: Image and Tradition across Five Centuries* (Cambridge: Cambridge University Press, 2002); Stafford Poole, *Our Lady of Guadalupe: The Origins and Sources of a Mexican National Symbol, 1531–1797* (Tucson, AZ: University of Arizona Press, 1996); Taylor, *Shrines and Miraculous Images*, 97–115. While Poole is relatively skeptical regarding the extent of the cult in the sixteenth century, Brading and Taylor emphasize its rootedness in baroque religiosity.

[65] Poole, *Our Lady of Guadalupe*, 100–55.

tlatoani. At the same time, Becerra Tanco initiated a new round of historical ventriloquism among creole guadalupanists, based upon their shared reverence for the erudite ladino caciques of previous generations. He testified to having seen numerous items referencing the apparition in the library of don Fernando de Alva Ixtlilxochitl, who had died sixteen years earlier; a decade after that, he specified that one of the items had come from an alumnus of the College of Santa Cruz de Tlatelolco.[66] In 1689, don Carlos de Sigüenza y Góngora insisted that the original Nahuatl version of the Juan Diego story had been written by none other than the revered don Antonio Valeriano of Azcapotzalco; that it had belonged to Alva Ixtlilxochitl, who had produced an abridged Spanish version; and that all subsequent versions derived from those two accounts.[67] Thus did the major Guadalupan authors, over four decades, assign noble, indigenous American, Christian roots to their legend. By retroactively attributing the story to the educated ladino caciques of the sixteenth century, the creoles embraced them as their own compatriots and intellectual ancestors.

The Virgin of Guadalupe is the most famous, but stories of heavenly apparitions before pious Indians abounded in the seventeenth century, and creole authors similarly sought to root them in Mexican antiquity. That is, while the apparitions of the Lady of Guadalupe and other denizens of heaven symbolize the religious transformation of native peoples and the integration of America into Christendom, some authors, echoing the providentialism of the ladino caciques, de-emphasized rupture by portraying the miracles less as innovations brought about by the conquest, and more as organic outgrowths of the deepest currents of primordial Mexican history. With deliberate detail, the creole religious chroniclers clothed the apparition stories in the distinguishing marks of Mexican culture and geography: its language, its fauna, and even its food. One unspoken implication was that the Spaniards did not "introduce" Christianity to Mexico; the Lady of Guadalupe and her heavenly counterparts were already there, hidden in its caves and atop its mountains, working in the hearts of the people, and preparing the way for the triumphant arrival of the institutional Church.

Such a premise characterizes the works of the tireless creole Jesuit Francisco de Florencia (1619–95), who spent much of his life promoting the various cult traditions of his native Mexico at home and abroad, in

---

[66] Ibid., 130–46.
[67] Ibid., 166.

Rome as well as Spain. Like his friend and partner don Carlos de Sigüenza y Góngora – who provided access to the Alva Ixtlilxochitl collection – he was a highly effective voice for the increasingly self-aware creole elite, and he did much to synthesize and standardize what had theretofore been a series of heterogeneous traditions. In ways both subtle and overt, his creolizing treatment of several apparition stories linked contemporary Novohispanic spirituality, not to conquest-era transformations, but to the human tradition of ancient Mexico.

Significantly, Florencia began his 1688 account of the Guadalupe apparition, *North Star of Mexico* (*La estrella del norte de México*), not in Europe, nor even in central Mexico, but in Chicomoztoc, the primordial Seven Caves of Aztec legend. Premonitions of Guadalupe were even present at the 1325 founding of Tenochtitlan: When the refugees who would become the Mexica arrived at the place they would make their capital, they called it *Mexico*, which Florencia translated as "place at the center of the moon." This, he argued, was portentous, as it clearly referred to the image of the Lady of Guadalupe, who stands upon a crescent moon.[68] Similarly, Florencia's account of the growth of the cult at Tepeyac places native believers at the center of the story, and relegates Spaniards to the margins. "We should admire God," he wrote, as "by choosing an Indian as his instrument for the glorification of His mother, ensured that the first Spaniards would forget to write it down ... and that it would be the Indians who conserved its memory in their own writings and ... in their own manner of veneration."[69] According to the Jesuit, first in images and painted maps, and then in alphabetic texts in their own languages, the Indians preserved their memories of the apparition, many of which he had seen in the library of Alva Ixtlilxochitl, who had inherited them from his noble indigenous ancestors. Unfortunately, none of these records – "written with such elegance" – was ever published, because their owners could not afford the printing fees.[70] Always citing sources from the Alva Ixtlilxochitl collection, Florencia copied a song hailing Juan Diego attributed to don Francisco Plácido, a cacique of Azcapotzalco, as recorded by Chimalpahin.[71] The creole also insinuated a certain native proprietary relationship to the miraculous image itself. Imprinted as it

---

[68] Francisco de Florencia, *La estrella del norte de México, aparecida al rayar el día de la luz evangélica en este Nuevo-Mundo*... (Mexico: Imprenta de Antonio Velázquez, 1741), 2–3.

[69] Ibid., 108.

[70] Ibid., 107.

[71] Ibid., 104.

was on the coarse Mexican thread of *ayatl,* Florencia insisted that only
an Indian could have possibly received it, and "only Indian painters have
been able to copy the holy image" with any accuracy.[72] Taking this narrative logic to its extreme, Florencia even questioned whether the Mexican
Guadalupe had any relationship at all to the *other* Virgin of Guadalupe
in southwestern Spain. Instead, he suggested that the name was a Hispanic corruption of a Nahuatl word: While Juan Diego's uncle recalled
having seen the apparition at *quauhtlalapan* – "place of the trees near
the water" – the Spaniards heard "Guadalupe," because they were ignorant of Nahuatl and because many of them were from Extremadura, and
acquainted with the other Guadalupe there.[73]

Florencia's 1685 account of the apparition of the Virgin of the Remedies (*Los Remedios*), *The Miraculous Discovery of a Hidden Treasure
(La milagrosa invención de un tesoro escondido)*, contains similar creolizing emphases, and likewise minimizes the role of Spaniards in the
origins of a colonial cult, instead relocating the spiritual substance of
the story to an entirely indigenous milieu and landscape. Soon after the
conquest, a righteous, Spanish-aligned cacique named don Juan de Tovar
Sequauhtli had a vision of the Virgin of the Remedies alongside St. James
as he traversed the countryside. He informed the local Franciscans but
they did not believe him. Later, while hunting, he found a small statue
of the Virgin under a maguey, "a plant well-known in this land"; crying
with joy, he called her *cihuapilli* ("my lady") and brought her back to his
house, where he venerated her in secret for ten years, offering her chocolate, tortillas, and other iconic staples of the indigenous diet. Florencia
elaborated upon the Mexican character of these gifts, as well as on the
depth of don Juan's piety and devotion. But the Virgin did not want to
be kept secret, and kept disappearing and returning to the same maguey
where don Juan had found her. Finally, the cacique understood, informed
several native and Spanish authorities, and a church was built to house
her on that spot.[74]

Florencia's account of a Tlaxcalteca apparition story likewise indi-
genizes the cult via numerous analogies and exegetical allusions to
iconic Mexican foods, animals, and plants. In his 1692 *Account of the*

---

[72] Ibid., 108–9.

[73] Ibid., 109–10. Stafford Poole discusses and critiques such attempts to give Nahuatl roots
to the name Guadalupe. See Poole, *Our Lady of Guadalupe,* 31–32.

[74] Francisco de Florencia, *La milagrosa invención de un thesoro escondido en un
campo...* (Sevilla: Imprenta de las Siete Revueltas, 1745), 1–10.

Marvelous Apparition of St. Michael Archangel (Narración de la maravillosa aparición del archángel San Miguel), Florencia recounted how St. Michael appeared to a Tlaxcalteca teenager named Diego Lázaro and his family, guiding them to a hidden spring with miraculous healing powers. When the humble Diego, fearing that he would not be believed, failed to spread the story of the apparition, the archangel infected him with the *cocoliztli*, the hemorrhagic fever that ravaged postconquest Mexico. The spring, meanwhile, emerged from beneath a hill that local people had, since the beginning of time, called *tzopiloatl*, or "water of vultures"; this was providential and indicative of heaven's plans, argued Florencia, because just as the spring rid the human body of death, the vulture cleanses the world of its filth and rot.[75]

Florencia openly speculated as to why the denizens of heaven preferred to honor Mexico's Indians rather than its Spaniards. When Spaniards appeared in Florencia's stories, they were skeptics and outsiders whose cynicism is proven wrong, or "people of reason" who confirmed the veracity of miracles experienced by Indians. In framing the events as inherent to an American, indigenous context, Florencia imagined a Mexican Church with native, perhaps even preconquest origins. Thus, while Church doctrine arrived in the wake of the conquest, the spirit that animated it reflected a divine plan eons in the making. Heaven had sown it, centuries earlier, among the magueys, waters, and native peoples of Mexico; blossoming forth upon the arrival of the institutional Church, they responded joyously with gifts of tortillas, chocolate, and *atole*, and preserved the memory of the events in their paintings, oral histories, and dances.

Florencia was not the only creole of his era to Mexicanize their religious tradition by giving it an indigenous "face" – sometimes literally; the Jesuit minister to the Nahuas, Nicolás de Segura, described the Lady of Guadalupe as an "Indian" virgin in 1741, noting that her appearance was akin to those of Mexico's caciques, whom he perceived as whiter than macehuales.[76] Others engaged in providentialism, locating Christian portents in the distant past. Sigüenza famously echoed the Franciscan contention that the Apostle St. Thomas had preached in Anahuac centuries earlier; his main source was Manuel Duarte, a Portuguese Jesuit who had reached his conclusions by way of native pictorial records.[77] Fray

---

[75] Ibid., 14–15.
[76] See Taylor, *Shrines*: 125–26.
[77] Sigüenza's text, now lost, was titled *Phoenix of the West, the Apostle St. Thomas Found Under the Name Quetzalcoatl*. Duarte's essay is *Pluma rica*; he gave it to Sigüenza upon

Balthasar de Medina engaged in ornate baroque hermeneutics to locate pre-Hispanic prophesies of the Church's eventual arrival and triumph. The name "Mexico," he wrote, was a corruption of the Hebrew *mashiah*, or "messiah." Thus was Mexico's destiny written, in its own name, centuries before the conquest.[78] Even Joseph Antonio de Villaseñor y Sánchez (1746), a viceregal surveyor who generally eschewed the excesses of baroque exegesis, wove providentialism into his history; God Himself had inspired Moctezuma's "donation" to Carlos V.[79] The creole vision imagined Mexican Christianity to be as ancient as Mexico itself.

An Otomí-Franciscan vision: the stone cross of Querétaro

The unique Otomí conquistador culture of the Bajío offers an exceptional example in which elite indigenous memories, in tandem with the advocacy of local friars, resulted in a patriotic legend celebrated and hailed at the summit of creole society. Ironically, the legend may have origins, not in the strength of indigenous Christian devotion, but in Spanish fears of its weakness and heterodoxy. John Tutino notes that Franciscans in the early to mid seventeenth century, although allied with the Otomí elite, actively sought to combat what they perceived as residual idolatry by promoting new forms of baroque cult devotion.[80] One of them, the miraculous stone cross of the Sangremal, became a means by which creoles in Querétaro and elsewhere appropriated the Otomí conquistador legacy for their own patria.

Hailing from Tula and claiming to be related to the Mexica Emperor Moctezuma, don Nicolás de San Luis Montañez was, along with his kinsman don Fernando de Tapia Connin, one of the original leaders to migrate into the region. And like don Fernando, in 1557 Viceroy Velasco I commissioned don Nicolás to help pacify the region, offering lands in return and titling him "Captain of the Chichimeca Frontier." He subsequently bore himself as an Indian hidalgo, settling and managing

---

leaving for the Phillippines in 1680. Octavio Paz, *Sor Juana, or, the Traps of Faith*, trans. Margaret Sayers Peden (Cambridge, MA.: Harvard University Press, 1988), 40–41; More, *Baroque Sovereignty*: 76–80.

[78] Balthasar de Medina, *Chrónica de la S. Provincia de S. Diego de México de Religiosos Descalços de N. S. P. S. Francisco en la Nueva España* (México: Juan de Ribera, 1682), 231v.

[79] Joseph Antonio Villaseñor y Sánchez, *Theatro americano: descripción general de los reynos y provincias de la Nueva España*, 2 vols. (México: Viuda de Joseph Bernardo de Hogal, 1746–48). v. 1, 7–8.

[80] Tutino, *Making a New World*: 116–19.

lands near San Juan del Río, carrying weapons, and donning Spanish attire.[81] Don Nicolás is the protagonist of an influential history of the conquest of Querétaro known as the "Relación de don Nicolás de San Luís Montañez," a first-person account from the late-seventeenth century that falsely purports to be the conqueror's own from 1555 (although it may have been based on earlier records and oral memories). Transcribed and loosely copied multiple times, like other texts celebrating Indian conquistadors its initial purpose was to recast don Nicolás as a hero of Mexican Christianity, thereby elevating the standing of his heirs and descendants.

Like the account of Francisco Martín de la Puente examined in Chapter 5, the "Relacion de don Nicolás de San Luis" is quasi-mythical – David Wright calls it "fantasy" – as it is nonlinear and blends legend with precise details such as names and dates.[82] One of its many variations records that in 1522 no fewer than twenty-one Otomí caciques from Tula, Xilotepec, and Tlaxcala – including don Fernando de Tapia and the narrator himself – descended into the region of Querétaro conquering and pacifying 25,000 "barbarous Chichimeca Indians" on behalf of Carlos V. For a time they pursued the Chichimecas through the mountains and valleys, founding pueblos and enticing the locals to join them while punishing those who refused to submit to Castile and its religion. On Sunday, July 25 – the feast day of the Spanish patron Santiago (St. James) – don Nicolás's "army" (*ejército*) confronted a group of Chichimecas on a hillside, accompanied by a Spanish priest.

And that day the sun stopped, as it was the will of God to make this miracle for the lord apostle Santiago so that the sun would stop, although the Christians had already won and all were exhausted from so much fighting with the barbarous Chichimeca Indians, and it was getting late, and the priest father knelt to his knees praying, begging our Lord God and the Holy Virgin on behalf of the Catholics who were fighting for the faith, warring against the barbarous Chichimeca Indians. Earlier on Sunday morning before the sun had set, we began to make war; it was the day of the lord Santiago, and the lord Santiago also appeared . . . and God assured that we emerged well, not a single Catholic was in danger; the Catholics merely came away very roughed up (*maltratados*) and bloodied, their faces covered in blood, such that it was unknown who were the Chichimecas, because the barbarians also became bloodied, and two [Chichimeca] captains called don Lobo (Wolf) and don Coyote fell into dismay and exhaustion.[83]

---

[81] Captaincy of don Nicolás de San Luis, Tenochtitlan, May 1, 1557, in Fernández de Recas, *Cacicazgos*, 313–14.

[82] See Wright, *Querétaro en el siglo XVI*, 26–34.

[83] "Relación de Nicolás de San Luis Montañez," in Frías, *La conquista de Querétaro*, 66–67.

Either before or during the battle – it is unclear from the convoluted narrative – a "captain of the Chichimecas" saw the forces arrayed against him, and "called for peace, saying in a loud voice 'we want peace' three times, 'we want this war to end,'" before surrendering to don Nicolás de San Luis.[84] At that point, the leader accepted baptism with the name don Juan Bautista Criado, learning the sign of the cross and the *Pater Noster*, the *Ave María*, the *Credo*, and other recitations. His wife was also baptized, becoming doña Juana Chichimecas Criado, followed by the rest of his contingent.[85] At that point, don Juan Bautista requested that a cross of white, red, and maroon stone be placed upon the hill as a permanent landmark.[86] When the cross arrived, masses were sung in its praise, and a series of miracles occurred. Don Nicolás fell to his knees "giving thanks to God and the Most Holy Virgin upon seeing such a lovely and holy cross, as it seemed we were in heaven (*gloria*) when a white cloud carried by four angels appeared, very beautiful, casting shade upon the holy cross." Upon seeing this, "the barbarous Chichimeca Indians received the most holy cross very eagerly, and they began dancing . . . and shooting arrows into the air, shouting with joy." The hill became known as the Sangremal.[87]

A related seventeenth-century account, which Serge Gruzinski has called the "Anonymous Relation," likewise tells the story of the stone cross while hailing the heroics of don Nicolás, although it dates the events to 1502.[88] In this narrative, the Otomí – called the "Catholics" – confront the Chichimecas, but offer gifts and friendship in lieu of hostilities. The Chichimeca chief responds well to the warm diplomacy, and calls on his people to embrace the new alliance: "My sons, the Catholics come in good faith, offering us baptism and marriage and gifts of blankets and clothing to bring us to an agreement with them. . . . I say they come

---

[84] Ibid., 71.

[85] Ibid., 65–66.

[86] Ibid., 62–63.

[87] Ibid., 73–74.

[88] A partial translation by Serge Gruzinski is in Serge Gruzinski, "Mutilated Memory: Reconstruction of the Past and the Mechanisms of Memory among Seventeenth-Century Otomís," in *Colonial Spanish America: A Documentary History*, eds. Kenneth Mills and William B. Taylor (Wilmington, DE: Scholarly Resources, Inc., 1998), 218. Gruzinski refers to it as the "Anonymous Account" (*Relación anónima*) of Querétaro, and calls it a source of "exceptional worth," given the near-complete absence of colonial documents written in Otomí. Serge Gruzinski, "Mutilated Memory: Reconstruction of the Past and the Mechanisms of Memory Among 17th-Century Otomís," *History and Anthropology* 2, no. 2 (1986), 338.

in good faith seeking agreement."[89] According to the Otomí accounts, Christian Querétaro was the work of God, St. James, and don Nicolás de San Luis Montañez.

The "Relación de don Nicolás de San Luis" and the "Anonymous Relation" are further examples of cacique self-fashioning through history, intended to burnish the reputation of revered ancestors. Indeed, Serge Gruzinski suspects they were written by the descendants of don Nicolás so as to emphasize his deeds over those of the more successful and renowned Tapias.[90] Yet these stories did not appear *ex nihilo*; they reflected both historical events and spiritual concerns, particularly with regard to their emphasis on the stone cross. Spanish conquerors frequently placed crosses on hilltops and other landmarks to assert possession as well as mark boundaries. Early documents pertaining to a 1536 dispute between the encomendero Hernando Pérez de Bocanegra and the caciques of Xilotepec may shed light on the events in question. In the early 1530s, the region was thrown into upheaval by Nuño de Guzmán's notorious campaigns to pacify western Mexico, provoking a series of conflicts between Spaniards, their native allies, and independent local groups. Guzmán sent his lieutenant, Maximiliano de Angulo, to take possession of the diverse Chichimeca settlements the Nahuas called Tlachco (Querétaro), which had recently swelled with Otomí refugees from Xilotepec escaping the encomiendas. There were some skirmishes and many people fled to the backcountry, but at least two local leaders sued for peace and agreed to Angulo's terms. The settlements were assigned to encomiendas, and a cross was placed on the hilltop outside Querétaro, both to mark boundaries as well as signal possession on behalf of Nuño de Guzmán.[91]

This Spanish mode of territorial possession may have resonated in unforeseen ways. William Taylor notes that longstanding Otomí traditions already associated the cross with certain natural and divine powers, and that colonial Otomí Christianity attributed many beneficial, protective, and redemptive qualities to the symbol.[92] Intriguingly, the indigenous testimonials of 1536 emphasize the importance of the cross well beyond what is explicitly prompted by the legal inquiries, hinting

---

[89] "Anonymous Relation," in Gruzinski, "Reconstructions of the Past," 220.

[90] Gruzinski, "Mutilated Memory," 339–40.

[91] See Cacique don Luis of Xilotepec vs. Encomendero Hernán Pérez de Bocanegra, Mexico, 1535–41, AGI-J 124, N.1, unpaginated.

[92] Taylor, *Shrines*, 85–89; see also William Taylor, "Placing the Cross in Colonial Mexico," *The Americas* 69, no. 2 (2012).

that such syncretism may have been at work in Querétaro. Bocanegra's inquest simply asked local witnesses to confirm whether, once peace had been secured, Nuño de Guzmán took legal possession of the settlements in the king's name, with no mention of any cross. Yet most native witnesses – both Otomís and Chichimecas, some baptized, some unbaptized, from diverse communities in the region, including Querétaro, Apaseo, and Bocanegra's encomienda in Acámbaro – centered their responses to this question on the placement of the cross. The cacique of Querétaro, don Fernando Bocanegra – many details suggest that this was likely none other than don Fernando de Tapia Connin, who had adopted the names of his godfather – reported witnessing the cross, but also noted that it had since been taken down.[93] Olin, the baptized cacique of Querétaro's Chichimecas (he did not remember his Christian name) told a rather descriptive tale of violence averted. War had been raging in the area, he said, but when the men on horseback arrived most of his people fled to the mountains, and he did not offer resistance. Rounding up the people that remained, the Spaniards declared that "from this day forward you all shall serve Nuño de Guzmán," and they placed crosses along the hills to mark the boundary between Guzmán's administrative territories of Jalisco (Nueva Galicia) and those of Mexico.[94]

The seventeenth-century Otomí accounts invoke these memories. Yet during the era of baroque myth-making, Querétaro's Franciscans would appropriate and reinterpret the story to attribute divine and marvelous origins to what was an increasingly creole, Spanish-speaking town within an older community led by those who prided themselves on conquering Otomí origins. Memories of the Otomí-Franciscan nexus were everywhere. Don Fernando de Tapia had built the first churches and Franciscan buildings; his children had founded the Convent of Santa Clara de Querétaro, where doña Luisa del Espíritu Santo was abbess; and Otomí patronage had beautified Querétaro's many churches and sanctuaries.[95] It was a unique heritage that the Franciscans fully embraced. Juan de

---

[93] Don Fernando Bocanegra's testimony of 1536 parallels don Fernando de Tapia's probanza of 1569 in several ways; both tell of hunger and hardships after fleeing Xilotepec for Querétaro, and both remember forming a close alliance with the encomendero Hernando Pérez de Bocanegra. Testimony of don Fernando Bocanegra, AGI-J 124, N.1, Querétaro, 1536, unpaginated.

[94] Probanza of Hernando Pérez de Bocanegra, Mexico, 1535–41, AGI-J 124, N.1, unpaginated.

[95] Tutino, *Making a New World*: 112–20.

Torquemada himself hailed don Diego and doña Luisa de Tapia and their role in the foundation of Santa Clara de Querétaro, which he described as exceedingly wealthy and prosperous. "The foundation of this convent is very fortunate," he wrote, "because although [Querétaro] was founded by Indians, there are now many Spaniards living there."[96] In 1682, the prolix Franciscan chronicler Balthasar de Medina summarized the attitude vividly in his own account of the convent:

> Today 120 religious live in this virginal cloister, sustained by the ample rents secured by [don Diego de Tapia], this memorable benefactor worthy of the greatest praise, as beyond his heroic services to God in giving Him on earth this pure choir of virgins, he served His Majesty our king (as did his father before him, don Fernando de Tapia) as Captain General against the Chichimecas, enlisting many men at his own cost for their pacification, winning many souls with new discoveries.[97]

Yet Torquemada – who chronicled examples of marvelous crosses in Tlaxcala and elsewhere – did not mention the stone cross of Querétaro.[98] Its tale appeared in print for the first time in a 1639 chronicle by Alonso de la Rea, a local Franciscan, who wrote that the encomendero Hernando Pérez de Bocanegra had installed a wooden cross at the top of the Sangremal to honor the heavenly image that had inspired the local people to submit peacefully and accept baptism. But the native converts were unsatisfied with such a poor imitation of the original vision, and constructed an entirely new one out of stone, extracting the materials from nearby quarries. Their zeal, combined with several unexplainable marvels, soon confirmed that their labors were endorsed in heaven. First, the heavy stones somehow became very light as the native masons hauled them up the steep hill. Next, after the cross had been installed, it began to tremble and change shape, and a supernatural hand perfected its proportions. The townspeople soon discovered that the cross had therapeutic properties. It revived a young girl who had seemingly died. Another woman, pregnant, fell from the belfry while ringing the bells of the cross's sanctuary. But she arose unhurt, laughed, and gave birth within a month. The author's own stepfather had managed to heal himself twice by applying shavings off the cross to his skin: First, after breaking bones in a horseriding accident,

---

[96] Torquemada, *Monarquía indiana*: v. 6, 53.
[97] Medina, *Chrónica*: 254r–54v.
[98] Torquemada, *Monarquía indiana*: v. 5, 299–307.

and second, after his palate had been pierced by falling rocks, "such that he had to eat and drink through his nose."[99]

The creole adaptation of the legend quickened after 1680. In that year, don Carlos de Sigüenza y Góngora described the cross in his *Glorias de Querétaro*, disseminating the story of Querétaro's "peaceful" conquest to a much broader audience.[100] In 1683, the Franciscans chose the cross as the animating symbol of their new apostolic college, established to train missionaries destined for the northern frontiers; one of the institution's founding members was, not coincidentally, fray Damian Mazanet, a Spanish acquaintance and correspondent of Sigüenza.[101] With the stone cross in its sanctuary, the eponymous Colegio de Propaganda Fide de la Santa Cruz de Querétaro produced a steady flow of erudite and patriotic Franciscans eager to spread the news of their marvelous treasure. In the spirit of the age, a search for confirmatory documentary evidence began: the older, the nobler, and the more indigenous, the better. The Franciscans soon reported finding old Otomí documents, including the "Relación de Nicolás de San Luis," in their library, and represented them as "ancient" accounts of miraculous portents. In 1716 an anonymous friar at the college published a homage to the cross; citing Sigüenza, "ancient tradition," and "many other authentic manuscripts preserved in the archives," he described its miracles and credited it with the conversion of "innumerable Gentiles who offered lying veneration to false gods."[102] The following year, in 1717, the guardian of the college, Joseph Díez, commissioned a copy and translation of the "Anonymous Relation," giving it the very patriotic title "Origen de la Santíssima Cruz de Milagros de la ciudad de Querétaro" ("Origins of the Most Holy and Miraculous Cross of the City of Querétaro"). In 1722, another friar, Francisco

---

99 Alonso de la Rea, *Crónica de la Orden de N. Seráfico Padre San Francisco, Provincia de San Pedro y San Pablo de Mechoacán en la Nueva España* (Zamora, Michoacán: Colegio de Michoacán / Fideicomiso Texidor, 1996), 191–94. See also Valentín Frías, *Leyendas y tradiciones queretanas* (Mexico: Plaza y Valdés, 1989), 138–39.

100 Carlos de Sigüenza y Góngora, *Glorias de Querétaro* (Mexico: Viuda de Bernardo Calderón, 1680), 28–30.

101 See the "Letter of fray Damián Massanet to don Carlos de Sigüenza, 1690," in Herbert Eugene Bolton, ed. *Spanish Exploration in the Southwest, 1546–1706* (New York: Charles Scribner's Sons, 1916), 353–87. Mazanet also played a role in spreading the legend of the Spanish Franciscan nun sor María de Jesús de Agreda, the "Lady in Blue" who, through bilocation, was said to have encouraged the Christianization of native groups in modern-day New Mexico and Texas.

102 Anonymous, *Novena a la Santíssima Cruz* (México: Herederos de la Viuda de Francisco Rodríguez Lupercio, 1716), n.p.

Xavier de Santa Getrudís, produced yet another paean to the cross based on the Otomí accounts. It identifies don Nicolás de San Luis of Tula as the hero of the Christian armies, and tells of vicious fighting lasting throughout the day before St. James and the cross brought an end to the battle.[103] Today, a large heroic portrait of don Nicolás hangs in the Museo Regional de Querétaro, bearing an excerpt from the account of Santa Getrudís.[104]

Isidro Félix de Espinosa (1679–1755) was a true son of Querétaro; born into a local creole family, he professed with the Franciscans in 1697 and spent several decades evangelizing in their missions in Texas before returning to serve as guardian of the Colegio de Propaganda Fide.[105] In 1746 he published a landmark chronicle of the Franciscans' entire network of missionary colleges, and dedicated it to the stone cross for which his institution was named. Espinosa's primary contribution to the legend was to replace don Nicolás de San Luis with don Fernando de Tapia as the hero. He faced a problem: The Tapias were ideal as patriotic creole icons, noble Christian caciques whose legacy as city founders was ubiquitous and visible throughout Querétaro. Yet don Nicolás, not don Fernando, was the protagonist in the main Otomí account of the miraculous cross. Espinosa resolved the issue with an opportunistic nod to the new epistemologies of the age, which emphasized skepticism and reason, even as he indulged in historical ventriloquism and the creoles' characteristic reverence for cacique authorities. To uncover the "true facts," he explained, he had consulted various indigenous sources, including "an account of the Indians maintained by a cacique of this place"; however, as they differed in some of their details, he had to balance and weigh them against one another to resolve contradictions. To these ends, he claimed to have found "authentic and ancient" papers pertaining to don Fernando and don Diego de Tapia among the records of the Convent of Santa Clara. These items convinced him that, although earlier Otomí-Franciscan accounts told that the

---

[103] Francisco Xavier de Santa Getrudís, *Cruz de piedra, imán de devoción* (Querétaro: Ediciones Cimatario, 1946).

[104] The portrait is reproduced in Ilona Katzew, "Stars in the Sea of the Church: The Indian in Eighteenth-Century New Spanish Painting," in *The Arts in Latin America, 1492–1820*, eds. Joseph J. Rishel and Suzanne L. Stratton (New Haven: Yale University Press, 2006), 346. I thank Robert Haskett for informing me of this painting.

[105] Enrique Brito Miranda, Introduction to Isidro Félix de Espinosa, *Crónica apostólica de los Colegios de Propaganda Fide* (Querétaro: Gobierno del Estado de Querétaro, 1997), xiii–xxi.

cross had appeared before don Nicolás de San Luis, in reality that honor belonged to don Fernando de Tapia.[106] His work, vetted and praised by some of Mexico's highest-ranking men of letters, conclusively spread the legend of Querétaro's stone cross to the rest of creole New Spain.[107]

"A realm apart": Tlaxcalteca exceptionalism and creole historiography

Another elite indigenous tradition that proved influential in the creole project to Mexicanize their Church came from Tlaxcala. As we have seen, during the sixteenth century Tlaxcalteca leaders worked tirelessly to ensure that their services during the conquest did not go unremunerated, and built a reputation as the king's most loyal and valuable native subjects. In the seventeenth century this idea accumulated additional dimensions, especially the idea that Tlaxcalteca religiosity was without peer. It was largely the domain of the region's most prominent families, who cultivated it within their campaigns to promote Tlaxcala within the viceregal order. The result was a singular narrative of destiny and providence, a self-advocating ethno-municipal sensibility that Jaime Cuadriello has termed *tlaxcaltequidad*, or Tlaxcalteca-ness. Not only did Tlaxcalteca leaders celebrate their ancient heritage and their services to Castile, they imagined their special place in New Spain – as indicated by a bevy of explicit royal exemptions and privileges – as arranged and endorsed in heaven itself.[108]

The religious dimension of Tlaxcalteca exceptionalism was present from the beginning, most famously expressed in Motolinia's story of the Tlaxcalteca children martyred by their revanchist parents. As we have seen, the tale of the boy-martyrs – repeated by both Muñoz Camargo and Torquemada – had become a fixture in both Tlaxcalteca and creole lore, immortalized in paintings, plays, and local memory. In Tlaxcala specifically, it was hailed as proof of the altepetl's uniquely virtuous character;

---

[106] Ibid., 3.

[107] The censor was Dr. Bartolomé Felipe de Itta y Parra, former rector of the Royal University. The religious censor, meanwhile, was Dr. Juan José de Eguiara y Eguren, perhaps the most revered intellectual of his time, best known for his ambitious (and unfinished) *Bibliografía mexicana* (1755), which aspired to list every work of scholarship ever printed in New Spain.

[108] According to Cuadriello, tlaxcaltequidad offered "an ideological possibility for renegotiation (or liberation?) in the midst of a context of 'domination.'"Cuadriello, *Glories*: xxi.

creoles, meanwhile, invoked the story to defend Mexican Christianity from outsiders.[109] Yet the idea that Tlaxcala was distinguished by its extreme piety continued to evolve in the seventeenth century, acquiring ever more flourishes and symbols. A major milestone was the work of the cacique-priest don Manuel de los Santos y Salazar, who adapted the themes of Sigüenza and other creole contemporaries to his own community. That is, by coloring creole legends with his own sensibilities as a patriotic cacique, he promoted news of miraculous or portentous events from the early colonial period indicating that Tlaxcala and its people were specially favored in heaven. For example, in 1691 don Manuel's patron, the bishop of Puebla Manuel Fernández de Santa Cruz, invited Francisco de Florencia – the great herald of creole legends – to promote the cult of St. Michael in Tlaxcala. (Florencia, in turn, dedicated his account to the bishop.) The cacique was working as a priest in eastern Tlaxcala when the Jesuit traveled through the region collecting news of Diego Lázaro and his miraculous well.[110] Yet while Florencia's chronicle was, like his other apparition accounts, intended to proclaim New Spain's divine and marvelous origins, don Manuel's understanding of the St. Michael apparition was far more local, and rooted in a Tlaxcalteca identity that went well beyond the colonial era. According to the cacique-priest, all the events of Tlaxcalteca history – its proud preconquest record of independence, its exemplary piety, and even its beneficent climate – were the results of divine providence. Projecting the Christian God into the Mesoamerican past, don Manuel implied in 1711 that God and the angels had underwritten Tlaxcala's hard-won independence from the Mexica. He wrote that preconquest Tlaxcala had been "a realm apart since its origin and foundation"; its independence and distinctiveness nurtured and sustained by heavenly favor, it "never [fell] subject to another American empire." That divine benevolence continued to bless Tlaxcala after the Spanish conquest was evidenced by miracles such as the apparition of St. Michael to Diego Lázaro. Addressing the archangel directly, don Manuel gratefully affirmed that "without a doubt, [Tlaxcala] and its whole province are beneath your protection."[111]

Don Manuel was also involved in the promotion of yet another symbol of Tlaxcala's divine favor, the Virgin of Ocotlan, whose image was

[109] Robert Haskett, "Conquering the Spiritual Conquest in Cuernavaca" (paper presented at the American Society for Ethnohistory, Eugene, OR, Nov 13, 2008).

[110] See Dedication to Bishop Fernández de Santa Cruz, in Florencia, *Maravillosa aparición*: n.p.

[111] Santos y Salazar, *Computo*, 226.

held to have appeared in 1541 to an Indian of Santa Isabel Xiloxoxtla in Tlaxcala. According to legend, the man was suffering from one of the terrible sicknesses of the era, and the virgin healed him with water from a spring in a pine grove, or *ocotlan*. Following her instructions, he later led the Franciscans to the spot, where they found the trees aflame, yet unconsumed. Upon chopping the largest of the burning trees, they encountered a carved image of the Virgin Mary, which they placed in a nearby temple. That don Manuel de los Santos would feel a special affinity for this particular legend is unsurprising, as the image was venerated in his particular corner of Tlaxcala. He had been raised in his father's village of Topoyanco, very near to Xiloxoxtla and just down the road from the parish of San Lorenzo, where the image was originally housed.[112] The *Historia cronológica* of don Juan Buenaventura Zapata y Mendoza, the Salazars' family friend, describes three occasions, in 1662, 1676, and 1682, in which the statue was brought out in processions to celebrate civic achievements (such as the completion of a bridge) or to protect Tlaxcala against misfortune. Upon taking responsibility for the manuscript in 1689, don Manuel lovingly dedicated it to the Virgin of Ocotlan, placing it under her protection "so it shall not suffer the disdain and forgetfulness of time."

These are the first explicit references to the cult of Ocotlan in all of colonial literature. Neither Motolinia (who was in Tlaxcala in 1541) nor Torquemada mentioned the devotion. Yet through the combined sponsorship and patronage of the Puebla diocese and the Tlaxcalteca cabildo – the patricians of which saw themselves as the patriotic stewards and guardians of Tlaxcalteca history and corporate integrity – the image would gain fame toward the end of the seventeenth century, and become firmly associated with the civic identity of Tlaxcala. Don Bernabé de Salazar – don Manuel's father – was one of the city councilmen who had arranged the processions of 1662. In the early 1670s, the diocese appointed the first permanent chaplain to protect and beautify the cult. In the 1680s, a new sanctuary was built. Sometime after 1689, don Manuel de los Santos related the core miracle story for the first time. He placed it in a primordial setting, "a primitive time, when the hill

---

[112] Probanza of don Manuel de los Santos y Salazar, Salazar Family Papers, Cuapiaxtla, 1707, ff. 47r–47v; see also Camilla Townsend, *Here in this Year: Seventeenth-Century Nahuatl Annals of the Tlaxcala-Puebla Valley* (Stanford: Stanford University Press, 2009), 25–28.

was still covered with pines," and couched it within the arcane eso-
tericism typical of Mexico's creole antiquarians – the frustrated sense
that a great forgetting had occurred, leaving only fragmented clues as to
the precise origins of the divine immanence they knew to exist in their
midst. The cacique-priest expressed disappointment that don Juan Zapata's manuscript contained no information about the miracle in the pine
grove. He had heard of an "ancient text" in the possession of "a cacique
of this city," but he had not been able to find it. "Time has deprived us" of
such knowledge, he lamented, "leaving behind only a remote and obscure
tradition."[113]

The unpublished and uncirculated manuscript of the *Historia
cronológica* would not effectively spread knowledge of the legend, however. That was left to the Mazihcatzins of the eighteenth century, a noble
lineage of Tlaxcala that boasted of numerous educated clergymen as well
as cabildo officers and other community leaders. One of their relatives,
the Br. don Manuel Loayzaga, authored the first complete history of the
apparition in 1745, setting the facts as they are generally known today.
He was the chaplain in charge of the sanctuary of Ocotlan for over four
decades between 1716 and 1758; during that time, his kinsmen and compatriots assisted him as he beautified the church into a fine example of
baroque Mexican aesthetics. As Jaime Cuadriello has detailed, during
Loayzaga's time the Mazihcatzins commissioned multiple paintings and
sculptures in honor of the Virgin of Ocotlan, all of which represented her
as a symbol of Tlaxcala's special link to heaven. They also built a shrine
honoring the native commoner to whom the virgin had first appeared in
his home village of Xiloxoxtla, and even claimed him as a Mazihcatzin,
one of their own ancestors.[114]

That Loayzaga's *History of the Very Miraculous Image of Our Lady
of Ocotlan* (*Historia de la milagrosíssima imagen de Nuestra Señora de
Ocotlan*) was as much a patriotic as a pious account is revealed in the first
chapters, as the author began not with the pine grove, but by invoking
the old trope of Tlaxcalteca loyalty and retelling Motolinia's account of
Cristobalito Acxotecatl and the other boy-martyrs. "It was the Tlaxcalteca," he explained, "who not only embraced the faith with all of their
hearts, but who united with the conquistadors to fight against hell in favor

---

[113] Santos y Salazar, "Imagen de la Virgen de Ocotlan," in Zapata y Mendoza, *Historia
chronológica*: 81.
[114] Cuadriello, *Glories*: 150–61.

of the Cross of Christ [and who] shed blood over almost the entire land."
Thus was heaven moved to show a sign of its special love for Tlaxcala,
and thus did the Virgin of Ocotlan make her appearance.[115] Echoing don
Manuel de los Santos (and creoles like Sigüenza and Espinosa), Loayzaga
lamented that so few of his contemporaries were aware of the miracle
of Ocotlan, and that so little material evidence of the apparition had
survived. He chastised his countrymen for having allowed such glorious
events to sink into obscurity.[116]

After 1745, the five major symbols and motifs of Tlaxcalteca exceptionalism – Tlaxcala's ancient tradition of independence and republicanism, its contributions to the fall of Tenochtitlan, the boy-martyrs, the well
of St. Michael, and the Virgin of Ocotlan – were cited at the summit of
Novohispanic politics to defend the creole agenda. That is, what began
as local traditions of ethno-municipal patriotism, nurtured by a patrician
Tlaxcalteca nobility, were adapted and redeployed in creole circles and
controversies as evidence of the deep piety of native peoples and New
Spain in general. In 1757, fray Joseph de Leyza, the abbot of the Franciscan college at Tlatelolco, cited the Tlaxcalteca martyrs as proof that
native peoples everywhere could achieve the virtue necessary for joining
the priesthood. It was for the eternal glory of all Indians, he wrote, that
the three boys "gave their lives for the law of Jesus Christ."[117] During
the same proceedings a statement by the Mexico City Audiencia likewise referenced the children to argue in favor of a renewed effort to
educate young caciques throughout the Americas.[118] The Franciscan José
Mariano Díaz de la Vega argued the same in 1782; citing each of the
Tlaxcalteca legends, he insisted that such glories proved that "the Indians
were never irrational, and were always worthy of all the sacraments, and
what is more, heaven has honored [them] with many very special favors."

Tlaxcalteca exceptionalism survived to the end of the colonial period,
even as other pre-Hispanic identities had begun to fracture before larger
categories of caste and class. As the cabildo of Tlaxcala proclaimed in
1759, its caciques "have since ancient times conserved the luster of their
nobility and ancestry," and were distinguished because their forebears
"served [Carlos V] with the aid they gave to his general . . . don Fernando

[115] Manuel de Loayzaga, *Historia de la milagrosíssima imagen de Nuestra Señora de
     Occotlan* (Tlaxcala: Instituto Tlaxcalteca de la Cultura, 2008), 20.
[116] Ibid., 34.
[117] Information of Fr. Joseph de Leyza, Mexico, June 27, 1757, AGI-MX 1937, f. 216.
[118] Statement of the Mexico City Audiencia, Mexico, June 17, 1757, AGI-MX 1937,
     ff. 160–61.

Cortéz, for the increase of his realms and dominions [and] likewise in
the propagation of our Holy Catholic Faith, as in this Noble City [of
Tlaxcala] the Holy Doctrine in this New World had its beginnings."
This history, they continued, "has honored, ennobled, and exempted
this Tlaxcalteca Nation."[119] Even as late as 1810, after Father Miguel
Hidalgo's *grito* heralded the beginning of Mexico's war of independence,
the cabildo declared that "Tlaxcala does not forget what it was and is,
preserving in its heart the same noble sentiments that so propitiously
served that invincible general Fernando Cortés."[120] Meanwhile, portraits
of the three martyred children continued to hang in a place of honor in
Tlaxcala's storied cabildo chamber; according to the cacique don Nicolás
Faustino Mazihcatzin y Calmecahua (Escovar) in 1773, "it was to the
glory of Tlaxcala the actions of these three boys, its sons."[121]

Conclusion

In 1766, Dr. don Luis de Torres of the Metropolitan Cathedral politely
asked his compatriots to restrain the flood of Guadalupe sermons. The
topic was "of great and loving interest to all Mexican hearts," he conceded, "yet at the same time the most repetitive in our pulpits, and almost
exhausted."[122] He was wrong.

The creole *patria* that emerged in the eighteenth century was built atop
the myths and legends forged in the seventeenth. Seen holistically, behind
the bombast and gongorisms of baroque Mexican oratory lies a certain
vision of New Spain's origins, a half-articulated longing to replace memories of bloodshed and rupture with more uplifting stories of providence
and Christian transformation. Unlike more organic national or group
identities, Novohispanic creolism derived not from a shared history or

---

[119] Declaration of the Governor and Officials of Tlaxcala, Mar 16, 1759, AGN-VM 234,
Exp. 3, ff. 13–17.

[120] Cabildo of Tlaxcala, 1810, "El ayuntamiento de Tlaxcala ofrece todos sus recursos
para combatir la revolución iniciada por el cura Hidalgo," in Juan Evaristo Hernández
y Dávalos, Colección de documentos para la historia de la guerra de independencia de
México de 1808 a 1821 (Universidad Nacional Autónoma de México, 2007), 2.

[121] Mazihcahtzin y Calmecahua, "Descripción del Lienzo de Tlaxcala," 67. In most contemporary documents, don Nicolás's name is given as Mazihcatzin y Escovar.

[122] Dr. don Luis de Torres, Approbation of *Sermon de Nuestra Señora de Guadalupe que
el día 6 de Julio . . . hicieron los cavalleros hacendados para impetrar el socorro de las
aguas necessarias a la fertilidad de los campos* by Francisco Xavier Rodríguez (México:
Imprenta del Br. D. Joseph Antonio de Hogal, 1766), n.p.

language, but rather a self-conscious emotional link to the Mexican land-scape and its history. Creole belonging, then, was not a passive condition of having been born in Mexico, but rather something one affirmed through active homage to a recognized set of icons and symbols, the most important being the Virgin of Guadalupe. The power of guadalupanismo, however, was not merely as a vector of religious and social solidarity, but also in how its legend linked late-colonial Spanish speakers to the numinous and marvelous immanence that writers like Florencia attributed to Mexican antiquity and its native traditions. The Virgin of Guadalupe did not cast down idols and reduce pagan temples to rubble; she invited Indians into her loving embrace. By validating, rather than eradicating, the deep legacy of Mexico – by transforming it into a cradle of Christian zeal – Lady Guadalupe and her heavenly counterparts enabled the creoles' reinvention. No longer were they conquering foreigners; they were compatriots and heirs.

Accordingly, other stories that likewise attributed divine and peaceful origins to New Spain – or otherwise de-emphasized the role of violent conquest – were common in eighteenth-century sermons and liturgical writings. In Zacatecas in 1721, an Augustinian friar named Joachin de Vayas told that the local Zacatecos, although "wild," "had given themselves peacefully without a single instrument of war."[123] This was the pride of all the people of Zacatecas, that by heavenly design "it was conquered and won without any bloodshed."[124] In 1766, the Jesuit Francisco Xavier Rodríguez wrote that the Virgin Mary was the true conqueror of the New World, and the weapons of the conquistadors merely confirmed a spiritual transformation that had already occurred. "Even before this New World metropolis surrendered to the Spanish forces," he proclaimed, "it had already surrendered itself to [the Virgin's] power" by way of the image that Cortés had placed in the Great Temple of Tenochtitlan. "This was how [Mary] took possession of these vast domains, before Spanish forces conquered the terrain."[125] The results were profound, he concluded; while in Europe hundreds of years separated Christ and Constantine, and heretics ran amok for centuries after that, in New Spain, by contrast, "there remains not a single vestige of paganism," idolatry,

[123] Joachin de Vayas, *Sermon panegyrico que en la fiesta annual que acostumbra celebrar la muy ilustre, opulenta, y leal Ciudad de Nuestra Señora de las Zacatecas en memoria de su conquista...* (México: Francisco de Rivera Calderón, 1721), 4–5.

[124] Ibid., 29.

[125] Francisco Xavier Rodríguez, Dedicatory preface to *Sermon de Nuestra Señora de Guadalupe...*, n.p.

or heresy.[126] The Lic. don Ignacio Luis de Valderas Colmenero, a secular priest and advocate with the audiencia, invoked a related idea before the archbishop and the other heads of the Mexican Church in Querétaro in 1755. Referencing Sigüenza y Góngora, Torquemada, and Querétaro's peaceful conquest, Valderas preached that the Church had established itself in Mexico twenty-five years *before* the arrival of the conquistadors. Millions of Christians already existed in Mexico, and it was they who ultimately enabled both Cortés's swift victory as well as the subsequent spread of the faith into other regions.[127] In such reckonings, the Mexican Church was only obliquely related, if at all, to the conquest of Tenochtitlan.

[126] Ibid., ff. 14–15.
[127] Ignacio Luis de Valderas Colmenero, *Sermon del príncipe de los apóstoles nuestro padre S. Pedro...* (México: Imprenta Nueva de la Bibliotheca Mexicana, 1755), 22–26.

7

Cacique-letrados

An Indian gentry after 1697

Two small canvases painted with the arms of his ancestors
three old cassocks and a shoulder cape (turca) of old flannel
a nice cape with purple trim
twelve silver buttons
a large silver salt container and eight small spoons
two silver-plated coconut [chalices] (cocos guarnecidos de plata)
an inkwell and a bronze lamp
fifty-four books in quarto, many old but in decent condition
two bound volumes in manuscript
a nice cedar chest with several bundles of paper and other manuscripts
two small images of Our Lady of Guadalupe, painted on wood

Partial inventory of the possessions of Lic. don José Luis Santiago de
Salazar y Tapia, priest of San Hipólito Soltepec, 1724[1]

We cannot deny the truth of the ignorance and rusticity [of the Indians,
nor] that this is so deeply ingrained . . . that it is impossible to remedy. Yet
we have also seen from many instances that, with careful attention to their
cultivation, they have acquired a perfectly Christian and political character.
Some have also received sufficient education to reach the minor [clerical]
orders, while here and there an admirable few have even attained the higher
[ranks], their talents matching those of many literate Spaniards.

Cabildo of the Collegiate Church of Our Lady of Guadalupe, 1754[2]

Historians have described the eighteenth century as a time of "re-
Indianization" in the native sphere – a backlash, in part, against crown

---

[1] Inventory of the estate of Lic. don José Luis de Santiago de Salazar y Tapia, deceased,
Soltepec, Apr 12, 1724, Salazar Family Papers, f. 51.
[2] Statement of the Cabildo of the Royal Collegiate Church of Nuestra Señora de Guadalupe,
Mexico, June 28, 1754, AGI-MX 1937, f. 135.

reforms hostile toward the cultural separateness of native communities.[3] Sensing threats to local autonomy and integrity, many native leaders responded by asserting the inviolability of the Indian republic and the importance of maintaining its strictly indigenous character, as well as by carving out and presiding over what Mónica Díaz calls "hybrid places within the colonial order": Lay, civic, and professional corporations parallel to and modeled after, yet discrete and semi-independent from their Spanish counterparts.[4] These included already established institutions like the cacique college of San Gregorio, but also militias, confraternities, guilds, and even convents with exclusively indigenous memberships. Such organizations were efforts at both inclusion and autonomy: They were a means to participate in the broader colonial society while still resisting the encroachment of Hispanic outsiders and culture into local life.[5] As the presumptive leaders of any Indian corporations, caciques in particular favored their establishment, as they offered opportunities to exercise the authority that they considered their noble obligation and birthright.[6]

A less-understood, contemporaneous phenomenon – related to yet distinct from re-Indianization – involved fewer numbers, yet was disproportionately consequential in the development of Mexican creolism and identity. Responding to a new set of crown incentives, some upwardly mobile cacique families traversed the social and linguistic divide to pursue positions of authority and "honor" within the Hispanic sphere itself, with the institutional Church, the viceregal bureaucracy, or both. Securing such positions was not only vocational, but also part of a pragmatic social and economic strategy, as the honor of official service to God and king promised many benefits, not the least of which were salaries, pensions, legal privileges, and social distinctions. Alongside their mestizo and creole compatriots, ambitious caciques eagerly sought to place sons as priests or crown agents, as in addition to income and honor, it could help facilitate the upward mobility of other relatives.[7] Like re-Indianization, caciques who aspired to honorable offices resisted the slow erosion of their status,

[3] Matthew D. O'Hara, *A Flock Divided: Race, Religion, and Politics in Mexico, 1749–1857* (Durham, NC: Duke University Press, 2010), 56–59.

[4] Mónica Díaz, *Indigenous Writings from the Convent: Negotiating Ethnic Autonomy in Colonial Mexico* (Tucson, AZ: University of Arizona Press, 2010), 11.

[5] For discussions of such associations, see Schroeder, "Jesuits, Nahuas, and the Good Death Society in Mexico City, 1710–1767."; Lockhart, *The Nahuas* 221–29; Martínez Baracs, *Gobierno de indios*: 480–502.

[6] Haskett, "Two Worlds."

[7] Rodolfo Aguirre Salvador, *El mérito y la estratégia: Clérigos, juristas, y médicos en Nueva España* (México: Plaza y Valdés, 2003), 11.

yet in this case they did so by asserting a traditionally Hispanic mode of prestige.

Honor is, by definition, exclusive. The immediate prerequisite for any honorable vocation was education, and thus the Royal University and its affiliates became the entry point for ambitious or well-connected caciques. Traditionally, however, the university was also a primary site of social and ethnic exclusion, its doors open only to those with the approved genealogical credentials, meaning Old Christian Spanish.[8] Yet a series of imperial laws culminating in 1697 shifted the official metrics of honor in a way favorable to caciques, such that many soon began sending their sons to matriculate in Spanish institutions of higher education. Emerging, degrees in hand, they hoped to join the proud and credentialed ranks of the *letrados* ("lettered ones") – the pen-wielding, erudite gentry of the early modern Hispanic world.

This was also a realm overwhelmingly dominated by creoles. The admission of caciques into lettered institutions thus facilitated contact between the two segments of colonial society that laid claim to the Mexican legacy. Thus, while their numbers were tiny, the cacique-letrados had an outsized influence over erudite perceptions of Mesoamerican history and of Indians and indigeneity in general – particularly those educated and formed within urban Jesuit institutions such as San Gregorio.

This chapter examines the legal incorporation of the indigenous nobility into the "honorable" segment of Hispanic society, as well as a number of individual lineages that both precipitated and reflected the phenomenon. It charts a shift that occurred in the late-seventeenth century with regards to the cultural and legal meaning of indigenous ancestry, one that would accelerate under the Bourbon monarchs in subsequent decades. Specifically, while the ideals of confederated empire associated with the Hapsburgs encouraged caciques to be natural lords – local authorities whose positions derived from Mexican antiquity – it also excluded them from the imperial bureaucracy. However, the Bourbon agenda favored the reinvention of the native elite as Hispanic gentlemen. Indigenous blood, especially if noble, was no longer shameful, but indigeneity itself – in terms of language, dress, and customs – was deemed dishonorable. In other words, under the Hapsburgs, Indians could be caciques of lineage, but not Hispanic gentlemen, whereas the Bourbons encouraged caciques to be Hispanic gentlemen, but not Indians. In a way parallel to the creoles' inclination to envision an unbridgeable gulf

---

[8] Poole, "Church Law."

between the admirable Mesoamerican past and their lowly native contemporaries, Bourbon policies valued elite indigenous genealogies, but only inasmuch as their descendants were not recognizably indigenous. This shift in the significance of Indian blood in creole discourse reflects a Jesuit influence; whereas early colonial Franciscans most consistently emphasized the caciques' piety and pedigree, late-colonial Jesuits also hailed them as men of letters whose genius ennobled the Novohispanic patria.

Once again, with regards to Mexican historical identity the incorporation of caciques into the lettered realm required presuming and asserting both rupture and continuity. Cacique gentlemen derived access to honorable institutions from preconquest genealogical distinctions, yet they were also compelled to sever that genealogy from the mosaic of colonial conceits regarding the innate inferiority, idolatry, and infidelity of native peoples.[9] Yet this transformation alluded to a deeper continuity: They were, they insisted, gentlemen of quality faithfully administering the civic and spiritual life of New Spain, just as their ancestors had centuries earlier in a different kind of society.

Cacique honor and the "Indian bishops" of New Spain

To early modern Spanish jurists and administrators, the question of whether Indians could be "honorable" was ambiguous – an echo effect of the perennial debates regarding the essential "nature" and rationality of America's native peoples. As a cultural as well as legal classification, honor was less a fixed status with clear criteria than an informally and locally negotiated reputation. It was, therefore, also a language that late-colonial caciques were required to master in order to remake themselves into Indo-Hispanic gentlemen, as it was both exclusionary and inclusionary toward Indians in different ways, and a central feature of the colonial construction of Indianness among both native as well as non-native subjects. A brief examination of the Iberian ideal of honor, as well as how it was applied to elite Indians in New Spain, will provide essential context.

In the early modern Hispanic world, honor was an umbrella concept connoting a wide variety of esteemed personal and genealogical qualities, especially a legitimate birth, a reputable lifestyle, and impeccably Christian credentials. Yet in both law and practice, honor was usually defined in the negative: Honorable people were those untainted by dishonor and

[9] Díaz, *Indigenous Writings from the Convent*: 9–10.

shame, meaning illegitimacy, vulgarity, and immorality. As a legal or intellectual concept, it was first and foremost a religious ideal: Those suspected of imperfect Christian orthodoxy or who had attracted attention from the Inquisition suffered from "infamy," the most egregious form of dishonor.[10] Meanwhile, as an informally determined social quality, dishonor was gendered: Female shame revolved almost entirely around ideals of sexual chastity, while male dishonor accrued from base activities associated with the peasantry such as manual labor, gambling, and drunkenness.[11] Crucially, honor was a hereditary trait; regardless of one's own moral credentials, honor required an entire family tree free of dishonor. The genealogical element of honor was most famously expressed in the peculiar Iberian ideal of "blood purity," which asserted the inferiority of the "New Christian" descendants of Jews and Muslims and the "cleanliness" of those "Old Christians" in whom the ancient blood of Visigothic Hispania presumably remained intact.[12] Nobility, also a genealogical quality, did not bear directly on theories of honor – one could be an honorable peasant or a dishonorable hidalgo – yet noble ancestries were generally accepted as *prima facie* evidence of honor.[13] In short, honor was no single thing, but rather the absence of a wide variety of disqualifiers, only a minority of which one might actually control.

Most importantly, early modern Castilian law and custom enshrined honor as a prerequisite for many civic and ecclesiastical ranks – a legacy of the self-interested campaigns by some in the fifteenth century to remove rivals from desirable posts by impugning their "impure" Jewish and Muslim ancestors. Honor requirements primarily affected the middling segments of society; grandees and kings were above suspicion – and many indeed would have been considered "impure" had their genealogies been subjected to real scrutiny – while peasants and laborers were simply excluded by custom and presumption.[14] The aspirations of rural hidalgos and the upwardly mobile urban merchant class, however, often led through the clergy and the royal bureaucracy. Those who hoped to gain

---

[10] Stafford Poole, "The Politics of *Limpieza de Sangre*: Juan de Ovando and his Circle in the Reign of Philip II," *The Americas* 55, no. 3 (1999): 369, 88.

[11] Paul H. Freedman, *Images of the Medieval Peasant* (Stanford: Stanford University Press, 1999); Ruiz, *Spanish Society*: 39–43, 52–53.

[12] Albert A. Sicroff, *Los estatutos de limpieza de sangre: Controversias entre los siglos XV y XVII*, trans. Mauro Armiño (Madrid: Taurus, 1985); Ruiz, *Spanish Society*: 68–70, 99–107; Ruiz, "Discourses of Blood and Kinship."

[13] See Böttcher, *El peso de la sangre*.

[14] King Fernando the Catholic, for example, had converso ancestors. Ruiz, *Spanish Society*: 69–70; Elliott, *Imperial Spain, 1469–1716*: 221–22.

access to such dignified and gentle positions needed to represent themselves as genealogically and socially honorable, whether through shrewd litigation or simply by adopting a conspicuously noble lifestyle untainted by manual labor and overtly commercial activities. Thus, it was in this segment of society where the precise contours of honor were debated, contested, and taken seriously.

This was the "lettered" world, honorable not only for its inherent connections to the monarchy and the papacy (the two ultimate sources of authority), but also because it involved pens, salaries, and the intellect rather than plows, wages, and muscle.[15] Letrados were first and foremost functionaries of the early modern state, yet one of their most characteristic features was a lofty pretension to the "honorable life." In contrast to the vulgarity of common labor and the crudeness of commerce, letrados – so aptly satirized by Cervantes in the *Quixote* – preferred to represent themselves as guardians of the Good, the True, and the Beautiful: gentlemen on horseback, defenders of the Church, and devotees of poetry and the life of the mind.[16] This also made them highly status-conscious: jealous of their titles and distinctions, fiercely competitive amongst one another, and sensitive to any perceived slights to their honor as gentlemen. While subject to a discrete set of rules and traditions, the secular clergy were letrados as well, as their careers likewise began in the university, and many secular professionals such as lawyers were also clergymen. Priests, meanwhile, were no less concerned with worldly issues such as pensions and rank.[17] The intersection of mundane administration with medieval literary and aristocratic ideals, embodied by the omnipresent letrados, was an iconic feature of Spanish America.[18]

Yet even as letrados proliferated – when the frontiers stabilized, would-be conquerors pursued lettered offices instead – their prestige derived from exclusivity. The most important barrier was education, as lettered vocations required credentials, or *grados*. Grados, meanwhile, were only available to those who could prove "merit," meaning genealogical purity and social honor. Indeed, the Royal University in Mexico City was originally established in the 1550s to secure the loyalties of the

---

[15] Aguirre Salvador, *El mérito y la estratégia*: 85–105.

[16] Ruiz, *Spanish Society*: 70–74.

[17] For the social history of the secular clergy, see John F. Schwaller, *The Church and Clergy in Sixteenth-Century Mexico* (Albuquerque, NM: University of New Mexico Press, 1987); William Taylor, *Magistrates of the Sacred: Priests and Parisioners in Eighteenth-Century Mexico* (Stanford: Stanford University Press, 1996).

[18] The classic portrait of Spanish–American letrados is Rama, *The Lettered City*.

restive conquistador-encomendero class by providing dignified careers in the Church and crown bureaucracy for their children. Blood strictures preserved the cachet of grados by preventing the development of a meritocracy that could threaten the creoles' supremacy. Due primarily to this link between lineage and education, those who boasted of bachelor's degrees *(bachilleratos)*, law degrees *(licenciados)*, and doctorates *(doctorados)* did not merely signal erudition, but also membership in an elite caste born, as it were, to wield authority.[19]

The complex demographics of America confounded Spanish theorists of honor. The New World and its peoples did not share Iberian history; there was no Visigothic golden age, and there had been no Jews or Muslims tainting precontact bloodlines, obviating there the cornerstones of Iberian notions of genealogical quality. Yet imperial administrators and observers nonetheless translated and applied standards of honor to the Americas, thereby ascribing all manner of qualitative interpretations to the social categorizations we today name "race." In this way, Iberian notions of social, religious, and genealogical merit rationalized the construction and preservation of concentric colonial hierarchies that favored Spaniards over non-Spaniards. While "Spanish" blood was meaningless in Iberia, in the racial-ethnic crucible of Spanish America it signified honor more than any other quality.[20]

Native peoples occupied an ambiguous place in this regime. Presupposing a peaceful baptism, no claim of genealogical dishonor could be alleged, as they were not descended from Jews or Muslims, those who had heard yet rejected the gospel. Neither were they descended from Africans, and were therefore unsullied by the Curse of Ham or the shameful association with slavery. Accordingly, upon its inauguration the Royal University explicitly opened itself to native students.[21] In 1645, when the important Bishop of Puebla, Juan de Palafox y Mendoza (r. 1640–55), compiled new statutes for the university, he prohibited the matriculation of Africans and their descendants, yet conceded that "Indians, as vassals of His Majesty, can and should be admitted."[22]

---

[19] Aguirre Salvador, *El mérito y la estratégia*: 85; Margarita Menegus Bornemann, and Rodolfo Aguirre Salvador, *Los indios, el sacerdocio, y la universidad en Nueva España, siglos XVI-XVIII* (Mexico: Plaza y Valdés, 2006), 59–68.

[20] María Elena Martínez, "The Language, Genealogy, and Classification of "Race" in Colonial Mexico," in *Race and Classification: The Case of Mexican America*, eds. Ilona Katzew and Susan Deans-Smith (Stanford: Stanford University Press, 2009).

[21] Menegus Bornemann, *Los indios, el sacerdocio, y la universidad*: 12.

[22] *Constituciones de la Real y Pontificia Universidad de México*, 2nd edn. (Mexico: Zúñiga y Ontiveros, 1775), 132.

Nonetheless, few Spaniards seriously entertained the notion of Indian–Spanish equality, especially *vis a vis* their eligibility for offices of authority in the Church. That a native clergy might catalyze a self-perpetuating cascade of Christian conversions was an idea as old as New Spain itself; as a crown official wrote in 1525, one Indian priest would be as effective as fifty Spaniards in attracting others to the Church.[23] Yet as we have seen, such optimism and universalism quickly soured.[24] In 1555, just five years after allowing them into the university, Church authorities listed Indians, mestizos, and mulatos alongside the descendants of Jews and Muslims as those with tainted ancestries.[25] Thirty years later, while introducing Tridentine priorities into Mexico, they defined Indians as neophytes in the faith for at least four generations: not dishonorable, yet nonetheless presumed ineligible for ordination "without the greatest and most careful scrutiny."[26] Such conceits easily accumulated racial dimensions that echoed Iberian attitudes toward the descendants of Jews, despite Church doctrines to the contrary. An influential theologian expressed such sentiments in the 1660s, writing that "the bad seed" of idolatry had "spread such deep roots in the Indians it seems that the two became one flesh and blood." Even after generations in the Church, he continued, "they carry this vice in their blood, and drink it in their [mothers'] milk."[27]

Given such prejudices, native aspirants to the lettered realm, however accomplished, were burdened by indigeneity. Spaniards considered them at best rustic, naïve, and superstitious, and at worst innately idolatrous, "unreasonable" (*sin razón*), and unsuited for anything beyond manual labor. When exceptions were made, however, they were invariably on behalf of native noblemen. Caciques were Indians, yet they were also Christian nobles bearing explicit declarations of the king's favor. It was, in some cases, possible to overwhelm antinative conceits with the residual prestige of noble pedigree. The Franciscans, for example, explicitly denied their habit to native aspirants as of 1569, yet Francisco Morales discovered ten Indians and non-Hispanic mestizos among their order in

---

[23] Figuera, *Formación del clero indígena*: 367.

[24] Lino Gómez Canedo, *La educación de los marginados durante la época colonial: Escuelas y colegios para indios y mestizos en la Nueva España* (Mexico: Editorial Porrúa, 1982); Menegus Bornemann, *Los indios, el sacerdocio, y la universidad*: 25–33; Henry Kamen, *Philip of Spain* (New Haven: Yale University Press, 1999), 33–34, 83–84.

[25] Figuera, *Formación del clero indígena*: 381.

[26] *Concilio III Provincial Mexicano, celebrado en México en el año de 1585 . . . ilustrado con notas por el R. P. Basilio Manuel Arriaga, S.J. . . .* (México: Eugenio Maillefert y Compañia, 1859), 41–42; see also Poole, "Church Law," 644.

[27] Alonso de Peña Montenegro, *Itinerario para parochos de indios . . .* 2 vols. (Amberes: Henrico y Cornelio Verdussen, 1698), v. 2, 221.

the seventeenth century – all caciques who represented themselves as hidalgos rather than indios. The iconic surname "Moctezuma" proved especially useful.[28]

This culture of exclusion reflected baroque ideals of innate social hierarchy: Lettered institutions were for Spaniards and creoles. Non-Spanish aspirants, therefore, were compelled to obscure their non-Spanish blood. Three examples illustrate both the genealogical obfuscation of the seventeenth century as well as the changed meaning of Indian blood in later generations.

Dr. Juan Merlo de la Fuente of Tlaxcala (c. 1590 to after 1665) soared within the ecclesiastical hierarchy of his time. According to his probanza, Merlo excelled at the Royal University alongside "the most learned men of [New Spain]," and obtained a doctorate in Canon Law in 1628. He was offered a seat with the canonry of Tlaxcala the following year, and spent the next two decades examining local clergy in the doctrine. Merlo clearly captured the esteem of his colleagues and contemporaries, including the eminent Bishop of Puebla Juan de Palafox y Mendoza. The latter endorsed him "with much approval," elevated him to a prebendary of the cathedral, and eventually appointed him his own vicar-general, one of the highest-ranking figures in the diocese. His reputation was such that in 1644 King Felipe IV offered Merlo the see of Nueva Segovia (the Phillippines), which he declined.[29] Finally, in 1650 he was named Bishop of Honduras, where he ministered for fifteen years.[30]

Dr. Francisco de Siles was born in 1614 in Real del Monte, outside Pachuca (Hidalgo). He obtained a doctorate in Theology in 1645, and quickly became a canon with the Mexico City cathedral.[31] He was also a professor of Theology at the Royal University, where in 1655 he was elevated to the position of chancellor, just below the rector.[32] In 1669,

---

[28] Francisco Morales, O.F.M., *Ethnic and Social Background of the Franciscan Friars in Seventeenth-Century Mexico* (Washington, DC: Academy of American Franciscan History, 1973), 40–47. Morales lists several cacique-friars by name: Frays Ruy de Mendoza, Domingo Álvarez of Tlaxcala, Sebastián de Navarrete y Trejo (an Otomí of Xilotepec), Manuel de los Santos y Salazar of Tlaxcala, Miguel Osorio Moctezuma of Tlaxcala, and the brothers Diego and Antonio Valdés Moctezuma.

[29] Merits of Juan Merlo de la Fuente, Puebla, Feb 2, 1650, AGI-I 196, N.1, f. 1r.

[30] Royal Appointment of Dr. Juan Merlo de la Fuente As Bishop of Honduras, Madrid, Dec 30, 1650, AGI-I 456, L.A. 29, ff. 55v-56v.

[31] Doctor of Theology of Francisco de Siles, Mexico, Apr 8, 1645, AGN-Universidad 13, exp. 7, ff. 6–7; Royal Confirmation of Dr. Francisco de Siles as Canon of the Metropolitan Cathedral, Madrid, Nov 30, 1647, AGI-I 456, L. 27, ff. 205r-06v.

[32] Acts of Plenary Cloister of Royal University in Favor of Francisco de Siles, Mexico, Oct 13, 1655, AGN-Universidad 15, Exp. 38, ff. 55–56.

he was appointed Bishop of Nueva Segovia, although he died before the order arrived to Mexico.[33] Siles was one of the original promotors of guadalupanismo in New Spain. He was close to Miguel Sánchez, the priest who wrote the first Spanish account of the legend in 1648, and introduced the volume with a letter that explicitly linked the Virgin of Guadalupe to the still-inchoate creole patria; she was, he wrote, Mexico's Esther, the queen who saved her people, and she left her "creole image" behind as a sign that she would always intercede on behalf of "her patria."[34] Siles was also instrumental in the inquiries of the 1660s. It was he who traveled to Cuauhtitlan and obtained the testimonies confirming the authenticity of the legend and of the virtue of Juan Diego; he also supervised the experts' investigation of the image itself, in which a group of master painters affirmed that it transcended the skill of a human hand.[35]

Dr. Nicolás del Puerto's achievements were no less. Born in Santa Catarina Minas, south of Antequera (Oaxaca), he achieved a licenciado and a doctorate in Canon Law in 1638. In 1640, he was licensed to act as an advocate (*abogado*) before the audiencia chamber, eventually representing some of the most important creole corporate interests of Mexico City, including the Metropolitan Cathedral, the city cabildo, and the local Franciscan province. Archbishop don Juan de Mañozca (r. 1643–50) even named Puerto as his personal legal representative. He was a judge with the Inquisition, and in 1650 he joined the chapter of the Metropolitan Cathedral with the approval of the viceroy. In 1655, he became a rector of the Royal University, and the following year he was named a canon with the Metropolitan Cathedral and became its treasurer. In the 1660s, he was vicar-general in the archdiocese of Mexico under two archbishops, and was also involved, along with Siles, in the investigation and propagation of the Guadalupe legend. In 1670, he was honorably released from official teaching duties, although he continued to do so voluntarily for another three years.[36] His lifetime of services – which he not-unreasonably declared "the most qualified of any subject of the Indies" – bore its final fruit in 1678, when he was named bishop of his

---

[33] Medina, *Chrónica*: f. 252v.
[34] Francisco de Siles, letter of introduction to Miguel Sánchez, *Imagen de la Virgen María Madre de Dios de Guadalupe*... (Mexico: Imprenta de la Viuda de Bernardo Calderón, 1648). n.p.
[35] Brading, *Mexican Phoenix*: 70–80.
[36] Méritos de Nicolás del Puerto, Mexico, 1673, LL Latin American Manuscripts.

home diocese of Oaxaca.[37] His sinecure lasted two years, during which he erected a new seminary and battled suspected heresies in the mountains before dying of old age on August 13, 1681.[38]

Juan Merlo de la Fuente, Francisco de Siles, and Nicolás del Puerto were exemplars of the clergy-intelligentsia of baroque Mexico: educated, erudite, and politically skilled. They were also remembered as cacique Indians by later generations in New Spain, who hailed them as proof of the intellectual and moral capacity of native peoples. Yet despite their posthumous fame as "Indian bishops" – and despite their relatively well-documented lives at the summit of the lettered realm – their indigenous ancestries were both minimal and largely obscured during their own era, likely deliberately so. Indeed, it seems to have been taboo until decades later, when the legal and cultural meaning of indigenous ancestry had shifted in favor of Enlightenment-era ideals elevating education alongside genealogy as an indicator of merit. Ironically, at that point patriotic creole lore began to overexaggerate the native character of the bishops' predominantly Hispanic backgrounds.

In his probanza of 1650, Merlo is never referred to as *don,* but only *doctor,* although in other documents he does adopt the honorific. He does not mention his parents' names; merely declaring himself the "legitimate son of parents of known quality" from the Puebla diocese.[39] In Spanish probanzas from the era, this would have indicated humble (if honorable) origins; in the Novohispanic context, it suggests an attempt to elide a partially indigenous background. Merlo's relationship with Bishop Palafox is also suggestive, as the latter was a powerful ally to native hidalgos from the Tlaxcala-Puebla region.[40] A number of Merlo's younger relatives also found vocational success, largely via his coattails, and their records are similarly indicative of genealogical obfuscation.[41] Don Joseph Merlo de

---

[37] Viceroy Payo Enríquez de Rivera, Appointment of Dr. don Nicolás del Puerto as Bishop of Oaxaca, Mexico, Dec 18, 1678, AGI-M 50, N.41, f. 1.

[38] Record of the Death of Nicolás del Puerto, Antequera, Aug 13, 1681, AGI-M 52, N.39, ff. 1–5. See also Medina, *Chrónica:* 246v–47r. As bishop, Puerto directed the ongoing idolatry extirpation campaigns in the Sierra Norte (Villa Alta) that eventually provoked the Caxonos Rebellion of 1700. See David Tavárez, *The Invisible War: Indigenous Devotions, Discipline, and Dissent in Colonial Mexico* (Stanford: Stanford University Press, 2011), 171–72.

[39] Probanza of Dr. Juan Merlo de la Fuente, Feb 1650, AGI-I 196, N.1, f. 1r.

[40] Felipe IV to Viceroy Conde de Alba de Liste, Madrid, Feb 15, 1650, AGI-I 456, L.A. 29, ff. 69r–70v.

[41] Don Juan de Merlo de la Fuente, Bishop of Honduras versus the Dean and Cabildo of Puebla, Puebla, Mar 21, 1653, AGI-ECJ 171A, N.6, ff. 16–17, 21. After beginning his duties in Honduras, in 1653 Bishop Merlo gave power of attorney to his nephews don

la Fuente – a Nahuatl-speaker who did style himself *don* – acquired a bachillerato in the Royal University in 1646 and served as a priest in four parishes around Puebla between 1652 and 1673.[42] The young don Francisco Merlo de la Fuente went to Honduras with his uncle the bishop, who ordained him in 1659; two decades later, in 1680, he became schoolmaster at the cathedral of Nicaragua.[43] Don Francisco described his parents as "persons of quality and Old Christians," a designation that by itself reveals little.[44] Yet he listed his father Matías de Merlo without the *don*, unlike his mother doña Magdalena de la Fuente, which might suggest one of the creole-cacica matrimonial pairings common to the era.[45] Finally, don Juan Merlo de la Fuente, also from Puebla-Tlaxcala, was likewise ordained by his episcopal uncle and namesake in 1659; his subsequent career, lasting through at least 1704, was as a vicar, parish priest, and cantor in Honduras and Guatemala, as well as archdeacon in Chiapas. In 1684, the bishop of Chiapas approved a prebendary for him in Puebla so he could return home and care for four nieces, "poor and virtuous," who needed his support.[46]

Bishop Puerto's family history is somewhat less obscure. His probanza declares him to be "of noble parents," the son of Martín Ortíz del Puerto and doña María de Colmenares Salgado.[47] Ortíz was no cacique, nor was he indigenous. He was the grandson of Sancho Ortíz del Puerto, a regidor of Vizcaya (Spain), and the cousin of Captain Nicolás del Puerto, a contemporary encomendero of Mérida (Yucatan).[48] Although he avoided delving into his mother's ancestors, he testified that they were "among

Francisco and don Juan to represent him in an ongoing salary dispute he had with his former cathedral chapter in Puebla.

[42] Merits and Services of Br. don Joseph Merlo de la Fuente, Madrid, June 18, 1674, AGI-I 201, N. 81, ff. 614–15.

[43] Merits of don Francisco Merlo de la Fuente, Madrid, Oct 15, 1683, AGI-I 205, N.80, ff. 541–42.

[44] Native families who claimed to be "Old Christians" typically did so to stress their ancestors' immediate embrace of Christianity during the conquest. See Peter B. Villella, "'Pure and Noble Indians, Untainted by Inferior Idolatrous Races': Native Elites and the Discourse of Blood Purity in Late-Colonial Mexico," *Hispanic American Historical Review* 91, no. 4 (2011).

[45] Merits of Francisco Merlo de la Fuente, Honduras, July 8, 1665, AGI-I 120, N. 168, unnumbered.

[46] Merits of don Juan Merlo de la Fuente, Madrid, May 11, 1685, AGI-I 206, N. 36, ff. 320–21.

[47] Merits of Nicolás del Puerto, f. 1r.

[48] Merits of Nicolás del Puerto Colmenares, Mexico, Aug 22, 1664, AGI-I 120, N. 86; Juan de Zervantes vs. Nicolás del Puerto, Madrid, July 5–Aug 23, 1672, AGI-ECJ 958, unnumbered.

the first conquerors and settlers of the Indies" – a phrase that connoted Spaniards but which was also regularly deployed by the descendants of Indian conquistadors. Puerto's maternal grandfather was Julian de Colmenares, who married a local noblewoman named doña Ana Salgado. Julian himself was the son of Melchor de Alavés y Colmenares, an original member of Hernando Cortés's company, and doña María de Salas, the possibly mestiza daughter of Juan Rodríguez de Salas, yet another conqueror and encomendero in Oaxaca.[49] Bishop Puerto's indigenous background was, therefore, limited to distant ancestors on his mother's side who had participated in the elite conquistador-cacique marriages of the early colonial era – hardly a "pure Indian" (as one twentieth-century historian described him), but nonetheless distinguished from Spaniards according to the genealogical accounting of the era.[50]

The achievements of Bishops Merlo, Siles, and Puerto were celebrated among their lettered contemporaries, yet none mentioned indigenous ancestors.[51] Bishops Merlo and Puerto were, like those examined in Chapter 6, castizo-creoles who belonged to the Hispanic sphere, yet whose family trees included one or two native noblewomen; the indigenous heritage of Siles, if any, remains unclear. Such ancestries were unhelpful to their professional ambitions, and so went unremarked. This situation would soon change, however, and the posthumous memory of these bishops could not be more different. Specifically, eighteenth-century creoles declared them "indios" in service to a different agenda. Significantly, it was their Indianness that mattered: To creole advocates their merit derived less from nobility and pedigree – although it was taken for granted that they were caciques of lineage – and more from their scholarship and erudition. Their grados and rank proved that Indians, properly educated, could become great men of letters. Their achievements, moreover, reflected glory on all Indians, and therefore (by creole reckonings) on Mexico itself, their patria. By classifying them as Indian bishops and

---

[49] Merits of Francisco de Alavés, Mexico, May 18, 1567, AGI-P 68, N.1, R.8, ff. 3r–4v. Juan Rodríguez was encomendero of Mitla and Tlacolula; his wife was Ana Rodríguez.

[50] Mariano Cuevas, *Historia de la iglesia en México*, 5 vols. (México: Editorial Patria, 1946–7), t. III, 117. Cuevas praises Puerto as an "Indian of pure race of the pueblo of Santa Catalina in the mountains of Oaxaca," who, because he became bishop only at a very advanced age, was never able to give full expression to his great talents. Following eighteenth-century sources, some modern accounts continue to name Puerto, Merlo, and Siles as "Indians," perpetuating this misrepresentation. See, for example, V. de P.A., appendix to Francisco de Sedano, *Noticias de México* (México: J.R. Barbedillo y Ca, 1880), v. 1, 100–04; Guillermo Lohmann Villena, "The Church and Culture in Spanish America," *The Americas* 14, no. 4 (1958): 387.

[51] See Medina, *Chrónica*: 19.

identifying them as compatriots and forebears, eighteenth-century creoles both claimed ownership of and defended the Mexican legacy.

The legend of the Indian bishops was most clearly a Jesuit phenomenon, linked to their broader agenda in favor of Indian education. Its primary advocates were the Jesuit teachers of caciques and their students, both of whom cited the bishops as proof of the intellectual potential of Indians and as models for aspiring native letrados. In 1753, full-body portraits of Merlo, Siles, and Puerto, complete with biographical glosses, were placed in the sacristy of the Colegio de Niñas Indias de Nuestra Señora de Guadalupe, a new school for native girls administratively linked to the Colegio Seminario de San Gregorio.[52] There was a fourth portrait as well, but it gave no biographical information. In one of the many stories of hazy origins and mishandled artifacts that characterized creole legends, the Franciscan advocate for native education, José Mariano Díaz de la Vega wrote that an unnamed native artist had produced the portraits; when he died, his belongings were sent to auction, and the ignorant auctioneer erased the glosses (yet the unnamed bishop was no less deserving of our praise, assured Díaz.) Eventually, the four works – along with another depicting the seventeenth-century Peruvian playwright and cleric (and rumored mestizo), Juan de Espinosa Medrano, "el Lunarejo" – were acquired by an unnamed lay brother who donated them to the Jesuits.[53]

The retroactively indigenized memory of Puerto and Siles perhaps reflects their fame as pioneers of guadalupanismo. As for Merlo, it is possible that his reputation derived from his friend and patron, Bishop Palafox of Puebla. Palafox maintained a strong following in the eighteenth century that continued to commission new editions of his texts.[54] Along with citing Merlo, in its statement of 1754 the audiencia also excerpted a passage from Palafox's apologetic *Virtues of the Indian* (*Virtudes del indio*, 1650), in which he explicitly praised the genius of a cacique-priest he was acquainted with, "don Fernando de Figueroa, Indian, son and grandson of caciques."[55] However, if Palafox knew Merlo to have an

---

[52] Katzew, "Stars in the Sea of the Church: The Indian in Eighteenth-Century New Spanish Painting," 340; Schmidt Díaz de León, *Colegio Seminario*: 55–57.

[53] Díaz de la Vega, "Memorias piadosas," UCB M-M 240, ff. 138–39.

[54] Palafox was beatified in 1726, and his complete works were published in Madrid in 1762. See Genaro García, ed. *Don Juan de Palafox y Mendoza*, Documentos inéditos o muy raros para la historia de México (Mexico: Librería de la Viuda de Ch. Bouret, 1906), 19–25.

[55] Royal Accord of the Audiencia of Mexico City, Mexico, June 27, 1757, AGI-MX 1937, f. 165; Juan de Palafox y Mendoza, "De la naturaleza del indio," in ibid., 271. In the audiencia's statement, the surname "Figueroa" is given for the cacique-priest

indigenous heritage, it seems strange that his treatise would not likewise cite his close associate and vicar as an exemplary Indian. This incongruency went unremarked.

The legend spread. During a controversy over a proposed seminary for Indians in the 1750s (discussed in Chapter 8), the members of the collegiate chapter of the Villa de Guadalupe outside of Mexico City remembered Bishop Merlo as a cacique of Tlaxcala to argue in favor of the project. "We cannot deny the truth of [the Indians'] ignorance and rusticity," the members wrote, yet some have excelled in letters and erudition; "such was – to the glory of his nation – the illustrious Doctor don Juan de Merlo, Bishop of Honduras."[56] The Jesuit educator Juan de Mayora, of the cacique college of San Gregorio, cited Bishop Merlo alongside don Antonio Valeriano, and recalled a number of triumphant anecdotes from the Jesuits' network of schools to argue in favor of the project. In fact, he insisted, the two most capable people he had met in Mexico, of any caste, were Indians. There would be many more Bishop Merlos, he lamented, if only there were a sustained effort to educate native children.[57] The Mexico City Audiencia helped spread the legend as well; in 1757, the oidores declared that the great achivements of Bishop Merlo, along with the famous alumni of Santa Cruz de Tlatelolco, proved that "one cannot doubt [the Indians'] capacity for learning."[58]

The idea that three Indians had become bishops energized eighteenth-century advocates of native education, but it was also dear to New Spain's increasingly patriotic creoles. By the 1770s, the Indian bishops were firmly ensconced in creole lore, finding expression at the summit of colonial society. In 1775, the viceroy commissioned a new edition of the recently updated constitution of the Royal University. Since the university's foundation, read the introduction, no fewer than eighty-four of its alumni had risen to become archbishops and bishops, "among whom three have been Indians."[59] In 1782, Díaz de la Vega gave accounts of Merlo, Siles, and Puerto in his impassioned defense of the Indians, which circulated in

don Fernando, but modern editions of Palafox's work do not include this name. The audiencia in 1757 gave the title of the work as *Retrato del indio* (*Portrait of the Indian*), but it is almost universally known today as *Virtudes del indio*.

[56] Opinion of the Cabildo of the Royal Collegiate Church of Our Lady of Guadalupe, Villa de Guadalupe, 1755, AGI-MX 1937, f. 135.

[57] Statement of Juan de Mayora and San Gregorio de Mexico, Mexico, June 13, 1757, AGI-MX 1937, ff. 245–58.

[58] Royal Accord of the Audiencia of Mexico City, Mexico, June 27, 1757, AGI-MX 1937, ff. 164–65.

[59] *Constituciones de la Real y Pontificia Universidad de México*: 84.

manuscript.[60] Not only were the Indians ideal Christians, he wrote, some of them had been "exalted" to the level of bishop. As for the many who had distinguished themselves as priests and vicars, he wrote, "it would be almost impossible" to tell of them all, as "it would be to attempt to count the stars in heaven."[61]

The reforms of the 1690s

Among many elite Spaniards and creoles of the seventeenth century, indigenous blood signaled, if not dishonor, then a general inaptitude for the intellectual life that characterized the letrado ideal. Accordingly, Bishops Merlo, Siles, and Puerto – and, presumably, their peers with similar ancestries – seem to have intentionally obscured their non-Spanish ancestries in official correspondence and documentation. This contrasts starkly with the non-lettered realm, where indigenous and mestizo contemporaries were spending considerable energy and treasure investigating, publicizing, and even inventing their descent from the great lineages of Anahuac, largely to secure tribute exemptions and other privileges. Yet toward 1700, a drastic shift occurred in the perceived significance of native forebears, especially noble ones, one that made native ancestry marginally more acceptable within lettered institutions. The new attitude, however, did not reflect an increased acceptance of pluralism, but rather the opposite; it was part of a broader regime of intentional cultural homogenization, one that would accelerate under the Bourbons of the eighteenth century. In the late-colonial era, upwardly mobile caciques were afforded greater access to the lettered realm, but only if they simultaneously adopted Hispanic cultural norms. It was both the denial and embrace of indigeneity; they lived as Hispanic gentlemen even as they proclaimed a noble quality derived from Mesoamerican roots.

A series of laws in the 1690s both encouraged and facilitated the entry of caciques *qua* caciques into honorable offices. As we have seen, early colonial policies, exemplified by the ideal of quasi-segregation known as the "Two Republics," had favored the preservation and semiautonomy of indigenous social and political structures that were inoffensive

---

[60] Ilona Katzew gives a broad overview of Díaz's manuscript, especially with regards to its portrayal of Indians as a whole. Ilona Katzew, "That This Should Be Published and Again in the Age of the Enlightenment?": Eighteenth-Century Debates About the Indian Body in Colonial Mexico," in *Race and Classification: The Case of Mexican America*, eds. Ilona Katzew and Susan Deans-Smith (Stanford: Stanford University Press, 2009).

[61] Díaz de la Vega, "Memorias piadosas," f. 138.

to Catholic mores and Spanish authority. In the late-seventeenth century, however, royal agents became frustrated with the resulting cultural and linguistic diversity, seeing it as an impediment to a more centralized crown authority.[62] Hoping to Hispanize the native elite, in the 1680s they began demanding quotas for cacique boys in new (creole) seminaries.[63] This policy expanded in 1691, when the Council of the Indies stipulated that caciques make up one-fourth of all entrants to a new crown-funded seminary in Mexico City. The idea of cultivating a vanguard of Spanish-educated Indian leaders was not new, of course, yet unlike its sixteenth-century antecedants the emphasis was more on cultural than religious transformation. Once versed in "Christian doctrine, grammar, and the other letters necessary for the predication of the Holy Gospel," the Council argued, the learned caciques "will become great examples, helping already converted Indians to remain firm in the observance of our Holy Faith while bringing others into it more easily."[64] If in the sixteenth century Catholic doctrine was Nahuatlized, the provisions of 1691 were meant to culturally and linguistically Hispanize Nahuas who were already Christian.

Yet to educate caciques was to assume their honor, for only the honorable could receive grados. Did Spanish law finally, after almost two centuries, accept the *a priori* honor of Indians? The issue was temporarily ambiguous, as indicated by an example from 1696, when an Otomí nobleman from Querétaro, don Ignacio de Mendoza y Granada, applied for a bachillerato, and openly declared his cacique heritage. But it seems that such provenance was insufficient, and he felt compelled to remind university officials that Indians were not, technically speaking, forbidden from seeking grados.[65]

---

[62] See Menegus Bornemann, *Los indios, el sacerdocio, y la universidad*: 103–07; Martínez, *Genealogical Fictions*: 204–06; O'Hara, *Flock Divided*: 57–71; Taylor, *Magistrates of the Sacred*: 568, n. 80.

[63] Recommendations for the Formation of a Seminary in Nicaragua for the Children of Caciques, Madrid, Apr 13–15, 1685, in Koneztke, *Colección de documentos para la historia de la formación social de Hispanoamérica, 1493–1810, ser. 1,* v. 2, t.2, 759–64. *Seminarios* were grammar schools, not necessarily places where priests were trained (as in modern usage).

[64] The Council of the Indies Recommends the Foundation of a Seminary in Mexico City, Madrid, July 12, 1691, in ibid., v. 3, t. 1, 15–16.

[65] Probanza of don José Ignacio de Mendoza y Granada, Mexico, May 26–28, 1696, in Medina M. de Martínez, "Indios caciques graduados de bachiller en la universidad," *Boletín del Archivo General de la Nación* 10, no. 1–2 (1969): 14–15.

The ambiguity would soon be resolved. An oft-cited decree of March 26, 1697 clearly delineated where native peoples, both common and noble, were to fit within Spanish metrics of honor. Henceforth, caciques were legally equivalent to Spanish hidalgos, and therefore eligible for any position requiring honor, blood purity, and nobility, while native commoners were to be regarded as analogous to the peasants of Castile.

> Although in special cases Indians can assume ecclesiastical, secular, governmental, and political posts that by charter and law require limpieza de sangre and the quality of nobility, there is a distinction between Indians and mestizos who are descendants of the principal Indians called caciques and those descended from less principal Indians who are the tributaries and who during pagan times recognized vassalage; the former and their descendants deserve all the preeminence and honors, ecclesiastical as well as secular, that are customarily conferred upon the noble hidalgos of Castile, and they can participate in any *comunidades* (private or religious corporations) that by law require nobility, because it is the case that they in pagan times were nobles whose inferiors recognized vassalage and paid tribute, and whose particular nobility still remains in effect, retaining as much as possible their ancient rights (*fueros*) and privileges....And as for the lesser principales and their descendants in whom occurs blood purity as descendants of pagans without the admixture of any inferiors or other reprobate sect, these also deserve all the prerogatives and honors enjoyed by the pure-blooded of Spain known as the *estado general* ("general estate," or commoners).

The decree continued by reiterating crown preferences for the education of cacique children in seminaries and declaring that they should constitute one-fourth of all institutionally funded students. Its conclusion was strongly worded: All of the crown's vassals should receive what their inherent merit entitled them to, "without hindering those from the Indies who are descended from pagan times, and so that the natives, [having justified their merits], can solicit and assume the honors and benefices that are available."[66] The Bourbon kings retained and even extended this policy. Seventy years later, Carlos III (r. 1759–88) reiterated the 1697 decree and stipulated that all vassals of proven lineage and merit were to be considered for "honors and employment of luster... without hindering those from the Americas who have descended from pagan times."[67]

Yet while the higher education of caciques was part of an imperial push to reduce the cultural distance between the native and Hispanic spheres, they had another, perhaps unintended effect. Ironically, the 1697 decree compelled caciques to emphasize their elite preconquest heritages.

[66] Decree of Carlos II, Madrid, Mar 26, 1697, AGN-RC 27, Exp. 114.
[67] Decree of Carlos III, Madrid, Sep 11, 1766, AGN-RC 89, Exp. 42.

It opened honorable positions to caciques, not all Indians, which required native aspirants to prove not only their good character, but also their pedigreed descent from the royal lineages of ancient Mexico. For example, that same year a new primary school opened in Mexico City and, in accordance with the new law, explicitly invited cacique aspirants, so long as they proved themselves "untainted by any stains or bad races of Moors, Indians, and heretics."[68] One was eligible as a cacique of lineage, equal to Spanish hidalgos; absent such a heritage, they were *indios,* and deemed ineligible for grados. As a result, late-colonial descendants of the pipiltin regularly cited their precolonial ancestors to justify sinecures within colonial institutions.

Thus, unlike the "Indian" bishops of earlier decades, educated caciques after 1697 did not obscure their native heritages. Rather, they became cacique-gentlemen: Nahua, Otomi, and Zapoteca nobles faithfully executing the business of the king and Church while boasting openly of Mesoamerican ancestry. Thus, if historians are largely correct that by 1700 those called "caciques" hardly resembled the tribute-harvesting aristocrats of the sixteenth century and before, it is also true that the title became influential and important in other ways. In this case, it underlay the rise of a new Indian gentry. After over a century and a half of ambiguity, the value of cacique status within colonial institutions was finally clarified, quantified, and codified. With or without cacicazgos, those who could prove descent from the preconquest ruling class were henceforth explicitly eligible for honorable offices, one of the only real avenues of social mobility in the early modern Hispanic world. Along with tribute exemptions, this helped preserve the desirability of cacique status, and it is no coincidence that the decades immediately following 1697 saw a spike in native petitions for noble confirmation.

The decree of 1697 in the cacique agenda

The viceroy received the 1697 decree in July of the following year, and publicized it on August 28th. Soon, native elites from multiple regions began citing its language while requesting all manner of privileges, from tribute exemptions to the right to place daughters in convents.[69] Many even attached verbatim transcriptions. An extensive early example is the 1699 probanza of don Pedro Ramírez Vázquez of Tequixquiac, discussed

---

[68] Menegus Bornemann, *Los indios, el sacerdocio, y la universidad:* 119.
[69] Díaz, "'Es honor de su nación.'"

in Chapter 6. In October of that year, don Pedro commissioned a copy of the 1697 decree and, based on its provisions, attached it to his request for noble amparo. "By virtue [of the royal decree of March 26th]," his advocate declared, "my party [asserts] that he is...a cacique and principal, a son, grandson, and descendant by both lines of caciques and principales." Don Pedro carefully crafted his probanza to parallel and invoke the decree's internal logic: As one of ancient lineage, steadfast loyalty, and impeccable Christian virtue, his primordial rights remained intact, secured by the Spanish crown. He was the heir to don Pedro Quauhlitzilatzin and doña María Papan[tzin], "caciques during ancient times," and all his forebears had enjoyed both tribute exemptions and the tecpan compound of nearby Tepotzotlan – proof of his "immemorial...and very ancient nobility."[70]

The legal effects of the 1697 decree are also evident in how the examination represented don Pedro's Christian credentials. Rather than merely assert fidelity and virtue like previous generations, he invoked the Spanish language of honor and blood purity – a predictable effect of the new qualitative equivalency between caciques and Spanish hidalgos. Extending the 1697 decree to its logical conclusion, the examination declared don Pedro to be "a legitimate (born in wedlock) Indian, without mix or infection of any other blood or bad race." "Besides being a cacique," it continued, "don Pedro Ramíres is an Old Christian and descendant of such, [and none] of his ancestors, his wife, or children, have been punished nor implicated in the crimes of idolatry, superstition, Judaism, heresy, or any other [dishonor]." Moreover, he lived virtuously, and had never been arrested or seen intoxicated in public. In its favorable ruling, the audiencia also cited the 1697 decree. As a "descendant of caciques since antiquity," ruled the oidores, don Pedro enjoyed all the "rights, preeminences, and honors customarily conferred upon the noble hijosdalgo of Castile...in the form conceded by Your Majesty in your royal decrees, laws, and ordinances, and especially that of the 26th of March of the past year of 1697."[71]

Contemporary examples parallel the Tequixquiac case in rhetoric and style, and illustrate the rush of probanzas submitted in the wake of 1697. In May of 1701, the Zapoteca nobleman don Francisco de Mendoza y Rojas of Huaxolotipac (Oaxaca) similarly petitioned for amparo for

---

[70] Petition of don Pedro Ramírez Vázquez, Mexico, Oct 31, 1699, AGN-I 34, Exp. 126, f. 129–30.

[71] Ibid., f. 171.

himself and three sons. And like don Pedro of Tequixquiac, he or his procurador attached a full and verbatim copy of the 1697 decree, invoking its language and structuring the probanza according to its logic. Don Francisco was the direct heir to a long line of local leaders, he had married a Zapoteca noblewoman, and the local people respected him as their cacique. The audiencia's response likewise cited the 1697 decree, ruling that don Francisco and his sons should enjoy "all the privileges, honors, preeminences, and privileges (sic) that are customarily conferred upon the noble hijosdalgo of Castile."[72] Similarly, in 1734 don Julian Carrasco of San Gabriel de Etla (Oaxaca) invoked the 1697 decree in an elaborate probanza detailing his noble quality. Bound in red leather and lovingly beautified, the probanza's opening pages consist of a complete transcription of the decree.[73] This became a valuable heirloom for his son – who, as we will see below, made good use of it in a dispute several decades later (Figure 8).

Although not lettered, certain high-status trades also belonged to the honorable realm, their exclusivity enforced by laws and policed by guilds. In 1773, an aspiring gold embroiderer in Mexico City named don José Mariano Sánchez de Salazar y Zitlalpopoca – of the illustrious Salazar family of Tlaxcala – attached a copy of the 1766 update to the 1697 decree to his bid to join the gold- and silversmiths' guild, which due to the sensitive nature of handling precious metals required both nobility and honor for membership. Don José was a mestizo or castizo, but the Salazars still represented themselves as the heirs of tlatoani Citlalpopoca, tlatoani of Quiahuiztlan and Indian conquistador of Tlaxcala.[74] Lest there be any controversy over his blood quality, don José petitioned the viceregal overseer in his own hand, declaring:

I am a cacique and the legitimate son... of a distinguished family; and in conformity... with the royal decree of 11 September, 1766, based on earlier ones, in which Our Catholic Monarch... ordered that caciques be worthy [of consideration], declaring them apt for any employment and ecclesiastical or secular dignities customarily conferred upon the hijosdalgo of Castile, and able to participate in any community whose statues demand nobility.[75]

---

[72] Privileges of don Francisco de Mendoza y Rojas, Mexico, June 19, 1702, AGN-I 35, Exp. 126.

[73] Probanza of don Julian Carrasco, Antequera, May 21, 1734, AGN-BN 553, Exp. 8, ff. 64r–67v.

[74] License to Practice the Noble Art of Goldworking of don José Mariano Sánchez de Salazar Zitlalpopoca, Mexico, Jan 11, 1773–Mar 26, 1774, Salazar Family Papers, LC-MMC, ff. 82r–89v.

[75] Petition of don José Mariano Sánchez de Salazar Citlalpopoca, Mexico, June 31, 1773, Salazar Family Papers, LC-MMC, f. 82r.

FIGURE 8 Probanza of don Julian Carrasco of Etla, 1734. Mexico. Archivo General de la Nación, Fondo Bienes Nacionales 553, exp. 8, f. 63r.

With the law on his side, don José experienced little trouble in securing his license. He presented witnesses to his family's purity and commissioned a scribe in Tlaxcala to consult the noble registry and confirm his lineage. After a practical exam, the overseer accepted don José's purity and honor as a "cacique Indian and son of a mestiza who, in accordance with the royal cédula of 11 September 1766 and the royal laws it cites, should be admitted to" those civic, religious, and trade organizations reserved for people of honor. Ironically, in conceding to don José the license to operate his own workshop, the overseer stipulated that he only accept Spanish apprentices.[76]

The 1697 decree and its 1766 update remained ubiquitous and consequential in cacique interactions with the viceroyalty for generations. As late as 1810, the mestizo, Spanish-speaking Cortés Chimalpopoca family of Tlacopan sought noble amparo from the viceroy, citing their famous forebear, don Antonio Cortés Totoquihuaztli, whose coat of arms remained prominently displayed on their lintel. Overzealous tax collectors and disrespectful commoners, complained don José Jorge Cortés Chimalpopoca, were threatening the noble quality and privileges that were his birthrights. In recent decades, he lamented, he and his family had suffered "a thousand outrages against their privileges, being treated as macehuales or plebeians, [being] arrested for trifling reasons, [and] were listed on the tribute rolls." These were clear violations of his noble prerogatives, he argued, because as an heir to the ancient kings of Tlacopan he was, by royal fiat, entitled to the same honors as the "noble hijosdalgo of Castile, with whom the Sovereign equated the caciques [by] royal decree in the year 1697."[77]

The legal equivalence between caciques and hidalgos in the eighteenth century opened doors to ambitious native elites. Yet laws have only an oblique influence on culture, and conceits against the indigeneity of caciques survived, often representing obstacles to upward mobility. For example, many native letrados benefitted from a "loophole" in the regulations regarding who could receive ordination; while Tridentine convention held that all who were called to the priesthood should demonstrate financial independence, the crown often waived that requirement for those who could speak native languages, the pressing and perennial lack of which plagued the colonial Church. Such aspirants received ordination *a título de idioma*, "by right of language." Because this enabled the ordination of a less-wealthy cohort – including many of indigenous background – it acquired a negative stereotype among the secular clergy, who

---

[76] Practical Examination in the Art of Goldcasting of don José Mariano Sánchez de Salazar Citlalpopoca, Mexico, Mar 16, 1774, Salazar Family Papers, f. 87v.

[77] Probanza of don José Jorge Cortés Chimalpopoca, Mexico, Mar 26, 1810, in Fernández de Recas, *Cacicazgos*, 47–50, quote on 49–50. The date is given as 1818, but that is a transcription error, as the testimony was presented to the Viceroy Francisco Javier de Lizana y Beaumont, who governed between 1809 and 1810.

scorned those so ordained as rustic and uneducated.[78] Ordination a título de idioma also worked against Bourbon priorities of cultural homogenization; in 1770, for example, the Archbishop of Mexico Francisco Antonio Lorenzana proposed to end the practice, which he felt aggravated the "problem" of linguistic diversity in the Americas while also allowing less-qualified individuals to obtain curacies.[79] Thus, native clerics suffered discrimination in the form of a general presumption of inaptitude and incompetence. The resulting "insults and mockery" of haughty Spanish colleagues, lamented the audiencia report of 1757, unjustly prevented many native letrados from achieving their full potential in erudite vocations.[80]

Cacique-bachelors, Hispanic gentlemen

Importantly, the newly stipulated honor of late-colonial caciques afforded greater access to lettered vocations. Thus, in accordance with the reforms of the 1690s, a small but significant cohort of indigenous noblemen entered the university, the clergy, the royal bureaucracy, and other prestigious communities traditionally restricted to Spaniards and the creole elite. Cacica women, of course, could not follow this path, but parallel and related developments facilitated the establishment of three convents specifically for indigenous nuns by the mid eighteenth century.[81] Soon, a small subset of native elites could be found, quill in hand, drafting official documents or administering the sacraments within the lettered apparatus of New Spain. The inventory of the belongings of the Tlaxcalteca cacique and parish priest Lic. don José Luis Santiago de Salazar y Tapia, which opened the present chapter, illustrates the humble, yet learned and dignified lives and vocations of such men.

The numbers of cacique-letrados were tiny, but real; Margarita Menegus and Rodolfo Aguirre have accounted for over 200 indigenous students in Novohispanic colleges and seminaries between 1692 and 1822 – perhaps only a fraction of the total – the vast majority of whom listed themselves as caciques.[82] William Taylor, meanwhile, estimates that between one and 5 percent of the Novohispanic clergy during the eighteenth

---

[78] Taylor, *Magistrates of the Sacred*: 95–96.

[79] Francisco Antonio Lorenzana, *El que llega reverente a el Trono de la Magestad debe siempre confiar que en él están colocados la Clemencia y la Justicia.* . . . Mexico, Aug 18, 1770, HL Mexico Viceroyalty Collection, ser. 2, vol. 1, no. 25, f. 4.

[80] Opinion of the Mexico City Audiencia in Favor of an Indian Seminary, Mexico, June 27, 1757, AGI-MX 1937, f. 160.

[81] See Díaz, *Indigenous Writings from the Convent.*

[82] Menegus Bornemann, *Los indios, el sacerdocio, y la universidad*: 16–18, 123–24.

century was of native descent, almost entirely caciques.[83] Nor were such developments hidden from public view; in 1728, the monthly *Gazeta de México* reported that the Seminary College of Mexico City (established in the 1691 decree) hosted four cacique children, the Jesuits at the College of San Gregorio fourteen, while eleven matriculated (appropriately enough) with the Franciscans at the newly reopened College of Santa Cruz de Tlatelolco.[84] Perhaps unsurprisingly, there is a clear connection between the flow of native letrados-in-formation and the presence of Jesuits, especially around Tepotzotlan and in the urban bases of Mexico, Puebla-Tlaxcala, and Oaxaca.[85]

Yet while the legal climate had changed, the ultimate basis for the caciques' claim to privileges – the presumption of an historic Indo-Hispanic alliance and confederation under Church and crown – had not. Indeed, the 1697 decree reimagined native leaders, as the heirs to the Mesoamerican aristocracy, as natural members of the colonial administrative class. That is, the decree inserted caciques into the elite social script of Spanish hidalgos: Like the latter, the former deserved privileges by way of pedigree, a history of services to the crown, and a reputation for Christian virtue. Thus, not only did the reforms of the 1690s leave the fundamental logic of cacique petitions and probanzas unchanged, they encouraged renewed, amplified efforts to assert notions of continuity and harmony between New Spain and Mexico's native legacy. The erudite caciques were scions of Anahuac laboring diligently as gentlemen operatives of the crown and Church. Thus, the same themes of primordiality, fealty, and piety that defined early colonial arguments for patrimonial preservation and restoration survived, rearticulated as justifications for the presence of native elites within Spanish institutions of colonial administration. The petition of don Lucas de Zárate of Tlaxcala, who pursued a Bachelor's in Philosophy, exemplifies this synthesis of Mesoamerican pedigree and letrado vocation. In filing for his bachillerato at the Royal University in 1712, he presented Spanish witnesses who testified that he was

virtuous, studious, and diligent, of good lifestyle and habits, because his parents taught him well; they are noble republicans [meaning officers within the cabildo], caciques and principales from among the best of Tlaxcala, descendants of kings, with very pure blood, not newly converted nor plebeian Indians, nor accustomed

---

[83] Taylor, *Magistrates of the Sacred*: 87.

[84] *Gazeta de México* (Mexico City), Dec 13, 1728, in León, *Bibliografía mexicana del siglo XVIII*, pt. 2, sec. 1, 84–85.

[85] Aguirre Salvador, *El mérito y la estratégia*: 65.

to drunkenness or witchcraft, but mindful of God and their consciences; not of low vocations nor of common stock (*consejiles*), and he has been alcalde, and all of those of his lineage have obtained [honorable posts] and are regarded, held, reputed, and esteemed as nobles of clean and good blood.[86]

Thus did don Lucas identify the native kings of preconquest Mexico as the originators of "pure" bloodlines, hidalguía, and honor in New Spain. Under the new laws, there was to be no qualitative distinction between the nobles of America and those of Spain.

Similarly, in 1711 a minor cleric named don Teodoro Xallallatzin Villegas, the son of the governor of the Nahua sector of Puebla, declared himself "a descendant of the royal blood of the kings of Tlaxcala" who had "noble and priestly relatives," and therefore eligible for a Bachelor of Arts.[87] In 1717, don José Juárez of Tepeaca (Puebla) studied philosophy at the Jesuit College of San Ildefonso in Puebla, reminding his superiors that he was of sufficient "quality and blood (*naturaleza*)" for a Bachelor's degree, and should "not be prohibited from similar pretensions" in the future.[88] Predictably, the Moctezuma name retained its customary cachet; the Tlatelolca don Pascual de Roxas Mendoza, Austria, y Moctezuma – yet another descendant of the sixteenth-century governor don Diego de Mendoza Imauhyantzin – acquired a Bachelor's of Arts at the College of Santa Cruz in 1732 and was ordained in 1736. After serving vicariously for over a decade, he became parish priest in Atenango del Río (Guerrero). Predictably, he was careful to emphasize his distinguished descent from "the [ancient] kings of this very noble and imperial city" to those who determined his career track.[89]

Neither were grados and lettered offices limited to Nahuas. In 1713, a Jesuit in Oaxaca named Clemente Guillén reported that he had recently awarded six Bachelors of Arts to local caciques, whom he listed by name.[90] In 1719, don José Crisanto Vanegas de Monjarás, a minor-

---

[86] Testimony of José Camacho de Ita and Antonio Álvarez Águilar on Behalf of don Lucas de Zárate, Mexico, Feb 27, 1712, in Martínez, "Indios caciques graduados de bachiller en la universidad," 29.

[87] Probanza of don Teodoro Xallallatzin de Villegas, Mexico, Mar 4, 1711, in ibid., 38–40.

[88] Petition of don José Juárez, Puebla, Feb 23–26, 1717, in ibid., 21–22.

[89] Probanza of don Pascual de Roxas Mendoza Austria y Moctezuma, in Menegus Bornemann, *Los indios, el sacerdocio, y la universidad*: 276–81; see also Taylor, *Magistrates of the Sacred*: 123.

[90] Their names were: don Marcelino Velázquez, Miguel de Oceguera, Pedro Cortés, Leonardo Zárate, Rodrigo de la Cruz, and Antonio Félix de Solís; their institution was the Jesuit Colegio Seminario de Santa Cruz de Oaxaca. Certification of Clemente

orders cleric who styled himself "a very noble cacique of the diocese of Oaxaca," cited his cacicazgo alongside his scholarship and ordination in soliciting a Bachelor's in Philosophy.[91] In a relatively unique episode from 1770, the university accepted don José Antonio Ximénes Frías, a mestizo nobleman from Temazcalapa (Oaxaca), as a doctoral student – which, due to its elevated prestige, required closer genealogical scrutiny. Despite his mixed heritage, the faculty chair who examined his case noted that neither his Spanish nor his cacique ancestors impugned his honor.[92] Similarly, the Jesuit Colegio de San Martín in Tepotzotlan – the home institution of Andrés Pérez de Ribas, addressed in Chapter 6 – helped launch the careers of a number of cacique-bachelors from the Otomí populations of today's states of Hidalgo and México. Don Gregorio de la Corona was an Otomí nobleman of Ixmiquilpan (Hidalgo); he promoted his candidacy for a grado in the standard way, citing numerous ancestors who were "nobles as evidenced by the public offices they obtained as governors, Old Christians, and clean of all bad races."[93] In 1736, another Otomí cacique, don Manuel Ignacio Ramírez of Tequixquiac – a cousin of don Pedro Ramírez Vázquez, who maintained the tecpan of Tepotzotlan – received ordination; he went on to administer the sacraments for at least thirteen years in a number of parishes in today's México and Hidalgo states.[94]

The post-1697 legal climate had secondary effects as well, both benign and less so. As we have seen, native lords had long represented themselves as patrons of the Church, honoring their parishes with pious bequests and other endowments such as chantries. Yet after 1697, it became more possible for native donors to designate – like their Spanish counterparts – their own heirs as the beneficiaries of the chantries. It was a potential means of transgenerational wealth preservation, as well as a way to secure income for children and grandchildren. Yet like all benefices, such donations were subject to frequent disputes.

Guillén, Mexico, Mar 14, 1713, in Martínez, "Indios caciques graduados de bachiller en la universidad," 17–18.

[91] Petition of don José Crisanto Vanegas de Monjarás, Mexico, Apr 21, 1719, in ibid., 24–25.

[92] Genealogical Investigation of Br. don José Antonio Jiménez Frías, Indian, Mexico City, 1770, in ibid., 260.

[93] Merits of don Gregorio de la Corona, Mexico, 1718, in Menegus Bornemann, *Los indios, el sacerdocio, y la universidad*: 288.

[94] Merits of don Manuel Ignacio Ramírez, 1749, in ibid., 275–76. See also Honors and Privileges of don Pedro Ramírez Vázquez of Tequixquiac, Mexico, Oct 31, 1699, AGN-I 34, Exp. 126, ff. 129–30.

In 1701, a cacique from Ocotelolco (Tlaxcala) named don José Gregorio Sánchez founded a chantry with a principal of 2000 pesos (20 percent of his total assets), and appointed his son, a minor-orders cleric, as its first chaplain; when the latter died, the benefice passed to a likewise educated sibling. About two decades later, don José Gregorio died, and his widow, doña María Luisa Texis, assumed the family estate. In 1726, she attempted to dismantle the endowment and recover its principal, arguing that she had never desired the chantry but that her late husband had violently coerced her into binding her own resources to its foundation. She cited her indigeneity as a cause for leniency – a common means of taking advantage of Spanish prejudices – insisting that, if she had known how, she would have prevented her husband from misusing her dowry assets "as some Spanish women habitually do." Her advocate echoed this theme, citing various laws requiring leniency toward Indians due to their "incapacity and rusticity." Laws, he argued, should be applied somewhat less rigorously toward Indians than toward Spaniards. In its ruling, the ecclesiastical tribunal compromised by reducing the chantry by half and returning the rest to doña María Luisa.[95]

Another example comes from the Etla region of Oaxaca. In 1722, don Diego Gonzalez y Chavez, a Zapoteca cacique of San Juan Guelache, and his wife, a Mixtec cacica from Cuilapan named doña Josefa María de Zarate, established a chantry anchored to nine small wheatfields and a share of a mill.[96] In the charter, the two caciques represented themselves as impeccably devout and honorable. Neither they nor any of their predecessors had ever practiced idolatry or otherwise violated Catholic orthodoxy; in their own words, they were, they insisted, "pure and noble Indians, untainted by inferior idolatrous races."[97] They stipulated that their son, Joseph, was to become the first chaplain once he had completed his education. After him, the endowment was to benefit, in perpetuity, future descendants of the founders.[98] The chantry passed through two generations without complications, but five decades later it fell vacant; as

---

[95] Petition and Prueba of doña María Luisa Texis, Puebla, Oct 30, 1726, AGN-BN 197, Exp. 8.

[96] Charter of the Chantry of Etla, Oaxaca, 1722, AGN-BN 553, Exp. 8, ff. 1-35v. William Taylor estimates the cacicazgo of San Juan Guelache at over 200 acres, including three houses, five house plots, a one-half interest in a wheat mill, and thirty-two pieces of arable land scattered around the area. Taylor, *Landlord and Peasant*: 63; Taylor, *Magistrates of the Sacred*: 126–30.

[97] Charter of the Chantry of Etla, Oaxaca, 1722, AGN-BN 553, Exp. 8, ff. 2–2v.

[98] Charter of the Chantry of Etla, Oaxaca, 1722, AGN-BN 553, Exp. 8, ff. 34–35v.

there were no obvious heirs, it became the focus of a raucous round of competitive cacique self-fashioning.

Three local families, varying in wealth, nobility, and education, came forward to claim the chantry on behalf of their sons, two of whom were merely boys. In dueling statements before an ecclesiastical judge, the fathers proclaimed their nobility while impugning that of their rivals. The winner was don Fernando Antonio Carrasco y Badillo, the son of the Zapoteca nobleman don Julian Carrasco, discussed previously. To establish his young son's eligibility for the honorable benefice, don Fernando revealed his family's treasured heirloom: The leather-bound 1734 probanza his father had commissioned in response to the 1697 decree, which attested to the family's "noble quality, hidalguía, legitimacy, and purity of blood."[99] The probanza was an archetypal expression of the caciques' preferred historical identity. It told that don Fernando's elite lineage originated with "Xsiqueguezagaba'a," a conquest-era Zapoteca ruler known to locals as "Lord of the Well."[100] Upon the arrival of Cortés into Oaxaca, this lord demanded baptism under the name don Julián and became a fierce ally of the Christians. Over the next several years, he and his brother personally supplied and led thousands of local warriors in the Spanish pacification of southern New Spain. The Carrascos of Etla, boasted the probanza, had been honored ever since as "Old Christians" whose diligence and valor had anchored the success of the crown and Church in Oaxaca.[101] The judge accepted the Carrascos' bid, due primarily to the legal authority of their notarized proof of nobility, purity, and honor. Thus, don Julián Carrasco's probanza – full of tales of ancient Zapoteca lords, Indian conquistadors, and early colonial conversions – had the intended effect: It secured his grandson a modest, but salaried, position in the parish church.[102]

Other conflicts were less complex. Some organizations had quotas regarding the number of subsidized positions reserved for caciques, sometimes stated in their charters, or sometimes established by statute. As few native families, caciques or not, could afford to support many years of educational formation, this meant competition for the few spots

[99] Probanza of don Julián Carrasco, Antequera, May 21, 1734, AGN, BN 553, Exp. 8, ff. 63–77, quote from 69r.
[100] Ibid., 77.
[101] Ibid., 75.
[102] Assessment of the Promotor Fiscal of Oaxaca, Oaxaca, 1775, AGN-BN 553, Exp. 8, ff. 156v–63v. For a more detailed account of the dispute and its links to late-colonial notions of blood purity, see Villella, "Pure and Noble Indians."

available. Such was the case of don Pedro Zacarias, a cacique of Azcapotzalco who in 1757 sought access to the Seminary College of Mexico City. As he stated in his petition, the seminary, which was under royal patronage, was required to reserve one-fourth of its funded seats for the children of caciques.[103] He was denied entry, however, because the final slot had already been filled. The 1697 decree had created opportunities, but demand would always exceed supply.

Unsurprisingly, the prominent families of Tlaxcala produced their fair share of upwardly mobile cacique-gentlemen. Jaime Cuadriello extensively details the activities of the Mazihcatzins, many of whom obtained grados and were ordained; tracing themselves to preconquest tlatoque, they used their positions within the Church to promote Tlaxcalteca art and civic pride.[104] Don Nicolás Joseph Faustino Mazihcatzin y Escovar (d. 1793), for example, was both a cabildo officer in Tlaxcala as well as a minor-orders cleric with bachilleratos in Theology, Sacred Canons, and Jurisprudence. Along with other relatives, he cultivated and patronized lay corporations in Tlaxcala that expressed and disseminated his vision of Indian Christianity. As we will see in Chapter 8, don Nicolás also joined the efforts of contemporary native letrados to solicit crown support for new cacique seminaries. In 1788, don Nicolás published a small manual promoting the veneration of St. Nicholas, his "saintly namesake." Representing himself as a devout "indio cazique," he declared one of his objectives to be the conversion "to Our Holy Catholic Faith [of] all the nations of the world."[105]

The Salazars of Tlaxcala also found success in lettered hierarchies. Don Manuel de los Santos y Salazar administered the sacraments in various Tlaxcalteca parishes between 1685 and his death in 1715. Due to his high regard in the Puebla diocese, several younger relatives were able to follow his example. His brother don Nicolás Simeon served vicariously under don Manuel in San Lorenzo Cuapiaxtla from 1693 to 1710 before assuming control of the parish until his own death in 1733.[106] Along with don Manuel, don Nicolás interacted with several prominent advocates of

---

[103] Petition of don Pedro Zacarias to the Real Colegio Seminario de Mexico, Mexico, 1757, AGN-BN 982, Exp. 50.

[104] See Cuadriello, *Glories*.

[105] Nicolás Joseph Faustinos Mazihcahtzin y Escovar, *Día seis de cada més, que se reza al esclarecido y gloriosísimo señor San Nicolás Obispo el Magno* ... (Puebla: D. Pedro de la Rosa, 1788).

[106] Ordination of Nicolás Simeon de Salazar, Puebla, 1692–93, Salazar Family Papers, ff. 24r–26r.

the emerging creole patria, such as the Bishop Manuel Fernández de Santa Cruz and the linguist Francisco de Aédo y Peña, and he published a pair of doctrinal manuals in 1715 and 1718.[107] Two nephews, meanwhile, don Agustín Flores Corona Citlalpopoca and don Antonio Marcial de Salazar, served vicariously under don Nicolás at Cuapiaxtla.[108] All together, the parish of Cuapiaxtla was administered by members of the Salazar family for forty years, where they oversaw the construction of its first church. A third nephew, don Santiago Salazar y Tapia, acquired a licenciado and became priest of San Hipólito Soltepec, where his uncle don Manuel began his career many years earlier.[109]

Yet one of the most successful Salazars was don Miguel Aparicio Sánchez de Salazar Quapiotzin (b. 1691), the nephew and intellectual heir of don Manuel de los Santos. Don Miguel, from the Tlaxcalteca community of Teolocholco, studied with the Jesuits at San Ildefonso in Puebla, where he joined the minor-orders clergy in 1711 (Figure 9). He then relocated to the Royal University in Mexico City where he received a bachelor's in Holy Scriptures in 1715 and a licenciado in Canon Law in 1717. As he advanced, he capitalized on his uncle's merit by temporarily replacing his father's name "Sánchez" with "Santos" and emphasizing the connection in his probanzas.[110] Yet don Miguel clearly aspired to a secular rather than ecclesiastical vocation, and eventually became an advocate with the Mexico City Audiencia. Yet don Miguel of Teolocholco remained dedicated to his Tlaxcalteca patria even from his comfortable position among Mexico City's gentry, performing legal services on behalf of his cousins in the Tlaxcalteca cabildo and continuing the genealogical-historical investigations of his uncle don Manuel.[111]

In 1762, don Miguel authored four short poems in honor of the four conquest-era tlatoque of Tlaxcala, likely for public recitation. They are

---

[107] Nicolás Simeon Sánchez de Salazar, *Directorio de confesores* (Puebla: Viuda de Miguel de Ortega Bonilla, 1715). See also "Nicolás Salazar Mazihcatzin Citlalpopoca," in José Mariano Beristáin de Souza, *Biblioteca hispano-americana* (Mexico: Alejandro Valdés, 1821), v. 3, 92.

[108] Grados and Ordination of Antonio Marcial de Salazar, Salazar Family Papers, ff. 39r–45r; Salazar Genealogy, f. 74v;

[109] Inventory of the estate of Lic. don José Luis de Santiago de Salazar y Tapia, deceased, Soltepec, Apr 12, 1724, Salazar Family Papers, f. 51

[110] Bachelor of Arts of Miguel Aparicio Santos de Salazar y Quapiotzin, Puebla, Feb 23, 1711, Salazar Family Papers, f. 72.; Merits of Miguel Aparicio Santos y Salazar, Puebla, 1711, in Martínez, "Indios caciques graduados de bachiller en la universidad," 36.

[111] Salazar Family Genealogy, f. 74r; Power of Attorney to Miguel Aparicio Sánchez de Salazar, Mexico, Jan 31, 1727, Salazar Family Papers, ff. 65r-66v; Martínez Baracs, *Gobierno de indios*: 480–502.

FIGURE 9 Minor orders certificate of don Miguel Aparicio Sánchez de Salazar y Quapiotzin from the Jesuit Colegio de San Ildefonso, Puebla, 1711. Salazar Family Papers, Miscellaneous Manuscript Collection, Library of Congress, Washington, DC.

archetypal expressions of late-colonial Tlaxcalteca patriotism, inasmuch as they credit the success of the conquest entirely to the heroism and Christian zeal of Tlaxcala's four conquest-era kings, including don Bartolomé Citlalpopoca, the Salazars' own ancestor. By both quiet religiosity and fierce valor, Tlaxcala's Christian tlatoque delivered the New World to Carlos V. The Spaniards and other native groups simply play no role in these accounts, leaving the impression that the conquest was an exclusively Tlaxcalteca endeavor in both its inspiration and execution.

The Invincible and Christian King don Vicente Xicotencatl –

> *Your valor is explained*
> *Don Vicente, because it was such*
> *That it filled the world with terror*
> *By merely its public fame*
> *And much more when applied*
> *To spread out that feat*
> *For which you went to war*
> *Indomitable, to fight for God,*
> *And only by you,*
> *Was New Spain won.*[112]

The Very Christian King don Lorenzo Mazihcatzin –

> *Noble, Eminent, and Valorous*
> *Don Lorenzo, whose name,*
> *Because it astonishes the enemy,*
> *Eternalized your fame,*
> *Because you eagerly accepted*
> *Belief in God, which is the first step,*
> *And then, with all dedication,*
> *As a sign of gratitude*
> *To His Law you promised*
> *To convert the entire world.*[113]

The Eminent and Catholic King don Gonzalo Tlahuexolotzin –

> *"Valiant Rooster," named you*
> *The Tlaxcalteco Senate*
> *Because the boom of your war cry*
> *Would deafen America,*

[112] Miguel Aparicio Sánchez de Salazar, "The Invincible and Christian King don Vicente Xicotencatl," Mexico, July 1, 1762, Salazar Family Papers, f. 56.
[113] Miguel Aparicio Sánchez de Salazar, "The Very Christian King don Lorenzo Mazihcatzin," Mexico, July 1, 1762, Salazar Family Papers, f. 57.

And as you fought for God:
It was easy to make it quake,
I hope that today will be found
The valor of don Gonzalo,
That struck fear into the Infidels,
And another Rooster to sing to them.[114]

The Very Loyal and Christian King don Bartholomé Sitlalpopoca –

How can I eulogize you,
O invincible Bartolomé,
When during the conquest
Your valor surpassed that of Mars
(If any comparison could be made).
Such things will never be repeated,
I argue for no small reason,
Because, with your undying love
You gave to Carlos V
All that amounts to a New World.[115]

Conclusion

There were very few cacique-letrados in New Spain. Their numbers were statistically tiny, and only a handful rose above minor or provincial positions.[116] However, the native elites who obtained grados and secured positions of honor demand our attention, because they straddled one of the major divides in colonial society. As Spanish-speaking ladinos with grados, the cacique-letrados were understood as latter-day analogs to the still-celebrated Nahua intellectuals of postconquest Tlatelolco. Yet they differed in an important way: Unlike the alumni of Tlatelolco, they did not merely lead the Indian republics, they also entered the circles of viceregal and Church administration. They embodied the Jesuits' ideal: They were the heirs to Anahuac, excelling in Christian letters.

Like their sixteenth-century predecessors, the cacique-letrados invoked the old ideals of alliance between the noble lineages of Mexico and the Spanish crown. Yet the social and political context had changed, and thus so did the implications of Indo-Hispanic mutuality. During the sixteenth century, the ladino cacique-governors told stories of unity to secure noble

[114] Miguel Aparicio Sánchez de Salazar, "The Eminent and Catholic King don Gonzalo Tlehuexolotzin," Mexico, July 1, 1762, Salazar Family Papers, f. 58.

[115] Miguel Aparicio Sánchez de Salazar, "The Very Loyal and Christian King don Bartholomé Sitlalpopoca," Mexico, July 1, 1762, Salazar Family Papers, f. 59.

[116] Taylor, *Magistrates of the Sacred*: 569, n. 81.

recognition, while later generations did so to preserve privileges such as tax exemptions. However, the same heritage that justified cacique distinction *vis a vis* native commoners – their descent from preconquest rulers – also prohibited their participation in lettered hierarchies, as the legal ideal of the Two Republics and Church conventions regarded viceregal and ecclesiastical administration as Spanish spaces. It should not surprise us that of all the high-ranking Indians of the colonial era – from the ladino caciques of the sixteenth century to the cacique-letrados of the eighteenth – the "Indian bishops" of the seventeenth century were among the few who did *not* openly proclaim native origins. Only after 1697, when caciques and hidalgos were declared legally and qualitatively equal, could preconquest noble origins fulfill the criteria for letrado honor.

Thus, by bringing them into colleges, seminaries, and the university, Bourbon-era policies envisioned caciques as Hispanic gentlemen with Mesoamerican roots. This differs from those whom James Lockhart has termed the "post-Nahuas," plebeian people who spoke Spanish, lived within the Hispanic cultural sphere, and did not consider themselves "Indians," yet whose everyday customs derived much from Nahua traditions. Cacique-letrados, in contrast, moved within the Hispanic world but explicitly represented themselves as the noble heirs to pre-Hispanic lineages. In other words, like contemporary creoles, they claimed Aztec Mexico as a noble heritage, but not a cultural identity.[117] In this way, the cacique-letrados both embodied and contributed to the tendency in Mexican creolism to envision a sharp disjuncture between ancient Anahuac and contemporary indigenous society. As we will see, this also brought them – and their perspectives on Mexican history – closer to the urban creoles of Mexico City and the major provincial cities, with significant consequences for the trajectory of creole discourse in the eighteenth century.

[117] Lockhart, *The Nahuas*, 450–51.

8

Cacique-ambassadors and the "Indian nation" in Bourbon Mexico

That is how the Empire
Of the Noble Zapoteca ended,
Absent any martial uproar
Clamoring through their land....
[Today] they venerate, with
The most humble displays
Of a vassal's love and fealty,
The royal name of their sovereign [in Spain]....
They revere the judges,
They honor the officials,
As well as the Roman Church
And its sacred religious orders....
The genius that
Distinguishes men from beasts:
This is amply found in [them],
Unlike others who are inferior.
He who applies himself to science
And the other noble arts,
If he does not exceed the Europeans,
Will at least become their equal.

Don Patricio Antonio López, 1740[1]

[Of the Indian lord I told my countryman:] "Never have I dealt with a man
of his class more alert, more Christian, more humble, or accommodating;
and what is more, God has bestowed upon him several clear abilities, and
instructed him in all manner of science, art, and reason...." "And with

[1] Patricio Antonio López, "Mercurio yndiano," Hubert Howe Bancroft Collection, MSS M-M 131, Bancroft Library, University of California, Berkeley, ff. 60–62.

regards to history, and the events of this realm – what is the nature of his
enlightenment?" asked my countryman. "Ah, my friend," I responded, "it
is so extensive and excellent, that he need not envy many who are deemed
sages and scholars."

José Joaquín Granados y Galvez, 1778[2]

"[My ancestors] did not know the teachings of Pythagoras, Boethius, Chrysippus, Protagoras, Nichomachus, Thales, or Euclid," explains an unnamed, fictional *indio*, as he relaxes one afternoon beside the Río de la Laja in Guanajuato, in one scene from José Joaquin Granados y Gálvez's 1778 *American Afternoons (Tardes americanas)*. However, he continues, they did know how to manipulate numbers for society's benefit – for example, in commerce, to keep time and record history, and to measure and divide their lands.[3] Though unfamiliar with the study of rhetoric, they had a highly developed tradition of oratory, and quickly recognized and accepted the genius of Demosthenes, Cicero, Horace, Virgil, and Ovid once introduced to them.[4] And although they were ignorant of "the celestial principles of Theology," they did understand that "there was but one solitary, invisible Cause and origin of all things."[5]

With these apologetic images, the *indio* – sometimes called the "American" – discusses the culture and history of pre-Hispanic central Mexico. He is responding to his friend – a well-read, cosmopolitan "Spaniard" (*español*), who, like many of his contemporaries, doubted the sophistication of Mesoamerican civilization. Where was proof of the "light" of Mexico's antiquity, he asks, given the widespread sloth and drunkenness of his indigenous contemporaries?[6] Did not the evidence suggest instead an innate irrationality and savagery? Going futher, did not native barbarity suggest that the American continent itself was incapable of supporting an enlightened society?[7] After all, the Spaniard continued, the creoles (or "Indian Spaniards") were a notoriously undistinguished group of layabouts and knaves among whom the great scholar Benito Feijoó could find only three examples of scientific genius.[8] Over a series of afternoons,

---

[2] Granados y Gálvez, *Tardes americanas*: preface.
[3] Ibid., 96.
[4] Ibid., 87.
[5] Ibid., 97.
[6] Ibid., 12.
[7] For the classic history of eighteenth-century theories of the "degeneracy" of the American continent, see Antonello Gerbi, *The Dispute of the New World: the History of a Polemic* (Pittsburgh: University of Pittsburgh Press, 1973 (1955)).
[8] Granados y Gálvez, *Tardes americanas*: 399.

the indio educates his misinformed Spanish friend about Mexican antiquity, and gradually convinces him of Anahuac's greatness – and therefore the contemporary value and future potential of its heir, New Spain.

Granados y Gálvez was a Spanish priest aligned with the crown, but *Tardes americanas* was a staunch defense of creole identity and culture.[9] His was an extreme case of historical ventriloquism, as he articulated the primary themes of eighteenth-century Mexican creolism – an emotional identification with Anahuac coupled with a defense of New Spain's baroque culture of saint veneration and Marian devotion – via the lips of an educated, Christian, noble Indian. Thus does the author establish his own credibility by appealing to the presumed expertise of the ladino cacique – a premise that, as we have seen, stretched back through the seventeenth-century religious chroniclers to the Franciscan investigators of the early colonial era. To creoles and supporters such as Granados, the epistemological authority of ladino caciques derived from both Mexican antiquity and Christian revelation, from both tradition and reason. Unbaptized natural lords were perhaps superior to their vulgar compatriots, but they remained blinded by idolatry and superstition. Christian macehuales, on the other hand, were like the peasants and laborers of Spain: free vassals of good standing, but hardly masters of reason and science. Educated Christian Indians of ancient lineage, however, were both noble and enlightened. In this sense, the creole vision regarded ladino caciques as innate authorities on questions pertaining to America and its peoples. In *Tardes americanas*, the narrator begs the indio "to dispel my ignorance by instructing us in the history, civility, rituals, and customs of the ancient Indians"; the latter graciously complies, noting that his knowledge "not only comes from the books and authorities, but also from the immemorial traditions passed from parents to children among [his] ancestors."[10]

Granados y Gálvez ventriloquized the perspective of a fictional *indio*, but real-life examples of such educated noble Indians were not uncommon in his world. Given the creole epistemology that privileged ladino caciques, the small, but visible vanguard of lettered Indians that emerged after 1697 played a significant role in late-colonial disputes pertaining to native peoples. Some indeed lent their voices, as men of erudition and

[9] Granados y Gálvez dedicated *Tardes americanas* to his uncle, José de Galvez, one of Carlos III's primary agents in charge of implementing modernizing reforms in Spanish America in the 1770s.
[10] Granados y Gálvez, *Tardes americanas*: preface.

pre-Hispanic pedigree, to late-colonial controversies and debates conventionally restricted to Spanish thinkers and writers. Scholars have only recently begun to explore this phenomenon in greater depth. As Alcira Dueñas has recently documented with regards to educated Andeans in Peru, such men mastered and deployed the knowledge and formal discursive practices of the colonizers to challenge and deconstruct the moral and legal foundations of indigenous subjugation.[11] They were Indians, but they were also colonial thinkers, steeped in a polemical realm defined by blended systems of meaning; as Gabriela Ramos and Yanna Yannakakis have argued, native intellectuals creatively adapted and manipulated their own symbolic and epistemological tools as well as those of the colonizers to "negotiate collective and individual identities, and the terms of colonial rule."[12]

Yet even the cacique-intellectuals who did not openly or explicitly critique colonial injustices – or, as was more common, who lamented moments of injustice yet blamed only the malice or corruption of individual officials – represented an existential challenge to colonial conventions. Erudite caciques were, in themselves, small but meaningful subversions of a fundamental rationalization of Spanish–American colonialism: The ubiquitous notion, increasingly racialized in Enlightenment-era debates, that those labeled "Indians" were, like sheep, innately irrational and incapable of self-government.[13] The agents of the Church and the crown, meanwhile, occupied precisely the opposite social role: They were the shepherds, the intellectual class tasked, by right of education and vocation, with defining and policing what was Good and what was True for all (to say nothing of their disproportionate political and social clout). Native letrados, then, were already subversive before uttering a single word. This implicit understanding explains why Granados expressed creole sentiments via a fictional ladino cacique rather than a creole.

---

[11] Alcira Dueñas, *Indians and Mestizos in the "Lettered City": Reshaping Justice, Social Hierarchy, and Political Culture in Colonial Peru* (Boulder, CO: University Press of Colorado, 2010), 2–4.

[12] Gabriela Ramos and Yanna Yannakakis, eds. *Indigenous Intellectuals: Knowledge, Power, and Colonial Culture in Mexico and the Andes* (Durham: Duke University Press, 2014), 14.

[13] For the contours of these debates as part of the European Enlightenment, see Pagden, *The Fall of Natural Man: The American Indian and the Origins of Comparative Ethnology*, 2nd edn. (Cambridge: Cambridge University Press, 1986), 57–108; Alain Milhou, "El indio americano y el mito de la religión natural," in *La imagen del indio en la Europa moderna* (Sevilla: Escuela de Estudios Hispano-Americanos, 1990); Cañeque, *The King's Living Image*: 186–212; Martínez, "The Language, Genealogy, and Classification of "Race" in Colonial Mexico."

Another dimension also informs the history of cacique-letrados, one that is at once larger and smaller than abstract ideals of justice and colonial modes of self-advocacy. Many of the intellectual activities of native thinkers were also vocational, articulated within familiar letrado rituals of upward mobility. Thus, they were both personal and local while also socially conscious and universal, functioning on two levels simultaneously: By contesting the doctrine of indigenous inferiority – by seeking to reshape what it meant to be "Indian" in New Spain – they were also challenging those who resisted their ascent within lettered institutions. Conversely, by insisting on their right to occupy positions of honor, they upset and upended the doctrine of indigenous inferiority. Their immediate goals of vocational advancement informed, and indeed compelled, their criticisms of Spanish America's social and ethnic hierarchy.

This intimate, vocational undercurrent within the caciques' contributions to eighteenth-century debates helps explain their broad diversity of perspectives. Like previous generations, local concerns and pragmatic considerations flavored how erudite caciques represented Mexican history, leading to an eclectic and varied corpus. In part this is explained by their general inclination, inherited from their predecessors, to conceive of themselves along ancestral and class lines rather than as "Indians" or some other pan-indigenous identity. However, certain eighteenth-century controversies in the creole and Hispanic realm prompted them to adopt precisely such a posture, however reluctantly, by presuming them to possess esoteric, insider knowledge of native history and calling upon them to share it. Only when compelled to speak, as intermediaries, on behalf of what was termed "the Indian nation" – *nación* being one of the early modern Hispanic anthropological categories most closely resembling contemporary understandings of biological "race" – did they adopt the Spaniards' reductive conception of native peoples as "Indians."[14] This distinguishes the lettered caciques of New Spain from some Andean counterparts, who, as Dueñas demonstrates, more effectively constructed

---

[14] In early modern Iberia and Spanish America, "race" (or *raza*) did not exist in the biological or genetic sense that we have inherited from the nineteenth century, as both it and *nación* connoted a host of other factors, including class, region of origin, religion, and "blood" (meaning ancestral roots). Nonetheless, nación often functioned in ways largely indistinguishable from modern notions of race inasmuch as it signaled an innate "nature" (*naturaleza*) inherited and passed on to descendants. See James H. Sweet, "The Iberian Roots of American Racist Thought," *The William and Mary Quarterly* LIV, no. 1 (1997); Martínez, *Genealogical Fictions*: 59, 142–70; Schwaller, "Defining Difference in Early New Spain," 105–07; Ruiz, "Discourses of Blood and Kinship."

and expressed pan-indigenous perspectives.[15] This could help explain the more radically critical nature of the Andean texts.[16] It also underscores the novelty and critical potential of those native Mexican leaders who found themselves cast as ambassadors of "the Indian nation" as a whole.

Thus it is useful to consider the cacique-intellectuals of New Spain individually rather than as members of a coherent movement. They represented only themselves, were motivated by a variety of professional concerns, and beyond several important episodes regarding the establishment of Indian-only educational opportunities, generally did not collaborate on any broadly shared agenda. Nonetheless, they faced similar vocational and intellectual challenges and obstacles, and their role within creole and Hispanic debates derived largely from their presumed expertise as guardians of the secrets of Mexican antiquity. This chapter examines several discrete examples of their efforts, and highlights their place within eighteenth-century controversies over the rights and potential of native peoples as well as the precise nature of the Mexican legacy.

Cacique authority in late-colonial Mexican creolism

One of the longest-running controversies in the early modern Hispanic world, the question of the "nature" and intellectual and moral capacity of native peoples, reappeared with vigor during the eighteenth century. This was partially the result of the reemergence of the cacique-creole archive into the public eye. As we have seen, upon his death in 1700, don Carlos de Sigüenza y Góngora willed almost his entire collection of "Indian antiquities" – the Alva Ixtlilxochitl library plus other items pertaining to Mexica history – to the Jesuit college of San Pedro y San Pablo in Mexico City, to which the cacique school of San Gregorio was attached. A pivotal moment came in the 1730s and 1740s, when the Italian Aztecophile Lorenzo Boturini Benaduci (1698–1755) compiled the single most important collection of Mesoamerican texts and artifacts in

---

[15] It should be noted, however, that the majority of the Andean nobility – those that did not overtly engage in polemics – did continue to express ethnic divisions rather than adopt pan-indigenous identities. See Garrett, *Shadows of Empire: The Indian Nobility of Cusco, 1750–1825*: 75–113; David Cahill, "Ethnogenesis in the City: A Native Andean *Etnia* in a Colonial City," in *City Indians in Spain's American Empire: Urban Indigenous Society in Colonial Mesoamerica and Andean South America*, eds. Dana Velasco Murillo, Mark Lentz, and Margarita R. Ochoa (Portland, OR: Sussex Academic Press, 2012).

[16] Dueñas, *Indians and Mestizos in the "Lettered City"*: 5–7, 65–84.

colonial history. Seeking empirical evidence substantiating the apparition of the Virgin of Guadalupe, Boturini contacted native cabildos throughout central Mexico and scoured their archives and church basements for "Indian" manuscripts – the older the better, with a preference for the pictorial and native-language texts that he considered more authentic. He also copied and circulated large portions of the Jesuits' entire Alva Ixtlilxochitl-Sigüenza collection, including the major cacique chronicles. In 1743, Boturini – who was as inept at handling royal personalities as he was successful as a collector – was forced to return to Spain, and the viceroy confiscated his "Indian museum," showing it to select audiences over the next several decades.[17] Thus a new era began in creole historiography; almost every subsequent innovation in Mexican historiography would reference items from the Boturini museum, the Alva Ixtlilxochitl-Sigüenza collection, or both. These items raised new questions about Indian history while also providing its defenders with vast amounts of new and curious evidence upon which to base their apologias.

Whereas in earlier generations, the debate over native rationality revolved around religious issues – such as which sacraments were appropriate for Indians and how to deliver them – in the mid eighteenth century, it centered increasingly on the value and potential of education.[18] The controversy arose again in the 1720s with the establishment of the new convent of Corpus Christi in Mexico City, a community with viceregal patronage originally founded exclusively for cacica women. As Mónica Díaz and others have chronicled, the convent became possible because some advocates argued that native noblewomen were capable of upholding the precepts of chastity and modesty required of nuns.[19] Perhaps predictably, supporters of the convent – including Juan Ignacio Castoreña y Ursúa, the outspoken cleric and former associate of the late Sigüenza

---

[17] For a detailed bibliographical-biographical account of Boturini, see Giorgio Antei, *El caballero andante: vida, obra, y desventuras de Lorenzo Boturini Benaduci, 1698–1755* (México: Museo de la Basílica de Guadalupe, 2007).

[18] See, for example, the 1713 priestly manual of the Augustinian friar Manuel Pérez, as well as the dueling *pareceres* (opinions) that introduce it. Pérez concludes that, whether or not the Indians were inherently capable of reason, "priestly care can relieve them, to a degree, from their rusticity." Manuel Pérez, *Farol indiano, y guía de curas de indios* (Mexico: Francisco de Rivera Calderón, 1713). quote from 94.

[19] For the history of Corpus Christi, see Díaz, *Indigenous Writings from the Convent*; Asunción Lavrín, "Indian Brides of Christ: Creating New Spaces for Indigenous Women in New Spain," *Mexican Studies/Estudios Mexicanos* 15, no. 2 (1999); Ann Miriam M.S.M Gallagher, "The Indian Nuns of Mexico City's *Monasterio* of Corpus Christi, 1724–1821," in *Latin American Women: Historical Perspectives*, ed. Asunción Lavrín (Westport, CT: Greenwood Publishing Group, 1978).

y Góngora – cited Sigüenza's account, culled from Alva Ixtlilxochitl, regarding the cihuatlamacazque priestesses of Tenochtitlan. As ancient Mexico had produced exemplars of female virtue, its descendants, as "noble maidens," could and should be allowed to take the sacred veils and habits of nuns.[20]

Unlike cloistered nuns, however, male clergy held positions of direct spiritual, moral, and temporal authority over the laity. The education and formation of indigenous men, therefore, raised additional concerns. Could proper instruction help Indians overcome their apparently inborn "rusticity" to become masters of reason? Could such education thereby alleviate the much-lamented poverty and squalor of native communities? Or was that misery the inevitable and immutable fate of an inferior caste? On one side were those we might call the "pessimists," largely among the upper levels of the secular clergy, who considered the Indians innately irrational, and who thus opposed indigenous education as a waste of resources. This position, a rather tedious and familiar expression of eighteenth-century essentialism, characterizes a scornful 1755 report of Archbishop Rubio y Salinas, who insisted that all Indians, even those who received careful instruction, were consumed by "drunkenness, lust, and cruelty." Those who did succeed in obtaining curacies, he argued, frequently tainted the sacrament of confession by soliciting sex in the confessional. And while few may have lived virtuously, "not one has proven eminent in any [lettered] discipline... and what is more, nor can they even write well."[21]

Standing opposed to such pessimism and hostility were the "apologists," largely drawn from the Franciscans and Jesuits who had the most experience with cacique education. Offended and upset at such scorn, they defended both the Indians and the Mexican legacy in two discrete ways: by proclaiming the sophistication of Anahuac, and by extolling the piety and intellectual achievements of individual Christian Indians. To the apologists, to defend the character of the Indians and the ancient civilizations they had built was to defend New Spain, the patria of the creoles who had invested in Anahuac as their own heritage. While both modes of apology drew their substance from creole interpretations of the Alva Ixtlilxochitl-Sigüenza and Boturini collections, in practice they appealed

[20] "Fundación y progresos del Combento de Corpus Xti de México," UCB M-M 240, ff. 132–46, quote from 136.
[21] Statement of Archbishop Manuel de Rubio y Salinas, Mexico, Apr 30, 1755, AGI-M 1937, f. 88.

to two very different sets of native sources, and amount to distinct, if heavily overlapping strains of patriotic discourse. As we will see, in later decades these strains aligned with and predicted deeper rifts among creoles, yet during the mid eighteenth century both rebuked the pessimism and scorn of the archbishop and other likeminded Spaniards.

Among the apologists, those who emphasized the sophistication of ancient Anahuac – beginning with Boturini himself – we might term the "antiquarians." Echoing Sigüenza y Góngora (and Torquemada before him), Boturini typified this brand of apologia by insisting that Mexican antiquity "could not only match the most celebrated [legacies] of the globe, but exceed them."[22] That its "excellence" was not universally recognized was a problem of sources, not a lack of substance; "although many European authors" had written about Mexico, they were ignorant of the vast corpus of materials produced by the Indians themselves, such as the painted manuscripts and the histories of don Fernando de Alva Ixtlilxochitl and Chimalpahin.[23] Several contemporaries echoed these sentiments, including José Antonio de Villaseñor y Sánchez, whom the viceroy commissioned in 1746 to produce a monumental geographical-historical account of New Spain. Familiar with the Jesuits' collection of Mesoamerican treasures inherited from Sigüenza, Villaseñor opened his text with a history of Anahuac that essentially reproduced the historical visions of the cacique-chroniclers – for example, Nezahualcoyotl's Tetzcoco was an American Athens, and Tlaxcala exemplified republican virtues.[24] Meanwhile, the creole lawyer and acolyte of Boturini, Mariano Fernández de Echeverría y Veytia (1718–80), explicitly declared Alva Ixtlilxochitl's account of Anahuac to be authoritative, and a conclusive refutation of "the errors of the Spanish historians."[25]

Although his own works were unpublished, Echeverría corresponded widely with elite creole contemporaries, and his vision was comparatively influential.[26] Perhaps his closest intellectual heir was Antonio de León y Gama, a creole archeologist and antiquarian who worked with the remnants of the Boturini collection and corresponded with indigenous nobles such as don Nicolás Faustino Mazihcatzin y Escovar of Tlaxcala. Unlike his baroque predecessors, León y Gama was less interested in the

[22] Boturini Benaduci, *Idea*: 2.
[23] Ibid., 151–52.
[24] Villaseñor y Sánchez, *Theatro americano*: v. 1, 155, 306–07.
[25] Mariano Fernández Echeverría y Veytia, *Historia antiqua de Méjico* (Mexico: C.F. Ortega, 1836). 35–36.
[26] Brading, *The First America*: 386–88.

"moral history" of those whom he called "our Mexicans," but rather the nature and degree of their mastery of science and the mechanical arts. In this realm, he wrote, the Aztecs were second to none; while European authors had faulted them for lacking recognizable forms of calculus and geometry, León y Gama pointed to their advanced architecture and irrigation systems, and argued that they had clearly developed their own, "ingenious" mode of manipulating values, "the autonomous invention of the Toltecs and Mexicans, [who] did not need to learn anything from other nations."[27] Elsewhere, he blamed the repeated flooding that plagued early colonial Mexico City on the Spaniards' refusal to learn from and adopt Aztec models of drainage and irrigation.[28] Most famously, in 1790 León y Gama investigated newly uncovered Mexica artifacts – including the iconic "solar stone" and statue of Coatlicue held today in the National Museum of Anthropology– and portrayed his project as a kind of national self-discovery. He explained that his research was motivated by his desire to reveal how far the erudite world had misjudged Mexico's Indians. Importantly, León y Gama framed his apologia for Anahuac as a defense of New Spain's creoles, noting that those who denigrated native antiquity did so only to diminish the "glorious deeds wrought in [its] conquest."[29]

The most influential apologetic antiquarian of the era, however, was the creole Jesuit Francisco Xavier Clavijero (1731–87). Clavijero was well-versed in the cacique-creole vision; he taught at the caciques' school of San Gregorio, and spent many years familiarizing himself with the Alva Ixtlilxochitl-Sigüenza collection in the attached Jesuit library. Unsurprisingly, like his Jesuit colleagues and peers at San Gregorio he became an outspoken defender of native rationality.[30] After the expulsion of the Jesuits in 1767 he went to Italy, where in 1780 he published his *History of Ancient Mexico* (*Storia antica de Messico*), the most complete and influential work of preconquest Mexican history since Torquemada's *Monarquía indiana* 165 years earlier.[31] Although Clavijero affected a mild and

[27] Antonio de León y Gama, "Fundamentos y operaciones de la arithmética mexicana," HL Manuscript 4297, f. 22.

[28] Antonio de León y Gama, "Geometría, hidraulica, mecánica, y geografía de los Mexicanos," HL Manuscript 4297, ff. 27.

[29] Antonio León y Gama, *Descripción histórica y cronológica de las dos piedras...* (Mexico: Alejandro Valdés, 1832), 4.

[30] Ernesto Burrus reconstructs which items of the Alva Ixtlilxochitl-Sigüenza collection Clavijero would have seen before 1767. Ernest J. Burrus, "Clavigero and the Lost Sigüenza y Góngora Manuscripts," *Estudios de cultura nahuatl* 1(1959).

[31] Brading, *The First America*: 453–62.

academic tone, the patriotic resentment of an exile swirls beneath his text. Thus it was only with Clavijero that the subversive potential of patriotic Mexican antiquarianism – largely suppressed in earlier creole histories – truly surfaced: If Mexico's Indians had once been prosperous and industrious but no longer were, something had clearly obstructed their progress. But what? In singing the praises of Tenochtitlan, Sigüenza himself had glossed over and depolemicized the issue by blaming alcohol – an anodyne but ultimately inadequate explanation.[32] Clavijero, in contrast, mischievously compared the "Aztecs" to the contemporary Greeks as examples of how foreign subjugation might ruin the creative and dynamic spirit of a people: "He who contemplates the current state of the Greeks," he wrote, "will not be persuaded that they had been the great sages that we know they were."[33] Left mostly unelaborated in this analogy was the rather shocking historical equation of the Spanish in Mexico with the Turks in Greece.[34]

The second strain of creole apologetic literature to derive from the Boturini and Alva Ixtlilxochitl-Sigüenza collections was that of the "cultivators," those who defended the Indians less by reference to ancient grandeur and more by hailing their postconquest achievements in Christian works and virtues. The cultivators, largely Jesuits and those educated by Jesuits, argued that the poverty and misery of native communities was not the result of innate irrationality, but rather a "lack of cultivation." They alluded to Luke 8, which compares the gospel to a seed that might flourish and bear fruit on fertile ground, but which comes to naught when scattered upon uncultivated ground. With good doctrine and good instruction, the Indians could – and had, on numerous occasions – prove themselves admirable Christians and people of reason.

The Jesuit Juan de Mayora, Clavijero's colleague at San Gregorio, articulated this sensibility succinctly in 1757. After almost two centuries of experience in Indian education, he argued, he and his colleagues knew the Indians' "rusticity and barbarity" were not innate, but rather the result of "a lack of cultivation and instruction." He supported this contention by echoing Alva Ixtlilxochitl's description of ancient Tetzcoco as a place of great learning and culture; Tetzcoco was the Indians' "university," and the "general archive" where the Aztecs preserved their histories,

---

[32] Sigüenza y Góngora, *Parayso occidental*: f. ixr.

[33] Francesco Saverio Clavigero, *Historia antigua de México: Sacada de los mejores historiadores españoles, y de manuscritas y pinturas antiguas de los indios*... trans. Francisco Pablo Vázquez (Mexico: JR Navarro, 1853), 381.

[34] See Pagden, *Spanish Imperialism and the Political Imagination*: 104.

annals, and genealogies. He was also familiar with the sixteenth-century Franciscan investigations, and cited the *huehuetlatolli* (sayings of the elders) – first recorded in Nahuatl by friar Andrés de Olmos and his cacique informants – as evidence of the sophisticated moral sensibilities of Anahuac.[35] He followed with a series of anecdotes drawn from the Jesuits' network of schools, and especially his home institution of San Gregorio, evidence of how industrious, honest, and genteel Indians might become with the proper education. Indeed, he insisted, his experience with the collegians at San Gregorio had taught him that profanity, greed, vanity, and ambition were entirely unknown among the Indians, who were naturally inclined toward humility, poverty, and obedience.[36]

The cultivators' attitude spread among the Jesuits' many creole students. Dr. Andrés de Arce y Miranda was an eminent cleric from Puebla who taught with the Jesuits in Mexico City; he was also elected bishop of Puerto Rico, but declined. In 1766, he lambasted his compatriots and fellow clergy in the harshest terms; if the Indians suffered from ineptitude and ignorance, it was no fault of their own, he insisted, but because they had never received proper "cultivation." This was clear from their histories, which proved that such vices were unknown in Anahuac. Anticipating the reasoning that would later energize Clavijero, he clarified this logic explicitly and passionately: The "drunkenness, falsehood, and theft" plaguing native communities, "all derive from our own bad example," he wrote, as "mistreatment by those who call themselves 'reasonable' has infected them." Indeed, he continued, the further away from major Spanish cities, "the less malicious" he found the Indians. Blessed by their remoteness and distance from corrupting Spanish influences, they "maintained their native innocence" and exemplified Christian virtue.[37]

The Franciscan José Mariano Díaz de la Vega also argued for cultivation, as his impassioned 1782 defense of the Indians revolved almost entirely around anecdotes of exemplary piety. He lamented that, almost as soon as Christ had arrived to liberate America from idolatry, evil men among the conquerors had begun abusing and ruining its native people.

---

[35] On Andrés de Olmos and the *huehuetlatolli*, see Baudot, *Utopia and History in Mexico: The First Chroniclers of Mexican Civilization (1520–1569)*: 217–45. Mayora cited a 1601 version of the speeches published by fray Juan Baptista Viseo.

[36] Statement of Juan de Mayora, Mexico, June 13, 1757, AGI-M 1937, ff. 241–58.

[37] Dr. Andrés de Arce y Miranda, approbation of Andrés Miguel Pérez de Velasco, *El ayudante de cura, instruido en el porte a que le obliga su dignidad, en los deberes a que le estrecha su empleo . . .* (Puebla: Colegio Real de San Ignacio de la Puebla 1766). n.p.

Given the Indians' natural predilection for humility and virtue, wrote Díaz, the conquest could have inaugurated a golden age of Christian brotherhood. Unfortunately, selfish Spaniards had denied the Indians the exercise of reason – and then, seeing the results, had the temerity to conclude that they were innately "irrational and incapable of society and human commerce."[38] Working from the Boturini collection and citing the great baroque myth-makers – including Florencia, Sigüenza, Espinosa, and Loayzaga (whom he must have known personally from his time in Tlaxcala) – Díaz heralded the entire mosaic of patriotic Indo-Christian legends. In detailing and praising marvels such as the Virgin of Guadalupe, the boy-martyrs of Tlaxcala, the Virgin of Ocotlan, and the stone cross of Querétaro, he exhorted his fellow creoles and Spaniards to acknowledge the special link between heaven and Mexico, and the Indians as its representatives. Proof of the Indians' worthiness and rationality, moreover, lay not only in their many direct contacts with the divine, but also in a tradition of admirable Christian scholarship exemplified by, among others, the "Indian bishops" of the seventeenth century and the many cacique authors of the Boturini collection.[39]

The old conceit of innate indigenous inferiority had, during the Enlightenment, taken on a "scientific" character in pessimistic European and Spanish writings, in which the perceived flaws of Indians were attributed to "nature" rather than the devil or some other supernatural mischief. Yet a more optimistic strain of Enlightenment attitudes offered a rebuttal: faith in the potential of education. Referencing the treasures of the cacique-creole archive, the patriotic apologists reframed the issue as one of history rather than nature: What the pessimists described as innate wretchedness was in reality the outcome of centuries of abuse and neglect. Yet who, ultimately, was at fault? Who had failed to "cultivate" the Indians? A handful of indigenous noblemen lent their voices to this debate, speaking explicitly as representatives of Mexico's native peoples and their antiquity.

---

[38] Díaz de la Vega, "Memorias piadosas," f. 1.

[39] See Díaz de la Vega, "Memorias piadosas," ff. 137–60. Díaz mentioned the authors of the native accounts that Sigüenza y Góngora had bound together with Alva Ixtlilxochitl's histories, including don Antonio Valeriano, Chimalpahin, and don Gabriel de Ayala of Tetzcoco. He also listed a number of authors from the Boturini library, including don Juan Buenaventura Zapata y Mendoza, "an Indian named Antonio" who wrote annals of Tula, another unnamed Indian – probably Cristobal del Castillo – who authored a Mexica history, "the lords of Culhuacan" who produced Nahuatl annals, and an anonymous author of a history of Tlaxcala (mostly derived from Torquemada).

Zapoteca Virgil: the case for Indian equality

Don Patricio Antonio López, a nobleman from Oaxaca, was a well-read Zapoteca patriot with a love for poetry. Educated among the Jesuits of Puebla and Mexico City, don Patricio carved out a lettered career in the viceregal court between 1723 and 1754, during which time he wrote apologias of native history in both prose and verse. While residing in Puebla in the early 1720s, he began angling for honorable positions in a most "letrado" of ways: by publishing a series of poems designed to ingratiate and capture the attention of colonial officials. His tactic worked; literate in Zapoteca, Nahuatl, Castilian, and Latin, he was appointed interpreter to the highest ecclesiastical and secular tribunals in Mexico City.[40]

Crucially, don Patricio also played an intimate role in Boturini's antiquarian project. In the late 1730s, the Italian asked the cacique-interpreter to visit native cabildos and noble households on his behalf, begging them to share with him their treasured heirlooms. If they revealed to don Patricio their "maps and ancient manuscripts," he promised, the Virgin of Guadalupe would show gratitude and protect "her children the Indians from all evils."[41] Don Patricio's participation in assembling the Boturini museum places him at the heart of the neo-Aztec consciousness within Novohispanic creolism that the project reflected and promoted. He examined the same manuscripts, testimonies, and painted maps, and was familiar with the work of such men as Alva Ixtlilxochitl, Sigüenza, and don Manuel de los Santos y Salazar. It also advanced his letrado career. After Boturini's exile, in 1745 the oidor Domingo de Valcárcel praised don Patricio's linguistic and literary skills, and commissioned him to inventory and catalog the collection he had helped to compile.[42] This was a high honor indeed, as it gave don Patricio personal access to and control over a highly sensitive and controversial subject, central Mexican history.[43] In 1749, don Patricio petitioned for and received viceregal recognition for his work in curating Boturini's museum.[44]

---

[40] José Fernando Ramírez, *Biblioteca de autores mexicanos*, vol. 17 (México: V. Agüeros, 1898), 27–37.

[41] Antei, *El caballero andante: vida, obra, y desventuras de Lorenzo Boturini Benaduci, 1698–1755*: 161–62.

[42] John B. Glass, *The Boturini Collection: The Legal Proceedings and the Basic Inventories, 1742–1745* (Lincoln Center, MA.: Conemex, 1981), 113.

[43] See Patricio Antonio López, "Inventario de los documentos recogidos a don Lorenzo Boturini por orden del gobierno virreinal," *Anales del Museo Nacional de Arqueología e Etnografía*, 5a época 3, no. 1 (1925).

[44] Glass, *The Boturini Collection*: 122.

Don Patricio was a viceregal official, but he was also a Zapoteca noble-man who leveraged his proximity to colonial power circles to make an intellectual case for Indian equality within late-colonial deliberations on racial difference. Although he wrote as an "Indian" before "Spaniards," his underlying perspective was more complex, as he aspired to a more integrative vision of himself and his society. He sought to bridge and unite, to erase contradictions rather than straddle; his main rhetorical mode was analogy and equivalence rather than ambivalence or ambigu-ity. That is, he portrayed pre-Hispanic Mesoamerica and Spain as cultural equals with fully parallel and directly comparable historical experiences. That idea allowed him to circumvent the colonial doctrine of native infe-riority and argue, paradoxically, for Indian equality within a Spanish order built on conquest. He, the man himself, was the message: Erudite, noble, proudly indigenous, and loyal to the king, his very existence – and his deep command of the neo-scholastic canon of early modern Spain – were powerful affronts to the ideology of Indian inferiority. And he knew it, overtly comparing himself to another poet: Virgil, whom he portrayed as having likewise emerged from a rustic provincial backwater to become one of Rome's literary titans.[45]

Don Patricio's literary identity had three primary components. The first, and most explicit, was his role as an interpreter. Don Patricio roman-ticized interpreters as indispensable bridges between humanity's various divisions; their labor, he argued, was what enabled peace and good gov-ernment. Alexander the Great would have been wholly unsuccessful with-out interpreters to bind his diverse armies, he argued, and the polyglot Roman Senate would have fallen to pieces without its cadre of skilled lin-guists. Don Patricio took Mercury, the god of interpreters and eloquence, as his personal literary avatar; indeed, his *magnum opus*, a poetic history of Mesoamerica he presented to the newly arrived viceroy in 1740, bore the self-referential title of *Indian Mercury (Mercurio yndiano)*.[46] "I am by vocation / like that son of Jove / Mercury (I say), he who was / The interpreter to the gods (Figure 10)."[47]

Don Patricio's emphasis on the importance of interpreters hearkens to the second aspect of his literary mission. Until recently, interpreters have been largely absent from histories of the colonial world – a deaf-ening silence considering that (as don Patricio insisted) they were both

[45] Patricio Antonio López, "Mercurio yndiano," Mexico, 1740, UCB M-M 131, f. 22.
[46] López, "Mercurio yndiano," ff. 23–27.
[47] Ibid., f. 31.

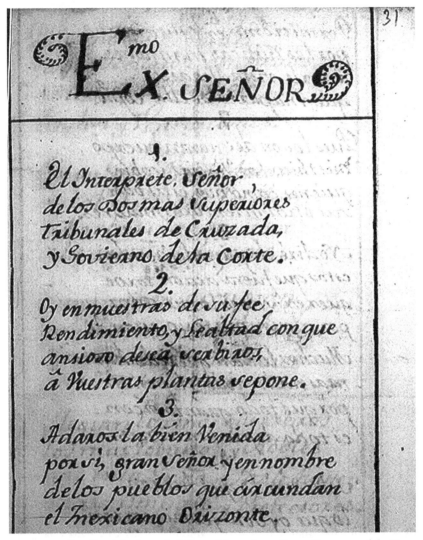

FIGURE 10 Don Patricio Antonio López, *Mercurio yndiano*. Courtesy of the Bancroft Library, University of California, Berkeley.

ubiquitous and indispensable to the everyday functioning of such a vast and diverse polity. Yet as Yanna Yannakakis and others have shown, interpreters were thinkers and agents in their own right, despite their pretensions to "mere" translation. Like all colonial subjects, they had ambitions and interests, as well as loyalties and enmities – all of which influenced the fulfillment of their duties.[48] Yet there was also a deeper and less predictable phenomenon: Interpreters are also, almost by definition, compelled to become ambassadors, who in colonial situations are simultaneously collaborators with the colonizers as well as apologists for their own brethren. Ambassadors facilitate colonial domination by participating in its structures, yet they are also well-placed to defend the colonized within the colonizer's own formal and intellectual structures.[49] Accordingly, don Patricio explicitly understood his role as interpreter to go well beyond translation; he was also the "Mexicans'" emissary to the Spanish world. He wrote his "Indian Mercury," he explained, both as a service to the crown – explaining indigenous history to the viceroy – as well as to proclaim the "natural" patriotic sentiment that all good people harbor in their hearts. Citing Cicero, he mused that "the Indians – and the Patricios – should . . . look to the good of their patria."[50]

Finally, the ambassadorial component of his position as interpreter led to the third of don Patricio's modes of self-representation – his presumption to speak for all "Indians." This was somewhat artificial, as we have seen, as caciques rarely adopted the Spanish category of *indio* except when accommodating colonial officials. The *Mercurio* opened by offering the viceroy a welcome on behalf of the entire native population: "The interpreter, lord . . . / Today as a sign of the faith, / Submission, and loyalty with which / He anxiously desires to serve you, / At your feet he kneels, / To bid you welcome / Both personally, great lord, and in the name /

---

[48] See Yanna Yannakakis, *The Art of Being In-Between: Native Intermediaries, Indian Identity, and Local Rule in Colonial Oaxaca* (Durham and London: Duke University Press, 2008); John Charles, *Allies at Odds: The Andean Church and Its Indigenous Agents, 1583–1671* (Albuquerque, NM: University of New Mexico Press, 2010); de la Puente Luna, "The Many Tongues of the King: Indigenous Language Interpreters and the Making of the Spanish Empire."

[49] Enrique Flores and Beatriz Mariscal Hay have addressed these aspects of don Patricio's work from a literary perspective, contextualizing him within the Mexican tradition of popular poetry and song. See Enrique Flores, "Patricio Antonio López, indio romancista (Romancero vulgar del siglo XVIII novohispano)," *Revista de dialectología y tradiciones populares* 46(1991); Enrique Flores, "Un romance de Patricio Antonio López," *Revista de Literaturas Populares* 1, no. 1 (2001); Enrique Flores, "Patricio López, Poeta e intérprete," in *La otra Nueva España: la palabra marginada en la colonia*, eds. Mariana Masera et al. (México: Universidad Nacional Autónoma de México, 2002); Beatriz Mariscal Hay, "La "embaxada por los indios" del cacique zapoteca Patricio Antonio López," *Caravelle* 76–77 (2001).

[50] Patricio Antonio López, *Triumphos aclamados contra vandoleros* . . . (Puebla: Viuda de Miguel de Ortega, 1723). Introduction. See also López, "Mercurio yndiano," ff. 2–4.

Of all the pueblos scattered across / The Mexican horizon."[51] Thus, while reserving special consideration for what he called "[his] Zapoteca Nation," he explicitly argued for the equality of all those called "Indians," including those of Peru.[52] Tellingly, don Patricio's inclination to speak for all native people grew more rather than less prominent as he rose within the viceregal court; while primarily a stylistic flourish in his early poetry from the 1720s, it was the entire basis for the *Mercurio yndiano* of 1740, written at the precise moment that he was helping Boturini locate Mexico's hidden trove of "Indian antiquities."

Beyond patriotism, don Patricio was open and explicit with his literary motivations. The first was simply vocational, reflecting his lettered ambitions: In the 1720s, he sought access to honorable positions in the viceroyalty. In the prologue to a 1726 commemoration of the execution of a band of criminals, he described the properties of a just governor. One of them was attention to capabilities more than blood – to delegate positions of authority to those who "by their qualities, works, and virtues deserve them, so that they may sustain themselves [by them]," even if they were Indians. He stated his objective on the frontispiece to the poem, signing it "don Patricio Antonio López, cazique of the Zapoteca Nation in the valleys of Antequera, [who] seeks to occupy . . . the position of Solicitor and Agent of Indian Affairs."[53]

Don Patricio's second stated objective was a defense of "the Indian nation" against "the opprobrium and criticisms and hateful words that are uttered to slander" it, which, he argued, were ultimately "more injurious" and shameful than any other oppression and injustice.[54] This cannot be separated from his antiquarianism, as he penned the *Mercurio yndiano* at the same time he worked as co-curator of the Boturini museum. His primary emphasis was a call for the equality of Indians under Spanish rule, expressed as the legal equivalency of Indians and Spaniards and the eligibility of native nobles for positions of honor reserved for hidalgos. Essentially, don Patricio desired the full realization of the spirit of the 1697 decree, which he not coincidentally copied in full and incorporated into the materials he delivered to the viceroy. He was particularly resentful

[51] López, "Mercurio yndiano," f. 31.
[52] Patricio Antonio López, "Breve apologético en defensa general de los yndios naturales de este reino y del otro del Perú," Mexico, 1740, UCB M-M 131, f. 91.
[53] Patricio Antonio López, *Triumphos que la real justicia ha conseguido de otros 40 vandoleros con los hechos en la vida . . .* (México: Herederos de la Viuda de Miguel de Rivera, 1726). n.p.
[54] López, "Breve apologetico," f. 96.

of the failure of Spaniards to respect the caciques' noble blood. "Caciques / Are the seigneurs of Indians," he wrote in 1723; and although "They by writs and laws / Enjoy hidalgo exemptions," they remained scorned and "disregarded by those who / Only seek nobility in whiteness."[55]

To bolster the case for equality, the cacique-poet attacked the notion of Indian irrationality in two ways: first, by documenting the sophistication and virtue of native societies both before and after the Spanish conquest, and second, with a *tour de force* of neo-scholastic erudition. The heroes and luminaries of Greco-Roman mythology, classical philosophy, and the Church canon are ubiquitous in don Patricio's poetry, and the rhetorical effect resembles that of the treatises of sor Juana Inés de la Cruz: In both cases, the highest principles of early modern logic were deployed effectively by those – an Indian and a woman – presumed to be incapable of it.[56] His analogies, meanwhile, allowed him to portray preconquest Mesoamerica as the cultural and civilizational equivalent to ancient Greece, Rome, and even pre-Christian Spain. The "Spaniards," he reminded his readers, were likewise initially considered barbarians by the Romans.[57]

His apology also involved exposing and lamenting native suffering. In a 1724 paean to the short-lived Luis I (r. 1724), don Patricio proclaimed the king's responsibility to be the care and protection of the weak, which in America meant the "humble and mute" Indians. He called on the new monarch to remove abusive officials from the colonies, writing "Observe, as [the Indians] are like humble silkworms, / And it is not just that they be worked to the bone (*se desentrañen*) for you; / Liberate them from this and other / Inflicted abuses / That malice, disguised as / Good governance, has introduced."[58] Somewhat incongrously, in the *Mercurio yndiano*, the cacique-poet alternated descriptions of the Indians' brilliance and sophistication with colonial stereotypes depicting them as phlegmatic, submissive, childlike, and innocent: "They are content with the little / That they acquire from their labors, / Because most of them live free / Of greed and ambition. / Humble and grateful / I continue listing their beneficence, / They are obsequious without flattery, / Cautious without insincerity."[59]

---

[55] López, *Triumphos aclamados contra vandoleros*...unpaginated.

[56] See Electa Arenal and Amanda Powell, Introduction to de la Cruz, *The Answer / La Respuesta*: 19–25.

[57] López, "Mercurio yndiano," ff. 15–17.

[58] Patricio Antonio López, *General aclamación de la lealtad mexicana* (México: Juan Francisco de Ortega Bonilla, 1724). n.p.

[59] López, "Mercurio yndiano," f. 62.

Indians were deemed "wretched" (*miserable*) in Spanish law, deserving of special charity and consideration – but such representations coexisted uneasily with claims of indigenous equality, and indeed had formed the paternalistic core of the moral defense of Spanish superiority over Indians for centuries.[60] Don Patricio did not acknowledge any tensions.

Finally, despite his pretense to the contrary, don Patricio ultimately failed to achieve a pan-indigenous perspective. He postured as the ambassador of the Indians, but the "Indian nation" was a Spanish invention, and it was not his beloved patria; Oaxaca was. As was common in contemporary Hispanic letters, don Patricio adopted an authorial perspective devoted to his birthplace or "little patria." Meanwhile, like many of his cacique forebears, don Patricio derived a certain moral authority by placing his Zapoteca ancestors in historical opposition to Tenochtitlan, envisioned as the ultimate source of pre-Hispanic barbarism and idolatry. A major plot element in the *Mercurio yndiano* was the heroic stand of the Zapoteca against the tyranny of the Mexica; indeed, the Zapoteca were, in his account, the "scourge" of Moctezuma.[61] Don Patricio also located his defense of the Indians within the portion of the poem dealing with his native Oaxaca, which effectively, if not explicitly, limits the apologia to the Zapoteca.[62]

Don Patricio Antonio López was a Zapoteca cacique, a letrado, and an interpreter, and his primary objective was to make the case for Indian equality. Mesoamerican grandeur is the primary theme of the first third of the *Mercurio yndiano*. His apologetic agenda is clear from the beginning: "In pagan times they were / Sociable, in contrast to / The barbarism that many today / Attribute and assume of them."[63] The poet portrays preconquest America as sociologically similar to medieval or classical Europe, with a clear and rational hierarchy of "three estates" governed by well-meaning monarchs. The "mazehuales" (sic) were the laborers, akin to the peasantry or townspeople of Europe – and like them, they suffered the brunt of bad government and corrupt officials. The "pili" (pipiltin), meanwhile, were those later known as "caziques, which corresponds / In Castilian to hijodalgo / Or duke, marquis, or count." The "theuhtes" (teteuctin), meanwhile, "were those / Elders, or senators /

---

[60] Cañeque, *The King's Living Image*: 186–212.
[61] "Mercurio yndiano," f. 37.
[62] Ibid., ff. 60–66.
[63] Ibid., f. 33.

Who in the king's councils / Governed his actions. / These today in every pueblo / Compose the republics / Who by the simple name / Of principales are known."[64] Overall, society was ordered, sophisticated, and just. Government officials prioritized the common welfare, and the countryside blossomed and prospered. Commerce flourished and produced great cities, which in turn led to enlightenment, wisdom, and virtue. Malice was punished and goodness was rewarded, and a benign host of learned judges "guarded justice / Toward the rich as well as the poor."[65]

The peace and prosperity of the land was threatened, however, by the ambitious tyrant Moctezuma, who sought to enlarge his dominions south and southeast toward Guatemala. But his plans were foiled when the king – whom the poet never names – led a coalition of Zapoteca and Mixteca in a heroic resistance. The Spaniards arrived in the midst of this ongoing clash, and their appearance allows don Patricio to stress Zapoteca services to Spain and its Church. He reimagines the establishment of Spanish rule in Oaxaca as bloodless and peaceful, as a collaborative and voluntary alliance rather than a conquest or subjugation. "When the Extremaduran Scipio [Cortés] / Crossing the salty sea / Sounded in Mexico / His terrifying canons / The king learned of it / From his two-faced deities, / And with heroic resignation, / Arranged to give himself in peace."[66] The Spaniards were powerful, but what impressed the Zapoteca ruler the most was the spiritual truth they carried with them. One of the king's counselors explains,

> *The general of a great king of whom I speak*
> *Carries an effigy upon*
> *A cross upon a hill, and*
> *His image is upon their banners.*
>
> *The King of Kings they say he is*
> *Who created the first man, and who*
> *Lives because He died*
> *On the cross, on that hill.*
>
> *And they adore Him as their God*
> *And it would be well to fear Him,*
> *As he that dies for others*
> *For God is justly adored.*

[64] Ibid., f. 34.
[65] Ibid., ff. 32–37, quote from 32.
[66] Ibid., f. 53.

> *For Him and His divine law*
> *They will give, say these men,*
> *Their lives and souls, until*
> *He is adored in these regions.*[67]

Don Patricio also insists that the Zapoteca leader transferred his kingdom to Carlos V, thereby echoing and adapting to Oaxaca the sixteenth-century fantasy of imperial continuity symbolized by Moctezuma's supposed donation to Cortés. Assessing the strength and power of the Spaniards and the justice of their cause, the king proclaims

> *And so I am determined that*
> *Tomorrow, before dawn*
> *When those mountains are turned golden*
> *By the brilliant rays of the sun*
>
> *To Mexico my emissary*
> *Will depart, and prostrate himself*
> *Before the general, and offer him*
> *My scepter, crown, and court.*
>
> *And with all willingness*
> *And sincere heart*
> *We will serve his king,*
> *Thereby today achieving peace.*
>
> *I will renounce into his hands*
> *If he wishes to come and take it*
> *All that of my nation*
> *I inherited from my elders.*[68]

In this version of history, the Zapoteca, unlike the Mexica, "submitted to royal obedience of their own accord, without ever having been conquered."[69] It was, once again, an erasure or denial of conquest, by which the poet challenged one of the most important rationales for native subjugation under Spanish law. His Zapoteca compatriots, he argued, were full partners in the Christian civilization of New Spain, as their ancestors had helped establish it.

The poetry of don Patricio Antonio López thus achieved a precise balance between criticism (of greedy or immoral officials) and praise

---

[67] Ibid., f. 55.
[68] Ibid., f. 56.
[69] Ibid., ff. 1–2.

(of the king and the Church). Minus the story of the Zapoteca king's peaceful repentance, don Patricio's paean to Mesoamerica and criticism of colonial exploitation would have been rather more subversive. Conversely, had he chosen to accept and express colonial stereotypes of native barbarism – even in a positive way – he could not have derived honor from his native ancestry, nor would it have served his immediate purpose of a lettered vocation. Europeans were familiar with the trope of the "noble savage," but noble savages were not models of erudition, literacy, and eloquence, nor were they good candidates for promotion within letrado circles. Thus, as it had for many creoles and caciques before, frequent analogies between Mesoamerica and ancient and medieval Europe enabled and fortified the balance of proindigenous and procolonial ideas apparent within don Patricio's poetry. Far from barbarians, the people of Mesoamerica were virtuous and rational like the Romans; they merely required the truth of Christian revelation to achieve moral wholeness. "Once the light of the Holy Doctrine shone upon them," wrote don Patricio, "they began to flourish in virtue, letters, and arms . . . and many are the memorable deeds that some achieved."[70] These accomplishments, however, were restricted only to Indians within a discretely indigenous context; in a seemingly discordant aside in the prologue, the poet exhorts the reader not to understand his rhymes as a defense of mestizos, insisting that, unlike the Indians, most mestizos were "lacking in talent and [had] little knowledge . . . of erudite studies."[71] Don Patricio critiqued colonial representations of Indians, but he was no liberal; he was a product of the eighteenth-century urban cacique culture that prized indigenous autonomy and adhered to the ideal of the Two Republics.

Don Patricio thus echoed the sixteenth-century ladino caciques such as don Hernando Pimentel Nezahualcoyotl and don Antonio Cortés Totoquihuaztli, both of whom lamented the loss of their patrimonies and their mistreatment by Spaniards yet strategically praised their own conquest as liberation from idolatrous darkness. Yet this ambivalence was always unstable. Was it possible to declare Indian equality without adopting an explicitly critical tone toward colonial institutions and practices derived from conquest and built upon the presumption of Indian inferiority? As we will see, other eighteenth-century cacique-intellectuals – likewise concerned with improving the lot of native communities – rejected

---

[70] Ibid., f. 21.
[71] Ibid., f. 28.

don Patricio's carefully moderated perspective, opting instead for a more accusatory narrative of decline, explicitly contrasting preconquest prosperity with postconquest misery.

Unrefined diamonds: the critique of Spanish misrule

A unique episode from the mid eighteenth century illustrates the critical potential of stories of Mesoamerican greatness, especially when unmoderated by allusions to conquest-era collaboration. A group of central Mexican elites led by cacique-priests appealed to native history to both challenge Enlightenment-era "science" regarding the innate inferiority of America's native peoples while also contributing to late-colonial deliberations on imperial reform. By contrasting the grandeur of Anahuac with the penury of contemporary native communities, they compelled Spanish officials to consider an uncomfortable idea: That far from "liberating" or "civilizing" barbarous peoples, Spanish rule had ruined a once-prosperous society. The argument mirrored those of contemporary creole apologists such as the Jesuits or Díaz de la Vega, yet in this case it was the Indian leadership articulating the premise. Thus it was not a patriotic defense of "Mexico" against peninsular scorn, it was a far more pragmatic call for the inclusion of Indians in the secular and ecclesiastical governance of New Spain.

Br. don Julian Cirilo de Castilla Aquiahualcateuhtle was a cacique and priest from Tlaxcala. After traveling to Spain in 1752, don Julian – a "direct descendant of the noble senators of Tlaxcala in New Spain" – logged a *memorial* with the Council of the Indies "in the name of all the nations that inhabit that vast empire."[72] Memoriales were extended petitions, a means by which subjects informed the king of broad injustices and solicited crown support.[73] According to its author, its purpose was to inform the king of the "utterly impolitic and helpless state" of the native peoples of contemporary Mexico. He described indigenous

---

[72] The memorial was titled, "Los yndios de la Nueva España suplican a vuestra merced se sirva edificarles un colegio privativo a su nación en que pueda su juventud intruirse en todas letras y política . . . ." First Memorial of Br. don Julian Cirilo de Castilla, Apr 27, 1752, AGI-M 1937, ff. 14–22. Aquiahualcateuhtle was the name of a conquest-era leader whose descendants had earned noble titles. See Concession of Arms of Don Pablo de Castilla, Madrid, Aug 16, 1563, in Villar Villamil, *Cedulario heráldico*: no. 132.

[73] Allan J. Kuethe and Kenneth J. Andrien, *The Spanish Atlantic World in the Eighteenth Century: War and the Bourbon Reforms, 1713–1796* (New York: Cambridge University Press, 2014), 10.

pueblos as abject and miserable, invoking some of the worst conceits and stereotypes of drunkenness, vice, and superstition. However, unlike contemporary pessimists, don Julian argued that the "vulgarity" and "rusticity" of native communities was anomalous rather than innate, the result of centuries of social breakdown stemming from a "lack of cultivation," a dearth of opportunities for education and moral development. "Without cultivation, even the richest diamond is worthless," he explained.[74]

Don Julian contrasted the poverty and misery of his contemporaries with a positive vision of pre-Hispanic Mexico culled largely from Juan de Torquemada. The Indians were clearly capable of rational self-government, because they had governed themselves rationally in the past. "During pagan times," he wrote, "[the Indians] lived in such strict accordance with their laws, that in their observance and politics they rivaled even the Romans." Virtue flourished as vice and immorality met harsh consequences. "The ancients punished inebriation with the death penalty," for example, "and only in instances of illness or necessity were they excused from the rigor of the laws."[75] This declinist account of history was an indictment of Spanish misrule. As it had been for the sixteenth-century ladino caciques, the rhetorical force lay in the contrast between what came before and what followed. Under the viceroys, Mexico's native communities had shrunk and become mired in poverty, isolation, and a host of social maladies. Something traumatic had clearly occasioned this devastation, although don Julian initially left his audience to reason for themselves what, precisely, that was.[76]

Don Julian's proposed solution involved the equal participation of native people in secular and ecclesaistical governance. Once again history provided his argument with evidence – in this case, the immediate postconquest period, which he portrayed as a sort of Christian golden age in which native leaders contributed to a broad flourishing of learning and enlightenment in Mexico. For one all-too-fleeting historical moment, Franciscan evangelizers and ladino caciques had together mastered the sciences and liberal arts. The achievements of the Tlatelolca cacique-scholars proved that God had endowed all nations, including Indians, with the same human rationality.[77]

---

[74] First Memorial of Br. Don Julian Cirilo de Castilla, f. 17.
[75] Ibid., ff. 19–20.
[76] Ibid., ff. 14–22.
[77] Second Memorial of don Julian Cyrilo Castilla, 1779, AGI-M 1937, ff. 824–828.

The cacique offered solutions in accordance with this belief. He revived the old idea to train a vanguard of Indian priests to spearhead a moral and social revival in native communities. To these ends, don Julian proposed the erection of a new seminary in the Villa de Guadalupe just north of Mexico City, where the children of caciques would learn "all manner of virtues and letters." Once educated and ordained, they would spread throughout the land, "guiding their countrymen and compatriots to the wisdom they [currently] lack."[78] With this plan, don Julian was both responding to and participating in the reformist spirit of the mid eighteenth century, centered around the Bourbon monarchy. In their important confidential report of 1748, for example, the Spanish naval officers Jorge Juan and Antonio de Ulloa insisted that the formation of a native clergy would be the best way to inspire Indians to "abandon vice" – and, moreover, that they would do so joyfully and of their own accord.[79] Thus, when the Consejo de Indias considered don Julian's proposal in 1754, the ideological climate was not uniformly hostile to the idea. Furthermore, he had prominent allies in the Hispanic sphere, particularly among the Jesuits and Franciscans who supported native education. In 1757, the Mexico City Audiencia lent support as well, citing the usual symbols of native potential: the fame of the Colegio de Santa Cruz de Tlatelolco, the 1697 decree, the boy-martyrs of Tlaxcala, and Bishop Juan Merlo de la Fuente. The failure of many Indians to acquire grados even after 1697 was due less to nature, it argued, but to a hostile culture of antinative "insult and scorn" in Novohispanic seminaries and colleges.[80]

Yet don Julian had enemies as well: The "pessimists" among the secular clergy who objected to the notion that Indians could join their ranks. Archbishop Rubio y Salinas rejected the project on the grounds that Indians were incapable of scholarship and letters. "Not a single one has been seen to obtain an excellent grado in this university," he reported in 1755,

---

[78] First Memorial of don Julian Cirilo de Castilla Aquiahualcateuhtle, f. 15. The complete story of the failed project, along with transcriptions of the two petitions of don Julian, is Margarita Menegus Bornemann, "El Colegio de San Carlos Borromeo: Un proyecto para la creación de un clero indígena en el siglo XVIII," in *Saber y poder en México, siglos XVI al XX*, ed. Margarita Menegus Bornemann (México: Universidad Nacional Autónoma de México, 1997). See also O'Hara, *Flock Divided*: 72–80. O'Hara contextualizes the project within Bourbon-era debates over the secularization of Novohispanic parishes.

[79] Jorge Juan and Antonio de Ulloa, *Discourse and Political Reflections on the Kingdoms of Peru*, trans. John J. TePaske and Besse A. Clement (Norman, OK: University of Oklahoma Press, 1978), 175.

[80] Real Acuerdo of Mexico to King Fernando VI, Mexico, June 27, 1757, AGI-M 1937, ff. 159–73.

nor to excel in any faculty such as to deserve credit as a good student."[81] A royal fiscal mostly agreed, insisting that Indians were happier as servants and laborers and had no inclination for intellectual rigor and scholarship. Besides, he sneered, "they are, in general, dirty and impolitic, and inclined toward lies and sneakiness, [and] they do not have the best discretion, nor the best control of their conduct, nor good prudence."[82] During the fifteen years that don Julian remained in Madrid, he watched in sadness as his project fell victim to political reticence and bureaucratic inertia. The royal appetite for reform faltered in the late 1750s as modernizing proponents fell from grace and Spain struggled with yet another war.[83] In 1766, the Consejo even tried to purchase don Julian's silence with a comfortable sinecure in Guadalajara, the home diocese of his wealthy sponsor in Spain, but the cacique remained true to his proposal and rejected the offer.[84]

A new phase began in 1767 with the expulsion of the Jesuits. Although the Society had supported the project, they left behind numerous properties that might have served for the proposed community. A charter was drawn up in which a new royal college for caciques would be established – not coincidentally, in or near the ex-Jesuit school of San Gregorio – and don Julian returned with it to Mexico the following year.[85] Yet the idea went nowhere, stymied by squabbles over expropriated assets, and high-level resistance to the plan's implicit acceptance of native cultural autonomy.[86] The new Archbishop Lorenzana, as we will see, desired a more culturally and politically homogenous colony, and was extremely hostile to the ideals of the Two Republics. In 1779, more than twenty-five years after he had first engaged the imperial behemoth, a frustrated, angry, and aged don Julian submitted yet another memorial, this one far more acerbic and overtly critical.[87] Whereas in his first petition he had left the cause for the Indians' lack of cultivation largely unstated and

---

[81] Archbishop Manuel José de Rubio y Salinas to Fernando VI, AGI-M 1937, f. 88.

[82] Report of Fiscal Antonio Andreu to Fernando VI, Mexico, 1755, AGI-M 1937, ff. 225–28.

[83] On the "pause" in the reformist agenda during the 1750s, see Kuethe and Andrien, *The Spanish Atlantic World*: 209–27.

[84] Offer of Prebendary to don Julian Cirilo de Castilla Aquiahualcateuhtle, Madrid, May 14-Sep 17, 1766, AGI-M 1937, ff. 549–54.

[85] Constitution and Curriculum for the Royal College of San Carlos Borromeo, 1769–76, AGI-M 1937, ff. 669–728.

[86] See Menegus Bornemann, "El Colegio de San Carlos Borromeo," 215–18; Schmidt Díaz de León, *Colegio Seminario*: 57–71.

[87] Second Memorial of don Julian Cirilo de Castilla Aquiahualcateuhtle, ff. 822–30.

implicit, in his new statement the cacique focused his ire on the secular clergy who were his peers as well as his main opponents, blaming them for the ills of native communities. It was they who had failed in the task of educating the Indians in "good practices and customs." Although the religious instruction of their parishioners was their most important duty, priests in charge of remote, rural communities were absent from their own parishes during most of the year. And when they did attend to their pastoral duties, they could not even speak the languages of or otherwise communicate with their parishioners. The resulting emotional distance led them to abuse their authority, pilfer church treasuries, and coerce Indians into personal service. Thus, lamented don Julian, the presence of corrupt priests in native communities was not only inadequate to the task of improving the Indians, it was actively harmful, leaving them in a state of vulgarity and ignorance rather than Christian virtue:

For the most part, [the Indians] cannot distinguish the malice of [the priests] from the sanctity, justice, and purity of our religion, such that the evangelical law does not animate them to love their neighbor as themselves, *only because he is an Indian* [don Julian's emphasis]. And therefore, they should not be instructed, as are all other nations, to correct their errors; and they should not have colleges in which to train, nor monasteries to praise God, because they were not raised for such things – a situation terrifying to merely pronounce, and which gives not even the slightest remorse to those who are at fault. . . . The more [the secular clergy] dominate, and the more they are obeyed, the more ignorant and proud they become, degrading the Indian people (*especie*) because they do not have this spirit, having ceded their kingdoms, their properties, and themselves to serve [the priests]. And for this, [the Indians] are deemed irrational.[88]

Unsurprisingly, the native elite of central Mexico, which included a number of educated caciques, supported don Julian's petition from beginning to end. During the original inquiries of the 1750s, the cabildos of Tenochtitlan and Tlatelolco contributed a statement endorsing the proposed seminary. Its primary author was yet another erudite cacique who claimed to speak on behalf of "all the nations that inhabit this vast empire," Br. don Andrés Ignacio de Escalona y Arias Axayacatzin y Temilo, the son of Nicolás de Escalona and Petra Arias of Tlatelolco and an alumnus of the Seminary College of Mexico, chartered during the reforms of the 1690s with a one-fourth quota for caciques. Don Andrés represented himself as a "direct descendant of the noble House of Collonacasco," a district of Tlatelolco. Despite his proud heritage, don Andrés came from rather humble conditions, and his studies (between

[88] Ibid., ff. 829.

1729 and 1736) were the result of the patronage of his godfather, Dr. Pedro Ramírez del Castillo of the Mexico City cathedral chapter.[89] However, he spoke for the Indian leadership; a number of Tlatelolca nobles signed his petition, including two members of the respected Mendoza Austria Moctezuma lineage, descendants of don Diego de Mendoza Imauhyantzin.[90]

Don Andrés's primary objective was the renewal of the old promise of Santa Cruz de Tlatelolco for the "good government of these realms and the welfare of the souls of their native inhabitants."[91] Like don Julian Cirilo de Castilla Aquiahualcateuhtle, don Andrés told a history of decline to challenge the widespread belief in innate indigenous inferiority. He pointed out that the population of New Spain was hardly a twentieth of its former size, and that despite all the best protective efforts of the crown, "all the remedies that have been established in favor of the natives have resulted in their harm."[92] Empowered by their access to education, the early ladino caciques had been wildly effective evangelizers. "The caciques and other lords of this district of Santiago Tlatelolco were the first to give themselves and their treasures to ensure peace and tranquility," he wrote, thereby enabling "the greatest conversion in the least amount of time ever known in our Holy Mother Church."[93]

The bulk of don Andrés's treatise engaged contemporary debates over the most effective means of religious administration in native communities. Training a native vanguard was necessary, he argued, to overcome the considerable obstacle of linguistic diversity in the Americas, the subject of much ongoing controversy, as we will see. Who better to translate and eloquently explain the mysteries of the faith to native flocks than shepherds drawn from their own compatriots, specifically trained for the task? He also declared the need for Christian compassion toward the least of the world's peoples, especially those, like the Indians, whose existence was largely wretched, and cited the first American saint, Santa Rosa of Lima – "our very venerated and holy compatriot" – in calling for special mercy and concern.[94]

---

[89] Br. D. Andrés Ignacio Escalona y Arias, Tlatelolco, in "Solicitud para la reapertura del Colegio de Santiago Tlatelolco," *Boletín del Archivo General de la Nación 6*, no. 1 (1935): 23. See Menegus Bornemann, *Los indios, el sacerdocio, y la universidad*: 206, 42, 52.

[90] Ibid., 36.

[91] Ibid., 25.

[92] Ibid., 27.

[93] Ibid., 26.

[94] Ibid., 27–33, quote from 32–33.

Don Andrés concluded his brief by directly criticizing, like don Julian Cirilo, the presumption of innate indigenous inferiority. Significantly, he did so by revisiting the infamous Valladolid Controversy of 1550, which pitted the great Dominican defender of Indian rights, Bartolomé de Las Casas, against Juan Ginés de Sepúlveda's quasi-Aristotelian philosophy of a "natural" hierarchy of slaves and masters among humans. Following Las Casas, don Andrés portrayed America's native peoples as "humble, meek, and pacific," and "worthy of the greatest compassion due to their poverty and misery."[95] Sepúlveda, meanwhile, he scorned as "blind and pernicious" in his attacks on the virtue of Indians. Thus, although don Andrés superficially echoed the paternalistic image of native peoples as virtuous by way of simplicity, his argument worked on a deeper, shrewder level. In referencing and exploring the sophisticated philosophy and theology debated at Valladolid, he showcased his own erudition even as he clothed it in a humble appeal to a respected Church authority. This also preempted the objections he foresaw based on the presumption of Indian irrationality; it was not his own opinion, but that of Las Casas, Bishop of Chiapas.[96]

During the renewed deliberations after 1767, the native elites of central Mexico involved themselves again in the long incubation of don Julian Cirilo's project. In April 1770, the "current and past governors of San Juan Tenochtitlan and Santiago Tlatelolco" drafted a letter to Carlos III indicating their support for the creation of a native priestly vanguard. Like the two cacique-priests, the cabildo officers claimed to speak on behalf of "all of the Indians" of New Spain, and wielded Christian universalism against the notion of innate indigenous inferiority. They argued that an oppressive web of cruelty and prejudice had for centuries squandered "the talents and facilities which God has given to us, as to all men," and they called upon the king's mercy to relieve the Indians' "unhappy state" of ignorance and poverty. Returning to the theme of cultivation, they cited the great universities of Europe to illustrate how education enriches and ennobles societies; deprived of such institutions, they argued, native people were doomed to be forever scorned as idolatrous, savage, and superstitious. How could they liberate themselves from accusations of irrationality, they asked, if they were denied the opportunity to become masters of reason in the first place? Not only was this deprivation immoral, they argued, it was a violation of Spain's own laws.

[95] Ibid., 33.
[96] Ibid., 34.

Citing the 1766 update to the 1697 decree, they noted that caciques were equivalent to hidalgos, and therefore deserved the same opportunities.[97]

Yet as before, the rhetorical gravity of the letter lies in the caciques' account of history – in their portrayal of their non-Christian ancestors, whom they remembered fondly and admiringly. "The histories," they wrote, "record that, in pagan times, boys and girls, young men and women, were educated according to Natural Law, in schools, with extreme care and diligence." These memories, of course, contrasted sharply with their contemporary circumstances, and were especially painful, they noted, "considering our current lack of all instruction."[98] They accused (unnamed) forces in the colonial world of mendaciously inventing the myth of Indian unreason – "the insidious malice of having denied [our] rationality" – precisely to prevent them from ever transcending their lowly state. To the cabildo, the fact that some were resisting don Julian's proposal merely confirmed their suspicions of a conspiracy to perpetuate indigenous wretchedness. "The continuous experience of almost three centuries," they lamented, "has demonstrated that all of the relief that the Catholic monarchs have provided, pitying their miseries... has not had any effect."[99]

Don Julian also enlisted the support of his fellow Tlaxcalteca nobles. Beginning in 1770, the cabildo contributed several letters to the effort written by don Nicolás Faustino Mazihcatzin y Escovar, the minor-orders cleric who corresponded with creole antiquarians.[100] Predictably, don Nicolás and his compatriots invoked Tlaxcalteca exceptionalism, reminding the king of Tlaxcala's services during the conquest 250 years earlier, and noted that the proposed college was proper recompense for those who had sacrificed so much for the crown. "To deny us [this college]," they wrote, "is the greatest injury that we will have ever received." Yet like don Julian, in a second letter of 1774 don Nicolás and the other officers also transcended the specifically Tlaxcalteca narrative to speak for the "Indian nation" as a whole. We should recognize this as a telling shift and a departure from Tlaxcalteca convention. Tlaxcala's leaders – including the Salazars and the Mazihcatzins in other contexts – were normally inclined to exalt Tlaxcala precisely by differentiating it from

---

[97] Representation of the Republics of Tenochtitlan and Tlatelolco, Mexico, Apr 11, 1770, AGI-M 1937, ff. 836–37.

[98] Ibid., f. 836–37.

[99] Ibid., f. 840.

[100] Representation of the Cabildo of Tlaxcala, Tlaxcala, Feb 3, 1770, AGI-M 1937, ff. 833–34.

other native pueblos, casting it as unique in both its ancient heritage
and its colonial privileges, all within a consistently triumphant tone. Yet
for a brief moment in 1774 they set aside Tlaxcalteca exceptionalism to
echo the declinism of don Julian and their counterparts in Tlatelolco and
Tenochtitlan, faulting a "lack of cultivation" for native poverty:

> Every defect that we execute against God, against ourselves, and against our supe-
> riors originates from our ignorance and poor education, which violates even our
> rational nature, and deprives us of Reason and the talents that are the foundations
> upon which we should be serving the One Sovereign who gives and takes away
> Empires and Kingdoms, and with which we can reconcile our volition with our
> compatriots and monarch. Lacking such abilities, what [progress] can we expect
> in the future?[101]

Cacique-letrados and royalist propaganda

In the same way that they might be powerful voices of criticism, erudite
Indian elites could lend legitimacy to colonial efforts to strengthen and
consolidate crown control. When crown operatives successfully commissioned or acquired the support of cacique-letrados, they were able to
co-opt the perceived epistemological authority of Christian native lords
and cloak royalist agendas within a pro-Indian, neo-Aztec guise. Such
was the program of the Archbishop of Mexico, Francisco Antonio de
Lorenzana y Butrón (r. 1766–72), an important executor of the sweep-
ing administrative reforms of Carlos III (r. 1759–88). Although sometimes remembered as an exemplar of Christian compassion and charity,
Lorenzana exhibited an extreme paternalism toward native people that
ultimately aimed to centralize crown control over indigenous lives and
squelch local traditions of autonomy.[102] In this he echoed a long tradition
in Spanish imperialist thought that justified colonialism by infantilizing
native peoples and advocating their subjugation to a benevolent despo-
tism. Wrote Lorenzana, "our kings love [the Indians] dearly, and in their
laws have always looked out for their welfare... such that they should
be very obliged to him, and should strive to serve him as the most loyal
vassals."[103]

---

[101] Letter of the Cabildo of Tlaxcala, Tlaxcala, Mar 20, 1774, AGI-M 1937, ff. 843–44.
[102] See, for example, Francisco Antonio Lorenzana, *A todos los fieles de este nuestro
arzobispado salud y gracia*... Mexico, 1772, HL, Mexico Collection.
[103] Francisco Antonio Lorenzana, *Reglas para que los naturales de estos reynos sean felices
en lo espiritual y temporal*... Mexico, 1768, HL Mexico Collection, ff. 2r–2v.

Yet while many predecessors who shared his belief in Indian irrationality – including the pessimist Archbishop Rubio y Salinas – had
scorned or disregarded Mesoamerican history as irrelevant or unimpor-
tant, Lorenzana researched the history so he could appropriate it for his
own purposes. Indeed, Lorenzana hailed Boturini as a great man who
"revealed" Indian history to the modern world.[104] Soon after arriving
into Mexico, he assembled a team of linguistic experts to examine the
Boturini museum and the remnants of the Alva Ixtlilxochitl-Sigüenza collection left by the exiled Jesuits. Two years later he published a new
History of New Spain. Although primarily a reprint of the second and
third letters of Hernando Cortés, the work contained graphic and historiographical elements derived from the Indian antiquities, including the
"Book of Tributes" associated with *Codex Mendoza* and an adaptation
of the Las Navas-Guevara calendar wheel of Tlaxcala studied by don
Manuel de los Santos y Salazar (Figure 11).[105]

Yet unlike Boturini and the creole apologists who followed him, Lorenzana did not defend Anahuac and the character of native peoples; his
project was to revive and strengthen the conqueror's vision at a time
when creole discontent was on the rise.[106] Despite his many appeals
to the wisdom of caciques such as don Fernando de Alva Ixtlilxochitl,
Lorenzana misrepresented and sanitized them by ignoring their critical
and pro-indigenous dimensions. Reproducing none of the characteristic
ambivalence of the cacique-chroniclers, the archbishop celebrated the fall
of Tenochtitlan as the end of America's dark age and the inauguration
of a new era of enlightenment, salvation, and good government that ben-
efited Indians above all. Lorenzana did not disguise his message, noting
that while Spaniards were loyal to the crown by nature of birth, the Indians needed to be taught to love the king. By republishing the letters of
Cortés, he intended to clarify "the goodness of the conquest" and how

---

[104] Lorenzana, *Historia de Nueva-España, escrito por su esclarecido conquistador Hernán
Cortés*: A2r–A2v.

[105] Ibid., 2–3.

[106] One of the archetypal statements of creole grievance, a statement by the Mexico City
cabildo logged on May 2, 1771, called for creole equality *vis a vis* peninsular Spaniards,
and the equality of New Spain *vis a vis* the other kingdoms of the Spanish crown. See
"Representación que hizo la ciudad de México al rey D. Carlos III en 1771 sobre
que los criollos deben ser preferidos a los europeos en la distribución de empleos y
beneficios de estos reinos," in *Historia de la guerra de independencia de México*, ed.
Juan Evaristo Hernández y Dávalos (Mexico: Instituto Nacional de Estudios Históricos
de la Revolución Mexicana, 1985).

FIGURE 11 Calendar wheel derived from Tlaxcalteca original studied by don Manuel de los Santos y Salazar, in Francisco Antonio Lorenzana, *Historia de Nueva-España*, 1770. Huntington Library, San Marino, CA.

the Indians' lives had been "improved by the lights of the Faith."[107] This inverted the declinist narratives of the creole apologists and caciques such as don Julian Cirilo de Castilla Aquiahualcateuhtle.

---

[107] Preface to ibid., n.p.

Lorenzana did not have the linguistic, historical, or cultural knowledge necessary to master the Boturini collection. That job he delegated to others. He listed three people who aided his research; the first two were experts in Nahuatl, Huasteca, and Otomí in Mexico City, and the third was don Domingo José de la Mota, a cacique of Tenochtitlan and a parish priest in Tochimilco (Puebla). As a member of the elite Nahua culture and memory of central Mexico – the bishop lauded his linguistic ability as "the most elegant style" – don Domingo's knowledge was critical to Lorenzana's work.[108]

Don Domingo was from Santa Cruz Acatlan, on the outskirts of Mexico City. His parents exemplified the mixed results of the Hispanization policies that animated the decree of 1697: Even as they received formal educations and adopted Spanish language and dress, they operated primarily as leaders within the Indian republic, their skills devoted to the administration and preservation of a discretely indigenous civic and religious sphere. Claiming "pure blood" as a descendant of the royal houses of Tenochtitlan, Tetzcoco, Tlacopan, and Tlalnepantla, don Domingo's father, don Alexandro Antonio de la Mota, had been rector of the Jesuits' cacique college of San Gregorio. His mother, doña Sebastiana Paula de Chávez, was likewise of noble lineage, and boasted that her niece had taken the veil, as Sister Gregoria de Christo, in the new convent of Corpus Christi for cacica women.[109] Exemplifying the scholarly trajectory of the family, two of don Domingo's brothers also received ordination, don José Antonio and don José Manuel.

Don Domingo's own lettered career was by turns both typical and extraordinary. He likely began his studies with the Jesuits of San Gregorio where his father worked. After receiving two bachilleratos at the Royal University before 1730, don Domingo was ordained and licensed to administer the sacraments in both Spanish and Nahuatl in 1733. For the next four years, he served vicariously in Teoloyucan, north of Mexico City, where he survived the devastating *matlazahuatl* epidemic of 1736; once immune, he traveled throughout the region providing Last Rites to the mortally ill. In 1740, he relocated to the remote parish of Tepecuacuilco (Guerrero), where he remained vicar for the next eight years. During this time don Domingo's two brothers, now ordained, arrived to assist with the parish.[110] In 1748, he was transferred again,

---

[108] Ibid., 176.
[109] Probanza of don Alexandro Antonio de la Mota, Mexico, Feb 14, 1744, AGI-I , 239, N.6, ff. 79v–81v.
[110] Menegus Bornemann, *Los indios, el sacerdocio, y la universidad*: 253.

to Zacualpan (México), where he was vicar, ecclesiastical judge, and the author of several pamphlets on proper religious practice in Nahuatl and Spanish.[111] In 1753, he requested a promotion, and six years later received his own parish in Yautepec (Morelos).[112] It was there that don Domingo caught the eye of Church luminaries. A semiheretical popular devotion had arisen in the area, and in 1761 the cacique-priest and his two brothers set out to uncover it and punish its leaders. The confrontation turned violent, and the leader of the cult bit off don Domingo's finger.[113]

If the maimed hand of don Domingo José de la Mota symbolized the extent of his alignment with the elite and Hispanic realm over the popular and indigenous, so also did his collaboration with Archbishop Lorenzana. As a cacique of lineage, he lent legitimacy to Lorenzana's project that it could not have otherwise earned, given the esoteric historical knowledge that indigenous nobles were presumed to possess. To enlist a native nobleman in his royalist agenda was a direct challenge to the epistemological authority of the creoles, who preferred to think of themselves as the heirs, whether literally or symbolically, to the Indian nobility and therefore as the true experts on the history of their patria. It is no coincidence that the exiled Jesuit Clavijero, who had read Lorenzana's history, highlighted the archbishop's mistranslations of pictographic materials to de-legitimize his native collaborators. Too much time had passed, and contemporary caciques such as don Domingo were simply no longer capable of deciphering the artifacts of Anahuac; that was best left to the creole antiquarians.[114]

Another of Lorenzana's major objectives was to extinguish linguistic pluralism in New Spain, which he considered detrimental to the king's authority and an obstacle to the modernization of his empire.[115] A decree of 1770 established this as official royal policy, and Lorenzana prioritized it as one of his most important tasks.[116] He was woefully unsuccessful;

---

[111] One of these is titled *Mes fructuoso, de sagradas meditaciones repartidas por todos sus días* (México: Herederos de María de Rivera, 1755). I have not been able to track any copies of this item.

[112] Merits of Domingo José de la Mota, Mexico, May 5, 1753, AGI-I 238, N.31, ff. 507r–09v.

[113] For accounts of this conflict, see William Taylor, "Morelos: un ejemplo regional de sacerdotes, feligreses, e insurrección," *Historias* 40(1998): 63–65; Serge Gruzinski, *Man-Gods of the Mexican Highlands*, trans. Eileen Corrigan (Stanford: Stanford University Press, 1989), 170–72.

[114] Cañizares-Esguerra, *How to Write*: 245.

[115] Dorothy Tanck de Estrada, *Pueblos de indios y educación en el México colonial, 1750–1821* (México: El Colegio de México, 1999).

[116] See Lorenzana, *El que llega reverente . . . .*

erudite institutions did not heed his call – some maintained and even added specialists in native languages – and the people responded mostly with consternation and resentment.[117] In 1810, the viceregal regime finally relented, and commissioned a new Nahuatl grammar, *Art of the Mexican Language (Arte de la lengua mexicana)*, the first in forty years.[118]

The author of the new grammar was don Rafael Tiburcio Sandoval y Moctezuma (d. 1817), a secular canon in central Mexico and a Bachelor in Theology who had taught Nahuatl to aspiring clergy in Tepozotlan, the Royal University, and the Collegiate Church of Guadalupe.[119] He was also a mestizo of noble Tenochca heritage and yet another product of the Jesuits' Colegio Seminario de San Gregorio. He had attained some fame as an effective instructor of Nahuatl, and belonged to a coterie of creole intellectuals and clergy who had resisted Lorenzana's restrictions on native languages by preserving a semi-underground culture of study. Indeed, in the dedicatory preface to his work he criticized the decree of 1770; yes, the Indians should learn Spanish, he conceded, but this should not require the disappearance of their own languages, especially when souls were at stake.[120] Thus we might place don Rafael alongside contemporary patriotic antiquarians such as Antonio de León y Gama, but as an alumnus of San Gregorio he was also linked to the lettered indigenous culture of late-colonial Mexico City.

Sandoval lent his facility in Nahuatl to viceregal counter-insurgency during the independence period. Soon after the arrival of Viceroy Francisco Javier Venegas de Saavedra (r. 1810–13) in September of 1810, Father Miguel Hidalgo gave his famous cry for Mexican independence. To preempt Hidalgo's appeal to the native population, Venegas quickly commissioned Nahuatl translations of two statements of royal benevolence, and printed and distributed them throughout New Spain.[121] According

---

[117] A royal order of 1778, for example, required the Collegiate Church of Guadalupe to permanently maintain four prebendaries trained in Nahuatl, one in Otomí, and another in Mazahua. Royal Instructions for the New Statutes of the Collegiate Church of Guadalupe, Mexico, July 18, 1778, AGN-RCO 114, Exp. 127.

[118] Rafael Tiburcio Sandoval, *Arte de la lengua mexicana* (México: Manuel Antonio Valdés, 1810).

[119] Proceedings to Fill Two Vacant Canons in the Mexican Language in the Collegiate Church of Guadalupe upon the Death of Dr. don Manuel Burgos y Acuña and don Rafael Tiburcio Sandoval, Mexico, 1817–1818, HL Mexican Records Collection 71111.

[120] Sandoval, *Arte de la lengua mexicana*: preface.

[121] *Ayamo moyolpachihuitia in Totlatocatzin Rey D. Fernando VII*, LL Latin American Manuscripts. The first words of the document read, "Our beloved ruler, King Fernando VII, has not yet been satisfied."

to Mark Morris, Sandoval was their likely translator. Intentionally circumventing decades of Bourbon centralization policies, the documents invoke the old Hapsburg ideal of composite monarchy, stressing direct vassalage and reciprocity between a loving, paternalistic crown and its loyal indigenous communities.[122]

Facing the insurgents, royalists continued to enlist educated Indians in their propaganda efforts, exhorting native communities to remember the great benevolence of their king. In 1811, a small pamphlet appeared, ostensibly the sermon of an unnamed native priest in Valladolid (Morelia). The sermon condemned Hidalgo's uprising by emphasizing the special love between Indians and the Spanish crown. The sermon might be a forgery, but the pamphlet nonetheless exemplifies the propaganda value of loyal native leaders; by ventriloquism – by placing the royalist agenda on the lips of an Indian priest – the crown's supporters presumed his authority to speak for "the Indian nation" and appropriated it for their own agenda. The sermon invoked the common image of the king as a "father" of his people, protecting and caring for his children. Indians needed the king, argued the priest, because he was their best defense against the greed and malice of Spaniards, foreigners, and heretics. "My children ... enjoy the tranquility that the laws ensure you, and the paternal government that holds your allegiance," he urged. The priest continued, warning against Hidalgo's seductive lies about independence and equality. He foresaw that in a liberal society without a benevolent king's protection, the Indians would suffer most: "In a chaos in which injustice, vengeance, hate, and anarchy reign ... the weakest and least astute will be the first to be sacrificed, just as in the sea the smallest fish is devoured by the largest."[123]

Importantly, the speaker avoided stating any ethnic affiliations, instead representing himself as an Indian looking out for the best interests of all Indians. Miguel Hidalgo and the other insurgents, on the other hand, he portrayed as alien flatterers and seducers who harbored nothing but scorn for native folk. While speaking the language of equality in public, in his private thoughts he disdained them, calling them "foolish Indians (*mentecatos*)" and "barbarous idiots," and laughing at their gullibility – drawn,

[122] Mark Morris, "Language in Service of the State: The Nahuatl Counterinsurgency Broadsides of 1810," *Hispanic American Historical Review* 87, no. 3 (2007): 451.

[123] "Proclama de un cura indio del obispado de Valladolid, a todos los padres curas y vicarios indios, y a nuestros hijos los caziques gobernadores y demas indios de esta America" (Mexico: n.p., 1811), 5.

as they were, "like flies to honey" by his empty promises of fraternity.[124] In Hidalgo's eyes, the priest argued, "we [Indians] are nothing but beasts of burden, stupid animals, a race deserving of extinction, [kindling] for the fire that he eventually wants to ignite in this America."[125]

Most spectacularly, the priest portrayed loyalty to the king as the very essence of being Indian. This was a particularly vivid *reductio ad absurdum* of the ideal of native loyalty, one that equated fealty with indigeneity itself. To betray the king, he argued, would be to betray the Indians' proud and ancient tradition.

> Oh barbarous and frenetic slaves (*agavillados*)! Do you wish us to violate and profane this soil, which has gone unstained by the disloyalty [of Indians] for three centuries, and without public apostasy against God, against His divine mother – our guardian (*amparo*), protector and sweet *conquistadora*? Do you wish for the most humble children of the religion, the most meek and pacific vassals of the Spanish monarchy, the citizens most privileged by the laws of our loving and beloved sovereigns...that we come to aid you in your crime and the most scandalous apostasy, sacrilege, and atrocity that history has seen...? This is the language of our heart, and every one of us will die to seal with our blood the fidelity and love we have for our God and our King.[126]

Conclusion

While the appearance of cacique-letrados – as well as the royal decree of 1697 – envisioned a natural harmony and alignment between Mexico's natural lords and the imperial regime, their professional and cognitive location along the seams of a major social and ethnic divide revealed a far more ambivalent reality. While in the abstract a cacique-letrado represented the full culmination and realization of the spirit of the 1697 decree – equality between Spanish and native hidalgos – in a more visceral way the social and linguistic presence of erudite Indians within the lettered world often intensified their otherness as Indians, a reality that neither viceregal insignias nor Church incomes could entirely assuage, and probably exacerbated. This is best witnessed in their tendency to be funneled into "ambassadorial" roles, speaking to Spaniards on behalf of an inorganic "Indian nation."

The arguments of the cacique-intellectuals paralleled those of contemporary creole apologists largely because they were participating in

---

[124] Ibid., 4.
[125] Ibid., 2.
[126] Ibid., 6–7.

the same disputes. Some, like Granados y Gálvez, invoked the old ideal of Indian–Spanish alliance (best symbolized by the conquistador-cacica marriages that he lauded), in which two grand civilizations, inspired by the truth of Christianity, had eagerly joined themselves under one wise and benevolent king. Others, however, emphasized decline in the style of Clavijero: an antiquity marked by order and sophistication followed by colonial-era ruin. From there, it was a rather short cognitive distance – if also a major ideological leap – to the explosive notion that the Indo-Hispanic culture and society of New Spain was, in the historical sense, un-Mexican. Such an idea, of course, would unravel almost three centuries of cacique-creole assertions to the contrary.

9

Conclusion

Although our pueblo is presently very small, in past ages it . . . surpassed all the other provinces in antiquity and nobility. . . . The annals of the elders tell us that it was founded 1,525 years ago, [while] all those who are noble and honored in every pueblo recognize universally that their origins trace back to Azcaputzalco.

Governors of Azcapotzalco, 1561[1]

Inspired by the supreme love I have for my Patria, [my work contains] very important information, not the least estimable of which is an explication of the [year-count] and history of the Chichimecas, who we call today Mexicans, *from just after the Flood to the present time.*

Carlos de Sigüenza y Góngora, creole scholar, 1684[2]

The general disinterest we endure with regards to Mexican antiquities [is] the residue left by our barbarous Spanish fathers, who strove to cast a dense veil over the events of the conquest and the government of our indigenous ancestors.

Carlos María de Bustamante, statesman, 1826[3]

Every Mexican bears within him this continuity, which goes back two thousand years. It doesn't matter that this presence is almost always unconscious

---

[1] Letter of don Hernando de Molina, don Baltasar Hernández, and the cabildo of Azcapotzalco to King Felipe II, Azcapotzalco, Feb 10, 1561, in PRT, 218.

[2] Sigüenza y Góngora, *Parayso occidental*: f. 1xr.

[3] Carlos María de Bustamante, *Necesidad de la unión de todos los mexicanos contra las asechanzas de la Nación Española y liga europea, comprobada con la historia de la antigua República de Tlaxcallan* (México: Imprenta del Águila, 1826), HL Mexican Records Collection, f. 16.

*and assumes the naïve forms of legend and even superstition. It is not some-
thing known but something lived. The Indian presence means that one of
the facets of Mexican culture is not Western.*

Octavio Paz, 1979[4]

Guardians of Mexican antiquity

The native nobility, once reconstructed as loyal Christians, played a key
role within the development of Mexican creolism, as they enabled and
validated the selective appropriation of American history that characterized the creole patria. In the creole imaginary, indigenous commoners
had no claim to a prestigious heritage, but the caciques were heirs to
Nezahualcoyotl, Moctezuma, and the great chieftains of Anahuac. The
commoners were rustic and superstitious, perhaps idolatrous, but the
caciques embodied a legacy of noble virtue and sophistication. Eager for
a proud American tradition to call their own, creole antiquarians delved
into the artifacts and memories of the Indian nobility, heralding them as
windows into their own heritage. By way of the caciques, who cast themselves as heirs to primordial Mexico as well as vassals of Spain and pious
Christians, creoles envisioned a patria built upon an intricate balance of
rupture and continuity. The caciques were ancient, but not pagan; they
were Christian, but not Spanish.

In short, the caciques' iconic blend of neo-Aztec and Hispano-Catholic
sympathies – one they forged not only as heirs to antiquity but also
as colonial subjects attuned to colonial laws and prejudices – allowed
creole patriots to identify with central Mexican civilization but not the
contemporary "Indians" whose ancestors had built it.[5] Once Tenochtitlan
had fallen, the Mexican legacy passed to the creoles, via the Christian
and ladino caciques whose histories they read and whose daughters they
married. According to Granados y Gálvez, contemporary Indians had
long since forgotten the wisdom of their ancestors; but "that portion
of Spaniards and masters of reason (*gente de razón*) who united with
[the native nobility] through the tight knot of matrimony form the body
of a distinguished Republic, enlightened, scientific, and full of talents."[6]
Colonial art reflecting these sentiments often juxtaposes creole heroes
and icons with Aztec symbolism in a visually exhausting melange of ideas

---

[4] Octavio Paz, "Mexico and the United States," in Paz, *The Labryinth of Solitude and Other Writings*: 362–63.

[5] Jorge Cañizares-Esguerra has detailed the stark qualitative distinctions that Spanish American creoles were inclined to draw between native nobility and commoners. See Cañizares-Esguerra, "Creole Colonial Spanish America."

[6] Granados y Gálvez, *Tardes americanas*: 229–30.

that both derived from and asserted the creoles' increasingly self-aware identity as "Mexicans" (Figure 12). The creoles envisioned themselves as the new teteuctin, Mexico's native-born hereditary leadership and the natural guardians of its ancient legacy against the hostility of "foreigners" and peninsular Spaniards. In New Spain, many late-colonial creoles had become – to paraphrase the old saying regarding the patriotic descendants of the Anglo-Norman conquerors of Ireland – "more Mexican than the Mexicans themselves".

Mexico is, of course, not the only place where Native American history helped harness and define a non-native political identity, yet it serves as a particularly deep, intense, and mostly unmatched example of the phenomenon at the national level.[7] The creole attachment to the idealized, often Christianized portrait that caciques painted of Mexican history ensured a cacique presence at all stages in the development of creole historiography. The early Spanish authors consulted with the postconquest natural lords, and their histories reflected cacique concerns with genealogy and ethnic ancestry. The letters of the early ladino caciques are rich with Franciscan influences, as are the native and mestizo chronicles of subsequent generations. The great legends arising from the baroque era, including the Guadalupe story and the marvelous foundation of Querétaro, were explicitly founded upon cacique testimonials. The core of the creole "archive" of the late-seventeenth and eighteenth centuries – that trove of patria-defining material best represented by the Mesoamerican collections of don Carlos de Sigüenza y Góngora and Lorenzo Boturini Benaduci – consisted of the cacique chronicles and their associated materials. The archive itself, moreover, was a collaborative achievement, as Boturini relied upon countless native leaders to assemble the most original components of his museum. He was especially indebted to the elite native culture of Tenochtitlan and Tlatelolco – the Jesuit-educated "enlightened Indianists" who administered the Indian republic – to say nothing of don Patricio Antonio López, the Zapoteca Virgil. Don Patricio himself built upon Boturini's project; once commissioned to inventory the Italian's materials in 1745, he took the entire collection into his own home, where he copied several items, including a calendar wheel that had once belonged

---

[7] Anthony Pagden notes that, while Mexican creoles embraced Aztec history as a unifying symbol, in South America Simón Bolívar explicitly rejected neo-Inca symbolism in favor of a more universalist republicanism. In the United States, indigenous legacies are largely invisible at the national level, but are quite prominent (and often controversial) in regional and local forms of patriotism and identity, as evidenced by university mascots and state flags such as those of New Mexico and Oklahoma. Pagden, "Identity Formation in Spanish America."; Pagden, *Spanish Imperialism and the Political Imagination*: 117–53.

Nombra la afortunada Mexico por Patron prin-
cipal al Biena.° Felipe de Jesus, á quien le dis
la Cuna

FIGURE 12 Two princes, one indigenous and one European, venerate San Felipe de Jesús, the first Mexican saint, atop the symbol of the founding of Tenochtitlan. From José Montes de Oca, *Vida de San Felipe de Jesús*, 1801. Courtesy of the John Carter Brown Library at Brown University.

to Sigüenza.[8] Furthermore, while the creole archive was built upon native texts, it also influenced how late-colonial caciques understood their own history. Don Manuel de los Santos y Salazar derived information and inspiration from Sigüenza and his contemporaries, and likewise lamented the great forgetting of the seventeenth century. Don Julian Cirilo de Castilla Aquiahualcateuhtle, meanwhile, explicitly derived his account of Anahuac from Juan de Torquemada.

Accordingly, while contemporary outsiders often presumed, erroneously, that the Indian nobility had largely disappeared, personal and textual contacts between certain native elites and creole antiquarians continued into the late-colonial period – most consistently between educated caciques and their Jesuit teachers. Yet such links survived even the Jesuits' expulsion. In the final decades of the eighteenth century, for example, Antonio de León y Gama worked not only with the remnants of the Alva Ixtlilxochitl-Sigüenza and Boturini collections, but also the papers of the late don Patricio López. He also participated in a circle of correspondence which included the prolific collector Diego García Panes and the Tlaxcalteca patriot, cleric, and cabildo officer don Nicolás Faustino Mazihcahtzin y Escovar.[9] García Panes, for his part, married into an elite creole family and traveled widely throughout Mexico, becoming familiar with its archeological legacy. He eventually befriended both Mariano Fernández de Echeverria y Veytia and the Tlaxcalteca nobility based upon their shared love for Mexican antiquity. His antiquarian labor, which contributed substantially to nineteenth-century historiography on both sides of the Atlantic, derived from both native and creole sources, including Alva Ixtlilxochitl, Tezozomoc, Zapata y Mendoza, don Manuel de los Santos, and the Tlaxcalteca caciques with whom he was personally acquainted.[10] The energetic García Panes, meanwhile, urged

---

[8] This was the famous wheel of Sigüenza's friend and collaborator, the Italian traveler Gemelli Careri (1651–1725). John Glass suggests that, due to the general blandness of don Patricio's inventory, the interpreter perhaps did not fully appreciate or understand the value of the Boturini museum, yet when we consider that he copied some materials (and elsewhere wrote glowingly and passionately on preconquest history), it may simply be that his terse, unemotional tone in the inventory reflected eighteenth-century bureaucratic expectations of disinterested objectivity. Glass, *The Boturini Collection*: 114, n. 7.

[9] Cuadriello, *Glories*: 56–58; Mazihcahtzin y Calmecahua, "Descripción del Lienzo de Tlaxcala."

[10] See Panes, *La conquista*: 20–21. García Panes produced an illustrated history of central Mexico and its conquest based on the Boturini library. He also copied the texts of the cacique-chroniclers and gave them to Juan Bautista Muñoz, the royal chronicler in Spain, who incorporated them into his grand collection at the Royal Academy of History in Madrid. The most influential Anglophone and Francophone historians of the nineteenth

the Tlaxcalteca leadership to protect its own antiquarian treasures. Accordingly, in 1773, don Nicolás Mazihcahtzin and the cabildo produced a new copy of the *Lienzo de Tlaxcala,* while don Nicolás's relatives in the priesthood commissioned new works honoring the great religious-patriotic legends of Tlaxcala: the apparition of St. Michael, the Virgin of Ocotlan, and the three boy-martyrs.[11] In 1787, don Nicolás informed León y Gama of his desire to write a new history of ancient Tlaxcala; however, he complained, it was proving difficult, as its most precious artifacts had been removed several decades earlier by none other than Lorenzo Boturini.[12]

Due in part to centuries of direct and indirect collaborations, many cacique perspectives and concerns were reflected in creole historiography and vice versa. Thus, it is difficult – and largely unhelpful – to assume a clear delineation between "creole" and "cacique" historical writing in New Spain, as both pertain to the overall story of Novohispanic self-representation and historical self-discovery.[13] The cacique don Patricio López, for example, perfectly replicated what Jorge Cañizares-Esguerra calls the "patriotic epistemology" of his creole contemporaries, which privileged the accounts of "Americans" (creole and elite indigenous) over European writers and historians.[14] Those who relied upon hearsay to write about American history from afar, argued the cacique, had been misled by the willfully distorted reports of early Spanish settlers seeking to justify their agenda of slavery and domination.[15] Half a century later, after studying the remnants of the Boturini collection – which included the papers of don Patricio – the creole Antonio de León y Gama declared that peninsular Spaniards and other outsiders were simply incapable of penetrating "the spirit of [the Indians'] paintings and other monuments."[16]

---

century, including William H. Prescott and Henri Ternaux-Compans, worked with the García Panes-Muñoz copies. See Gibson, *Tlaxcala in the Sixteenth Century:* 241–43, 49–50, 60.

[11] Cuadriello, *Glories:* 33–50.

[12] Mazihcahtzin y Calmecahua, "Descripción del Lienzo de Tlaxcala," 61.

[13] Even authorship is collaborative; see Danna Levin Rojo, "Historiografía y separatismo étnico: el problema de la distinción entre fuentes indígenas y fuentes españolas," in *Indios, mestizos y españoles: Interculturalidad e historiografía en la Nueva España,* eds. Danna Levin and Federico Navarrete (México: Universidad Nacional Autónoma de México, 2007).

[14] Cañizares-Esguerra, *How to Write:* 204–65.   [15] López, "Mercurio yndiano," f. 20.

[16] Antonio de León y Gama, "Otras ciencias y artes que cultivaron los mexicanos," HL Mexican Manuscripts Collection, f. 55; see also Mazihcahtzin y Calmecahua, "Descripción del Lienzo de Tlaxcala," 61.

In fact, one of the primary distinctions between Mexican creolism and cacique self-representation was crudely political rather than substantive: While both invoked the indigenous legacy and hearkened to an ideal of harmony within the Church and the Spanish crown, creoles were more concerned with promoting their own position *vis a vis* peninsular Spaniards than in subverting colonial social and ethnic hierarchies, while the opposite was true for caciques.[17] Creoles did not repeatedly brandish the royal decree of 1697 that equated native and Spanish nobility. That task was left to caciques such as don Patricio López, don Julian Cirilo de Castilla, and the small but ubiquitous cohort of would-be native letrados active in New Spain's colleges and seminaries.

Nineteenth-century echoes

Holistically speaking, the creole patriotism that matured in the eighteenth century incorporated an eclectic array of themes and symbols. It was pride in imperial Tenochtitlan, yet it was also love for the Virgin of Guadalupe and reverence for the Tlaxcalteca martyrs. It admired not only the fierce resolve of Cuauhtemoc and his Tenochca resistance, but also the supposed donation and baptism of Moctezuma. It was the Tetzcoca Athens as well as the Indian bishops, Tlaxcalteca republicanism and Querétaro's marvelous foundation, huehuetlatolli and Tloque Nahuaque. In short, it honored both Anahuac as well as its conquest and Christian transformation.

In practice, however, there were two overlapping strains of creole patriotism: one that emphasized ancient greatness, and another that praised the glories of Indo-Christian New Spain. During eighteenth-century debates over Indian rationality, both flavors of patriotic sentiment co-existed rather comfortably, expressed to varying degrees by both the "antiquarians" and "cultivators" discussed in Chapter 8. Francisco Xavier Clavijero, for example – most famous for his defense of ancient Mexico – also hailed achievements by colonial native scholars, insisting that many Indians had become priests and rectors and doctors, "and, as reports go, even a very learned bishop." This was, by definition, also praise for the Jesuits' successes in native education, which Clavijero insisted were proof that, given the opportunity, the Indians might produce "philosophers, mathematicians, and [clergymen] to rival the [best] in Europe."[18] Nonetheless,

---

[17] Dueñas, *Indians and Mestizos in the "Lettered City"*: 5.

[18] Clavigero, *Historia antigua de México: Sacada de los mejores historiadores españoles, y de manuscritas y pinturas antiguas de los indios* . . . 352–53.

these remained distinct modes of apology, as the antiquarians hearkened to antiquity, while the cultivators implicitly endorsed the Christian colonial culture that replaced it. The events of the early nineteenth century, when Spanish rule itself was under debate, placed these two tendencies within Mexican creolism in direct opposition.

In 1806, the eminent creole cleric and bibliographer José Mariano Beristain de Souza (1756–1817) wrote a short piece in praise of the Virgin of Guadalupe, still the reigning icon of the creole patria.[19] It was published in the *Diario de México,* a new daily periodical co-founded by Carlos María de Bustamante (1774–1848), a young creole lawyer from Antequera. Yet during the era of Mexican independence, these two creole patriots found themselves on opposite sides of the debate over Spanish rule; Beristain remained loyal to his death, while Bustamante eventually became one of the most outspoken nationalists of the postindependence era. The divergence between the two reverberated in their distinct interpretations of the Mexican legacy. In short, Bustamante was a patriot of Anahuac, while Beristain was a patriot of New Spain.

During the political crisis engendered by the 1808 French occupation of Spain, Beristain hailed his patria in familiar terms, casting New Spain as a global center of art, religious purity, and learning.[20] However, unlike predecessors such as Torquemada, Sigüenza, and Granados y Gálvez, all of whom argued that New Spain was also ennobled by its preconquest heritage, Beristain embraced the hostility that had more often characterized the creoles' opponents. "What were you, o Mexico?" he asked in 1809, "a crude and barbarous people, subject to despots who, after draining all the essence from their vassals and fattening themselves with the sweat of their brows, sacrificed their children on the impure altars of their abominable idols."[21] Following this logic to its conclusion, Beristain erased the pro-indigenous element from the creoles' beloved apparition stories. The Virgin of Guadalupe – whom creoles such as Francisco de Florencia had conspicuously interpreted as emblematic of heaven's abiding

---

[19] *Diario de México,* t. IV, n. 452, p. 477 (Dec 21, 1806); Esther Martínez Luna, *Estudio e índice onomástico del Diario de México: primera época (1805–1812)* (Mexico: Universidad Nacional Autónoma de México, 2002), 34.

[20] José Toribio Medina, *Don José Mariano Beristáin de Souza: Estudio bio-bibliográfico* (Santiago: Imprenta Elseviriana, 1897), xlvii–li.

[21] José Mariano Beristáin de Souza, *Discurso politico-moral y cristiano que en los solemnes cultos que rinde al santisimo sacramento en los dias del carnaval la Real Congregación de Eclesiásticos Oblatos de México* (Mexico: Doña María Fernández de Jaureguí, 1809), 7–8.

love for the Indians – Beristain reinterpreted as divine aid to the conquistadors, akin to the medieval Iberian image of St. James the Moor-Killer.[22]

Bustamante, meanwhile, precisely inverted Beristain's interpretation of Mexican history. Bustamante, the son and grandson of Spaniards, hailed Anahuac as the true heritage of his imagined nation, which he indeed wished to name "Anahuac."[23] The true savages of America, insisted Bustamante, were the invaders, not the natives; far from liberators, the Spaniards were tyrants, thieves, and liars. "Under the pretext of giving us heaven," he wrote in the first person, "they took away our land."[24]

Beristain and Bustamante each adopted one component of the old creole vision while discarding the other; the former embraced New Spain but not Anahuac, while the latter did the opposite. Beristain, the intellectual heir to the creole patriots of the early eighteenth century, praised viceregal Mexico City but scorned the Tenochtitlan that had preceded it. Bustamante, on the other hand, inherited the materials of Echeverría y Veytia and García Panes, and echoed their apologetic antiquarianism.[25] Yet unlike the latter two, Bustamante fully embraced the nationalist potential of declinist history, and regarded the colonial era as three centuries of foreign-imposed misery and ruin. Beristain hailed the Virgin of Guadalupe, but only as an endorsement of Mexico's conquest and transformation. Bustamante, by contrast, embraced "his" Aztec forebears, but named Indian conquistadors such as Ixtlilxochitl of Tetzcoco as "traitors" to "[his] patria."[26] Citing Alva Ixtlilxochitl, Tezozomoc, Chimalpahin, Muñoz Camargo, and Zapata y Mendoza, the creole nationalist wrote that Tlaxcala's ancient and admirable love of liberty had turned tragic, as they had enabled Spanish tyranny in exchange for "ridiculous blazons of nobility." "Although they defeated the Mexicans," he wrote, "they became in reality the vanquished."[27]

---

[22] José Mariano Beristáin de Souza (unattributed), *Diálogos patrióticos*, 15 vols. (Mexico: La oficina de doña María Fernández de Jaureguí, 1810–11), 35.

[23] See Florescano, *Historia de las historias*: 298–304. Florescano charts Bustamante's perspectives, his writings (including the *Diario de México*), and his experience during the war for independence and after.

[24] Carlos María de Bustamante, *Cuadro histórico de la Revolución Mexicana, comenzada en 15 de septiembre de 1810 por el ciudadano Miguel Hidalgo y Costilla, cura del pueblo de Dolores, en el obispado de Michoacán*, 2nd edn., 2 vols. (México: J. Mariano Lara, 1843), v. 2, xii.

[25] Carrera Stampa, "El *Teatro de Nueva España*," 405, 08.

[26] Bustamante, *Cuadro histórico de la Revolución Mexicana*, v. 2, xii.

[27] Bustamante, *Necesidad de la union de todos los mexicanos contra las asechanzas de la Nación Española*, 40–41.

Thus did both Beristain and Bustamante, in divergent ways, reject the ideal of continuity between colonial society and its native forebear, and therefore the centuries-old cacique-creole vision. The polarizing question of Mexican independence negated, and indeed inverted, the moral and legal potency of stories of Indo-Hispanic alliance. The colonial era was either an age of tyranny or liberation from savagery, but it could no longer be a collaborative achievement between Spanish and native Christians. Beginning in 1812, Mexican exiles in London, Philadelphia, and elsewhere beyond the reach of Spanish censors began republishing the works of Bartolomé de Las Casas, whose criticisms of the conquistadors were a textual cornerstone of the early modern critique of Spanish power.[28] In the prologue to an 1821 edition, the nationalist Servando Teresa de Mier praised Las Casas as a visionary, arguing that history had proven the truth of his fiery *j'accuse*. Because the conquest was invalid, argued Mier, the entire colonial era was an historical abomination, writing "what is not just in its origins does not become so with the passage of time."[29]

Nonetheless, the cacique-creole ideal of continuity between Anahuac and modern Mexico – shorn of its overtly royalist elements – continued to supply early nationalists with the symbols and themes by which to affix an ancient heritage to their fledgling nation. Thus did the historical longings of the Christian descendants of the Mesoamerican nobility contribute, by way of the creoles' journey of self-discovery, to the neo-Aztec emotional contours of modern Mexican nationalism, visible today within its national institutions, schools, and emblems. The eagle atop the nopal cactus – the Mexica symbol of imperial Tenochtitlan – has regaled the flag of Mexico since its foundation.

Meanwhile, other elements of the cacique-creole vision survived as well, mostly among nineteenth-century conservatives who sympathized with the colonial legacy. The great collector Joaquín García Icazbalceta (1824–94), for example, promoted the old stories of respect and cooperation between natives and the first Franciscans.[30] His correspondent José Fernando Ramírez (1804–71), meanwhile, compiled early codices attesting to the imperial destiny of Tenochtitlan alongside creole

---

[28] Isacio Perez Fernandez, *Inventario documentado de los escritos de fray Bartolomé de Las Casas* (Bayamón, Puerto Rico: CEDOC, 1981), 321–12, n. 126. Thanks to Hari Nair at the Universidad Nacional Autónoma de México for this reference.

[29] Servando Teresa de Mier, prologue to Bartolomé de Las Casas, *Breve relación de la destrucción de las Indias Occidentales* (Philadelphia: Juan F. Hurtel, 1821). xxxiv.

[30] Joaquín García Icazbalceta, *Don Fray Juan de Zumárraga, primer obispo y arzobispo de Méjico* (Buenos Aires: Espasa-Calpe, 1952).

sources lauding the icons of native piety such as the stone cross of Querétaro.[31] Echoing the cacique-creole collaborations of previous centuries, Ramírez's own labors relied upon the linguistic skills of Faustino Galicia Chimalpopoca (1805–77), a Nahua scholar of noble Tetzcoca lineage – and appropriately enough, one of the last alumni of the cacique college of San Gregorio de México, which had managed to preserve its indigenous character before finally closing its doors in 1856.[32] True to his intellectual heritage, Chimalpopoca saw himself obliged by blood and training to lead the native sector of Mexican society, promoting its welfare and preserving its integrity as an educated Indian of pedigree. These commitments led him to oppose liberal efforts to dismantle the remnants of the Two Republics. A supporter of the Second Mexican Empire, he served as the private Nahuatl tutor of Emperor Maximilian and his counselor on indigenous affairs.[33] He was, perhaps, the final representative of a venerable Mexican history of ladino cacique governors, interpreters, and ambassadors originating three centuries earlier with the Colegio de Santa Cruz de Tlatelolco and the restorationist policies of Viceroy Mendoza.

A new nation, an ancient people

In his classic account of utopian conceptions of native Andean civilization, Alberto Flores Galindo explores the "Inkarri myth," the perennial Peruvian longing to recapture the perceived harmony of Inca Tawantinsuyu, perhaps remade under Christian principles. Citing Friedrich Katz, however, he notes that Mexico developed no corresponding "Aztec utopia," no equivalent to the Andean longing for the return of the Inca. According to Katz, outside of a few intellectuals, memories of imperial Tenochtitlan held little motivating power, and inspired no radical agendas of restoration.[34] And indeed, while indigenism in Mexico today is highly critical of Western modernity – for example, contrasting the "deep

[31] Some of Ramírez's manuscript copies of these items are at the Bancroft Library in Berkeley, CA; see "Memorias de México," Bancroft Library M-M 240, University of California, Berkeley.

[32] Schmidt Díaz de León, *Colegio Seminario*: 151–52.

[33] On the life and activities of Galicia Chimalpopoca, see Kelly S. McDonough, *The Learned Ones: Nahua Intellectuals in Postconquest Mexico* (Tucson, AZ: University of Arizona Press, 2014), 88–110.

[34] Friedrich Katz, *The Ancient American Civilizations*, trans. K.M. Lois Simpson (New York: Praeger, 1972), 337–38.

Mexico" of its rural cultures from the "imaginary Mexico" of its urban business and political elites – few prominent thinkers look to pre-Hispanic civilization for viable alternative models, preferring instead the ideals of popular empowerment that animated the Revolution of 1910.[35] This does not mean, however, that there were no recurring visions of harmony within the vast scope of Mexican historical memory; indeed, Flores Galindo offers the Virgin of Guadalupe as Mexico's functional analog to the Peruvian idealization of the Incas, an inspirational symbol of unity and triumph.[36] Yet this book has argued that there were others as well as generations of postconquest indigenous leaders and their creole contemporaries ennobled themselves and their society by telling stories that promised to erase or ignore or transcend the social and cultural divisions of colonialism. With visions of Indo-Hispanic harmony they imagined a patria with pre-Hispanic roots, later named "Mexico" in a conscious allusion to the Aztec legacy.

Partially by way of the political efforts of native leaders and the patriotic longings of American Spaniards, then, modern Mexico emerged in 1821, not as a young society, but an ancient one. Early leaders in the United States did not hearken to an Algonquin or Iroquois legacy to define their new nation; Anahuac, however, was central to how the first Mexican nationalists understood themselves and their own heritage. "Like the Irish or the Greeks," observes David Brading, "the Mexicans could never forget the past."[37] This attitude – this powerful sense of belonging to an ancient, yet frustratingly elusive legacy – reflects Mexico's mestizo character, but many of its more explicit symbols and themes derived from the efforts of the colonial native nobility to carve out and reserve a space for themselves within the postconquest order. In part due to the caciques, Anahuac remained for many a time and place of origins, serving as a vibrant source of identity and unity, if rarely a template for the future.

The stories examined in this volume raise questions bearing upon some of the perennial tensions within Mexican nationalism – and nationalism in the Western Hemisphere more generally – regarding the ambivalent and unsteady place of indigenous peoples within the modern nation-state

---

[35] Guillermo Bonfil Batalla, *México profundo: una civilización negada* (Mexico: Editorial Grijalbo, 1990).

[36] Alberto Flores Galindo, *In Search of an Inca: Identity and Utopia in the Andes*, trans. Carlos Aguirre and Charles F. Walker (New York: Cambridge University Press, 2010), 6.

[37] David A. Brading, *The Origins of Mexican Nationalism* (Cambridge: Centre of Latin American Studies, 1985), 54–55.

and its supporting fictions. What does it mean if native subjects helped innovate and disseminate some of the deepest and most iconic themes of Mexican identity and pride – not merely regarding the genius of Nezahualcoyotl and the imperial destiny of Tenochtitlan, but also the general sense of proprietary admiration for a thriving and prosperous Anahuac? Does it matter today if, rather than reflecting timeless primordial memories, such images were often promoted by displaced Indian leaders seeking answers to the traumas, challenges, and imperatives of colonial rule?[38]

Scholars know that the construction of early Mexican nationalism – if not Mexican independence – was a predominantly creole endeavor.[39] Yet the creole nationalists themselves inherited and elaborated upon a synthetic Indo-Christian heritage that emerged, to a large degree, from the aspirations of the postconquest natural lords of central New Spain. The teteuctin and tlatoque lost their patrimonies, but their sense of antiquity survived in a different guise – one more existential and emotional than pragmatic or political – reminding generations of Spanish-speaking Mexican Christians of all backgrounds that their true origins lie in the grandeur of Anahuac By-the-Water, forever lost yet never forgotten.

[38] David Cahill raises parallel questions, noting that the concept of Inca authority that underlay the 1780 Great Rebellion of Túpac Amaru II – often considered an anti-colonial resurgence of pre-Hispanic, indigenous identities – may have had roots in sixteenth-century negotiations between the crown and allied Inca nobles, who were reconstructed as guarantors of the king's law in the Andes. See Cahill, "Becoming Inca."

[39] Eric Van Young, "In the Gloomy Caverns of Paganism: Popular Culture, Insurgency, and Nation-Building in Mexico, 1800–1821," in *The Making of Modern Mexico, 1780–1824*, ed. Christon I. Archer (Wilmington, DE: Scholarly Resources, 2003).

Works cited

Acuña, René, ed. *Relaciones geográficas del siglo XVI*. 10 vols. Mexico: UNAM, Instituto de Investigaciones Antropológicas, 1981–88.

Adorno, Rolena. "Court and Chronicle: A Native Andean's Engagement with Spanish Colonial Law." In *Native Claims: Indigenous Law against Empire, 1500–1920*. Edited by Saliha Belmessous. 63–84. New York: Oxford University Press, 2012.

"The 'Indio Ladino' as Historian." In *Implicit Understandings: Observing, Reporting, and Reflecting on the Encounters between Europeans and Other Peoples in the Early Modern Era*. Edited by Stuart B. Schwartz. 378–402. Cambridge: Cambridge University Press, 1994.

The Polemics of Possession in Spanish American Narrative (New Haven: Yale University Press, 2007).

Aguilar Moreno, Manuel. "The Indio Ladino as Cultural Mediator in the Colonial Society." *Estudios de cultura nahuatl* 33 (2002): 149–84.

Aguirre Salvador, Rodolfo. *El mérito y la estratégia: clérigos, juristas, y médicos en Nueva España*. México: Plaza y Valdés, 2003.

Alegre, Francisco Javier. *Memorias para la historia de la provincia que tuvo la Compañia de Jesús en Nueva España*. 2 vols. México: Talleres Tipográficos Modelo, 1940.

Altman, Ida. "Conquest, Coercion, and Collaboration: Indian Allies and the Campaigns in Nueva Galicia." In *Indian Conquistadors: Indigenous Allies in the Conquest of Mesoamerica*. Edited by Laura E. Matthew and Michel R. Oudijk. 145–74. Norman, OK: University of Oklahoma Press, 2007.

The War for Mexico's West: Indians and Spaniards in New Galicia, 1524–1550. Albuquerque: University of New Mexico Press, 2010.

Alva Ixtlilxochitl, Fernando de. *Obras históricas*. edited by Edmundo O'Gorman 2 vols Mexico: Universidad Nacional Autónoma de México, 1975.

Obras históricas. 2 vols México: Oficina tip. del Secretario de Fomento, 1892.

Alvarado Tezozomoc, Hernando de. *Crónica Mexicana*. Madrid: Dastin, 2001.

Anales de Tecamachalco, 1398–1590. Translated by Eustaquio Celestino Solís and Luis Reyes García. Mexico: CIESAS, 1992.

Anales de Tlatelolco. Translated by Rafael Tena. México, DF: CONACULTA, 2004.

Anderson, Benedict. *Imagined Communities: Reflections on the Origin and Spread of Nationalism*. New York: Verso, 1991 (1983).

Andrien, Kenneth J. *Andean Worlds: Indigenous History, Culture, and Consciousness under Spanish Rule, 1532–1825*. Albuquerque, NM: University of New Mexico Press, 2001.

Anónomo Mexicano. Translated by Richley H. Crapo and Bonnie Glass-Coffin. Logan, UT: Utah State University Press, 2005.

Antei, Giorgio. *El caballero andante: vida, obra,y desventuras de Lorenzo Boturini Benaduci, 1698–1755*. México: Museo de la Basílica de Guadalupe, 2007.

Arrillaga, Basilio, S.J. ed. *Concilio Provincial Mexicano, celebrado en México el año de 1585, confirmado en Roma por el Papa Sixto V, y mandado observar por el gobierno español en diversas reales órdenes*. México: Eugenio Maillefert y Compañia, 1859.

Assadourian, Carlos Sempat and Andrea Martínez Baracs, eds. *Tlaxcala: textos de su historia, siglo XVI*. Tlaxcala: Gobierno del Estado de Tlaxcala, 1991.

Asselbergs, Florine. *Conquered Conquistadors: The Lienzo de Quauhquechollan: A Nahua Vision of the Conquest of Guatemala*. Boulder: University Press of Colorado, 2008.

Baber, R. Jovita. "Empire, Indians, and the Negotiation for the Status of City in Tlaxcala." In *Negotiation within Domination: New Spain's Indian Pueblos Confront the Spanish State*. Edited by Ethelia Ruiz-Medrano and Susan Kellogg. 19–43. Boulder: University Press of Colorado, 2010.

"Law, Land, and Legal Rhetoric in Colonial New Spain: A Look at the Changing Rhetoric of Indigenous Americans in the Sixteenth Century." In *Native Claims: Indigenous Law against Empire, 1500–1920*. Edited by Saliha Belmessous. 41–62. New York: Oxford University Press, 2012.

Balbuena, Bernardo de. *La Grandeza Mexicana*. Mexico: Editorial Porrúa, 1980.

Baptista Viseo, Juan. *Sermonario en lengua Mexicana*. Mexico: Diego López Dávalos, 1606.

Barlow, Robert. *Tlatelolco: rival de Tenochtitlan. Obras de Robert Barlow*. México: Instituto Nacional de Antropología e Historia, 1987.

Baudot, Georges. "Nezahualcóyotl, príncipe providencial en los escritos de Fernando de Alva Ixtlilxóchitl." *Estudios de cultura nahuatl* 25 (1995): 17–28.

"Sentido de la literatura histórica para la transculturación en el México del siglo XVII: Fernando de Alva Ixtlilxóchitl." In *Reflexiones lingüísticas y literarias, Vol. II – literatura*, Edited by Rafael Olea Franca and James Valender. 125–37. México, D.F.: El Colegio de México, 1992.

Utopia and History in Mexico: The First Chroniclers of Mexican Civilization (1520–1569). Translated by Bernard R. Ortíz de Montellano and Thelma Ortíz de Montellano. Niwot, CO: University Press of Colorado, 1995.

Benton, Bradley "Beyond the Burned Stake: The Rule of Don Antonio Pimentel Tlahuitoltzin in Tetzcoco, 1540–45." In *Texcoco: Prehispanic and Colonial Perspectives*. Edited by Jongsoo Lee and Galen Brokaw. 183–200. Boulder: University Press of Colorado, 2014.

"The Lords of Tetzcoco: Sixteenth-Century Transformations of Indigenous Leadership in the Aztec Empire's Second City." Ph.D. diss., UCLA, 2012.

Beristaín de Souza, José Mariano. *Biblioteca Hispano-Americana*. Mexico: Alejandro Valdés, 1821.

Diálogos patrióticos (unattributed). 15 vols. Mexico: La oficina de doña María Fernández de Jareguí, 1810–11.

Discurso politico-moral y Cristiano que en los solemnes cultos que rinde al santisimo sacramento en los dias del carnaval la real congregación de eclesiásticos oblatos de México. Mexico: Doña María Fernández de Jaureguí, 1809.

Bhabha, Homi. *The Location of Culture*. New York: Routledge, 1994.

Bolton, Herbert Eugene, ed. *Spanish Exploration in the Southwest, 1546–1706*. New York: Charles Scribner's Sons, 1916.

Bonfil Batalla, Guillermo. *México profundo: una civilización negada*. Mexico: Editorial Grijalbo, 1990.

Boone, Elizabeth Hill. "Manuscript Painting in Service of Imperial Ideology." In *Aztec Imperial Strategies*. Edited by Frances Berdan. 181–206. Washington, DC: Dumbarton Oaks, 1996.

Stories in Red and Black: Pictorial Histories of the Aztecs and Mixtecs. Austin: University of Texas Press, 2000.

Borah, Woodrow. *Justice by Insurance: The General Indian Court of Colonial Mexico and the Legal Aides of the Half-Real*. Berkeley and Los Angeles: University of California Press, 1983.

Borgia Steck, Francis. "The First College in America: Santa Cruz de Tlatelolco." *The Catholic Educational Review* 34 (1936): 449–62, 604–17.

Böttcher, Nikolaus, Bernd Hausberger, and Max S. Hering Torres, eds. *El peso de la sangre: limpios, mestizos, y nobles en el mundo hispánico*. México: El Colegio de México, 2011.

Boturini Benaduci, Lorenzo. *Catálogo del museo histórico Indiano*. Madrid: Juan de Zúñiga, 1746.

Idea de una nueva historia de la América septentrional. Madrid: Juan de Zúñiga, 1746.

Brading, David A. *The First America: The Spanish Monarchy, Creole Patriots, and the Liberal State 1492–1867*. Cambridge: Cambridge University Press, 1991.

Mexican Phoenix: Our Lady of Guadalupe: Image and Tradition across Five Centuries. Cambridge: Cambridge University Press, 2002.

The Origins of Mexican Nationalism. Cambridge: Centre of Latin American Studies, 1985.

Prophecy and Myth in Mexican History. Cambridge: Centre of Latin American Studies, 1984.

Brian, Amber. "The Alva Ixtlilxochitl Brothers and the Nahua Intellectual Community." In *Texcoco: Prehispanic and Colonial Perspectives*. Edited by Jongsoo Lee and Galen Brokaw. 201–18. Boulder: University Press of Colorado, 2014.

"The Original Alva Ixtlilxochitl Manuscripts at Cambridge University." *Colonial Latin American Review* 23, no. 1 (2014): 84–101.

Burkhart, Louise M. "Pious Performances: Christian Pageantry and Native Identity in Early Colonial Mexico." In *Native Traditions in the Postconquest World*. Edited by Elizabeth Hill Boone and Tom Cummins. 361–80. Washington, DC: Dumbarton Oaks, 1998.

The Slippery Earth: Nahua–Christian Moral Dialogue in Sixteenth-Century Mexico. Tucson, AZ: University of Arizona Press, 1989.

Burrus, Ernest J. "Clavigero and the Lost Sigüenza y Góngora Manuscripts." *Estudios de cultura nahuatl* 1 (1959): 59–90.

Bustamante, Carlos María de. *Cuadro histórico de la revolución Mexicana, comenzada en 15 de Septiembre de 1810 por el ciudadano Miguel Hidalgo y Costilla, cura del pueblo de dolores, en el obispado de michoacán*. 2nd edn. 2 vols. México: J. Mariano Lara, 1843.

Cahill, David. "A Liminal Nobility: The Incas in the Middle Ground of Late Colonial Peru." In *New Worlds, First Nations*. Edited by David Patrick Cahill and Blanca Tovías. 169–95. Portland, OR: Sussex Academic Press, 2006.

"Ethnogenesis in the City: A Native Andean Etnia in a Colonial City." In *City Indians in Spain's American Empire: Urban Indigenous Society in Colonial Mesoamerica and Andean South America*. Edited by Dana Velasco Murillo, Mark Lentz, and Margarita R. Ochoa. 32–47. Portland, OR: Sussex Academic Press, 2012.

Calvi, María Vittoria. "El diálogo entre españoles e indígenas en la XIII relación de Fernando de Alva Ixtlilxóchitl." *Quaderni ibero-americana* 72 (1992): 621–39.

Cañeque, Alejandro. *The King's Living Image: The Culture and Politics of Viceregal Power in Colonial Mexico*. New York: Routledge, 2004.

Cañizares-Esguerra, Jorge. "Creole Colonial Spanish America." In *Creolization: History, Ethnography, Theory*. Edited by Charles Stewart. 26–45. Walnut Creek, CA: Left Coast Press, 2007.

How to Write the History of the New World: Histories, Epistemologies, and Identities in the Eighteenth-Century Atlantic World. Stanford: Stanford University Press, 2001.

Puritan Conquistadors: Iberianizing the Atlantic, 1550–1700. Stanford: Stanford University Press, 2006.

Carrasco, Pedro. "The Civil–Religious Hierarchy in Mesoamerican Communities: Pre-Spanish Background and Colonial Development." *American Anthropologist* 63 (1961): 483–97.

"Indian–Spanish Marriages in the First Century of the Colony." In *Indian Women of Early Mexico*. Edited by Susan Schroeder, Stephanie Wood, and Robert Haskett. 87–104. Norman: University of Oklahoma Press, 1997.

"Los linajes nobles del México antiguo." In *Estratificación social en la mesoamérica prehispánica*. Edited by Pedro Carrasco and Johanna Broda. 19–36. México: Centro de Investigaciones Superiores, Instituto Nacional de Antropología e Historia, 1976.

The Tenochca Empire of Ancient Mexico: The Triple Alliance of Tenochtitlán, Tetzcoco, and Tlacopan. Norman: University of Oklahoma Press, 1999.

"The Territorial Structure of the Aztec Empire." In *Land and Politics in the Valley of Mexico: A Two-Thousand-Year Perspective.* Edited by H.R. Harvey. 93–112. Albuquerque, NM: University of New Mexico Press, 1991.

Carrasco, Pedro, and Jesús Monjarás-Ruiz, eds. *Colección de documentos sobre coyoacán.* 2 vols. México: Centro de Investigaciones Superiores, 1976.

Carrera Stampa, Manuel. "El teatro de Nueva España en su Gentilismo y Conquista, Diego Panes." *Boletín del archivo general de la nación* XVI, no. 3 (1945): 399–428.

Castañeda de la Paz, María. "Apropriación de elementos y símbolos de legitimidad entre la nobleza indígena: el caso del cacicazgo tlatelolca." *Anuario de estudios americanos* 65, no. 1 (2008): 21–47.

"Central Mexican Indigenous Coats of Arms and the Conquest of Mesoamerica." *Ethnohistory* 56, no. 1 (2009): 125–61.

Conflictos y alianzas en tiempos de cambio: Azcapotzalco, Tlacopan, Tenochtitlan, y Tlatelolco (siglos XII-XVI). México: Universidad Nacional Autónoma de México, Instituto de Investigaciones Antropológicas, 2013.

"El Códice X o los anales del grupo de la Tira de la Peregrinación."Copias, duplicaciones, y su uso por parte de los cronistas." *Tlalocan* XV (2008): 183–214.

"Historia de una casa real. Origen y ocaso del linaje gobernante en México-Tenochtitlan." In, *Nuevo mundo, mundos nuevos* (2011). Published electronically, Jan 31, 2011. http://nuevomundo.revues.org/60624.

Castillo, Cristóbal de. *Historia de la venida de los Mexicanos y de otros pueblos e historia de la conquista.* Translated by Federico Navarrete Linares. Mexico: Cien de México, 2001.

Cedulario Indiano recopilado por Diego de Encinas. Facsimile edn., 4 vols. Madrid: Ediciones Cultura Hispánica, 1945 (1596).

Chamberlain, Robert S. "The Concept of the *Señor Natural* as Revealed by Castillian Law and Administrative Documents." *Hispanic American Historical Review* 19, no. 2 (May 1939): 130–37.

Chance, John K. "The Caciques of Tecali: Class and Ethnic Identity in Late Colonial Mexico." *Hispanic American Historical Review* 76, no. 3 (1996): 475–502.

"Indian Elites in Late Colonial Mesoamerica." In *Caciques and Their People: A Volume in Honor of Ronald Spores.* Edited by Joyce Marcus and Judith Francis Zeitlin. 45–65. Ann Arbor, MI: University of Michigan Museum of Anthropology, 1994.

"The Noble House in Colonial Puebla, Mexico: Descent, Inheritance, and the Nahua Tradition." *American Anthropologist* 102, no. 3 (2000): 485–502.

Charles, John. *Allies at Odds: The Andean Church and Its Indigenous Agents, 1583–1671.* Albuquerque, NM: University of New Mexico Press, 2010.

Chimalpahin Cuauhtlehuanitzin, Domingo Francisco de San Antón Muñon. *Annals of His Time: Don Domingo de San Antón Muñón Chimalpahin Quauhtlehuanitzin.* Translated by James Lockhart, Susan Schroeder, and Doris Namala. Stanford: Stanford University Press, 2006.

Codex Chimalpahin: Society and Politics in Mexico Tenochtitlán, Tlatelolco, Texcoco, Culhuacán, and Other Nahua Altepetl in Central Mexico. Translated by Arthur J.O. Anderson and Susan Schroeder. 2 vols. Norman: University of Oklahoma Press, 1997.

Chipman, Donald E. *Moctezuma's Children: Aztec Royalty Under Spanish Rule, 1520–1700.* Austin: University of Texas Press, 2005.

Christensen, Mark. *Nahua and Maya Catholicisms: Texts and Religion in Colonial Central Mexico and Yucatan.* Stanford: Stanford University Press, 2013.

Clavigero, Francesco Saverio. *Historia antigua de México: sacada de los mejores historiadores Españoles, y de manuscritas y pinturas antiguas de los Indios...* Translated by Francisco Pablo Vázquez. Mexico: JR Navarro, 1853.

Clendinnen, Inga. *Aztecs: An Interpretation.* Cambridge: Cambridge University Press, 2000.

Cline, Howard F. "The relaciones geográficas of the Spanish Indies, 1577–1586." *Hispanic American Historical Review* 44, no. 3 (1964): 341–74.

Cline, Sarah L. *Colonial Culhuacán, 1580–1600.* Albuquerque: University of New Mexico Press, 1986.

Colección de documentos inéditos, relativos al descubrimiento, conquista y organización de las antiguas posesiones Españolas de América y Oceanía, sacados de los archivos del reino, y muy especialmente del Indias. 42 vols. Madrid: Real Academia de la Historia, 1864–84.

Connell, William F. *After Moctezuma: Indigenous Politics and Self-Government in Mexico City, 1524–1730.* Norman, OK: University of Oklahoma Press, 2011.

Constituciones de la Real y Pontificia Universidad de México. 2 edn. Mexico: Zúñiga y Ontiveros, 1775.

Conway, Richard. "Nahuas and Spaniards in the Socioeconomic History of Xochimilco, New Spain, 1550–1725." Ph.D. diss., Tulane University, 2009.

Cook, Noble David. *Born to Die: Disease and New World Conquest, 1492–1650.* New York: Cambridge University Press, 1998.

Cooper, Frederick. *Colonialism in Question: Theory, Knowledge, History.* Berkeley: University of California Press, 2005.

Cortés, Hernán. *Letters from Mexico.* Translated by Anthony Pagden. New Haven: Yale University Press, 2001.

Cortés, Rocío. "The Colegio Imperial de Santa Cruz de Tlatelolco and its Aftermath: Nahua Intellectuals and the Spiritual Conquest of Mexico." In *A Companion to Latin American Literature and Culture.* Edited by Sarah Castro-Klaren. 86–105. Malden, MA: Blackwell, 2008.

Cruz, Juana Inés de la. *The Answer/la respuesta.* Translated by Electa Arenal and Amanda Powell. New York: The Feminist Press, 1994.

Cruz Rangel, José Antonio. *Chichimecas, misioneros, soldados, y terratenientes: estrategias de colonización, control, y poder en Querétaro y la Sierra Gorda, siglos XVI–XVIII.* México: Archivo General de la Nación, 2003.

Cuadriello, Jaime. *The Glories of the Republic of Tlaxcala: Art and Life in Viceregal Mexico*. Translated by Christopher J. Follet. Austin: University of Texas Press, 2004.

Cuevas, Mariano. *Historia de la iglesia en México*. 5 vols. México: Editorial Patria, 1946–7.

Curcio-Nagy, Linda A. *The Great Festivals of Colonial Mexico City: Performing Power and Identity*. Albuquerque, NM: University of New Mexico Press, 2004.

Díaz del Castillo, Bernal. *The Conquest of New Spain*. Translated by J.M. Cohen. London and New York: Penguin, 1963.

Díaz, Mónica. *Indigenous Writings from the Convent: Negotiating Ethnic Autonomy in Colonial Mexico*. Tucson, AZ: University of Arizona Press, 2010.

"'Es honor de su nación': Legal Rhetoric, Ethnic Alliances, and the Opening of an Indigenous Convent in Colonial Oaxaca." *Colonial Latin American Review* 22, no. 2 (2013): 235–58.

Dibble, Charles "The Nahuatlization of Christianity." In *Sixteenth-Century Mexico: The Work of Sahagún*. Edited by Munro Edmunson. 225–33. Albuquerque: University of New Mexico Press, 1974.

Diel, Lori Boornazian. *The Tira de Tepechpan: Negotiating Place under Aztec and Spanish Rule*. Austin: University of Texas Press, 2008.

Documentos para la historia de México, 3a Serie. Vol. 1. Mexico: Vicente García Torres, 1856.

Domínguez Torres, Mónica. "Emblazoning Identity: Indigenous Heraldry in Colonial Mexico and Peru." In *Contested Visions in the Spanish Colonial World*. Edited by Ilona Katzew. 97–115. Los Angeles: Los Angeles County Museum of Art, 2011.

Dorantes de Carranza, Baltasar. *Sumaria relación de las cosas de la Nueva España*. Mexico: Editorial Porrúa, 1987.

Douglas, Eduardo de Jesús. *In the Palace of Nezahualcoyotl: Painting Manuscripts, Writing the Pre-Hispanic Past in Early Colonial Period Tetzcoco, Mexico*. Austin, TX: University of Texas Press, 2010.

"Our Fathers, Our Mothers: Painting an Indian Genealogy in New Spain." In *Contested Visions in the Spanish Colonial World*. Edited by Ilona Katzew. 117–31. Los Angeles: Los Angeles County Museum of Art, 2011.

Dueñas, Alcira. *Indians and Mestizos in the "Lettered City": Reshaping Justice, Social Hierarchy, and Political Culture in Colonial Peru*. Boulder, CO: University Press of Colorado, 2010.

Durán, Diego. *History of the Indies of New Spain*. Translated by Doris Heyden. Norman, OK: University of Oklahoma Press, 1994.

Earle, Rebecca. *The Body of the Conquistador: Food, Race, and the Colonial Experience in Spanish America, 1492–1700*. New York: Cambridge University Press, 2012.

The Return of the Native: Indians and Myth-Making in Spanish America, 1810–1930. Durham: Duke University Press, 2008.

Echeverría y Veytia, Mariano Fernández de. *Historia antigua de Méjico*. Mexico: C.F. Ortega, 1836.

Los calendarios Mexicanos. Mexico: Museo Nacional, 1907.

Elliott, J. H. *Imperial Spain, 1469–1716.* London: Penguin, 2002 (1963).

Escalante Gonzalbo, Pablo. "The Painters of Sahagún's Manuscripts: Mediators between Two Worlds." In *Sahagún at 500: Essays on the Quincentenary of the Birth of Fr. Bernardino De Sahagún.* Edited by John F. Schwaller. 167–91. Berkeley, CA: Academy of American Franciscan History, 2003.

Espinosa, Isidro Félix de. *Crónica apostólica de los colegios de Propaganda Fide.* Querétaro: Gobierno del Estado de Querétaro, 1997.

Evans, Susan T. "Architecture and Authority in an Aztec Village: Form and Function of a Tecpan." In *Land and Politics in the Valley of Mexico: A Two-Thousand-Year Perspective.* Edited by H.R. Harvey. 63–92. Albuquerque, NM: University of New Mexico Press, 1991.

Fernández de Recas, Guillermo S., ed. *Cacicazgos y nobiliario Indígena de la Nueva España.* México, D.F.: Instituto Bibliográfico Mexicano, 1961.

Figuera, Guillermo. *La formación del clero indígena en la historia eclesiástica de América, 1500–1810.* Caracas: Archivo General de la Nación, 1965.

Fisher, Andrew B., and Matthew D. O'Hara, eds. *Imperial Subjects: Race and Identity in Colonial Latin America.* Durham: Duke University Press, 2009.

Florencia, Francisco de. *La estrella del norte de México, aparecida al rayar el día de la luz evangélica en este nuevo-mundo...* Mexico: Imprenta de Antonio Velázquez, 1741. (1688).

La Milagrosa invención de un Thesoro escondido en un campo... Sevilla: Imprenta de las Siete Revueltas, 1745. (1685).

Narración de la maravillosa aparición que hizo el Arcángel San Miguel a Diego Lázaro de San Francisco. 2 vols. Sevilla: Tomás López de Haro, 1692.

Flores, Enrique. "Patricio Antonio López, Indio romancista (Romancero vulgar del siglo XVIII Novohispano)." *Revista de dialectología y tradiciones populares* 46 (1991): 75–116.

"Patricio López, poeta e intérprete." In *La otra Nueva España: la palabra marginada en La Colonia.* Edited by Mariana Masera et al. 235–52. México: Universidad Nacional Autónoma de México, 2002.

"Un romance de Patricio Antonio López." *Revista de literaturas populares* 1, no. 1 (2001): 7–24.

Flores Galindo, Alberto. *In Search of an Inca: Identity and Utopia in the Andes.* Translated by Carlos Aguirre and Charles F. Walker. New York: Cambridge University Press, 2010.

Florescano, Enrique. *Historia de las historias de la nación mexicana.* México, D.F.: Taurus, 2002.

"La reconstrucción histórica elaborada por la nobleza indígena y sus descendientes mestizos." In *La memoria y el olvido: segundo simposio de Historia de las Mentalidades.* México, D.F.: Instituto Nacional de Antropología e Historia, 1985.

Memory, Myth, and Time in Mexico: From the Aztecs to Independence. Translated by Albert G. Bork and Kathryn R. Bork. Austin: University of Texas Press, 1994.

Freedman, Paul H. *Images of the Medieval Peasant.* Stanford: Stanford University Press, 1999.

Frías, Valentín, ed. *La conquista de Querétaro*. Querétaro: Escuela de Artes del Señor San José, 1906.

Frye, David. *Indians into Mexicans: History and Identity in a Mexican Town.* Austin: University of Texas Press, 1996.

Gallagher, R.S.M., Ann Miriam. "The Indian Nuns of Mexico City's Monasterio of Corpus Christi, 1724–1821." In *Latin American Women: Historical Perspectives.* Edited by Asunción Lavrín. 150–72. Westport, CT: Greenwood Publishing Group, 1978.

García de Valdeavellano y Arcimis, Luis. *Orígenes de la burguesía en la España Medieval.* Madrid: Espasa-Calpe, 1969.

García, Genaro, ed. *Don Juan de Palafox y Mendoza, documentos inéditos o muy raros para la historia de México.* Vol. 7. Mexico: Librería de la Viuda de Ch. Bouret, 1906.

México en 1623, por el Bachiller Arias de Villalobos. Edited by Genaro García, Documentos ineditos o muy raros para la historia de México. Vol. 12. Mexico: Librería de la Viuda de Ch. Bouret, 1907.

García Icazbalceta, Joaquín, ed. *Colección de documentos para la historia de México.* Vol. 2. México: Antigua Librería, 1866.

Nueva colección de documentos para la historia de México: Pomar-Zurita, relaciones antiguas (siglo XVI). Mexico: Editorial Salvador Chávez Hayhoe, 1941.

García Icazbalceta, Joaquín. *Don Fray Juan de Zumárraga, primer obispo y arzobispo de Méjico.* Buenos Aires: Espasa-Calpe, 1952.

García Loaeza, Pablo. "Deeds to Be Praised for All Time: Alva Ixtlilxochitl's *Historia de la nación chichimeca* and Geoffrey of Monmouth's *History of the Kings of Britain.*" *Colonial Latin American Review* 23, no. 1 (2014): 53–69.

"Estratégias para (des)aparecer: la historiografía de Fernando de Alva Ixtlilxochitl y la colonización Criolla del pasado prehispánico." Ph.D. diss., Indiana University, 2006.

García Quintana, Josefina. "Fray bernardino de Sahagún." In *historiografía novohispana de tradición Indígena.* Edited by José Rubén Romero Galván. 197–228. México: Universidad Nacional Autónoma de México, 2003.

García Ugarte, María Eugenia. *Breve historia de Querétaro.* Mexico: Fondo de Cultura Económica, 1999.

Garduño, Ana. *Conflictos y alianzas entre Tlatelolco y Tenochtitlan, siglos XII a XV.* México, D.F.: Instituto Nacional de Antropología e Historia, 1997.

Garrett, David T. *Shadows of Empire: The Indian Nobility of Cusco, 1750–1825.* Cambridge: Cambridge University Press, 2005.

Gerbi, Antonello. *The Dispute of the New World: The History of a Polemic.* Pittsburgh: University of Pittsburgh Press, 1973 (1955).

Gerhard, Peter. *A Guide to the Historical Geography of New Spain.* London: Cambridge University Press, 1972.

Gibson, Charles. "The Aztec Aristocracy in Colonial Mexico." *Comparative Studies in Society and History* 2 (1960): 169–96.

The Aztecs under Spanish Rule: A History of the Indians of the Valley of Mexico, 1519–1810. Stanford: Stanford University Press, 1964.

"Conquest, Capitulation, and Indian Treaties." *American Historical Review* 83, no. 1 (1978): 1–15.

"The Identity of Diego Muñoz Camargo." *Hispanic American Historical Review* 30, no. 2 (1950): 195–208.

"Llamamiento general, repartimiento, and the empire of Acolhuacán." *Hispanic American Historical Review* 36, no. 1 (1956): 1–27.

Tlaxcala in the Sixteenth Century. Stanford, CA: Stanford University Press, 1967 (1952).

Glass, John B. *The Boturini Collection: The Legal Proceedings and the Basic Inventories, 1742–1745.* Lincoln Center, MA.: Conemex, 1981.

Gómez Canedo, Lino. *La educación de los marginados durante la epoca colonial: escuelas y colegios para Indios y mestizos en la Nueva España.* Mexico: Editorial Porrúa, 1982.

Gonzalbo Aizpurú, Pilar. *Historia de la educación en la epoca colonial: el mundo indígena.* México: El Colegio de México, 1990.

Gonzales, Michael J. "Imagining Mexico in 1910: Visions of the Patria in the Centennial Celebration in Mexico City." *Journal of Latin American Studies* 39, no. 3 (2007): 495–533.

González de Cossío, Francisco. "Tres colegios Mexicanos: Tepotzotlán, San Gregorio, y San Ildefonso." *Boletín del archivo general de la nación* XX, no. 2 (1949): 199–249.

Granados y Gálvez, José Joaquin. *Tardes Americanas: gobierno gentil y Católico: breve y particular noticia de toda la historia Indiana: Sucesos, casos notables,y cosas ignoradas, desde la entrada de la gran nación tolteca a esta tierra de Anáhuac, hasta los presentes tiempos, trabajadas por un Indio y un Español.* México, D.F.: Porrúa, 1987 (1778).

Gruzinski, Serge. *Man-Gods of the Mexican Highlands.* Translated by Eileen Corrigan. Stanford: Stanford University Press, 1989.

"Mutilated Memory: Reconstruction of the Past and the Mechanisms of Memory Among 17th-Century Otomís." *History and Anthropology* 2, no. 2 (1986): 337–53.

Harris, Olivia. "The Coming of the White People: Reflections on the Mythologization of History in Latin America." *Bulletin of Latin American Research* 14, no. 1 (1995): 9–24.

Haskett, Robert S. "Conquering the Spiritual Conquest in Cuernavaca." Paper presented at the American Society for Ethnohistory, Eugene, OR, November 13, 2008.

"Conquering the Spiritual Conquest in Cuernavaca." In *The Conquest All Over Again: Nahuas and Zapotecs Thinking, Writing, and Painting Spanish Colonialism.* Edited by Susan Schroeder. 226–60. Portland, OR: Sussex Academic Press, 2010.

"Dying for Conversion: Faith, Obedience, and the Tlaxcalan Boy Martyrs in New Spain." *Colonial Latin American Review* 17, no. 2 (2008): 185–212.

"Indian Town Government in Colonial Cuernavaca: Persistence, Adaptation, Change." *Hispanic American Historical Review* 71, no. 3 (1987): 203–31.

Indigenous Rulers: An Ethnohistory of Town Government in Colonial Cuernavaca. Albuquerque: University of New Mexico Press, 1991.

"Living in Two Worlds: Continuity and Change among Cuernavaca's Colonial Indigenous Ruling Elite." *Ethnohistory* 35, no. 1 (1988): 34–59.

"Paper Shields: The Ideology of Coats of Arms in Colonial Mexican Primordial Titles." *Ethnohistory* 43, no. 1 (Winter 1996): 99–126.

Visions of Paradise: Primordial Titles and Mesoamerican History in Cuernavaca. Norman, OK: University of Oklahoma Press, 2005.

Hernández y Dávalos, Juan Evaristo. *Colección de documentos para la historia de la guerra de independencia de México de 1808 a 1821*. Universidad Nacional Autónoma de México, 2007.

Hicks, Frederic. "Xaltocan under Mexica Domination, 1435–1520." In *The Caciques and Their People: A Volume in Honor of Ronald Spores*. Edited by Joyce Marcus and Judith Francis Zeitlin. 67–85. Ann Arbor, MI: University of Michigan Museum of Anthropology, 1994.

Himmerich y Valencia, Robert. *The Encomenderos of New Spain, 1521–1555*. Austin: University of Texas Press, 1996.

Horcasitas, Fernando. "Los descendientes de Nezahualpilli: documentos del cacicazgo de Tetzcoco (1545-1855)." *Estudios de cultura nahuatl* 6 (1978): 145–85.

Horn, Rebecca. *Postconquest Coyoacan: Nahua–Spanish Relations in Central Mexico, 1519–1650*. Stanford, CA: Stanford University Press, 1997.

Jenkins, Keith. *Re-Thinking History*. New York: Routledge, 1991.

Jiménez Abollado, Francisco L. "Don Diego Luis Moctezuma, nieto de hueytlatoani, padre de conde: un noble indígena entre dos mundos." *Anuario de estudios Americanos* 65, no. 1 (2008): 49–70.

Jiménez Abollado, Francisco Luis, and Verenice Cipatli Ramírez Calva. *Pretensiones señoriales de Don Pedro Moctezuma Tlacahuepantzin Yohualicahuacatzin: desafíos y vicisitudes de un mayorazgo, 1528–1606. Estudio y fuentes documentales*. Pachuca: Universidad Nacional Autónoma del Estado de Hidalgo, 2011.

Juan, Jorge, and Antonio de Ulloa. *Discourse and Political Reflections on the Kingdoms of Peru*. Translated by John J. TePaske and Besse A. Clement. Norman, OK: University of Oklahoma Press, 1978.

Kamen, Henry. *Philip of Spain*. New Haven: Yale University Press, 1999.

Kartunnen, Frances. "Indigenous Writing as a Vehicle for Postconquest Continuity and Change in Mesoamerica." In *Native Traditions in the Postconquest World*. Edited by Tom Cummins and Elizabeth Hill Boone. 421–48. Washington, DC: Dumbarton Oaks, 1998.

Katz, Friedrich. *The Ancient American Civilizations*. Translated by K.M. Lois Simpson. New York: Praeger, 1972.

Katzew, Ilona, ed. *Contested Visions in the Spanish Colonial World*. Los Angeles: Los Angeles County Museum of Art, 2011.

"Stars in the Sea of the Church: The Indian in Eighteenth-Century New Spanish Painting." In *The Arts in Latin America, 1492–1820*. Edited by Joseph J. Rishel and Suzanne L. Stratton. 335–48. New Haven: Yale University Press, 2006.

"'That This Should Be Published and Again in the Age of the Enlightenment?': Eighteenth-Century Debates About the Indian Body in Colonial

Mexico." In *Race and Classification: The Case of Mexican America*. Edited by Ilona Katzew and Susan Deans-Smith. Stanford: Stanford University Press, 2009.

Kauffmann, Leisa A. "Figures of Time and Tribute: The Trace of the Colonial Subaltern in Fernando de Alva Ixtlilxochitl's *Historia de la nación chichimeca*." *The Global South* 4, no. 1 (2010): 31–47.

"Hybrid Historiography in Colonial Mexico: Genre, Event, and Time in the 'Cuauhtitlan Annals' and the 'Historia de la nación chichimeca'". Ph.D. diss., University of Illinois at Urbana-Champaign, 2004.

Kellogg, Susan. *Law and the Transformation of Aztec Culture, 1500–1700*. Norman, OK: University of Oklahoma Press, 1995.

Kerpel, Magaloni. "History under the Rainbow: The Conquest of Mexico in the Florentine Codex." In *Contested Visions in the Spanish Colonial World*. Edited by Ilona Katzew. 79–95. Los Angeles: Los Angeles County Museum of Art, 2011.

Klein, Kerwin Lee. "On the Emergence of Memory in Historical Discourse." *Representations* 69, Winter (2000): 127–50.

Koneztke, Richard, ed. *Colección de documentos para la historia de la formación social de Hispanoamérica, 1493–1810, Ser. 1*. 3 vols. Madrid: Consejo Superior de Investigaciones Científicas, 1953–1958.

Kranz, Travis Barton. "Sixteenth-Century Tlaxcalan Pictorial Documents on the Conquest of Mexico." In *Sources and Methods for the Study of Postconquest Mesoamerican Ethnohistory, Provisional Version*. Edited by James Lockhart, Lisa Sousa, and Stephanie Wood. Eugene, OR: University of Oregon Wired Humanities Project, 2007. http://whp.uoregon.edu/Lockhart/index.html.

"Visual Persuasion: Sixteenth-Century Tlaxcalan Pictorials in Response to the Conquest of Mexico." In *The Conquest All over Again: Nahuas and Zapotecs Thinking, Writing, and Painting Spanish Colonialism*. Edited by Susan Schroeder. 41–73. Portland, OR: Sussex Academic Press, 2011.

Kuethe, Allan J. and Kenneth J. Andrien. *The Spanish Atlantic World in the Eighteenth Century: War and the Bourbon Reforms, 1713–1796*. New York: Cambridge University Press, 2014.

Las Casas, Bartolomé de. *Breve relación de la destrucción de las Indias Occidentales* Philadelphia: Juan F. Hurtel, 1821.

Lavallé, Bernard. "Del indio al criollo: evolución y tranformación de una imagen colonial." In *La imagen del indio en la Europa moderna*. Seville: Escuela de Estudios Hispano-Americanos, 1990.

Lavrín, Asunción. "Indian Brides of Christ: Creating New Spaces for Indigenous Women in New Spain." *Mexican Studies/Estudios Mexicanos* 15, no. 2 (Summer 1999): 225–60.

"The Role of Nunneries in the Economy of New Spain in the Eighteenth Century." *Hispanic American Historical Review* 46, no. 4 (1966): 371–93.

Lee, Jongsoo. *The Allure of Nezahualcoyotl: Pre-Hispanic History, Religion, and Nahua Poetics*. Albuquerque: University of New Mexico Press, 2008.

León-Portilla, Miguel. *Bernardino de Sahagún: First Anthropologist*. Translated by Mauricio J. Mixco. Norman, OK: University of Oklahoma Press, 2002.

León, Nicolás de, ed. *Bibliografía Mexicana del siglo XVIII*. México: J.I. Guerrero, 1902–1908.

León y Gama, Antonio. *Descripción histórica y cronológica de las dos piedras*... Mexico: Alejandro Valdés, 1832.

Leonard, Irving. *Don Carlos Sigüenza y Góngora, a Mexican Savant of the Seventeenth Century*. Berkeley: University of California Press, 1929.

Lesbre, Patrick. "El Tetzcutzinco en la obra de Fernando de Alva Ixtlilxóchitl." *Estudios de cultura nahuatl* 32 (2001): 323–40.

Levin Rojo, Danna. "Historiografía y separatismo etnico: el problema de la distinción entre fuentes indígenas y fuentes españoles." In *Indios, Mestizos y Españoles: interculturalidad e historiografía en la Nueva España*. Edited by Danna Levin and Federico Navarrete. México: Universidad Nacional Autónoma de México, 2007.

Return to Aztlan: Indians, Spaniards, and the Invention of Nuevo México. Norman, OK: University of Oklahoma Press, 2014.

Lienhard, Martin. *La voz y su huella*. México: Ediciones Casa Juan Pablos, 2003.

Testimonios, cartas, y manifiestos indígenas desde la conquista hasta comienzos del, siglo XX. Caracas: Biblioteca Ayacucho, 1992.

Loayzaga, Manuel de. *Historia de la Milagrosíssima imagen de nuestra Señora de Occotlan* Tlaxcala: Instituto Tlaxcalteca de la Cultura, 2008. 1750.

Lockhart, James. "Double Mistaken Identity: Some Nahua Concepts in Postconquest Guise." In *Of Things of the Indies: Essays Old and New in Early Latin American History*. Edited by James Lockhart. Stanford, CA: Stanford University Press, 1999.

The Nahuas after the Conquest: A Social and Cultural History of the Indians of Central Mexico, Sixteenth through Eighteenth Centuries. Stanford, CA: Stanford University Press, 1992.

"Receptivity and Resistance." In *Of Things of the Indies: Essays Old and New in Early Latin American History*. Edited by James Lockhart. 304–32. Stanford: Stanford University Press, 1999.

Lockhart, James, ed. *We People Here: Nahuatl Accounts of the Conquest of Mexico*. Eugene, OR: Wipf & Stock, 2004.

Lockhart, James, Frances Berdan, Arthur J.O. Anderson, eds. *The Tlaxcalan Actas: A Compendium of the Records of the Cabildo of Tlaxcala, 1545–1627*. Provo, UT: University of Utah Press, 1986.

Lohmann Villena, Guillermo. "The Church and Culture in Spanish America." *The Americas* 14, no. 4 (1958): 383–98.

López-Portillo, José-Juan. "Another Jerusalem: Political Legitimacy and Courtly Government in the Kingdom of New Spain (1535–1568)." Ph.D. diss., Queen Mary University of London, 2011.

López Caballero, Paula. *Los títulos primordiales del centro de México*. México, D.F.: Consejo Nacional para la Cultura y Las Artes, 2003.

López Mora, Rebeca. "El cacicazgo de Diego de Mendoza Austria y Moctezuma: un linaje bajo sospecha." In *el cacicazgo en Nueva España y Filipinas*. Edited by Margarita Menegus Bornemann and Rodolfo Aguirre Salvador. 203–86. México: Universidad Nacional Autónoma de México, Plaza y Valdés, 2005.

López, Patricio Antonio. *General aclamación de la lealtad Mexicana*. México: Juan Francisco de Ortega Bonilla, 1724.

"Inventario de los documentos recogidos a Don Lorenzo Boturini por orden del gobierno virreinal." *Anales del Museo Nacional de Arqueología e Etnografía, 5a época* 3, no. 1 (1925): 1–55.

Triumphos aclamados contra Vandoleros...Puebla: Viuda de Miguel de Ortega, 1723.

Triumphos que la real justicia ha conseguido de otros 40 Vandoleros con los hechos en la vida...México: Herederos de la Viuda de Miguel de Rivera, 1726.

López Sarrelangue, Delfina Esmeralda. *La nobleza indígena de Pátzcuaro en la epoca virreinal.* Mexico: Universidad Nacional Autónoma de México, Instituto de Investigaciones Históricas, 1965.

Lorenzana, Francisco Antonio. *Historia de Nueva-España, escrito por su esclarecido conquistador Hernán Cortés.* México: Joseph Antonio de Hogal, 1770.

MacLachlan, Colin M. *Imperialism and the Origins of Mexican Culture.* Cambridge, MA: Harvard University Press, 2015.

MacLachlan, Colin M., and Jaime E. Rodríguez O. *The Forging of the Cosmic Race: A Reinterpretation of Colonial Mexico.* Berkeley: University of California Press, 1980.

Macmillan, Margaret. *Dangerous Games: The Uses and Abuses of History.* New York: Modern Library, 2009.

Mariscal Hay, Beatriz. "La 'embaxada por los Indios' del cacique zapoteca Patricio Antonio López." *Caravelle* 76–77 (2001): 277–87.

Martínez Baracs, Andrea. *Un gobierno de Indios: Tlaxcala, 1519–1750.* México: Fondo de Cultura Económica, 2008.

Martínez Baracs, Rodrigo. *La secuencia Tlaxcalteca: orígenes del culto a nuestra Señora de Ocotlán.* Mexico: Instituto Nacional de Antropología e Historia, 2000.

Martínez Luna, Esther. *Estudio e indice onomástico del diario de México: primera época (1805–1812).* Mexico: Universidad Nacional Autónoma de México, 2002.

Martínez, María Elena. *Genealogical Fictions: Limpieza De Sangre, Religion, and Gender in Colonial Mexico.* Stanford: Stanford University Press, 2008.

"The Language, Genealogy, and Classification of 'Race' in Colonial Mexico." In *Race and Classification: The Case of Mexican America.* Edited by Ilona Katzew and Susan Deans-Smith. Stanford: Stanford University Press, 2009.

Matthew, Laura E. *Memories of Conquest: Becoming Mexicano in Colonial Guatemala.* Chapel Hill: University of North Carolina Press, 2012.

Matthew, Laura E. and Michel R. Oudijk, eds. *Indian Conquistadors: Indigenous Allies in the Conquest of Mesoamerica.* Norman: University of Oklahoma Press, 2007.

Mazihcahtzin y Calmecahua (Escovar), Nicolás Faustino. "Descripción del lienzo de Tlaxcala." *Revista Mexicana de estudios históricos* 1, no. 2 (March/April 1927): 59–90.

Mazihcatzin y Escovar, Nicolás Faustino. *Día seis de cada mes, que se reza al esclarecido y gloriosísimo señor San Nicolás Obispo el Magno....* Puebla: Don Pedro de la Rosa, 1788.

McDonough, Kelly S. *The Learned Ones: Nahua Intellectuals in Postconquest Mexico*. Tucson, AZ: University of Arizona Press, 2014.

McEnroe, Sean F. *From Colony to Nationhood in Mexico: Laying the Foundations, 1560–1840*. New York: Cambridge University Press, 2012.

Medina, Balthasar de. *Chrónica de la s. provincia de S. Diego de México de religiosos descalços de N. S. P. S. Francisco en la Nueva España*. México: Juan de Ribera, 1682.

Medina, José Toribio. *Don José Mariano Beristaín de Souza: estudio bio-bibliográfico*. Santiago: Imprenta Elseviriana, 1897.

Megged, Amos. *Social Memory in Ancient and Colonial Mesoamerica*. New York: Cambridge University Press, 2010.

Megged, Amos, and Stephanie Wood, eds. *Mesoamerican Memory: Enduring Systems of Remembrance*. Norman, OK: University of Oklahoma Press, 2012.

Mendieta, Jerónimo de. *Historia eclesiástica indiana*. México: Antiguo Librería, 1870. www.cervantesvirtual.com/obra-visor/historia-eclesiastica-indiana-0/html.

Menegus Bornemann, Margarita. *Del señorío indígena a la república de indios: el caso de Toluca, 1500–1600*. México: Consejo Nacional para la Cultura y las Artes, 1991.

——— "El cacicazgo en Nueva España." In *El cacicazgo en Nueva España y Filipinas*. Edited by Margarita Menegus Bornemann, and Rodolfo Aguirre Salvador. 13–69. México: Universidad Nacional Autónoma de México, Plaza y Valdés, 2005.

——— "El colegio de San Carlos Borromeo: un proyecto para la creación de un clero indígena en el siglo XVIII." In *Saber y poder en México, siglos XVI Al XX*. Edited by Margarita Menegus Bornemann. 197–243. México: Universidad Nacional Autónoma de México, 1997.

Menegus Bornemann, Margarita and Rodolfo Aguirre Salvador, eds. *El cacicazgo en Nueva España y Filipinas*. México: Universidad Nacional Autónoma de México, Plaza y Valdés, 2005.

——— *Los indios, el sacerdocio, y la universidad en Nueva España, siglos XVI–XVIII*. Mexico: Plaza y Valdés, 2006.

Mignolo, Walter. *The Darker Side of the Renaissance: Literacy, Territoriality, and Colonization*. Ann Arbor, MI: University of Michigan Press, 1995.

Milhou, Alain. "El indio americano y el mito de la religión natural." In *La imagen del indio en la Europa moderna*. 171–96. Sevilla: Escuela de Estudios Hispano-Americanos, 1990.

Miller, Marilyn. "Covert mestizaje and the strategy of 'passing' in Diego Muñoz Camargo's *Historia de Tlaxcala*." *Colonial Latin American Review* 6, no. 1 (1997): 41–58.

More, Anna. *Baroque Sovereignty: Carlos de Sigüenza y Góngora and the Creole Archive of Colonial Mexico*. Philadelphia: University of Pennsylvania Press, 2012.

Morehart, Christopher T. "What If the Aztec Empire Never Existed? The Prerequisites of Empire and the Politics of Plausible Alternative Histories." *American Anthropologist* 114, no. 2 (2012): 267–81.

Morris, Mark. "Language in Service of the State: The Nahuatl Counterinsurgency Broadsides of 1810." *Hispanic American Historical Review* 87, no. 3 (2007): 433–70.

Motolinia, Toribio de Benavente. *Memoriales*. Madrid: Ediciones Atlas, 1970.

Motolinía's History of the Indians of New Spain. Translated by Francis Borgia Steck. Washington, DC: Academy of American Franciscan History, 1951.

Munch Galindo, Guido. *El cacicazgo de San Juan Teotihuacán durante la colonia, 1521–1821*. México: Instituto Nacional de Antropología e Historia, 1976.

Mundy, Barbara. *The Mapping of New Spain: Indigenous Cartography and the Maps of the Relaciones Geográficas*. Chicago: University of Chicago Press, 1996.

Muñoz Camargo, Diego. *Descripción de la ciudad y provincia de Tlaxcala de las Indias y del Mar Océano para el buen gobierno y Ennoblecimiento Dellas*. Edited by René Acuña. México: Instituto de Investigaciones Filológicas, Universidad Nacional Autónoma de México, 1981.

Historia de Tlaxcala. Edited by Alfredo Chavero. Mexico: Oficina tip. de la Secretaría de Fomento, 1892.

Muriel, Josefina. "La mexicanidad de don Carlos de Sigüenza y Góngora manifiesta en su *Paraíso occidental*." In *Carlos de Sigüenza y Góngora: Homenaje 1700–2000*. Edited by Alicia Mayer. 67–77. Mexico: Universidad Nacional Autónoma de México, 2000.

Nesvig, Martin Austin, ed. *Local Religion in Colonial Mexico*. Albuquerque, NM: University of New Mexico Press, 2006.

Nirenberg, David. "Enmity and Assimilation: Jews, Christians, and Converts in Medieval Spain." *Common Knowledge* 9, no. 1 (2003): 137–55.

O'Hara, Matthew D. *A Flock Divided: Race, Religion, and Politics in Mexico, 1749–1857*. Durham, NC: Duke University Press, 2010.

Olko, Justyna. "Remembering the Ancestors: Native Pictorial Genealogies of Central Mexico and Their Pre-Hispanic Roots." In *Mesoamerican Memory: Enduring Systems of Remembrance*. Edited by Amos Megged and Stephanie Wood. 51–69. Norman, OK: University of Oklahoma Press, 2012.

O'Sullivan John L. "The Great Nation of Futurity." *The United States Magazine and Democratic Review* 6, no. 23 (1839): 426–30.

Orozco y Berra, Manuel, ed. *Noticia histórica de la conjuración del Marqués del Valle*. Mexico: R. Rafael, 1852.

Oudijk, Michel R. and María Castañeda de la Paz. "El uso de fuentes históricas en pleitos de tierras: la Crónica X y la Ordenanza de Cuauhtémoc." *Tlalocan* 16 (2009): 255–78.

Ouweneel, Arij. "From 'Tlatocayotl' to 'Gobernadoryotl': A Critical Examination of Indigenous Rule in 18th-Century Central Mexico." *American Ethnologist* 22, no. 4 (1995): 756–85.

Owensby, Brian. *Empire of Law and Indian Justice in Colonial Mexico*. Stanford: Stanford University Press, 2008.

Pacheco, Torales. "Don Fernando de Alva Ixtlilxochitl, historiador Texcocano." In *Historia general del Estado de México*. Edited by Rosaura Hernández Rodríguez and Raymundo César Martínez. 143–77. Toluca: Colegio Mexiquense, 1998.

Pagden, Anthony. *The Fall of Natural Man: The American Indian and the Origins of Comparative Ethnology.* 2nd edn. Cambridge: Cambridge University Press, 1986.

"Identity Formation in Spanish America." In *Colonial Identity in the Atlantic World, 1500–1800.* Edited by Nicholas Canny and Anthony Pagden. 51–94. Princeton, NJ: Princeton University Press, 1989.

Lords of All the World: Ideologies of Empire in Spain, Britain, and France, C. 1500–1800. New Haven, CT: Yale University Press, 1995.

Spanish Imperialism and the Political Imagination: Studies in European and Spanish–American Social and Political Theory, 1513–1830. New Haven: Yale University Press, 1990.

Panes, Diego García. *La conquista: selección de láminas y textos de los tomos v y vi del teatro de Nueva España.* Mexico: San Ángel Ediciones, 1976.

Pastor, Beatríz. *The Armature of Conquest: Spanish Accounts of the Discovery of America, 1492–1589.* Translated by Lydia Longstreth Hunt. Stanford: Stanford University Press, 1992.

Paz, Octavio. *The Labryinth of Solitude and Other Writings.* Translated by Lysander Kemp, Yara Milos, and Rachel Phillips Belash. New York: Grove Press, 1985.

Sor Juana, or, the Traps of Faith. Translated by Margaret Sayers Peden. Cambridge, MA: Harvard University Press, 1988.

Peña Montenegro, Alonso de. *Itinerario para parochos de Indios...* 2 vols. Amberes: Henrico y Cornelio Verdussen, 1698.

Pérez-Rocha, Emma, ed. *Privilegios en lucha: la información de Doña Isabel Moctezuma.* Mexico: Instituto Nacional de Antropología e Historia, 1998.

Pérez de Ribas, Andrés. *History of the Triumphs of Our Holy Faith.* Translated by Daniel T. Reff, Maureen Ahern, and Richard K. Danford. Tucson: University of Arizona Press, 1999.

Pérez de Velasco, Andrés Miguel. *El ayudante de cura, instruido en el porte a que le obliga su dignidad, en los deberes a que le estrecha su empleo...* Puebla: Colegio Real de San Ignacio de la Puebla 1766.

Pérez Fernández, Isacio. *Inventario documentado de los escritos de Fray Bartolomé de las Casas.* Bayamón, Puerto Rico: CEDOC, 1981.

Pérez, Manuel. *Farol Indiano, y guía de curas de Indios.* Mexico: Francisco de Rivera Calderón, 1713.

Perry, Richard J. *From Time Immemorial: Indigenous Peoples and State Systems.* Austin, TX: University of Texas Press, 1996.

Pintura del gobernador, alcaldes y regidores de México: Códice Osuna. 2 vols. Madrid: Ministerio de Educación y Ciencia, Dirección General de Archivos y Bibliotecas, 1973.

Pizzigoni, Caterina, ed. *Testaments of Toluca.* Stanford: Stanford University Press, 2007.

Pomar, Juan Bautista de. "Relación de Texcoco." In *Relaciones geográficas del siglo XVI.* Edited by René Acuña. México: Universidad Nacional Autónoma de México, 1986.

Poole, Stafford. "Church Law on the Ordination of Indians and Castas in New Spain." *Hispanic American Historical Review* 61, no. 4 (1981): 637–50.

Our Lady of Guadalupe: The Origins and Sources of a Mexican National Symbol, 1531–1797. Tucson, AZ: University of Arizona Press, 1996.

"The Politics of Limpieza de Sangre: Juan de Ovando and His Circle in the Reign of Philip II." *The Americas* 55, no. 3 (January 1999): 359–89.

Powell, Philip Wayne. "North America's First Frontier, 1546–1603." In *Essays on Frontiers in World History.* Edited by George Wolfskill and Stanley Palmer. 11–31. College Station, TX: Texas A&M University Press, 1983.

"Presidios and Towns on the Silver Frontier of New Spain, 1550–1580." *Hispanic American Historical Review* 24, no. 2 (1944): 179–200.

Prem, Hanns J. "Spanish Colonization and Indian Property in Colonial Mexico, 1521–1620." *Annals of the Association of American Geographers* 82, no. 3 (1992): 444–59.

Prescott, William Hickling. *Mexico, and the Life of the Conqueror Fernando Cortés.* 2 vols. New York: Peter Fenelon Collier, 1898.

Puente Luna, José Carlos de la. "The Many Tongues of the King: Indigenous Language Interpreters and the Making of the Spanish Empire." *Colonial Latin American Review* 23, no. 2 (2014): 143–70.

Puga, Vasco de. *Provisiones, cédulas, einstrucciones para el gobierno de la Nueva España.* Facsimile ed. Madrid: Ediciones Cultura Hispánica, 1945 (1563).

Ramírez, José Fernando. *Biblioteca de autores mexicanos.* Vol. 17. México: V. Agüeros, 1898.

Ramos, Gabriela, and Yanna Yannakakis, eds. *Indigenous Intellectuals: Knowledge, Power, and Colonial Culture in Mexico and the Andes.* Durham: Duke University Press, 2014.

"Representación que hizo la ciudad de México al rey D. Carlos III en 1771 sobre que los Criollos deben ser preferidos a los Europeos en la distribución de empleos y beneficios de estos reinos." In *Historia de la guerra de independencia de México.* Edited by Juan Evaristo Hernández y Dávalos. 427–55. Mexico: Instituto Nacional de Estudios Históricos de la Revolución Mexicana, 1985.

Restall, Matthew. *The Maya World: Yucatec Culture and Society 1550–1850.* Stanford: Stanford University Press, 1997.

"The New Conquest History." *History Compass* 10, no. 2 (2012): 151–60.

"Spanish Creation of the Conquest of Mexico." In *Invasion and Transformation: Interdisciplinary Perspectives on the Conquest of Mexico.* Edited by Rebecca P. Brienen and Margaret A. Jackson. 93–102. Boulder, CO: University Press of Colorado, 2008.

Restall, Matthew, Lisa Sousa, and Kevin Terraciano, eds. *Mesoamerican Voices: Native-Language Writings from Colonial Mexico, Oaxaca, Yucatan, and Guatemala.* New York: Cambridge University Press, 2005.

Reyes García, Luis, ed. *Anales de Juan Bautista. Cómo te confundes? Acaso no somos conquistadores?* México, DF: Centro de Investigaciones y Estudios Superiores en Antropología Social, Insigne y Nacional Basílica de Guadalupe, 2001.

Rincón, Antonio del. *Arte Mexicana.* Mexico: Oficina Típ. de la Secretaría del Fomento, 1885 (1595).

Romero Galván, José Rubén. *Los privilegios perdidos: Hernando Alvarado Tezozomoc, su tiempo, su nobleza, y su crónica Mexicana.* Mexico City: Universidad Nacional Autónoma de México, 2003.

Romero Galván, José Rubén, and Rosa Camelo. "Fray Diego Durán." In *Historiografía novohispana de tradición Indígena.* Edited by José Rubén Romero Galván. 229–57. México: Universidad Nacional Autónoma de México, 2003.

Ruiz-Medrano, Ethelia. *Mexico's Indigenous Communities: Their Lands and Histories, 1500–2010.* Translated by Russ Davidson. Boulder, CO: University Press of Colorado, 2010.

Ruiz-Medrano, Ethelia, and Susan Kellogg, eds. *Negotiation within Domination: New Spain's Indian Pueblos Confront the Spanish State.* Boulder, CO: University Press of Colorado, 2010.

Ruiz de Alarcón, Hernando. *Treatise on the Heathen Superstitions that Today Live among the Indians Native to this New Spain, 1629.* Translated by J. Richard Andrews and Ross Hassig. Norman, OK: University of Oklahoma Press, 1984.

Ruiz, Teofilo F. "Discourses of Blood and Kinship in Late Medieval and Early Modern Castile." In *Blood and Kinship: Matter for Metaphor from Ancient Rome to the Present.* Edited by Christopher H. Johnson, Bernhard Jussen, David Warren Sabean, and Simon Teuscher. New York: Berghahn, 2013.

From Heaven to Earth: The Reordering of Castillian Society, 1150–1350. Princeton: Princeton University Press, 2004.

Spanish Society, 1400–1600. Harlow, England: Pearson Education Ltd., 2001.

Saavedra y Guzmán, Antonio de. *El peregrino Indiano.* Edited by María José Rodilla. Madrid: Iberoamericana, 2008.

Sahagún, Bernardino de. *General History of the Things of New Spain.* Translated by Arthur J.O. Anderson and Charles E. Dibble. 13 vols. Santa Fe, NM: School of American Research, 1950–1982.

Salomon, Frank. "Collquiri's Dam: The Colonial Re-Voicing of an Appeal to the Archaic." In *Native Traditions in the Postconquest World.* Edited by Elizabeth Hill Boone and Tom Cummins. 265–94. Washington, DC: Dumbarton Oaks Research Library and Collection, 1998.

Sánchez de Salazar, Nicolás Simeon. *Directorio de confesores.* Puebla: Viuda de Miguel de Ortega Bonilla, 1715.

Sánchez, Miguel. *Imagen de la Virgen María Madre de dios de Guadalupe...* Mexico: Imprenta de la Viuda de Bernardo Calderón, 1648.

Sandoval, Rafael Tiburcio. *Arte de la lengua Mexicana.* México: Manuel Antonio Valdés, 1810.

Santa Getrudís, Francisco Xavier de. *Cruz de piedra, imán de devoción.* Querétaro: Ediciones Cimatario, 1946 (1722).

Schmidt Díaz de León, Ileana. *El colegio seminario de Indios de San Gregorio y el desarrollo de la Indianidad en el Centro de México, 1586–1856.* México: Plaza y Valdés, 2012.

Schmidt, Peer. "Neoestoicismo y disciplinamiento social en Iberoamérica colonial (siglo XVII)." In *Pensamiento Europeo y cultura colonial.* Edited by Karl Kohut, and Sonia V. Rose. 181–204. Frankfurt and Madrid: Vervuert, Iberoamerica, 1997.

Schroeder, Susan. "Chimalpahin Rewrites the Conquest: Yet Another Epic History?". In *The Conquest All over Again: Nahuas and Zapotecs Thinking, Writing, and Painting Spanish Colonialism*. Edited by Susan Schroeder. 101–23. Portland, OR: Sussex Academic Press, 2011.

"Introduction: The Genre of Conquest Studies." In *Indian Conquistadors: Indigenous Allies in the Conquest of Mesoamerica*. Edited by Laura E. and Michel R. Oudijk Matthew. Norman, OK: University of Oklahoma Press, 2007.

"Jesuits, Nahuas, and the Good Death Society in Mexico City, 1710–1767." *Hispanic American Historical Review* 80, no. 1 (2000): 43–76.

"The Truth About the Crónica Mexicayotl." *Colonial Latin American Review* 20, no. 2 (2011): 233–47.

Schroeder, Susan, ed. *The Conquest All over Again: Nahuas and Zapotecs Thinking, Writing, and Painting Spanish Colonialism*. Portland, OR: Sussex Academic Press, 2011.

Schwaller, John F. *The Church and Clergy in Sixteenth-Century Mexico*. Albuquerque, NM: University of New Mexico Press, 1987.

Schwaller, Robert C. "Defining Difference in Early New Spain." Ph.D. diss., Pennsylvania State University, 2010.

"'For Honor and Defence': Race and the Right to Bear Arms in Early Colonial Mexico." *Colonial Latin American Review* 21, no. 2 (2012): 239–66.

Sedano, Francisco de. *Noticias de México*. México: J.R. Barbedillo y Ca, 1880.

Sicroff, Albert A. *Los estatutos de limpieza de sangre: controversias entre los siglos XV y XVII*. Translated by Mauro Armiño. Madrid: Taurus, 1985.

Sigüenza y Góngora, Carlos de. *Alboroto y motín de México del 8 de Junio de 1692*. Edited by Irving A. Leonard. Mexico: Museo Nacional de Arqueología, Historia, y Etnografía, 1932.

Glorias de Querétaro. Mexico: Viuda de Bernardo Calderón, 1680.

Glorias de Querétaro. Querétaro: Ediciones Cimatario, 1945 (1680).

Parayso occidental, plantado, y cultivado por la liberal benéfica mano de los muy Católicos, y poderosos reyes de España nuestros señores en su magnifico real convento de Jesús María de México. Mexico: Juan de Ribero, 1684.

Theatro de virtudes políticas que constituyen a un príncipe. Mexico: Viuda de Bernardo Calderón, 1680.

Triumpho parthénico que en glorias de María santíssima immaculadamente concebida, celebró la pontificia, imperial, y Regia Academia Mexicana... Mexico: Juan de Ribera, 1683.

Silvermoon. "The Imperial College of Tlatelolco and the Emergence of a New Nahua Intellectual Elite in New Spain (1500>–1760)." Ph.D. diss., Duke University, 2007.

Simpson, Lesley Byrd. *The Encomienda in New Spain: The Beginning of Spanish Mexico*. Berkeley: University of California Press, 1966.

Sociedad de Bibliófilos Españoles. *Nobiliario de conquistadores de Indias*. Madrid: Imprenta de M. Tello, 1892.

Sousa, Lisa, and Kevin Terraciano. "Historiography of New Spain." In *The Oxford Handbook of Latin American History*. Edited by José Moya. 25–32. New York: Oxford University Press, 2010.

"The 'Original Conquest' of Oaxaca: Nahua and Mixtec Accounts of the Spanish Conquest." *Ethnohistory* 50, no. 2 (2003): 349–400.

Sugawara, Masae. "Boturini y los manuscritos históricos sobre Tlaxcala." In *La escritura pictográfica en Tlaxcala*. Edited by Luís Reyes García. Tlaxcala: Universidad Nacional Autónoma de Tlaxcala, 1993.

Super, John C. *La vida en Querétaro durante la colonia, 1531–1810*. Mexico: Fondo de Cultura Economica, 1983.

Sweet, James H. "The Iberian Roots of American Racist Thought." *The William and Mary Quarterly* LIV, no. 1 (1997): 143–66.

Tanck de Estrada, Dorothy. *Pueblos de Indios y educación en el México colonial, 1750–1821*. México: El Colegio de México, 1999.

Tavárez, David. *The Invisible War: Indigenous Devotions, Discipline, and Dissent in Colonial Mexico*. Stanford: Stanford University Press, 2011.

"Nahua Intellectuals, Franciscan Scholars, and the Devotio Moderna in Colonial Mexico." *The Americas* 70, no. 2 (2013): 203–35.

Taylor, William. "Cacicazgos coloniales en el Valle de Oaxaca." *Historia Mexicana* XX, no. 1 (1970): 1–41.

Landlord and Peasant in Colonial Oaxaca. Stanford, CA: Stanford University Press, 1972.

Magistrates of the Sacred: Priests and Parisioners in Eighteenth-Century Mexico. Stanford: Stanford University Press, 1996.

"Morelos: un ejemplo regional de sacerdotes, feligreses, e insurreción." *Historias* 40 (1998): 47–82.

"Placing the Cross in Colonial Mexico." *The Americas* 69, no. 2 (2012): 145–78.

Shrines and Miraculous Images: Religious Life in Mexico before the Reforma. Albuquerque: University of New Mexico Press, 2010.

Terraciano, Kevin. "Competing Memories of the Conquest of Mexico." In *Contested Visions in the Spanish Colonial World*. Edited by Ilona Katzew. 55–77. Los Angeles: Los Angeles County Museum of Art, 2011.

The Mixtecs of Colonial Oaxaca: Ñudzahui History, Sixteenth through Eighteenth Centuries. Stanford: Stanford University Press, 2001.

"Three Views of the Conquest of Mexico from the Other Mexica." In *The Conquest All over Again: Nahuas and Zapotecs Thinking, Writing, and Painting Spanish Colonialism*. Edited by Susan Schroeder. 15–40. Portland, OR: Sussex Academic Press, 2011.

Torquemada, Juan de. *Los veinte y un libros rituales y monarquía Indiana . . .* 3rd edn., 7 vols. México: Universidad Nacional Autónoma de México, Instituto de Investigaciones Históricas, 1975–83.

Tovar, Juan de. *Historia y creencias de los Indios de México*. Madrid: Miraguano Ediciones, 2001.

Townsend, Camilla. "Burying the White Gods: New Perspectives on the Conquest of Mexico." *Hispanic American Historical Review* 108, no. 3 (2003): 659–87.

"Don Juan Buenaventura Zapata y Mendoza and the Notion of a Nahua Identity." In *The Conquest All over Again: Nahuas and Zapotecs Thinking, Writing, and Painting Spanish Colonialism*. Edited by Susan Schroeder. 144–80. Portland, OR: Sussex Academic Press, 2011.

"The Evolution of Alva Ixtlilxochitl's Scholarly Life." *Colonial Latin American Review* 23, no. 1 (2014): 1–17.

Here in This Year: Seventeenth-Century Nahuatl Annals of the Tlaxcala-Puebla Valley. Stanford: Stanford University Press, 2009.

Malintzin's Choices: An Indian Woman in the Conquest of Mexico. Albuquerque, NM: University of New Mexico Press, 2006.

Trabulse, Elías. *Los manuscritos perdidos de Sigüenza y Góngora.* México, D.F.: El Colegio de México, 1988.

Tutino, John. *Making a New World: Founding Capitalism in the Bajío and Spanish North America.* Durham: Duke University Press, 2011.

Umberger, Emily. "Art and Imperial Strategy in Tenochtitlan." In *Aztec Imperial Strategies.* Edited by Frances Berdan. 85–108. Washington, DC: Dumbarton Oaks, 1996.

Valle, Perla, ed. *Ordenanza del Señor Cuauhtémoc.* México: Gobierno del Distrito Federal, 2000.

Van Deusen, Nancy. *Global Indios: The Indigenous Struggle for Justice in Sixteenth-Century Castile.* Durham: Duke University Press, 2015.

Van Young, Eric. "In the Gloomy Caverns of Paganism: Popular Culture, Insurgency, and Nation-Building in Mexico, 1800–1821." In *The Making of Modern Mexico, 1780–1824.* Edited by Christon I. Archer. 41–65. Wilmington, DE: Scholarly Resources, 2003.

Vargas Betancourt, Margarita. "Caciques tlatelolcas y tenencia de la tierra en el siglo XVI." In, *Nuevo mundo, mundos nuevos* (2011). Published electronically, January 31, 2011. http://nuevomundo.revues.org/60635.

Velasco Murillo, Dana, Mark Lentz, and Margarita R. Ochoa, eds. *City Indians in Spain's American Empire: Urban Indigenous Society in Colonial Mesoamerica and Andean South America, 1530–1810.* Portland, OR: Sussex Academic Press, 2012.

Velazco, Salvador. *Visiones de Anáhuac: reconstrucciones historiográficas y etnicidades emergentes en el México colonial: Fernando de Alva Ixtlilxóchitl, Diego Muñoz Camargo, y Hernando Alvarado Tezozómoc.* Guadalajara: Universidad de Guadalajara, 2003.

Vetancurt, Fr. Agustín de. *Teatro Mexicano: descripción breve de los sucesos exemplares, históricos, políticos, militares, y religiosos del nuevo mundo occidental de Las Indias.* Vol. 1. Mexico: Doña María de Benavides, 1698.

Villar Villamil, Ignacio de. *Cedulario heráldico de conquistadores de Nueva España.* Mexico: Publicaciones del Museo Nacional, 1933.

Villaseñor y Sánchez, Joseph Antonio. *Theatro Americano: descripción general de los reynos y provincias de la Nueva España.* 2 vols. México: Viuda de Joseph Bernardo de Hogal, 1746–48.

Villella, Peter B. "Indian Lords, Hispanic Gentlemen: The Salazars of Colonial Tlaxcala." *The Americas* 69, no. 1 (2012): 1–36.

"The Last Acolhua: Alva Ixtlilxochitl and Elite Native Historiography in Early New Spain." *Colonial Latin American Review* 23, no. 1 (2014): 18–36.

"'Pure and Noble Indians, Untainted by Inferior Idolatrous Races': Native Elites and the Discourse of Blood Purity in Late-Colonial Mexico." *Hispanic American Historical Review* 91, no. 4 (2011): 633–63.

Von Wobeser, Gisela. *Vida eterna y preocupaciones terrenales: las capellanías de misas en la Nueva España, 1700–1821.* Mexico: Universidad Nacional Autónoma de México, 1999.

White, Hayden. *The Content of the Form: Narrative Discourse and Historical Representation.* Baltimore: Johns Hopkins Press, 1987.

Wolf, Eric R. "The Vissicitudes of the Closed Corporate Peasant Community." *American Ethnologist* 13, no. 2 (1986): 325–29.

Wood, Stephanie. "Collective Memory and Mesoamerican Systems of Remembrance." In *Mesoamerican Memory: Enduring Systems of Remembrance.* Edited by Amos Megged and Stephanie Wood. 3–14. Norman, OK: University of Oklahoma Press, 2012.

"The Social Vs. Legal Context of Nahuatl Títulos." In *Native Traditions in the Postconquest World.* Edited by Elizabeth Hill Boone and Tom Cummins. 201–32. Washington DC: Dumbarton Oaks, 1998.

Transcending Conquest: Nahua Views of Spanish Colonial Mexico. Norman, OK: University of Oklahoma Press, 2003.

Wright, David, ed. *Conquistadores otomíes en la guerra chichimeca.* Querétaro: Gobierno del Estado de Querétaro, 1988.

Querétaro en el siglo XVI: Fuentes documentales primarias. Querétaro: Gobierno del Estado de Querétaro, 1989.

Yannakakis, Yanna. *The Art of Being in-Between: Native Intermediaries, Indian Identity, and Local Rule in Colonial Oaxaca.* Durham and London: Duke University Press, 2008.

"Indigenous People and Legal Culture in Spanish America." *History Compass* 11, no. 11 (2013): 931–47.

"The Indios Conquistadores of Oaxaca's Sierra Norte: From Indian Conquistadors to Local Indians." In *Indian Conquistadors: Indigenous Allies in the Conquest of Mesoamerica.* Edited by Laura E. and Michel R. Oudijk Matthew. 227–53. Norman, OK: University of Oklahoma Press, 2007.

Zapata y Mendoza, Juan Buenaventura. *Historia cronológica de la noble ciudad de Tlaxcala.* Translated by Luis Reyes García and Andrea Martínez Baracs. Tlaxcala: Universidad Autónoma de Tlaxcala, 1995.

Zorita, Alonso de. *Life and Labor in Ancient Mexico: The Brief and Summary Relation of the Lords of New Spain by Alonso De Zorita.* Translated by Benjamin Keen. 2nd ed. Norman: University of Oklahoma Press, 1994. 1963.

Relación de la Nueva España. Edited by Ethelia Ruiz-Medrano, José Mariano Leyva, and Wiebke Ahrndt. 2 ed. 2 vols Mexico: CONACULTA, 2011.

Index

Cambridge Latin American Studies

General editor

Herbert S. Klein

Gouverneur Morris Emeritus Professor of History, Columbia University and Hoover Research Fellow, Stanford University